HENGISTBURY HEAD

The Whole Story

W. A. HOODLESS

Poole Historical Trust
2005

Previous Publications

The Pride of Poole, 1688-1851
An Album of Old Poole
Mansions and Merchants of Poole and Dorset
Brownsea Islander
Poole and World War II
A Portfolio of Old Poole
Ebb-Tide at Poole
History of the Town of Poole, 1839 (reprint)
The Sydenhams of Poole (booklet)
Art in Poole and Dorset
Victorian Poole
Poole after World War II 1945-1953
D-Day Poole (booklet)
The Spirit of Poole 1953-1963
Lifeboatmen Never Turn Back
Schools of Old Poole
Poole's Pride Regained 1964-1974
Poole Was My Oyster
For Nature, Not Humans
I Was There

First published 2005
ISBN 1873535600

Text edited for publication by Martin Blyth
Designed by Andrew S Arnold
Production by Graphic Editions, Poole
Printed and bound in Great Britain by Bath Press
Cover picture: **Hengistbury Head by Roger Holman**

CONTENTS

LIST OF ILLUSTRATIONS

Cover photograph by Roger Holman
Frontispiece of Warren Summer House by Christopher Hollick

I dedicate this book to my wife

"Susan"

Without whose kindness, support and patience

it would not have been possible.

PREFACE

MY INTEREST in Hengistbury Head stems from early childhood when I walked there aged three with my brother aged six from our home in West Southbourne. This may not have been the safest of enterprises because of unexploded ordnance still lingering from World War II. Indeed, it has been reported that a boy took home a box of grenades five years later! The atmosphere of this rather haunting headland has captured me ever since.

The story of Hengistbury Head has a great deal more than local interest, partly because so much has happened over such a long period and partly because of its unique character. During the process of research, it has been amazing just how much unexpected information, which adds to its attraction, has come to light. Indeed, it is my hope that a reader may open this book at random and be quite likely to say "How interesting! I did not know that!"

The headland is a place not only of beauty, but also one of controversy, significance and impact. It will always matter and always generate all kinds of feelings and opinions. Many of us get territorial about it, which is ridiculous. For example, it makes no difference whether you live nearby, or work there, or have responsibility for planning, or deal with erosion, or study geology: whatever your interest, you think you own it and are much better placed to decide its future than anyone else. My intention has been to give a summary of everything in a way that will help towards the care and conservation of this magnificent and important promontory.

The unspoiled charm of Hengistbury is one of its main aspects. There are no slot machines, pubs with piped music, traffic jams or any other of the downsides to so-called "modern living." I know that some feel it is overdeveloped, but such things as the car park and land train are rather low-key. If we disregard the Neolithic town and Iron Age port, which were a very long time ago, and also the World War II development, which has been removed, very little has ever been built east of the Dykes. Most of it is on Mudeford Sandbank for leisure purposes, the remainder merely including the Old Barn, the coastguard station and some stores in the Nursery Garden. This is likely to continue. West of the Dykes, since the purchase by Bournemouth, is a different story, with Broadway, car parks, the Hengistbury Head Centre, church, school, Hungry Hiker, golf facilities, shops and residential building. Nonetheless, provided nothing major is done in the future east of the Dykes, I believe it will remain a wonderful place having a sustainable balance between conservation and tourism.

Although much of this book does run roughly in date order, it is not purely about local history. Other things are included because they are important to understanding Hengistbury Head and its surroundings. Hence, in the interests of providing a context, the book sometimes goes beyond the Head itself to a wider geographical area or to matters, which are not closely related. A reader might wish to skip the sections on geology or even start on that concerned with the smuggling. My purpose has been to assist such "dipping-in" by making each chapter fairly self-contained even if this means a little duplication. Where dimensions are involved, I make no apology for these being imperial throughout.

If I had to provide very broad categories of content, they would be "technical," including some science and "general," covering history and human interest. Chapter headings are fairly clear to help direct the reader. The first draft of the book had some 250 footnotes and eight appendices to give sources or to amplify the text. To help readability, I have dispensed with everything except one appendix, by omitting many sources or just giving limited attribution. Other items have been abbreviated and included in the text. Nonetheless, there remain a few sections of more appeal to someone wanting a book of reference, e.g. that on the history of coastal defence.

Whilst I have taken much care in providing correct information, this is unlikely to be 100% accurate, if only because of the fact that few books achieve it. I would not, for example, claim to be a professional geologist. My hope remains that any errors are as few as can be expected, given the breadth of material. The precaution has been taken of verifying where possible, and certain parts of the book have been submitted in advance to specialists for comment. That said, any mistakes must remain my own. Certainly, I should be pleased to know (via the publisher) of anything which can be shown to be wrong. There is little to be done, however, when there exists a difference of professional opinion in a specialist field, or when my research becomes overtaken by new findings after publication. Where material is still in copyright, I believe that I have the permission of the owners to reproduce their material. I would be glad to be advised if I have unwittingly infringed any person's rights.

Finally, I would thank the many sources and people who have been a great help in making the book possible. Although this is necessarily not a complete list, helpful advice and comment has been freely given by many. In no particular order, these include Jim Hunter and John Lewis (Red House Museum), Jane Rutter, Michael Andrews, Olive Samuel and others at the Christchurch Local History Society, Sue Newman (concerning Tutton's Well), Basil Ratcliffe (Councillor), David Atkinson MP, Bernard Tull and Joan Turner (Hengistbury Residents' Association), Tricia Zimmerman (Hengistbury Head Centre), Tim Baber (Hengistbury Head Times), John Chaffey (geologist), Ian West (Southampton University), Nick Barton, Barry Cunliffe and Peter Hawes (all archaeologists), Ian Andrews and Martin Blyth (Poole Historical Trust), Mark Holloway (Ranger at the Head), Lawrence Popplewell (local historian), Sue Hogan, Robin Strides, Vic Derham, Roy Stuart, David Reeves and John Buckle (long established local families), Herbert Brewer (son of former gamekeeper), Tommy Tucker and Dave Gill from the Coastguard Service, Chris Austin (Christchurch Sailing Club), Bill Foster (Mudeford fisherman), Gary Foyle, Mike Hinton and Peter Holloway (all Christchurch Council), Frank Tyhurst (ex Christchurch Council), Colin Rudkin (House of Lords Record Office), Gordon le Pard (Dorset Coast Forum), Claire Pinder (Dorset County Council), David Rymill (Hampshire Record Office), Pat Law (Bournemouth Dowsers), David Harlow and Neal Turner (Bournemouth Council), Duncan Coe (English Heritage), Douglas Kite (English Nature), Phil Woodworth (Proudman Oceanographic Laboratory), Ian Surface (National Coastwatch Institution) and Bill Rees (local writer).

W A Hoodless

FOREWORD

HENGISTBURY HEAD has long deserved to be recorded comprehensively and in such a way as to interest all those who travel some way to enjoy its beauty as well as those who live nearby.
Thus I very much welcome this fine book.

I am privileged to have represented Bournemouth East for more than 25 years in the House of Commons. The constituency is any MP's dream! Bournemouth is Britain's finest seaside resort located in one of our most beautiful counties. Dorset's coast effectively stretches from Hengistbury Head westward to the recently UNESCO designated World Heritage site by Lyme Regis.

What a pity the new New Forest National Park does not include Hengistbury Head within its boundary as I had proposed, which would have provided it with the highest status of protection that it deserves!

Not long ago, there would not have been so much of the Head left to protect. In the spring of 1985, the Bournemouth Echo reported my warning to the inaugural meeting of the Bournemouth Centre of the National Trust at the Town Hall: "It is no exaggeration to say that the current rate of erosion will mean that by the year 2,000 the Head will have lost most of its prominence and the sea will have broken through at Double Dykes, thus rendering it an island."

Fortunately the Head remains intact because we were able to persuade the Government, which was facing great economic difficulties at the time, to agree to a coastal protection grant of over £4 million.

As we read in the book there would have been so much more of the Head today if the mining company had not been allowed to remove the ironstone at its base which was the beach's natural barrier to erosion in the 1850s.

I commend Bill Hoodless on the outstanding research he has undertaken to record this story of Hengistbury Head. It is very timely, as the establishment of a modern Visitors Information Centre for the student and the walker is being considered.

This book will give great pleasure to all those who appreciate Bournemouth's natural and historical heritage. It should challenge all of us to ensure its protection for posterity.

David Atkinson

INTRODUCTION

The fascinating story of Hengistbury

The curl of the breaker, the sound of the surf
The cry of the seagull, the spring of the turf
The scent of the weather, the clover and thyme
The sight of the Island illumined in lime.
Ah! Give me the Headland majestic and free
For the spell of its grandeur makes music for me

Kathleen Foley

I WANT TO GIVE a foretaste of the surprisingly exciting history of this headland. These are examples of some of extraordinary things about this place which are covered in detail in later chapters.

- Hengistbury was a major **smuggling** location at the end of the eighteenth century. It is believed that landers' parties hid their horses and waggons between the Dykes, before taking the contraband inland via Wick Lane. The Battle of Mudeford actually resulted in a fatal shootout at the Run, with one of the smugglers executed by hanging in due course.
- Due to the nineteenth century **mining** operation, which removed enormous quantities of protective ironstone, the headland is about half the size it should be, owing to the consequent erosion. Apart from this catastrophic impact on Hengistbury Head, the ironstone was won at the cost of some gruesome fatal accidents.
- Many schemes of **development** have been mooted. The retail store magnate Gordon Selfridge planned two castles, including one designed with a dome almost the size of St. Paul's Cathedral! A plan was drawn up for a prestige golf course over Warren Hill. Another proposal was for a marine drive or coastal road from a new bridge at Mudeford and over the top of the Head. Perhaps the worst idea was for a railway station in the lee of the headland and the creation of a deep water harbour to rival Southampton. The scheme to build a Classroom of the Future and Community Centre in Green Belt near to Double Dykes resulted in another controversy.
- There have been many **tragedies** ranging from a murder at White Pits to death from land mines at the end of World War II. Not least was the fatal crash (near what is now Broadway) of Charlie Rolls, joint founder of Rolls Royce, at the Bournemouth Centenary Airshow of 1910.
- Even the rather technical subject of **coastal defence** throws up its own dramas, as shown by the following extracts from local newspaper reports of the flooding that took place in 1916:

  "Raging seas tearing over low sandbank"; "Beat high over Haven Inn"; "Enterprise Tea Room, constructed of wood and corrugated iron, completely demolished and swept away"; "Water beating against houses at the Haven"; "Waves breaking all around making it impossible for inmates to venture out of doors"; "Mrs. Cutler and three children unable to get out of the door owing to raging surf sweeping round the house."

Hengistbury and its surrounding area seem destined always to be a place of interest, controversy and stories. The archaeologists have found it to be an internationally important site to tell us about pre-history.

We know it was once among the most important and prosperous Iron Age ports in the country. Even the geology has the capacity to surprise and interest, with the story of sediments laid down some 50 million years ago available for all to see in the cliff face of Warren Hill.

There is an absorbing explanation for the formation of the ironstones, without which Hengistbury would not exist. As for stories and controversy, the townspeople often seem to be at loggerheads with the council and there is no shortage of tales such as the Ghostly Horseman or the Dragon of Christchurch.

Finally, the wildlife is diverse and spectacular, having a unique combination of habitats within a relatively small land area. The enormous variety of fauna and flora contributes both to the beauty of the headland and its attraction for the tourist.

First impressions

Whether or not you are a first-time visitor, you immediately feel the peace and quiet of Hengistbury.

Having left the hustle and bustle of the town, you step out of the car into a wide expanse of level land close to the sea and only just above it. The chances are high that the weather is fairly windy and changeable! As you venture past the tranquil field east of Double Dykes, you are struck by a feeling of solitude and timelessness, despite the presence of others. During the slow climb up Warren Hill, it becomes increasingly clear that the Head will impart superb views (Fig.1) of both the expanse of Christchurch Harbour and a seascape running from the Isle of Wight to the Purbeck Hills. However, the breathtaking quality of the eventual outlook is only evident once the top is reached.

Why does it matter?

Perhaps there are two main reasons.

The modern world is probably more stressful than it has ever been. We need to hold on to as many antidotes to such things as we can. Owing to its atmosphere and attraction, I believe many people already see Hengistbury Head as a sort of antidote, which must be preserved. My hope is that this book may help. In short, my first answer is that it is important for us to keep, understand and use such a thing of beauty in the modern world.

If by doing so, we can also spend more time out of doors and see our position at the end of the chain of pre-history and history, so much the better in these rootless times. I don't believe the past is best viewed through rose-tinted spectacles, or hankered after in any way. But it is important to see our place in the scheme of things.

And so my second answer is that we will benefit from knowing about the amazing story of Hengistbury, which puts our own short lives into context and gives a sense of belonging.

Fig.1 ***Poole Bay from the headland***

(Author 2005)

This is just one of many photographs which could have been included, to show the sheer charm and superb outlook from this special place.

Description and prospects

Hengistbury Head, which is owned by Bournemouth Borough Council, lies at the relatively quiet eastern end of town. It is an undeveloped promontory surrounded on three sides by water and divided from the west by an Iron Age defence, an Ancient Monument known as the Double Dykes. There are two large car parks, a café and a considerable area of council land devoted to leisure pursuits such as golf, walking and kite flying in the open area between the Dykes and the residential part of Southbourne. The headland proper is east of Double Dykes.

Including Wick Fields, Hengistbury covers a land area of about 400 acres or 5/8ths of a square mile. Its latitude is 50° 43' North, longitude 1° 45' West and Ordnance Survey reference SZ 175905. Height above Ordnance Datum is 120 feet at the Triangulation Station on the top of Warren Hill. Winds are more frequent and much stronger than inland. Temperatures are lower in the summer and higher in the winter, whilst relative humidity is high and annual rainfall low. Tidal range is low, but a high Spring Tide combined with a surge in the Channel would cause a risk of a sea breach to Christchurch harbour near the low cliff at Double Dykes. Until a serious breach occurs, the tidal range in the harbour should remain at around 60% only of that outside it. The size of the headland is about half of that before the enormous erosion caused by the disastrous ironstone mining of the nineteenth century.

Just about the only concession to modernity is the land train, which runs along the narrow tarmac road from the Hungry Hiker café west of the Dykes to Mudeford Sandbank. Otherwise, it is a case of the visitor walking along the many footpaths, open land or the beach. Incidentally, it is rare for the beach to be impassable for walkers (due to sea conditions) right from the promenade in Southbourne, around the headland all the way to the end of the Sandbank. Refreshments and toilets are available both at the Hungry Hiker café by the Dykes and the Beach House Café near to the ferry jetty on the sandspit. If you go about halfway along the sandspit, you will find ferries available in the summer both to Mudeford Quay, and to Christchurch Quay and the pontoons by Wick Lane, Christchurch. Since this ferry arrives at the Christchurch side of the Stour, you need to use the separate Wick Ferry to reach Wick Lane, Southbourne.

You may purchase a nature trail, archaeological trail or wildlife booklet from the Ranger's Office in the Hungry Hiker building at the end of Broadway. Although there are no archaeological findings on display, there are public notices giving brief information about coastal erosion, ironstone mining, the Dykes and wildlife. At a summer weekend, when the tide is high, you would expect to see more than one dinghy race in the harbour and perhaps another race out in Christchurch Bay.

As for the longer term, provided there are no more incursions into the Green Belt, the whole area will probably continue successfully as a carefully managed wildlife haven and visitor attraction. However, one day, the inevitable change in climate will cause a breakthrough of the sea near the Dykes. Even with more groynes for coastal defence, Hengistbury is expected to become an island within about 100 years.

Getting to know the Head

If you are a first-time visitor, my recommendation is that a minimum of two walks (which can be followed from Fig.46) will be needed as an introduction to Hengistbury. The first is easier, quicker and arguably more spectacular: from the Dykes, over the top of the Head, down the steps at the end of it to the start of the Sandbank and back along the tarmac road taken by the land train. The main feature of this route is the view from the top. The second starts at the beach by Solent Beach car park in Southbourne Coast Road, goes all around the Head keeping to the beach and along the sea side of the Sandbank to the Run. It returns along the harbour side of the sandspit towards the flat land on the north side of the headland, and finally, along the footpath running at the southern edge of the harbour to the Dykes. (If there is a high tide, it is advisable to return to the Dykes by the tarmac road, because the harbour path can get too wet.) From the sea end of the Dykes, a walk on the cliff top will take our visitor back to the car park. The main features of this walk are the imposing high strata of the headland as seen from the beach and the changing views across the waters. Walking boots are best, particularly for the second one. I would describe the first walk as "reasonably easy" and the second as "at least moderate."

Prehistoric Times to Twenty-First Century

ONE

EARLY PREHISTORY

I wish I could bring Stonehenge to Nyasaland to show there was a time when Britain had a savage culture

Dr. Hastings Banda

THIS CHAPTER takes us through the Stone and Bronze Ages. It seeks to show the background over many centuries of occupation, nearly all signs of which have now disappeared to the casual observer. About the only clue left from the Bronze Age is the occasional tumulus, the most prominent being that by the ranger's cottage (Fig.14). During this period, Hengistbury moved from being a convenient site from which to hunt the migrating deer, to early mixed arable and pasture farming and finally a prestige cemetery. Perhaps the quote above is a little harsh, bearing in mind that Stonehenge was a great achievement for early man.

Archaeological record

There have been many professional digs over the last century. The usual motive is "rescue before disappearance!" Collections are widespread, partly in private hands and far from accessible. Despite these problems, the site has received the attention its importance deserves. The Red House Museum, Christchurch, has good displays, and the two monographs (see Bibliography) by Professor Barry Cunliffe and Dr Nick Barton, give most of the information. The 1932 OS map (Fig.2) marks a number of key finds.

J.P. Bushe-Fox carried out the first main excavation. This respected archaeologist believed that it would be over in a matter of weeks but had to continue for more than six months, 1911-1912, due to the extent of the finds. Some 58 sites were trenched, 42 acres were investigated and three barrows dug out. His scholarly report was published by the Society of Antiquaries of London in 1915.

Fig.8 shows the areas exposed by Bushe-Fox from the Iron Age settlement. It will be seen from this that there were at least 13 occupied areas, 14 dwelling sites, 5 hut circles, 8 hearths and a coin site largely sheltered in the lee of the Head. There are examples of much more detail not shown in the illustration:

- Site 3 included six fireplaces, not separately indicated.
- Sites 8 and 9 contained a hearth and cupellation hearth respectively.
- Sites 4 and 16 had remains of iron slag and "fireplaces probably," respectively.
- Site 18 included two dwellings, yielding loom weights, sandstone spindle whorl and a bronze spoon from the Roman period.

- Site 21 provided a series of hearths with six layers of burnt matter.
- Site 23 supplied a Kimmeridge shale bracelet.
- Site 29 was a rubbish pit from the Roman period nine feet deep.
- Site 31 was occupied from the earliest times to the fourth century AD and contained coins throughout, which had been distributed by both the plough and rabbits.
- Site 33 must have been particularly exciting due to the high density of finds: remains of dwellings, burnt clay, charcoal from oak and hornbeam, evidence of metal working but most of all the cache of over 3,000 coins.
- Site 36 had several burnt gravel layers, 48 and 49 both had ovens and 54 a workshop floor.
- Signs of hardened clay, bearing the impression of wattle indicated the position of the walls of village huts.

Bushe-Fox would have been aware that part of the large occupied area (his reference Site 1) had already been lost to the sea before his arrival. It was 55 feet wide and went inland 92 feet from the cliff. It has now completely eroded away, preventing any further research. Adjoining the sea end of the Dykes, on the eastern side, it was covered by 3 feet 10 inches of blown sand. Beneath this was a heavily burnt layer, one foot thick. It contained human bones, oak charcoal, bronze ornaments, corroded iron and burnt pre-Roman pottery.

The Cunliffe and Barton monographs give a much fuller picture, including chemical analysis and tables of slag residues, alloy objects and iron nodules; descriptions of pieces of shale, iron nails, blades, rods, bars and loops; assessments of coins, ditches, flints and so forth.

Barry Cunliffe led the 1980-1984 programme, which covered 3/4 of an acre and employed 15 to 20 volunteers for three weeks every July for five years. The area is shown as Site 1 on Fig.5. There were 814 layers, 505 features and 1,469 postholes. Even then, the site is only 4% of the extent of the Late Iron Age/Roman settlement area in Barn Field and Long Field.

Nick Barton researched the two big Stone Age camps on Warren Hill over the same period. One feature of the work done on the Old Stone Age site was the hand digging of 150 trial pits, each ten inches square, to the north of the main site.

An interim report in the professional press commented that the Head might contain the largest unmixed assemblage from the Upper Palaeolithic in the whole of the British Isles. It was a big investigation by any standards, including volunteers and archaeologists from several nations. The excavations yielded answers to old problems by use of new techniques. Apart from improved methods of dating, experimental work had come into favour, such as the deer and arrow experiment (Fig.3). Archaeologists also look at distribution factors such as frost and worms, produce scale drawings of flint scatters and use Accelerator Mass Spectrometry to date settlements.

Local historians owe a big debt to **Herbert Druitt.** By his death in 1943, he had amassed 2,450 boxes of archaeological artefacts, much of it from the Head and deposited at the Red House Museum. As soon as Gordon Selfridge purchased the Head, he appointed **H. St. George Gray** as consultant. Over seven years, 1918-1924, part of the Nursery Garden, land nearby and seven barrows were dug. There were ten north-south trenches 4 feet by 330 feet from the Batters to the harbour shore. Although the Red House Museum now holds some archives, no general plan survives. This means that it is not possible to locate the trenches properly. In 1957, **Angela Mace** excavated a Late Upper Palaeolithic site above Long Groyne, reporting in 1959. It was a more formal task after the **Calkin** finds of the previous few years.

In 1968, **Dr. J. Campbell** was employed to do a further rescue of the same site. He reported disagreement with the findings of Angela Mace. Since then, further research has rejected a number of Campbell's conclusions. The reason for the excavation by **Dr D. P. Peacock** in 1970, was yet another rescue: to see what could be found before the council's plan to consolidate the south shore of the harbour was put in hand. Protective gabions are now in place, although finds of pottery fragments are still possible, to the east of the old Holm Oak tree (mainly removed March 2005) marked on Fig.46.

In May 1997 (**Barton and Dumont**) and June 2001 (**Barton and Roberts**) further reports were made about re-colonisation and settlement of Britain at the end of the last glaciation and late glacial tanged assemblages, respectively. The latter refer to collections of pointed flintstones from the latest part of the Old Stone Age. Many of these were fixed to shafts and used as weapons.

The **Wessex Archaeology** report of December 2001 has cast a new light on the area west of the Dykes and north of Broadway. The initial site survey covered 12.7 acres on both sides of Broadway, with the main evaluation area being 6.2 acres on the pitch and putt and a section of the golf course to the west. There were

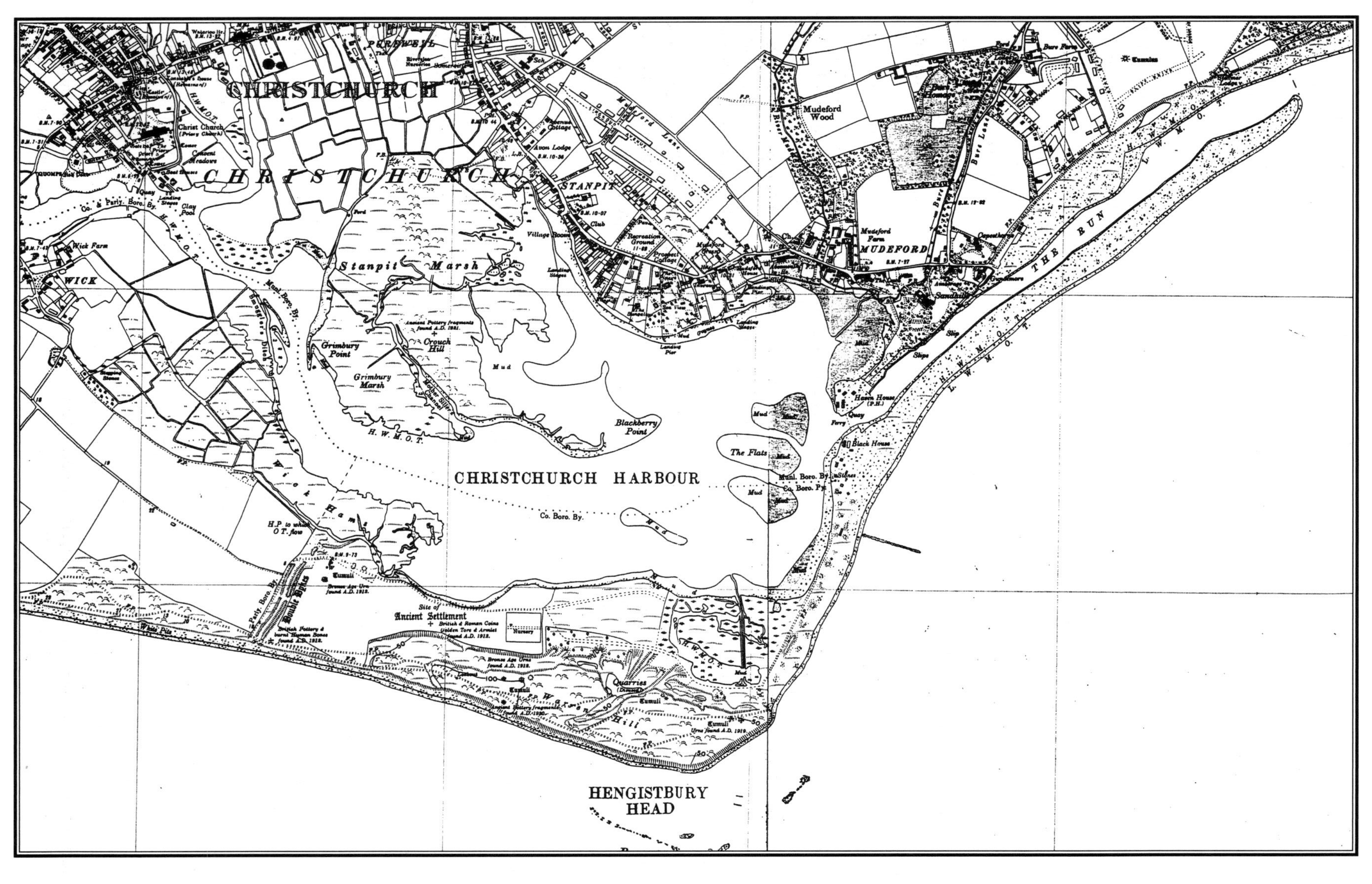

Fig.2 ***Extended Mudeford Sandbank and archaeological finds, 1932***

(Reproduced from the Ordnance Survey map of that date. © Crown Copyright. 1/10,560 scale before reduction)

This shows the area and finds before Hengistbury was opened up by the construction of Broadway. The Long Groyne was also still to be built, so explaining the enormous sandspit extension, caused by beach material drifting around the Head. About three years later, there was a storm breach in it at the Haven, so creating a shorter Run. The extension had not been sustainable but the resulting attractive lagoon saw a number of swimming tragedies.

eight trenches of 82 feet length dug by JCB over about a week. Finds ranged from the Middle Stone Age to the Middle Iron Age. The report makes clear that further things may have been found but for the time constraints. A possible burial urn meant that a Home Office licence was needed under the Burial Act 1857 before excavation. It is amazing to think that only now can we say the Iron Age people lived on both sides of Double Dykes. In October 2002, the widow of **Alessandro Nobli-Vitelleschi**, a regular walker on the Head, gave to the Red House Museum a large representative batch of flints from his private collection.

Stone Age

The Stone Age is divided into the **Old** (Palaeolithic from 500,000 years Before Present [BP]), **Middle** (Mesolithic from 9,700 BP) and **New** (Neolithic from 6,000 to 3,700 BP). Most of the Old Stone Age is the Lower Palaeolithic from 500,000 years BP; the Upper Palaeolithic started only 15,000 years BP. The earliest remains at Hengistbury are from around 12,500 years BP. In the absence of metalworking, mankind evolved slowly during the Stone Age.

Flint, an impure type of quartz in the form of silicone dioxide crystals, was a very convenient hard mineral for Stone Age Man. Flints have been found around Bournemouth dating back some 250,000 years, but these are not specific to Hengistbury Head. Nothing from this far back has yet been found at the Head. Such very old flints were thinly spread compared to the concentration at the Hengistbury Reindeer Camp 12,000 years ago (see below). It follows that Hengistbury may only have become attractive when the hunter-gatherers found it best to operate in teams.

At the start of the Upper Palaeolithic, the ice sheet from the last Ice Age began to recede. Before then, the whole of the country down to what is now London was covered in ice. It is thought (Barton and Dumont) that Europe was re-colonised from about 13,100 years BP, and it was another 500 years before sustained human activity was established in Britain. These people are believed to have hunted wild horses and reindeer. Flints with tanged points are typical of north-western Europe's Late Glacial technology. Hengistbury has the richest collection of these, the larger ones having close affinity to the Scandinavian Bromme type. A reasonable supposition is that the hunters expanded to the west across the dry bed of what is now the North Sea, into East Anglia and beyond.

In the Mesolithic period, the hunter-gatherers produced smaller flints as they sought smaller animals; the ground was warmer and trees were becoming established. The Neolithic was a time of early arable and pasture farming, when mankind was beginning to learn how to settle on the land instead of operate from camps.

Old Stone Age Reindeer Camp
(Late Upper Palaeolithic)

There was little human occupation in north-western Europe 20,000 years ago, the Late Glacial Maximum. Sea level was around 375 feet below its present level. It remained cold until at least 14,500 BP, with winters at –20° to –25°C and summers only up to 10°C. Although there was a temporary warm spell around 12,500 BP, when the climate in Britain was similar to that of today, there is no evidence that it had any effect on the establishment of the Reindeer Camp at this closing stage of the last Ice Age. The campsite is within part of the Head called the Eastern Depression, a dry stream valley now cut off by the retreating cliff face. Doubtless, many artefacts have been lost to erosion. Hengistbury is one of the very few Upper Palaeolithic sites which is on open land: nearly all finds in the country from this period are in caves.

In 1957, Angela Mace found 2,263 items including much worked flint by the cliff edge above the Long Groyne. Known as the Reindeer Camp (Ref. 29, Fig.46) ever since, the excavation was limited to an area of 85 square yards only. In 1968, Dr. John Campbell looked at a much larger area (about 160 square yards) and recovered another 4,400 flints. He disagreed with Mace, saying that virtually all the finds were much younger, many being Mesolithic. The site had been revisited due to its importance and risk of loss through erosion.

The most definitive work here started in 1980 on an area of about 115 square yards. By 1983, Barton and James had carried out six thermoluminescence tests on burnt artefacts. This dating technique measures emissions from radioactive material. The tests supported the Mace view by indicating a range of 1,200 years either side of around 12,500 years BP, i.e. well before the Mesolithic time. Moreover, the same conclusion was supported by flint re-assembly and a scrutiny of the vertical placement of flints in the ground.

Pepin noted in 1985 that 20,000 to 25,000 artefacts had been recovered from this period. Although the campsite was temporary, it was revisited many times during the hunting seasons, which coincided with the spring and autumn migrations of horses and reindeer. It is believed that the camp was up to about half an acre in extent. Due to the high number of retouched tools (649), Hengistbury was then said to be the largest known Late Upper Palaeolithic site in the country.

Since good flint was not easily available at the Head, large, good quality flint cobbles, probably from what is now the Isle of Wight, were transported to Hengistbury, and knapped on site. They were pre-formed by removing the ends. After striking, which produced "cresting," the blanks were made and the remaining core discarded. There are two types of flint: the elongated angle-backed trapezoidal Creswellian type and the straight-backed blade type found at Hengistbury. The former was used in caves and the latter at open-air sites. The earliest people, re-colonising Britain about 12,600 years BP, made Creswellian flints. This was probably before the Hengistbury hunter-gatherers at the Reindeer Camp, from which six tanged flints have now been dated to 12,295 BP, plus or minus 795 years.

A common tool of the period was a *burin* or *graver* used to carve bone or antler. They were made, used and discarded on the site. Some were found to have been heavily used along their edges and to have been frequently re-sharpened. It is likely that one use of the burin was to provide barbed hunting implements from antlers. Backed blades appear to have been used for cutting and for spears. Hafted scrapers were extremely efficient at de-fleshing deerskin hides, often requiring no sharpening even after three hours of continuous use. Pointed flint flakes were much bigger than those found at the Mesolithic site, implying they were used for spears. This is because the animals to be killed (reindeer and horses) were much bigger at this earlier time. Since the frozen ground meant that there were very few trees, the landscape was different from the later, warmer Mesolithic time.

All these tools were connected with hunting and consequent work. Hides were scraped, fires made to high temperatures, tools burnt in hearths and of course meat cooked. Flint knapping and production of blanks occurred away from the hearths. The tools found in Holland, Germany and France, were very similar, indicating much the same lifestyle, before the creation of the English Channel.

The Hengistbury campsite is an excellent vantage point over the flood plain, where herds of deer migrated to the west for spring calving. They could have been ambushed and driven into the waters of the rivers for the kill, a method historically verified as used in Siberia by the Nganasan tribe.

Middle Stone Age Archers' Camp

(Early Mesolithic: The Powell Site)

The main Mesolithic site on Hengistbury lies about 710 yards to the west of the Reindeer Camp. It is named after Ronald Powell, who found artefacts eroding out of the cliff top in 1977.

This site, (Ref.30, Fig.46) however, is not the only Mesolithic evidence in the area. Finds were discovered when the Coastguard Station was erected in 1975; near the quarry; along the northern edge of the headland; near the Old Stone Age site described above; at the Nursery; west of the Dykes; at Tuckton, Wick, Stanpit Marsh and along the Avon. In 2001, the Wessex Archaeology investigation of the pitch and putt site west of the Dykes revealed a small amount of Mesolithic material, including a blade, bladelet core and unfinished microlith. This shows that a Mesolithic campsite may have existed close to Double Dykes similar to one on the opposite side of the harbour.

Due to frozen ground, there was limited vegetation in Britain until the thaw of about 9,700 BP, when the Middle Stone Age started. Pine forests became established and man began to hunt smaller, mainly woodland species, instead of reindeer and wild horses. Flint tools became much smaller as a consequence of the wooded landscape. Prey for the Mesolithic hunter is now thought to include wildfowl, roe deer, wild cattle, beaver and wild pig. A very specialised set of tools was found at the Powell Site including scrapers, saws and small pointed flints. These microliths would have been for arrowheads and the larger flints for hide scraping and meat processing. The dating of five burnt flints at 9,750 BP (± 950 years), places this site around the Early Mesolithic, at a time when the coast was at least 12 miles away.

The main type of flint is likely to be either from the Stour or Avon valleys, or possibly from the now submerged Solent valley. In addition, some different flint occurs from a presently unknown source. As for the sandstone found here, this seems to have come from Devon, whilst the block of sarsen, weighing nearly nine pounds, could have been found in the Bournemouth area. The sandstone could have been used for grinding, skin stretching or hide working; the sarsen was probably a working surface block.

Between 1980 and 1983, 35,444 artefacts were found, comprising flakes, blades, bladelets, chips, cores and core fragments. Thick edged scrapers were used for woodworking. Thin edged ones were applied to hides.

Microdenticulates were employed in cutting soft plants, such as ferns. Microliths became arrowheads, plant knifes and even mounted drill bits. The limited variety of tools from the Powell Site is of specialised design for the purpose of hunting game. Other Mesolithic sites, which are lower lying and on the water's edge, have burins and adzes within their toolkits, implying more intensive maintenance and processing activity. It is likely that a single hunter-gatherer community used the Head for an annual settlement.

Hunter-gatherers of Hengistbury
(Old and Middle Stone Age)

Stone Age people were no less intelligent or capable than we are today; they were simply in an early stage of developing skills. They operated from temporary campsites due to the need to follow the food sources. A key worker was the knapper, who would produce the various weapons and implements to ensure survival. To knap simply means to strike a flint with precision in order to split off a flake. A skilled knapper can get over 50 blades from a single core in about 15 minutes. The knapper could go on to fashion hand axes, scrapers, arrow tips etc. Probably, willows were used for bows and arrow shafts, although pine and elm bows have been found in Europe. The sharply pointed flint heads were inserted and bound on to the shafts with cord made from animal tendons, and glue from a mixture of pine resin and beeswax.

Daily life at the Mesolithic campsite

It is quite likely that the flint knappers were women, who would be able to stay in relative safety by the campfire, look after the children and produce the meals. The men, with their greater strength, could then concentrate on hunting. Experiments have shown that a bow and arrow made by such methods is perfectly able to kill a deer. Fig.3 is a photograph of a suspended deer carcass after an arrow of Middle Stone Age type has been fired through it. If the arrowhead does not strike bone, it can pass right through, but if it is stopped by bone, the end may chip off in a fashion identical to arrowhead chips found at Hengistbury. The archer returned to the campsite with the body of his prey. Both bits of the arrowhead would then have been discarded at the campsite, only to be retrieved and matched up by the archaeologist today! The Mesolithic site provided

Fig.3
Fallow deer carcass pierced with Stone Age missile
(Copyright of Nick Barton. 1992)
Suspended carcass in the arrow-firing experiment. Any impact-shattered debris was caught on the underlying plastic sheet. The purpose was to learn about Stone Age man by repeating his hunting method. It showed that these primitive arrows were well able to do their job and that the flint heads could chip if they hit bone.

six instances of such animal bone impact. The dead quarry would have been returned to the camp for skinning, cutting up and eating. Work at the camp included many trades: knapping, processing animal skins for clothing and tents, extracting bones, sinews and antlers for tool-making, butchery, and, not least, cooking. In addition, it was necessary to fish and gather nuts, berries and roots. The campfire would have been very important for warmth, light, cooking, drying and keeping away dangerous animals.

New Stone Age
(Neolithic Period)

By the start of this Age, 6000 years BP, Britain was cut off from mainland Europe and was mostly deciduous woodland. Farmers cleared and burned the trees to grow wheat and barley and raise herds of cattle, sheep and pigs. Since grain could be stored, the tough nomadic life was not needed. No longer did people have to gather food from the wild and follow animal migrations just to survive. Knives, borers, scrapers, whetstones, fabricators, arrowheads, cores, retouched flakes and axes have been found. Such finds make Hengistbury one of the most important Neolithic sites in the south of England. It had workable, light soil, both to cultivate and to support animals. Clothing was of both skin and woven material at this time. The top of the Head and the slopes to north and west seem to have been occupied.

During the earliest part of this period, up to 4,000 BP, there were indications of early farming only. From the Late Neolithic, 4,000 BP to 3,700 BP, much highly decorated Grooved Ware has been found, both at the Head and at Crouch Hill, Stanpit. This Late Neolithic settlement is much less well known than the Iron Age town some 1,700 years later. Users of Grooved Ware had a more dominant position in society, because they were able to secure more of such exotic materials than were other people. The concentration of finds at Hengistbury means that it was an important part of the coastal plain and of high status. It is even possible that Hengistbury had its own henge from this time, but if so, it has long since been lost to the sea.

Bronze Age

From this point, I shall be using the time-scale of BC (Before Christ). The Bronze Age runs from about 3,700 BP to 2,700 BP, or from 1,700 BC to 700 BC. It is so called because of the invention of a metal alloy. Copper

Fig.4

Bronze Age Cinerary Urn found in important barrow by ranger's cottage

(Reproduced from Excavations at Hengistbury Head, Hampshire in 1911-12. Research Report No.3. Published 1915. J. P. Bushe-Fox. Courtesy of the Society of Antiquaries, London)

Known in 1915 as Barrow No.1 (Fig.8), this is now named Barrow 3. Still one of the most exciting finds of Hengistbury Head, the urn contained an Early Bronze Age Wessex burial of high status. The remains of a woman of about 20 were found together with an incense cup, gold cones and a pendant.

and tin were heated together to create bronze and provide a better range of implements. Those who could not afford the new material had to continue using flint artefacts, as indeed found by Gray in Bronze Age barrows.

Evidence shows that the Head was set aside by the community for human burial, i.e. as a cemetery without any obvious form of residential occupation. This is supported by the lack of Deverel-Rimbury pottery at the Head. The 13 tumuli or barrows originally found by Bushe-Fox were considered to be Early Bronze Age, implying that the land may have been abandoned for the rest of the Age. However, the 2001 excavation revealed a Late Bronze Age cremation burial west of the Dykes. But why use Hengistbury purely for burial? If Neolithic man had started arable farming, why not continue it with the improved implements of the Bronze Age? Although the current evidence indicates only cemetery use east of the Dykes, it is still reasonable to assume that some people were living in Barn Field and Long Field at that time and integral with the burial landscape.

In this context, certain finds are worth noting. Firstly, a broken **battle-axe** was dug up in July 1981 in the (Barton and Roe). It was likely that the axe was discarded after being broken, since very few examples exist of such axes from burials. The conclusion at the time was that Hengistbury was perhaps settled in the Early Bronze Age. Secondly, but of less weight, is the report held by Dorset County Council Ancient Monuments Records concerning an Early Bronze Age **flanged axe**. This was found in 1953 two feet below ground level, east of the quarry. A third and significant find, in the 2001 excavation west of the Dykes, is a **sherd** from what could be a pot from the Middle Bronze Age.

In summary, although the river valleys to the north and west were intensively occupied in the Middle and Late Bronze Age, the Head was probably occupied, but more sparsely, for several hundred years before the start of the Iron Age.

Bronze Age burial mounds and finds

The most prominent tumulus (approximately 100 feet wide and 7 feet high), known as Barrow 3 (Bushe-Fox Barrow No.1 in Fig.8) is just south of the ranger's cottage. It is a bowl barrow example of the burial during the Early Bronze Age of a rich member of a tribe, containing an inverted urn (13 inches high and 10.5 inches wide at the mouth, Fig.4) just 4 feet 3 inches below the surface. Contents were the cremated bones of a woman of about 20, an incense cup having ten perforations, three amber beads, two sheet gold cones, a rodent tooth and a halberd pendant. The pendant was a miniature weapon comprising a copper blade in an amber handle. Signs existed of oak charcoal. Some 21 flints were also recovered.

This "furnished Wessex burial" is one of only two found on the south coast and is considered to be of high status. It may be the last Hengistbury burial act of the Bronze Age. Although the barrow had already been opened in the eighteenth century, it seems these items were missed because they were placed off-centre.

One of the earliest signs of interest in the prehistory of the headland occurred in the eighteenth century. In his Description of 20 November 1777 to Gustavus Brander (Fig.52), Francis Grose says that "Near the northern extremity (of the Dykes) is a large barrow or tumulus, which was opened a few years ago when an urn and some human bones were found in it." It seems that much evidence has been lost due to unauthorised barrow excavations. Brander, a Swedish antiquarian and naturalist, was an important figure of the time, able to occupy his leisure time with scientific pursuits. It appears therefore that the Grose Description of Hengistbury Head was to a man interested in buying the headland. By the time of the 1791 Milne map, which shows the Brander name at Hengistbury, the ownership had passed to his family.

Other features of interest from the barrows are:

- Barrow 4 may have been robbed before 1911, because Gray found no burial evidence, but part of a Middle Bronze Age Collared Urn was discovered on the fringe in a 1958 telephone-cable trench.
- Barrow 6 had no central burial but evidence of five secondary ones, which had been disturbed, probably by rabbits.
- Barrow 7 had eight pockets of "burnt matter," two food vessels without cremation, three cremations in urns, two other vessels which disintegrated and some flint artefacts.
- Barrow 10 had been dug previously and no remains existed, except some flints, now in Taunton Museum. However, an Early Bronze Age axe was found nearby and might have accompanied a burial, since removed.
- Barrow 13 had a complete urn, inverted over 3 lbs. weight of bones together with other indications of cremations. (It was common practice to invert burial urns over cremations). The remains were of a woman over 40 years old.

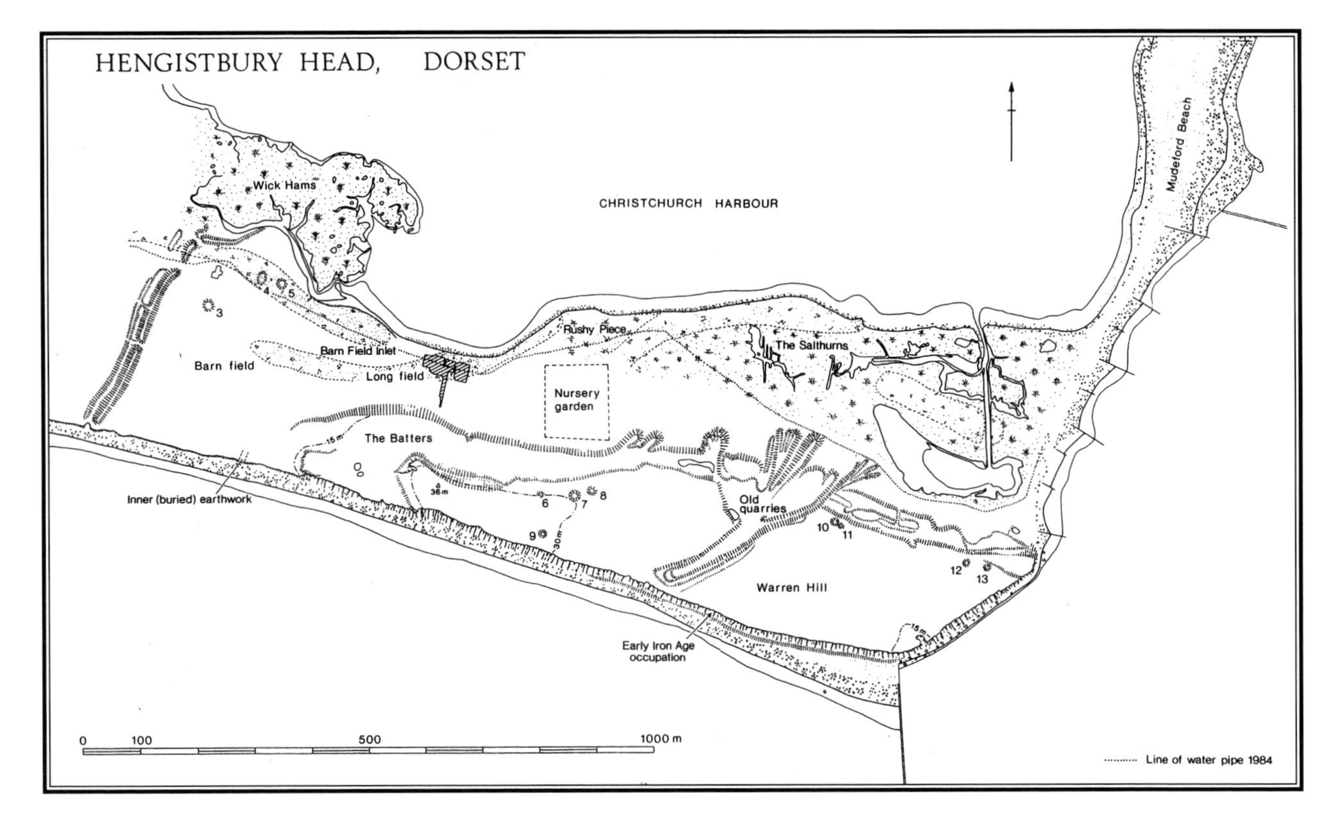

Fig.5 ***Excavation of Iron Age remains in Long Field***
(Reproduced by consent of Barry Cunliffe. 1987)
The position of the most significant Iron Age excavation yet made at Hengistbury is the hatched area known as Site 1. In addition, the barrows are numbered (in a way that supersedes the Bushe-Fox numbering) and the inner earthwork (bank and ditch, photograph at Fig.7) is marked.

In addition to the usually reported barrows, there may be the remains of a bowl barrow, not shown on Fig.5 with the other Bronze Age barrows, nor on the Ordnance Survey. The county council record from 1969 indicates that it is at the highest point of Warren Hill, being a large mound nearly 100 feet diameter and about 4 feet 3 inches high. As mentioned later, the mound could be the remnants of the old Warren Summer House (Fig.13).

The Wessex Archaeology excavation of 2001, west of the Dykes, made internationally important finds from the Late Neolithic/Early Bronze Age up to the Iron Age. One pit had a Collared Urn containing most unusual charred remains with well-preserved hazelnut fragments, shells and crab apples. Ten crab apples were discarded whole into the fire, instead of just the pips, so providing important information about using organic remains as offerings. A partial ring ditch was also found marking what is likely to be another barrow, not previously known. Another important discovery was a Late Bronze Age burial, including the efficiently cremated remains of a single adult human. Other undisturbed pyre sites may well exist in the area.

TWO

IRON AGE AND THE ROMANS

Human history becomes more and more a race between education and catastrophe.

H. G. Wells

BY THE IRON AGE, the stage had been reached where significant progress in civilisation occurred at the same time as military advance. Improving wealth and technical knowledge was marching hand in hand with the power of Rome.

Until recently, it was thought that the Celts spread from central Europe, bringing their iron-working skills. However, it is now felt that this country was already populated by the Britons and had been for many centuries. Trading contacts across the Channel meant that new technology was exported to the people already here. In the Late Iron Age, the trading community of Hengistbury was relatively rich and prosperous, having far more luxury objects than existed at a typical agricultural settlement. It may be that there was an Armorican trading community located at the Head. Hengistbury must have been attractive due to the ironstones available on the beach. Uses would have included swords, knives, farm implements and nails. A strong cohesive community can be imagined: people occupied houses in their own fenced plots and worked in the port or a local industry such as iron smelting.

The settlement began around the start of the Iron Age in 700 BC, but only strongly flourished when it became a major trading port about 100 BC. The decline of this very intensive period of occupation started with a typically ruthless Roman subjugation of the Veneti in Gaul after an uprising in 56 BC. Their navy was destroyed, many were slaughtered, many more were enslaved, and the whole area was put under Rome. It meant that trade with Hengistbury declined. Caesar had promoted shorter, more attractive trade routes to south-eastern England via the Seine and Rhine.

Although trade with the continent reduced, Hengistbury continued as a small Durotrigan town until the Roman invasion of AD 43. It is quite likely that this is the time of the Hengistbury coin mint, which would have helped local trade for the Durotrigans. Afterwards, it was a small village until abandonment of the settlement around the time of the final Roman withdrawal around AD 406. In summary, we can say that the greatest activity, which was initially intense but later declined, took place at the Head from roughly 100 BC to AD 43, compared to the low-key occupations before and after this time.

Early Iron Age
(700 - 400 BC)

The dating of specific sites is not clear enough to decide the extent of the Early Iron Age (EIA) occupation. Although it could have been anything from a large settlement to a single farm, it is most likely to have been something in between. Other nearby EIA sites are concentrated on or near the gravel of the Stour and Avon valleys, or on the chalk of the Isle of Purbeck.

In the seventh and eight centuries BC, there was much contact between Wessex and Armorica, including the exchange of bronze on a large scale. At the same time, very similar pottery extended from Wessex to the

Upper Thames valley, imputing great importance to the Dorset coast as a contact zone. It was an era of widespread contact, trade and consistency of ceramics. However, when bronze became much less important than iron, it was no longer exchanged and there was a big reduction in cultural contact. Hence, by the sixth and fifth centuries BC, we find distinct regional styles of pottery: it seems people were becoming more parochial.

Middle Iron Age
(400 - 100 BC)

There is some limited evidence of MIA occupation at Hengistbury, including circular stake built structures and typical MIA pottery. It seems that there was not much activity, and indeed, there may have been abandonment for a time. There was a tendency for MIA pottery to be found in direct association with imports from the Late Iron Age. Hence, there was perhaps no MIA occupation, or more likely, a short period only just pre-LIA. If this is right, it implies light agricultural use only for some 250 years up to 150 BC. The 2001 excavation yielded pottery evidence for occupation west of the Dykes probably for around the end of the MIA, although the vessel in question was strictly LIA type.

Hengistbury and the Late Iron Age trading revolution

The intense activity, from 100 BC onwards, took place against a background of economic and social change. Before then, there were small mixed farming communities, which had seen little change for as much as 1,000 years. Hill forts became increasingly important and well-defended centres to serve their rural catchment areas of typically 40 square miles. They provided protected storage and redistribution for local and foreign products, an administrative headquarters, and perhaps even legal and religious functions. Hengistbury could well have acted in this way.

Suddenly, the revolution started in the first century BC with the abandonment of the hill forts over most of Sussex and Hampshire. They were replaced by new enclosures sited to control trade routes, for example, on valleys overlooking river crossings. However, this did not happen in Dorset and nearby areas to the west, where the hill forts continued until being taken during the Roman invasion. While this partial relocation was going on, trade routes opened up with the continent. The process continued apace with coinage and markets, until south-eastern England had become an urban trading economy by AD 43. The significance of Hengistbury in all this change is its major role in starting up the continental trade with the south of England.

In summary, the evidence shows that Hengistbury rapidly developed one of the first important trading links between southern Britain and the continent.

Major port and one of first "towns" in Britain

Hengistbury may have been the first real urban community of the time, a prototype early English town, with its wide variety of industries, considerable relative size and wealth, and most of all, its high quality trading links. Poole Harbour was also the site of a major port. The so-called Green Island Causeway has been shown to be two quays, instead of a causeway, dating from the Middle Iron Age. Intriguingly, in one sense, it is the same story as at Hengistbury, of a thriving cross-channel port and community now virtually deserted and without signs of the past.

It is known that unstable flat-bottomed, high-sided boats were used around the time of Christ. Such shallow draught vessels with leather sails could not have been very safe and seaworthy, especially considering the lack of navigation aids for the twelve-hour crossing from Cherbourg. Imports to the settlement at the Head caused least difficulty, as they were heavy items such as wine and metal ore. But to avoid capsize when the same boats were used for exporting light goods, gravel ballast was probably added. Latest thinking is that the type of vessels used by the seafaring Veneti came to the harbour, although it remains the case that the remains of a Roman ship were found there in 1910. Many cattle were apparently butchered at the headland and their hides exported. It appears that this light cargo was probably supplemented by the gravel ballast from the hollows found in the 1980s to have been scooped out from the south side of the harbour, where cargo ships beached.

The Britons used woven clothing, were skilled in metalwork and were able to present a fearsome appearance to enemies, with woad tattoos and chalk in the hair. Spinning and weaving were carried on at

Hengistbury. Evidence (of post-holes) has been found for typical Iron Age storehouses. Thatched roundhouses were erected with walls both of wattle and daub and of split planks. Such dwellings had central hearths. Hengistbury Port was well located for trade with both this country and abroad. It was positioned at the boundary of the territories of the Durotriges and Atrebates (which became approximately Dorset and Hampshire respectively).

It is likely that food was generally imported to Hengistbury town, which relied on trade and industry for its survival. A summary of trade might be:

> *Exports* to have included cattle, skins, hunting dogs, craft-ware, corn, copper, gold, silver, iron goods, salt and probably slaves. Since the Roman Empire was based on slavery, it is a fair assumption that local people were forcibly sent to a slave market at Hengistbury.
>
> *Imports* to have included metals for melting down such as silver-rich lead from the Mendips; copper (having a high silver content) from Cornwall; copper from Devon and Cornwall, gold scrap from inland, and shale from Kimmeridge. There were also luxury goods such as wine, figs, Armorican pottery and manganese glass from the continent. The British trading links, to the west of the Head, are supported by finding pottery and some coins from those same three locations. Crops were also brought in from a wide area.

A considerable two-way business was conducted from Hengistbury with both British and foreign customers. From about 100 BC, life in southern Britain started to mirror that in mainland Europe. Gallic coins, bronzes from the Mediterranean, and wheel-thrown pottery were all used or copied locally. This import of continental culture took place partly through Hengistbury from north-western Gaul, and partly through south-eastern England from Belgica. South-eastern England prospered at the expense of south-western England, but

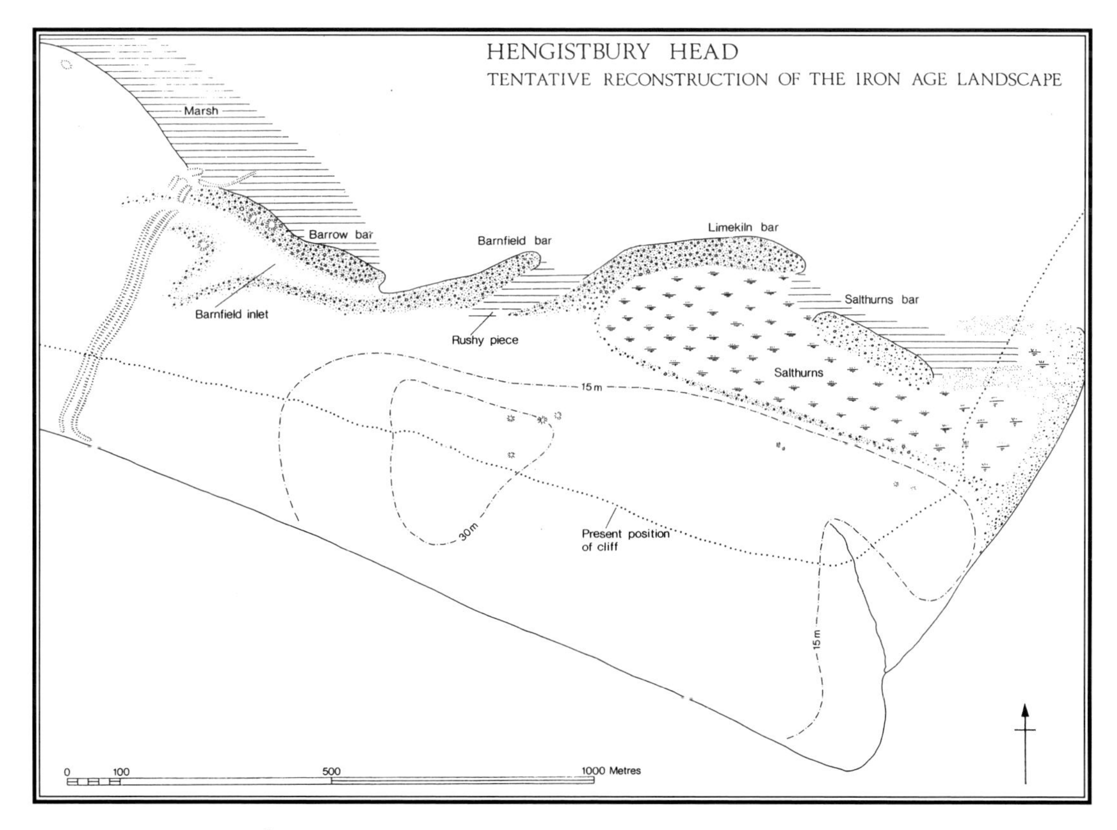

Fig.6 ***Tentative reconstruction of the Iron Age landscape***

(Reproduced by consent of Barry Cunliffe. 1987)

Simplified geomorphology in the first millennium BC. The Iron Age cliff position relates to the Mackenzie map of 1785 (Fig.11) and the present one to the latest OS maps. The shape of the south side of the harbour was different, in particular having an inlet in what is now Barn Field. My own view is that the headland was much larger in the first millennium than shown here.

Hengistbury continued to be an important market centre with excellent sea and river communications. It still imported some French pottery, albeit probably via the east coast. Perhaps this is the stage at which manufacturing expanded to fill the gap. It is known that the settlement existed at the time Vespasian swept through all the hill forts of the area in AD 43 to 44.

Landscape in the Iron Age

Fig.6 depicts the headland at about twice its current size, although my view is that it was much bigger. This is because Fig.6 assumes little coast erosion from the Iron Age to the eighteenth century. Certainly, there would have been large quantities of ironstones at the end of the headland, doubtless giving an appearance similar to that shown in Fig.38 and Fig.18. Wick Hams did not then exist, and four gravel ridges (Barrow Bar, Barnfield Bar, Limekiln Bar and Salthurns Bar) stood above marsh and water. Relative land level was much lower in Barn Field, allowing an inlet on what is now dry land. Other inlets were at Rushy Piece and Salthurns.

The shoals were probably laid down when the east flowing Stour deposited a river terrace. The tidal inlet at Barn Field has now gone, leaving only a slight depression in the ground level to show for it. In the Middle and Late Iron Ages, it would have flooded a number of times due to sea level rise or a succession of high tides, resulting in deposits of sands. Later, windblown sands and the gravel metalling, installed along the south shore of the harbour, would have caused further rises in ground level. It became possible for occupational activity to spread down to land below the old High Water Mark. A drying out of the inter-tidal range would be consistent with a change from the south shore being scoured to it attracting alluvium instead.

In the light of the 2001 report from Wessex Archaeology, we can imagine a continuous LIA occupation from a point west of the Dykes, along the shore to beyond Rushy Piece. Apart from boat ballast, the small gravel quarries on the south shore of the harbour probably provided material to raise further the ground level of the former Barn Field Inlet. Gravel was also used in an engineering operation to provide a simple "sloping hard" for the port. LIA remains show ditching and gullies, which do not seem to appear on the site earlier. It is possible that they were necessary by then due to a higher water table.

Another interesting landscape feature was included in the Barton monograph. The line of an old bank and ditch runs NW/SE for over 550 feet from the cliff, just east of the Reindeer Camp site. The low hump at ground level is just visible. Although perhaps we will never know for sure, it could be a Late Bronze Age or Early Iron Age field boundary. Considering the huge amount of erosion since then, such a boundary may have enclosed a much bigger area of land than can be seen today.

Defence of promontory by earthworks

Were the Dykes felt necessary to provide security for the headland from possible attack from the west? Times must have been uncertain, because of the need for the large number of hill forts built throughout Britain. Some say that they were probably found to be required for defence against people who had suffered a bad harvest. Another view is that they were needed to provide both protected storage and a trading/administrative centre to serve local farms. The latest theory is simply that a secure environment was needed for the benefit of traders coming to the port and the resident community. It is thought that the building of Double Dykes started in the period from around the seventh century BC. Although the north section of them now ends in flat marshes, this is due to a build-up of alluvial material since the Iron Age. When built, the north section would have reached the south shore of the harbour. However, finds made in 2001 show that some people lived to the west, presumably because at that particular time, the risk was much less.

Clearly, the banks (which were built of sand and gravel) and ditches would have been larger then, because there has been erosion by weather and trampling, and a lot of ditch filling from wind-blown sand. Measurements were taken in 1911 showing a height difference of 25 feet 6 inches in two places between the original base of the central ditch and the actual top of the main inner bank. If we assume a seven feet high wooden stockade on top, an attacker from within the ditch would be looking up to archers at about the height (32 feet 6 inches) of the ridge of a two-storey house. Indeed, it would be higher – some 40 feet at the time of the Iron Age – as this disregards the amount of top erosion. Imagine planning an infantry attack up such a high and steep slope, with arrows raining down.

The turf lines revealed in a 1911 photograph of the end of the Inner Dyke mean that it was probably built in three phases. On the other hand, the Outer Dyke appears to be a single gravel-based tip, without later work. The final completion of the defence is likely to have coincided with the most intense period of use, when the trading links were strongest, for about 100 years from 100 BC.

Fig.7 ***Iron Age defence bank and ditch east of Double Dykes***
(Author 2002)
The position of the ditch can be seen where it has been filled in with darker material. It is not known whether this structure, which is about 650 feet east of Double Dykes, went north to Barn Field Inlet, nor indeed whether it pre-dated the Dykes. At some stage however, it seems to have been a secondary defence system. See also Figs. 5 and 46.

War chariots, horses, swords and shields would have been used by attackers, whilst arrows, javelins, slingshot and spears would have been the defence. The accuracy of the sling is about twice the distance from the higher dyke to the ditch beyond the lower one, whilst the javelin is accurate from the higher dyke to the top of the lower one. An attacker under such fire between the Dykes would find it hard either to advance or retreat. A hoard of sling stones has been found near to the Dykes at Wick Hams.

I do not think the Dykes have been specifically investigated for remains, even in 1911. Despite the acid soil, 602 bone fragments have been found at the Head, implying that an excavation could prove fruitful. A good justification would have to be put to English Heritage, who decide what excavations may be carried out at this Ancient Monument. It is not known, therefore, whether the Dykes were ever stormed with much loss of life. However, it is interesting that one of the bridle bits for a pair of chariot horses has been found at Hengistbury, a find of sufficient importance to form the cover drawing of Prof. Cunliffe's 1978 book. Although a hill fort may have been a practical defence against attack, it was no match for the Romans, who took about 20 of them in this region after the invasion of AD 43.

There is another little-known defensive gravel bank and ditch, as shown on Figs. 5, 7 and 46, lying about 650 feet east of the Dykes. It is likely to have been a Late Bronze Age or Early Iron Age defence, which was either a separate system, or part of the main Dykes system. It is no longer visible from the cliff top, since at some time, the ditch was manually filled with gravel and blown material has obscured both bank and ditch. The base of the bank was at least 30 feet and the ditch over 20 feet wide and six feet deep. It can however be seen from the beach. Fig.7 is a photograph of the ditch, a bowl-shaped section of dark sandy soil. The full position of this inner defence earthwork has not been scientifically established. Geophysical methods were used without success to try and determine its landward extent. It may have simply run across to Barnfield Inlet as implied by a divining exercise

Evidence of trade and industry

This section gives some detail on the artefacts, which have been found and the forces, which lie behind them. The picture is one of many human skills developing from scratch within a co-operative community or "town," in order to achieve a better way of life.

Main Trading Patterns

After centuries of little trade, the Late Iron Age port of Hengistbury became very active about 100 BC as a direct result of the slow take-over of Gaul by Rome. As the people in northern Gaul lost their trading partners in the south, new outlets for their goods and a different source of raw materials were found in Britain. In addition, Rome had expanded to southern Gaul and created the province of Transalpina by 120 BC. This encouraged Italian traders to find markets for their wine in the north including Britain, in exchange for manpower and raw materials. Hence by 100 BC, Roman expansion was creating trading opportunities out of Hengistbury. The commerce worked by Italian goods destined for Britain being short-hauled to St. Servan (near St. Malo) and then taken across the channel by the Coriosolites of northern Brittany. Armorican goods in pots were added to these items for export to the Hengistbury/Poole contact area. British exports, such as Kimmeridge shale, made the return crossing to St. Servan. Many goods moved through a number of trading links before reaching Britain from the Roman world and vice versa.

The Roman conquest of Gaul was finally completed in 51 BC, so disrupting Hengistbury's trade with Gaul and Rome. It seems that Caesar concluded monopoly-trading rights with the Kent tribes as allies, following his reconnaissance of 55 BC and campaign of 54 BC. The disruption meant a decline in trade rather than a cessation. Not only was a lot of pottery imported, but amber has been found from France, Spain and Italy. Bushe-Fox opines that close links were demonstrated with pre-Roman Gaul in at least two ways: the fact that Caesar often fought with Britons serving in the Gallic army, and that a major reason for Gaul opposing Rome was a wish to keep trading with Britain.

Coins and Coin Mint

It must have been an exciting discovery when Site 33 (Fig.8) yielded Bushe-Fox a hoard of over 3,000 coins! There is a big variety, many of which are strongly suggestive of a mint. The precious and base alloys were all available at the Head. He concluded that there was "possibly a coin mint" at Hengistbury. Some now consider that it was probable. Many coins of the Hengistbury Hoard were in mint condition when buried, but badly decayed into silver chloride when found. The same site yielded valuable copper and silver ingots.

Celtic coins can be divided into Durotrigan, the local Dorset tribe, and Non-Durotrigan, which can be sub-divided into the British and the Gaulish, the latter coming from Gallia, Belgica and Armorica. The Non-Durotrigan British coins are mainly silver and appear to have been used for trade (50 BC to AD 100) from the south coast to the Thames valley. Those from Belgica may be payments to British mercenaries who fought with the Gauls against Caesar in almost all his campaigns. The Armorican coins imply trading activity with Gaul, or possibly a foreign presence at the port of Hengistbury.

As for the Durotrigan coins, the first phase of staters were made of silver and gold to a good standard of workmanship. Phase Two however produced coarser, debased silver/bronze coins. In addition, there are over 90 varieties of bronze stater. Of the 1,700 cast bronze staters found, 1,696 are known to have come from within a five-mile radius of Hengistbury. The Hengistbury Hoard included so many debased staters that it might well suggest a mint. There are also Durotrigan quarter staters (which again progressed from gold and silver to bronze) and a silver coin called a "starfish."

Including excavations and past finds, the Cunliffe monograph refers to 3,326 Celtic coins and only 107 Roman ones. Bushe-Fox found the Roman coins in Site 33, the earliest of which goes back to 91 BC. They have mainly been deposited at the British Museum and include gold, silver, bronze and silver/bronze. Since so few Roman coins were found, it is thought that the intensity of occupation was low during the third and fourth centuries AD.

Luxury goods

Late Iron Age brooches of bronze and iron have been catalogued and dated. Rings from chain belts and bracelets have also been found. One main find from site 33 was a twisted mass of gold. When disentangled, it was found to be a complete small torc, usable as an armlet, a gold strip and a fragment of another torc. It is probable that although some of these objects came from abroad, others were made locally. Other items include bridle bit, terret rings, fasteners, toggles, studs, silver/gold handle, Roman netting needle, bronze rings, rivets and pre-Roman glass beads/armlets of continental origin or inspiration. It was a prosperous society including wealthy traders.

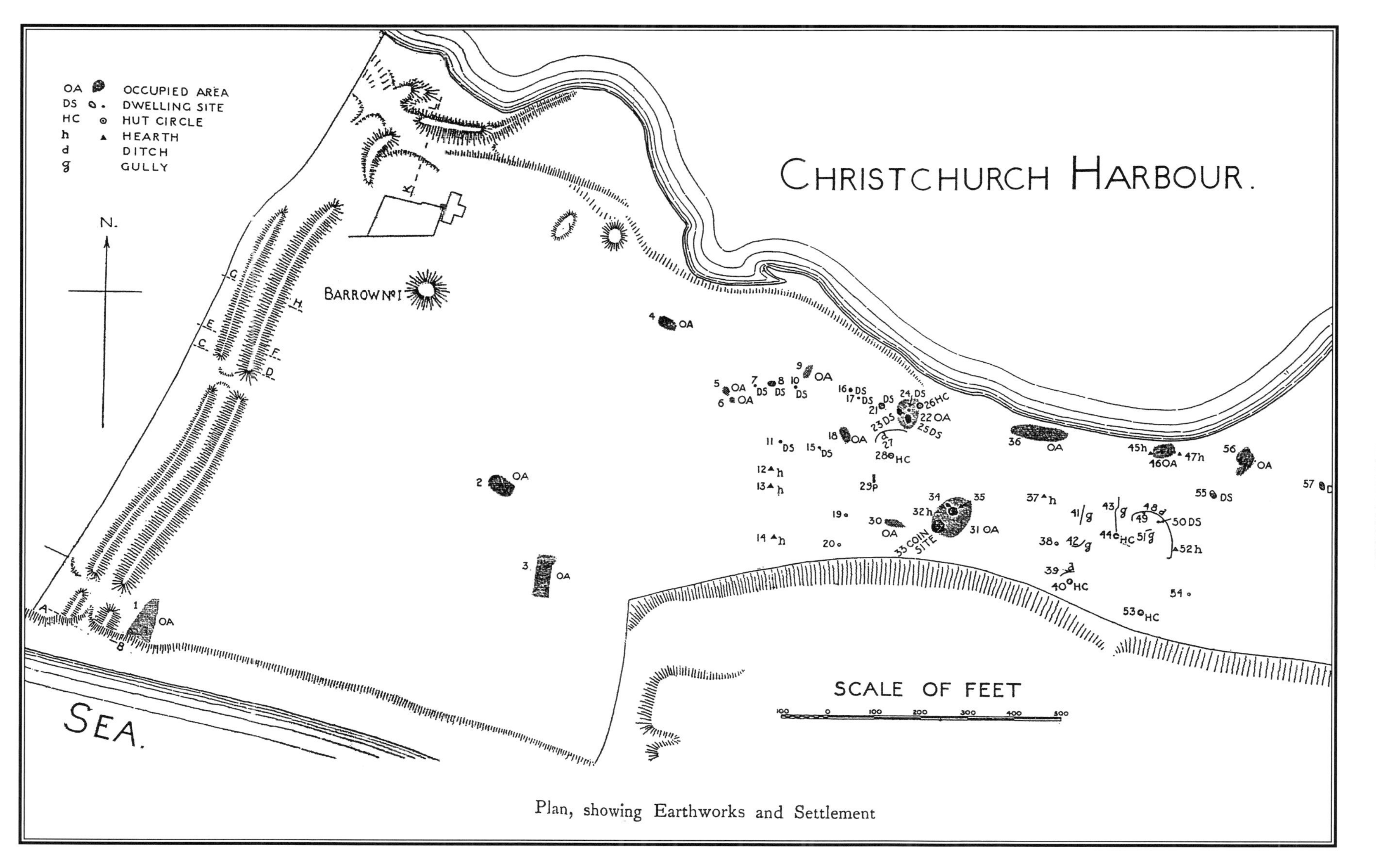

Fig.8 ***Iron Age settlement in Long Field***

(Reproduced from Excavations at Hengistbury Head, Hampshire in 1911-12. Research Report No.3. Published 1915. J. P. Bushe-Fox. Courtesy of the Society of Antiquaries, London)

A drawing showing the locations and types of archaeological finds. The coin site and Barrow No.1 are among the most important. This was the first comprehensive investigation of prehistoric Hengistbury. It is amazing now to realise that a thriving town and port existed in the lee of the headland.

Shale, stone, clay products and textiles

Baked clay slingshot has been found, implying hunting and/or defence. In addition, Kimmeridge shale was imported to the Head and initially hand turned on site. Later, lathes were in use. For example, eight out of 14 armlets are believed to have been lathe-turned there in the Late Iron Age. Shale spindle whorls have been found from throughout the period and 13 loom weights (the largest weighing about 4 lbs.) were recorded, made from baked clay. Since spinning and weaving was conducted, there was a fully functioning textile industry.

Some 112 fragments of quernstones were found. Both saddle and rotary types can be identified. Many are of Roman design. Although it may not be significant, since only four per cent of the main settlement site has been fully excavated, there is a quernstone evidence gap for the Middle Iron Age, raising the possibility of temporary abandonment, either of use or of corn grinding. Whetstones were essential for blade sharpening in the Iron Age and 32 of them were duly recovered.

Iron working

The iron ore on the beach was of good quality, and potting clay was available on the slopes of Warren Hill. Iron-smelting hearths have been found, at the top of Warren Hill and elsewhere. The strong winds from the cliff edge would have helped to generate the high temperatures needed, around 1,300° C. Unfortunately, the physical evidence of some hearths has now disappeared over the edge through erosion. Having made the iron implements, the tribe could trade them for farm produce, charcoal, etc., with those settled in the river valleys below. Experiments have shown that the Hengistbury iron ore, which contains aluminium, is much easier to smelt when mixed with one from Sussex. This does not mean such a mixture method was necessarily used: it could be that effective smelting of ironstones is simply a skill now lost to us.

Non-ferrous metal working

Bushe-Fox found a lump of 98.5% copper, weighing 5 lbs. 10oz. This is sufficient to prove a copper working industry. Another lump weighing 19 lbs. 8 oz. was an impure alloy of copper (50.45%), silver (46.43%) and gold (1.2%), (plus a small amount of foreign matter), indicating imports to Hengistbury for metalworking. The discovery of cupellation hearths for re-melting means silver purification. The process needs lead, traces of which have been found, probably imported from the Mendips. Alloys were certainly made. Crucibles were used for melting bronze, which was then cast. Copper was similarly melted, although it is not established whether artefacts were also likely to have been made. It has been proved by experiment that gold was tested on site.

Glass working

The site has yielded unworked purple glass, containing tin and manganese and opaque yellow tin-opacified glass. It is not yet certain that glass was worked at Hengistbury, in the absence of further finds, such as malformed armlets or beads, or crucibles with adhering residues.

Salt workings

Excavations have suggested that salt workings can be reasonably assumed on the northern shore of the settlement throughout the Iron Age. Kiln supports for evaporating troughs have been identified. Ceramic containers, to evaporate the water and/or to pack the salt, have also been discovered. These items have various shapes, such as that of a flower pot, truncated cylinder, rounded bowl and trough.

Other finds

A Breton palstave or axe was found by Bushe-Fox on site 33. It is of a type that was commonly used on both sides of the Channel, so demonstrating the trade in progress. A Sicilian axe has been found in the sea at Southbourne, again showing the distance of trading contacts.

Pottery

Early Iron Age pottery (700 BC to 400 BC) was identified from only a few of the Bushe-Fox sites and then described as Class A. It was widespread in central southern England and intimately connected with south-west France and the Pyrenees. The later part of this period has pottery in the Dorset tradition, whilst that from before 600 BC is much more widespread. More specifically, the earliest of the EIA material is the Kimmeridge-Caburn style, comprising large coarse and ovoid jars from the seventh and eighth centuries BC. The next type of pottery is still coarse, but differently decorated and more flared. It is called the Late All Cannings Cross-Meon style from the fifth and sixth centuries BC.

Pottery of very mixed types, believed to come from the Middle Iron Age (400 BC to 100 BC) was found at the Head from Hampshire (St. Catherine's Hill-Worthy Down), Wiltshire (Yarnbury-Highfield), and Dorset (Maiden Castle-Marnhull) ceramic styles. The use of Hengistbury as a market at this time would be consistent with the evidence. Late Iron Age pottery (100 BC to AD 400) named Class B by Bushe-Fox, was thought in 1915 to be from Hengistbury only. Then, in 1955, the same type, dated around 100 BC, was discovered in Normandy. Objects were not found from any later than the fourth century AD.

The whole period from eighth century BC to fourth century AD can be divided into two phases:

Phase One up to 100 BC, involved mainly locally handmade pottery, including both Early and Middle Iron Age. *Phase Two* reflected imports of better quality, which were locally copied on the potter's wheel. This phase can be subdivided as follows:

Late Iron Age 1 100 BC to 50 BC, when there was great contact with the continent. It included the impressive Dressel type 1A pots, which were tall, Italian jars, weighing over 3.5 stones and used for the transport of wine. Armorican ware came from three separate regions of northern France. Types included Black Cordoned, Rilled Micaceous and Graphite Coated. Distribution is known to be much less than the Dressel 1A amphorae.

Late Iron Age 2 from 50 BC onwards, when contact with the continent was much less, and can be described as the Durotrigan period. This was local to begin with, until the large kilns (e.g. that at Poole) took over from the second century AD.

The Dressel 1A vessels have been found in great number, showing a heavy trade when they were common in Europe (approx.100 BC to 50 BC). The number was so far in excess of other types of pottery that many cargoes of this wine were probably destined for inland. It is estimated that there may have been the remains of about a thousand of these vessels at the headland. On the other hand, there are only one sixth as many Dressel 1Bs at the Head, a type which dates from approximately 50 BC: but there are plenty of examples of this type in south-eastern England, showing that the Roman traders were forced to deal with tribes there almost exclusively.

Another pointer to the same conclusion is that from about 50 BC to AD 50, local pottery is mainly Durotrigan. Much of this was wheel-turned and decorated to a high standard. It is probable that French pottery was copied at the Head, and this may have been the first use of the potter's wheel in the country. However, imported pottery has also been discovered, coming from the Lizard, Devon, the Mendips, the Channel Islands, Normandy and Brittany. Late Iron Age imports from Gaul included plates, flagons and bowls. Some foreign material could even have originated with refugees from Caesar. The changes occurring about 50 BC, due to Caesar's Gallic campaign, are also emphasised with the start of imports of Catalan wine in Spanish ware (Dressel 1-Pascual 1) and that from western France, and the end of imports of Dressel 1A and pottery from Armorica. At this time, it seems that raw materials were imported and many pots and their contents exported from the site.

A key conclusion from the pottery record is the extremely high level of trade at the port of Hengistbury for the first 50 years of the Late Iron Age.

Evidence from bones and plants

Although, as mentioned previously, there is poor evidence of old bones from this site, due to acid soil, 602 fragments have still been identified. In the Late Iron Age, they mainly came from cattle, although pigs, sheep and horses also feature. Unlike most Iron Age sites, cattle were the most common animals at Hengistbury, followed by pigs and then sheep. Horses increased in Roman times. It is known that the Romans killed their cattle at a younger age than did native people.

Much land was given over to heath for fuel, building material and perhaps fodder. Arable crops were grown more inland, making Hengistbury a net importer of these in the Iron Age. Peas and flax were however grown there in the Late Iron Age. Indeed, at that stage, the Head seems to have switched from being mainly a consuming site to being a processing one.

The 2001 Wessex Archaeology excavation provided more information. Occupation west of the Dykes was shown by the discovery of pits containing the remains of Iron Age pottery. Since the pottery was accompanied by much charred grain, chaff and weed seeds, it implied domestic activity rather than burials. It follows that apart from the heath areas, arable land was cultivated and material was collected for fodder.

Significance of Iron Age Hengistbury

The Iron Age represents the first time that man used Hengistbury Head in a recognisably modern way. Its first use had been for intermittent campsites for the hunter-gatherers of the Old and Middle Stone Ages.

Although there had been some form of New Stone Age settlement, the people did not trade from a town as such, whilst the Bronze Age use had been mainly as a cemetery. It was also the last time that the Head was used residentially. All later use has related to agriculture, quarrying, defence and amenity.

It is hard to overstate the importance of a time when one of the first urban communities in the country was formed, a variety of industries set up, and a port established with many different cargoes and trading links. A prosperous, defended town existed in the lee of Warren Hill for up to 150 years before the Roman conquest.

Julius Caesar and the Celts

Julius Caesar's enormous influence even extended to the development of Hengistbury. Owing to the Romans' fear of the Germans, it was not hard for Caesar to justify his campaigning. He wanted to bring Gaul under Rome to prevent it from being overrun by the Germans, which would compromise the security of Rome. The Celts had originated as an aristocratic culture in eastern France and southern Germany in the fifth and sixth centuries BC, before migrating across Europe in the next two centuries. By Caesar's time, Celtic traditions dominated Gaul and Britain. In 55 BC and at the age of 45, he carried out an armed survey of Britain. He noted that the British reinforced the Gauls "in almost all of our campaigns." He made Commius the king of the Atrebates and sent him as an envoy to advise the tribes to seek the protection of Rome. The British reaction was to put Commius in chains and attack the Romans as they struggled to leave their ships in the waves.

The following year, Caesar crossed the Channel with five legions and 2,000 cavalry in 800 ships. He found a very large population with many cattle and farm buildings. Due partly to the risk of unrest in Gaul, Caesar did not try to consolidate his position. It is probable that he prohibited trade to places like Hengistbury in favour of re-routing it to the pro-Roman tribes of eastern England. Both invasions were diversions from the main task of subjugating Gaul, which took from 58 to 51 BC. It was 98 years before the Romans returned. Although the real invasion of Britain was in AD 43, with the military occupation lasting for some 363 years, the importance of Caesar to Hengistbury remains: a severe trade disruption.

The Roman invasion

It has been persuasively argued that Vespasian of the 2nd Legion captured the Isle of Wight and then landed at Hengistbury. This would have been more suitable than other sites due to the benefits of distance, tide, wind, landing beaches and harbour. There was a good route to the Severn along the Stour Valley, with its various oppida to capture, and the benefit of the Avon as a right flank protection. Whilst there is a paucity of information about the impact of the Roman occupation on Hengistbury, many commentators feel that it was not important enough for them to colonise fully. At the time of the conquest, the local tribe was still the Durotriges. The hoard of some 3,000 Durotrigan coins, found at Hengistbury , would probably have stayed in use for about 60 to 70 years from AD 43. The absence of later coins implies agricultural use only of the Head after this time. It is likely that Hengistbury was used as a small farm of minor importance for most of the Roman occupation, after which it was abandoned.

Early Roman harbour works

It is known that there was Roman involvement at Hengistbury well before the invasion. In 1985, Prof. Cunliffe discovered a massive programme of engineering on the south side of the harbour. Around 100 BC, a Roman harbour was formed, including a channel dug out in deep water, a sloping gravel ramp and a level gravel-topped platform. Apart from gravel, bones were used from cattle, horses and sheep. It gave very good archaeological potential for further investigation. These works, located at Rushy Piece, were to allow easy beaching of ships.

Roman finds

Roman pottery has been found together with some limited evidence of occupation, such as a Roman rubbish pit about ten feet deep, and some hearths. It is possible from the coin evidence that there was sporadic abandonment. One view is that the settlement was abandoned after the Roman attacks of AD 43 and 44, to be reoccupied towards the end of that century for a period of around 250 years, purely as a small farming settlement. The shoreline road was built along the south side of the harbour in the Late Iron Age before the Roman conquest. During the Roman period, it was maintained, with fields eventually being laid out to north and south of it in the fourth century AD. Research is able to show the field boundary ditches, which ran at right angles to the road down the slope to the harbour. They were re-dug many times.

Occupation evidence of ovens, pits and post-holes was discovered in Professor Cunliffe's Site 1, but nothing substantial. Iron slag and lumps of iron ore have been found spread around in Roman layers in the vicinity. Field drainage ditches have been found, as well as signs of Roman cultivation in the Nursery Garden. Other evidence of agricultural use includes spade marks and plough ruts. On Site 3, it was even possible to trace the northern edge of the Roman field system. Taken with plant remains analysis, the indication is of arable farming over a large amount of the low-lying part of the headland.

The remains of a Roman ship, a burnt wooden vessel or galley (with iron bolts) were discovered in Christchurch Harbour in 1910. The location of this vessel, which was first thought to be Viking, is uncertain. It may be in the north-eastern corner, close to the entry point of the Bure Brook, or perhaps at Blackberry Point. It contained a graceful, wheel-turned vase or incense cup, which was sent to the British Museum and identified as Roman. In the same vessel were found portions of a human skull, leg and arm. Sadly, David Chambers, a Southbourne antique dealer who discovered these things, perished in World War I and no further information is now to hand.

Whilst Hengistbury must have been a backwater compared to the Roman military supply base at Hamworthy, the coins mean that it could have been occupied much more intensively than as just a peasant farm. There are other indications of this. For instance, the centre of the Roman settlement has still to be identified, meaning that there is evidence still to find. There is also a concentration of first and early second century coins and a collection of Gallo-Belgic wares, samian pottery and brooches. This implies a greater use, at least up to the middle of the second century.

There is a general lack of finds dating from the late third and fourth centuries. The small amount of pottery and a few coins indicates a low level of occupation by that time, perhaps simply as a peasant farmstead near the western edge of the Nursery Garden. Thereafter, the marsh encroached in to the harbour and blown sand raised field levels. There followed a reversion to the wild for hundreds of years.

THREE

DARK AGES TO VICTORIAN TIMES

A viewe taken the 23, 24, 25 of june anno dni. 1574, ...
of the daungerous landing places uppon the sea coste from Bornemouthe, ...
Wee Finde more oon other like place within the same baye betwixt Redd Cliff, and Hensbury ende, called lowe lands....of Depthe viii or ix Fathem, having verye good ancorhold within the same.

Return from Earl of Southampton 8 July 1574,
enclosing a certificate of the dangerous places
for the landing of an enemy on
the coasts of Hampshire

Abandonment as a main habitation

UNDER the Romans, Hengistbury had the benefit of a mixed farming system continuing to the fourth century. Road access existed to the level crop growing fields on the south side of the harbour. By about AD 400, there are no indications that Hengistbury was occupied as a place to live. No doubt there would have been varying amounts of agricultural use, or hunting, but the withdrawal of the legions marked a long period of limited use or abandonment. It is likely to have been only fringe quality agricultural land in a sparse, mainly rural, economy, at a time when living on the coast was increasingly insecure due to raids from the Saxons. People moved inland to the fortified townships.

Over several hundred years prior to the Norman Conquest, the Saxons settled in the south. Although the Danes were successful in the north east of the country, King Alfred prevented a complete take-over, resulting in a somewhat different form of society and land management. For instance, in 1086, west Hampshire and east Dorset were found to have 20 to 25% of the population as serfs or slaves, whilst there were less than 5% of these under Danelaw in the north east. Nonetheless, the Saxons had managed to create a relatively wealthy, sophisticated and reasonably ordered society. It included a strict system of social and wealth grading, together with the necessary military, local and central administration. By this time, under ordered Saxon government, the use of Hengistbury would have depended mainly on how marginal the land was compared to better land in the river valleys. In this period also, it was likely to have been mainly disused.

The earliest event after the Romans left seems to have been the Pope sending St. Birinus to convert central England. In turn, Birinus sent priests to Wessex in the seventh century. They wisely chose the compacted gravel spit between the Avon and Stour to found a missionary church at Twynham, which has been spelt in various ways and derives from "where two rivers meet," or "between the waters" from the original Saxon *betweox thaem eam.* It was a wise choice of location due to defence advantages, river communications and potential as a fishing town. In recognition of its success, around 900, Alfred made the town a burgh. It was duly fortified and became a defensive settlement.

The Saxon boundaries of the town can be seen on the excellent Millennium Trail map (see Bibliography). Protection certainly appeared to be needed in view of the warlike methods of the Danes, including the practice of using an axe to strike open a victim's chest and then throwing the lungs over his shoulders to resemble a flying angel.

Following the Norman Conquest, Hengistbury Head became a small and unimportant part of Christchurch for hundreds of years. There were no strong political or economic reasons for the various owners, listed in a separate chapter, to take very much interest. When it was used, it is more likely to have been for pasture than arable. Certainly towards the end of the period covered in this chapter, there are reports of cattle, sheep and rabbits, whilst the owner found it best to have a gamekeeper in what is now the ranger's cottage (Fig.14). This fits in with the nature of the locality, in that Poole and Christchurch were simply small towns with little in between.

The Black Death hit Christchurch in July 1348 and probably caused the death of at least one third of the local population, the same proportion as in the rest of the country. A man could be healthy at the start of the day and be dead by lunchtime. Fields would have been left uncultivated, houses left empty, and essential bridges poorly maintained. On the other hand, the plague boosted the wages of the survivors and the numbers who paid a monetary rent, rather than a feudal service rent to their lords. This last must always have been a bone of contention, especially at harvest time, when the tenant had to help with harvest on his lord's land as a priority before his own. What would have been the impact of this increased freedom on Hengistbury? If the land was used at the time for stock farming, this may well have stopped if there were better farming opportunities opening up elsewhere due to depopulation.

Although in the eighteenth century there were farms at Tuckton and Wick, for example, Bourne Heath (or Pool Heath, now Bournemouth) was mainly heathland. The viability of arable cultivation east of the Dykes must have been doubtful. Also at this time and during the early part of the nineteenth century, it is thought that there was small-scale lime burning on the harbour shore and salt extraction at Salt Hurns.

In summary, the indications are that farming was very limited from the time of the Romans to that of the Victorians. Indeed, the main significance of the headland was probably as a military lookout. Hence, despite occasional threats of limited harbour improvements, or a new railway, the solitude of this place remained essentially unbroken for at least 1,400 years, until the rude disturbance of the peace by the nineteenth century mining operation described elsewhere. But now, I want to look more closely at the time following the Norman invasion.

Domesday and farming at Hengistbury

The impact of the Conquest on Hengistbury would have been the same as on the wider area. The amount of land adequate to support a peasant household was typically around 120 acres and known as a "hide." Since land quality varied, a hide could be more or less than this acreage. Moreover, it was a unit of assessment for taxation purposes. Indeed, one could imagine the Head amounting to just one hide, if that. A "virgate" was a quarter of a hide and a "plough" usually meant a team of eight oxen, as supplied by several households. A smallholder's annual income varied from three to eleven shillings only. The twenty years before Domesday in 1086 had been marked by famine, war and high taxation. One result was a big fall in land values. Times were hard. For example, any household farming the Hengistbury land in 1083 must have been less than happy about William the Conqueror's tax that year of six shillings per hide!

Perhaps the main feature of the feudal system was the sheer rigidity of the hierarchy. The King owned everything and granted most manors to Tenants in Chief such as Hugh de Port. In turn, sub-tenancies were granted by the Tenants in Chief, e.g. to Robert of Winkton. Beneath these, we have the manorial workers, each with their own duties and status, including Freemen, Socmen, Villeins, Bordars, Cottars, Radknights, Coliberts and the landless serfs. In 1086, both Twynham and Holdenhurst were royal domains with manorial workers directly under the Crown. Manorial grants were made later. It was a highly effective form of agricultural land management and taxation. For example, a villein would have around 30 acres of his own together with the obligation to work on his lord's land as a form of rent payment. Provided he performed his feudal duties, he did have security of occupation and the ability to hand on the land to his heirs. Although he was bound to the land and unable to leave it, such an obligation was probably not onerous in its day and there was little desire to move.

King William became increasingly involved in wars, which had to be financed. The Domesday Survey or Book aimed to show how much tax different estates paid, to record the lands and revenues of the lords, and to make a judicial statement about disputed land seizures. In order to assess the future taxability of the country, the listings were shrewdly made under people rather than property. But the Book does not specifically mention Hengistbury as within the ownership of either the Crown or the Church. Despite the tremendous detail of Domesday, this is unsurprising, because in 1086 it was just a small area of indifferent farmland or wasteland.

Even if it did amount to a hide, this would not have been separately identified any more than other hides were. However, it did then form part of Hampshire, the boundary of which remained the same until the 1974 local government reorganisation.

In 1086, there were four hundreds in this locality, i.e. "Sirlei", "Rodedic", "Bovre" and "Egheiete". It is fair to regard these as the "greater Christchurch" and including land as far as Milford and a section of the New Forest. Christchurch was then known as "Thuinam" or "Tuinam" and Holdenhurst, which included Hengistbury Head, was known as "Holeest". Both were part of "Egheiete" Hundred. "Egheiete" was divided into ten: "Tuinam", "Holeest", "Hurn", "Knapp", "Stanpit", "Hoburne", "Bashley", "Bortel" (which is Bosley) and two unnamed manors. In 1176, Holdenhurst ("Holeest") was made into a separate hundred, which was later known as the "Liberty of Westover". It included tithings west of the Stour, i.e. North Ashley, Muscliff, Muccleshell, Throop, Holdenhurst, Iford and Tuckton. The last-named would have incorporated Hengistbury. An 1832 map exists, which shows the headland within the tithing of Tuckton and Wick.

By 1263, Holdenhurst Hundred had embraced three others. By 1316, I believe most was within Christchurch Hundred, as far as and including Lymington, until 1593. Eventually, one may say that the boundaries of the Christchurch Hundred of 1881 appear to include some 40,030 acres (62.5 square miles) and the four Hundreds of 1086. Clearly, this whole matter is complicated and made no simpler by certain apparent mistakes of the Domesday Book clerk, e.g. some nine manors including Lymington were put in "Bovre" instead of "Rodedic". There is also some variation between published maps of Hundreds. Perhaps the main significance here is that the headland was part of an area that was comprehensively administered for hundreds of years. Incidentally, unlike the relatively modern name of Hengistbury, other local place names genuinely derived from Anglo-Saxon times. For instance, Wick normally meant a dairy farm and the suffix of Tuckton implies an enclosed farm.

Domesday says that the King then held Holdenhurst himself. In 1066, it had been assessed at 29 hides (including "seven" in the Isle of Wight) and half a virgate under Earl Tostig, who was King Harold's brother. (I have used inverted commas for the seven hides referred to above, because this appears to be a Domesday Book mistake: it should be three and a half.) This was reduced to 18½ hides on the mainland only (excluding 3½ hides transferred to the Forest) and half a virgate by 1086. Indeed, the value dropped from 44 pounds in the time of King Edward (1066) to 34 pounds later, and was 24 pounds in 1086, "but it pays £25 at 20 pence to the ounce. The land in the Forest is rated at £12 10s." Other information includes 181 acres of meadow, woodland for six swine from the pannage and a mill worth 15 shillings. "There is land for 20 ploughs; in the demesne are 4½ ploughs; there are 37 villeins and 25 bordars with 19 ploughs." Some 14 serfs, a chapel and three fisheries for the use of the hall are mentioned. The land of the canons of Twynham included the third part of the tithings (or tithes) of Holdenhurst. As for other manors, the king had taken land from Holdenhurst to include within the Forest with its much stricter laws. On these 3½ hides, 13 villeins and eight bordars had dwelt with eight ploughs and woodland for 129 swine from pannage.

Holdenhurst was larger than Twynham in both size and population, but would have looked to it for defence. Owing to poorer quality, much land would have been scrub only. In the more fertile valleys, households would have practised strip farming, with each farmer having both good and poorer land within his allocation. In general, however, it is likely that only the best land was farmed. A typical three-field rotation system could have had one fallow and the others down to wheat and barley respectively. A farmer could expect to have his strips reallocated each year and see cattle on the arable land after harvest. The relatively poor soil and small area of level land at Hengistbury meant that it was probably only used, if at all, as rough pasture east of the Dykes. Villagers may have used their feudal rights to put cattle on the pasture and pigs in the woodland. It is best viewed as a fringe part of the self-sufficient feudal manor, which itself amounted to a purely agricultural village of scattered hamlets.

Hengist and the renaming of the Head

From the Jutes are descended the men of Kent, the Wightwarians (that is, the tribe that now dwelleth in the Isle of Wight), and that kindred in Wessex that men yet call the kindred of the Jutes.

Anglo-Saxon Chronicle

Hengist and his brother Horsa were half Danes or Jutes, who invaded shortly after the Romans left. Although they certainly conquered Kent, there are conflicting views about how far to the west Hengist fought the Britons. Historians Stow and Speed thought that he made his second landing at the Head. It has been claimed that he seized the Isle of Wight and Hampshire coast before being killed in 488 and probably even buried on Hengistbury Head. However, the more generally accepted historical opinion is that his exploits never extended so far: more of this later. Hengist's alleged absence from this area is therefore some reason to cast doubt on the historical correctness of the name, Hengistbury Head.

A second reason for the general view, or received doctrine, is that the current name is quite a new one and not used initially. A document of 877 from Nursling, Hampshire, refers to "Hednesdene". According to Gibson's Saxon Chronicle, the promontory was where the English and the Danes made peace in 907. It was then known as "Yttingaford". Moreover, long after the conquest in 1066, Henry I granted the Manor of Christchurch to Richard de Redvers. Richard's son, Baldwin, then granted "Hednesburia" to the canons of Christchurch between 1107 and 1155. A twelfth century charter of confirmation describes it as "Hedenes Buria," a name considered to be derived from "Heddinesburh," or fort of Heddin. A Scandinavian legend tells that Hedinn, a Norse sea king, took captive the daughter of his great rival Hogin. He sailed with her from Norway to Britain, pursued by Hogin. When Hogin caught up, a great sea fight took place, possibly at what is now called Hengistbury Head. It was known as the "legend of the everlasting fight."

In 1300, the king was stated to have the right to the "second best sheep from every customary fold of Wick in Westover, the tenants in return having pasture for their sheep outside the ditch of Hednesburia," meaning headland stronghold. There is no mention of "Hengistbury," as one would expect, if it had been correctly named from the fifth century landing onwards. So far, we can say that the original name for the headland appeared to derive either from the legend of the sea fight with Hedinn over Hogin's daughter, or from the translation to headland stronghold. But as yet there is no link to Hengist.

By 1574, it was reported that the name, Hednes Buria, had been corrupted to Hensbury Ende. Following the 1660 Restoration, "Hynesbury" appeared. The suffix "bury" may be a corruption of "burh," meaning a fortified settlement, rather than implying any burial. The first sign of the current name came from certain old maps showing "hengistbury heade," starting with Speed (1611) Blome ("Hengist bury head" 1673) Morden (1695) Badeslade (1742) and Cary (1787-1825). The Milne map of 1791 shows Hengistbury or Christchurch Head. It has even been shown on a map of Mackenzie dated 1785 purely as Christchurch Head (Fig.11).

Before the mining operation, the Head used to have the appearance of a horse from seaward, giving rise to yet another historic name, Stone Horse Hill. I think that the enormous erosion of the headland has altered its appearance, because I have found it hard to visualise it as a horse, from the south. The background to this name, however, is very different from the story of Hengist's second landing. Although Hengist translates as "stallion" and Hengistbury has therefore been translated as "the fort of the stallions," this is most unlikely to have any connection with the name, Stone Horse Hill, which related to appearance only.

But what does the general view have to say about the translation? Since it is known that the stallion was an emblem for the warlike Saxons, does that imply the headland was once an armed camp for them? If it was, is this not ample justification for the current name? The answer is "no" because, failing evidence, this would be far too big a jump to make. Hence, none of this proves that the Head was correctly named after the fifth century invader. It follows from the above that Hengistbury Head is a relatively modern name dating from about 1600. This conclusion is historically firm in that previous names were essentially different from before the time of the Norman Conquest. Regardless of whether or not one accepts the received doctrine about the name being wrong, it is clear that from around this time, there was a change of name to Hengistbury.

In summary, therefore, the general view is that a somewhat misguided antiquarian may have concocted the current name around 1600, based on the unproved or false idea that Hengist was actually there at one time. Alternatively, there may have been a coincidental corruption from Hednes to Hengist – but for this approach, we have to imagine the generally illiterate local population making a big and surprising phonetic leap to the name of an invader of whom they had probably never heard. Historians and mapmakers would then have reflected common usage.

This is not the end of the story, because the general view is not universally accepted. Another theory promotes an opposite opinion, that the name is correct after all and not the product of some romantic antiquarian. Although the Danish name of "Hednes Buria", meaning headland stronghold, stood happily for centuries, it is quite valid and proper to rename a place based upon adequate research. Apart from this, the received doctrine is just not good enough, relying as it does upon either an unjustified attempt to discredit Stow and Speed, or an implausible name corruption. The phonetic leap mentioned above is most unlikely.

The alternative theory proceeds to show that there was good reason in Stow's time to change the name in tribute to the great English conqueror Hengist. If this is right, it overturns the general opinion and means that there is nothing wrong with the current name. Let us look at the evidence. The first Masonic lodge of

Bournemouth was founded in 1803 and known as the Lodge of Hengist. Its history (no doubt derived from sources which may no longer be available to us) refers to a peace conference held with the Britons by Hengist and a large, mainly Saxon, army on Salisbury Plain. The presumption, in that history, is of a landing by Hengist at Hengistbury and a journey up the Avon valley. One might also say that this means Hengistbury was probably the successful point of invasion for the Saxons. As such, they might be expected to name it after their fighting emblem, the stallion. In addition, if Hengist had died here, it would have been culturally appropriate to bury him in a mound on a coastal headland.

However, all this is a little too speculative for comfort. We have to return to the real issue, the historical correctness of the post-1600 name. For that, we need to go back to Stow's Chronicle about the lives of the brothers, as quoted by Benjamin Ferrey in his *Antiquities of Christchurch Priory* and various other sources. Although there is inevitably some conflict between sources, there is also much agreement. Accepting therefore an element of myth, legend and distortion, quite a tale can be unfolded, which is arguably mainly accurate.

In 443, Hengist and Horsa were successfully employed as mercenaries for King Vortigern's government against the Picts and Scots. Unfortunately, there was a pay dispute with the king when their military reinforcements arrived, with the brothers deciding to revolt and sack various cities in the 450s. It is possible that at this stage, they even made league with the Picts and Scots in order to fight more effectively from their Kent stronghold. At a battle with the Britons in Kent in 455, Vortimer, the king's son, killed Horsa. The town of Horsted was later named after him. Vortimer was a popular and enormously strong man. Legend has it that Vortimer felled Horsa with a tree, which he had uprooted for the purpose, having run out of other weapons.

It should be explained that there had been a lot of anger against Vortigern from both his family and the nobility. In the era of co-operation, Hengist had agreed to the marriage of his beautiful daughter Rowena to the king, exacting the whole of Kent as a dowry. Since he loved her so greatly, Vortigern, a Christian, would not listen to people's concerns about her paganism or their fears about the Saxons taking over the whole country with their steadily increasing immigration. In some desperation, the Britons turned to the great warrior, Vortimer, who scarcely felt duty-bound by the dowry. Following the death of Horsa, Hengist lost further battles with Vortimer, was driven back to Thanet and forced to leave the country.

While Vortimer lived, Hengist dared not return. But Rowena hated Vortimer for driving her father away. After many attempts to arrange his murder, she finally succeeded in having him poisoned. She immediately summoned Hengist. On learning of Vortimer's death, Hengist interrupted his task of building a castle in Holland and crossed the Channel with a large army. Whilst their previous victories meant that the Britons were ready to fight, Hengist cajoled them into a friendly peace conference near Stonehenge on Salisbury Plain on 1 May 473, saying that he would take back his daughter Rowena and depart.

Sadly for them, it was not at all friendly. The Saxons started a fight with weapons hidden under cloaks. It is said that these were produced on a shout from Hengist and 300 unarmed Britons were killed at once. Each Saxon made sure that his particular victim was next to him, and stabbed that person to death on hearing the signal. Vortigern, who had resumed his kingship, was deliberately spared. The coup was successful, with Hengist not only becoming the king of Kent, but also of Essex, Sussex and Middlesex as ceded by Vortigern.

Vortigern fled with Rowena and his various other wives (one of whom was his daughter by whom he had a child) to a remote castle in Wales. They died later in the flames of a siege. Hengist died in 488, according to one account beheaded by a clergyman who survived the massacre of the 300 Britons. Wherever this took place, Ferrey said that a castle or fortress stood at the Head in his honour. Hengist may have built it, or it may have been erected and named after him by his countrymen. Either way, it is extraordinary that a Saxon castle can be imagined at end of the Head, when it was a much longer ridge and a good fifteen centuries before the Selfridge plans for two castles.

However fascinating this story, how much of it is myth? We can say with some certainty that a big Saxon army crossed the channel for a conference on Salisbury Plain. It would have been known that the best landing place was around Hengistbury, and the shallow draught ships were suitable for Christchurch harbour. There was bound to have been an adequate Roman road to Salisbury. In short, the renaming was a reasonable geographical inference from Hengist's second invasion via the Avon valley, and the detailed information runs against the claim that he never ventured west of Kent. (When visiting the car park at Mudeford Quay today, one should be aware that the 1995/1996 reconstruction works revealed an ancient course of the Avon. One might even be passing above Hengist's route.) It is probable that an antiquarian was inspired by reading Stow's Chronicle, and persuaded the owner of Christchurch manor to change the name as a patriotic tribute to the first true Englishman, Hengist. A further indication about the likely location of Hengist's second invasion is that his ancestors' names (son of Wictgils, son of Witta) appear to be derived from the Isle of Wight.

As I have tried to show, it is not possible to be definite as to whether the general view that the 1600 renaming was wrong, or was quite justified. Yet there is also a possibility – one that does of course run against the general view – that the renaming was merely a reinstatement of the correct original name! A reference exists in the Anglo-Saxon Chronicle to a victory in 838 by the King of Wessex over the Danes and Cornish (or Welsh) at Hengestdwn. This name predates Hednesburia and incorporates "dune," which originally meant a long ridged hill, and later, a hill-fort built on a ridge. As explained in the chapter on erosion, I think that the ridge of Warren Hill extended way beyond Beer Pan Rocks in those days and "dune" would therefore be right, with or without a hill-fort.

This reinstatement theory is only one possibility, consistent with the 838 battle being located in Wessex between a pincer movement of Cornish forces and Danish ones from the north-east. But another explanation is that Hengestdwn was actually Hingston Down in Cornwall. This would overcome the problem with the suffix: "dwn" is Celtic, and therefore the entire name (applying to whatever location) may have existed before the Saxons arrived. As such, it could not have been in honour of Hengist. On the other hand, the suffix could be justified at Hengistbury as being a later Anglo-Celtic translation literally meaning the large sand "dune" below the Head. If this last option is correct, the name would not be pre-dating Hengist himself.

The renaming is controversial and will probably remain so. Whilst proponents of the general view might point to the lack of corroborating evidence for a journey up the Avon valley or the location of the 838 battle, those against might reject both the implausible phonetic leap and the unfair criticism of Stow.

Named after Hengist and Horsa

It can be fairly said that the large public house, opened on Broadway by the Dorset brewers Eldridge, Pope on 3 January 1940, was named the "Saxon King" after the famous Jute. It was originally to have been named either Hengist or Horsa. Although it was long since demolished for housing redevelopment, the connection continued with the new road name of Saxon King Gardens. Indeed, Horsa Road and Rowena Road in Tuckton must have been named after Hengist's brother and daughter respectively.

Although it is well known that a glider used in the Second World War during the D-Day landings in France was named after Horsa, there was also a World War II troop transport glider called the Hengist. It had an 80-foot wingspan and could be towed at 150 mph, fully loaded in a group of three, with 15 troops per glider including the pilot.

The French

You must consider every man your enemy who speaks ill of the king, and...you must hate a Frenchman as you hate the devil

Horatio Nelson (1758 – 1805)

In *Yes Minister*, Sir Humphrey Appleby memorably told his boss that the real enemy of this country was not Russia but the French. Although the minister, and no doubt the viewer, was surprised at this assessment, there is a great historical pedigree for the opinion. Perhaps Nelson would have approved verse 10 of Richard Warner's 48-verse poem, dated 1793, about Hengistbury Head:

In vain the straining vision seeks to ken
The opposing cliffs of Gallia's wretched shore,
Where Giant-like Rebellion stalks amain,
Bathing his purple feet in ROYAL GORE

The first thing to happen after the Romans left was a take-over by the Saxons and much later, the Normans. The fact that there was still a significant French element in the country cut little ice with France when the Hundred Years' War began in 1338. Although Lymington and Poole were burnt in the war, there seems to have been no direct effect on Christchurch, of which the agricultural Hengistbury was then part.

With the French threatening Southampton in 1457, invading the Isle of Wight and entering Spithead in 1545, invasion remained a risk. A sophisticated beacon system was set up to give warning and to allow defence forces to be mustered. A contemporary account claimed that it mustered them so effectively in 1545 that the French did not attempt to land. It was claimed that 25,000 men could be assembled by this means within two hours. By the time of the Armada in 1588, this defence system was well established, and the main Spanish general

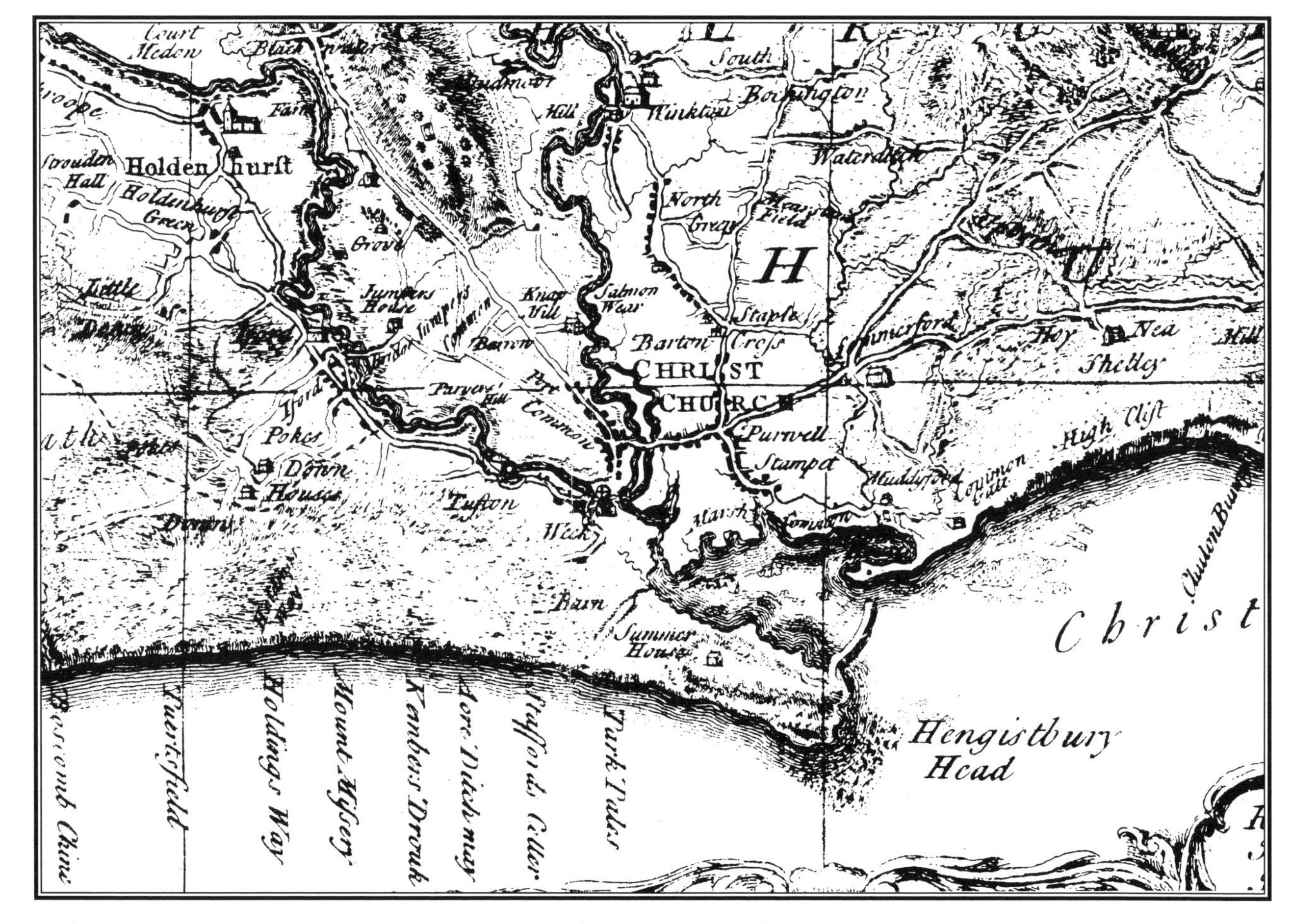

Fig.9 ***Place names in 1759***

(Isaac Taylor map. Reproduced by consent of Red House Museum)

Bournemouth, as such, did not then exist, being largely heath-land crossed by tracks. The tiny settlements of Tuckton, Wick and Iford can be identified however, together with some old coastal place names, now largely lost. The legendary derivation of Mount Misery (located at the sea end of the present Clifton Road) is contained in the chapter on smuggling. It is clear that Hengistbury Head was much larger than now and well protected by the skirt of ironstones, shown similarly in the 1785 map of Fig.11.

was contemplating the need to "fight battle after battle." A 1574 survey found Bournemouth was a very easy place for the enemy to land. Apart from the Head, beacons were also placed at St. Catherine's Hill, and the East Cliff, marked with a beacon on a 1539 map, and further west at Canford Cliffs and Constitution Hill.

Henry VIII ordered that shoreline positions, such as Hengistbury Head, required three beacons, hills behind the coast two, and inland sites just one. The code system enabled local forces to respond in the right numbers and to the locations under threat. For example, three columns of smoke would mean the enemy had landed at the port of that beacon, causing the nearest inland site to fire both of their beacons. Other sites would fire just one so that the defenders knew they had to march in the direction of the twin smoke columns, and from there to the invasion site showing three columns. Invasion scares continued relentlessly up to the Napoleonic Wars. We can imagine the dramatic and disturbing sight of three permanent structures at the top of Warren Hill. They were likely to have been made from tall oak posts, with a fire basket on the top approached by a ladder, and spare fuel barrels at the base.

In 1666, local seamen were asked about sites suitable for the French to land. They identified Hynesbury as a true stronghold, being surrounded by sea except for the landward side, which was entrenched. Clearly, the Dykes were still felt to have considerable merit for defence purposes in those days. The perceived risk was that at least 20,000 men could have camped there and held off all comers with large guns for up to two miles in all directions. There were only 100 men guarding it at the time, but the invasion never came.

At the time of the Napoleonic Wars, plans were laid for entrenchments at the Head as a first line of defence, with a second line at St. Catherine's Hill and a third from Ringwood to Wimborne. These defensive works were not built. During the 1890s, Hengistbury was found useful for summer training camps for the Royal Engineers and cavalry.

Development around the Head

I have included an extract from an eighteenth century map (Fig.9) to show that there was very little in the vicinity apart from Christchurch and some small villages or hamlets. Tuckton, Wick and Iford were tiny in those days. The Barn may be the ranger's cottage, but the map is not quite clear on this. There are some intriguing place-names: Park Pales, Staffords Celler, Acre Ditchmay, Kembers Drouk, Mount Misery and Holdings Way. These run from just east of the Dykes to west of what is now Clifton Road. Their stories are now mainly lost, although the chapter on smuggling gives the legendary derivation of Mount Misery. It has also been said that Staffords Celler was a smuggler's cave, needed due to a lack of good hiding places in this area. It has since been eroded away. The picture at the start of the nineteenth century remains a remote promontory, separated by water from the ancient town of Christchurch and by largely unpopulated heath land from Poole to the west.

Fig.10, which derives from a map of 1811, was an illustration apparently produced due to the Bournemouth centenary celebrations in 1910. Like the 1759 map in Fig.9, it shows that Bournemouth was still mainly open country at that time. We know however that a large Summer House (Fig.13) had been erected on the highest point of the Head by then. Descriptions, from around the time of the Christchurch Inclosure Act of 1802, refer to a vast desolate heath of probably 20 square miles. The public roads were few, but there existed many wheel tracks in what is now Bournemouth, mainly used to cart turf, for fuel, to the nearest houses. Such turf, cut from one to four inches thick, was the only fuel available for most houses. Otherwise, tracks were used by smugglers or by those driving over the heath for sea bathing. A small number of sheep and cattle were farmed. The picture is completed by a small public house with stables by the sea.

The feelings at the centenary must have included optimism and confidence. The immense horror of two world wars was part of an unknown future. Instead, it was a time of patriotism, Empire Days, and the legacy of the sheer success of the Victorians, typified by Bournemouth's fast expansion. Although the Hengistbury air-show might have been the most dramatic form of celebration, this map was just as important, in its own way, demonstrating as it does the transformation of the area from country to town.

From the middle of the nineteenth century, the expansion of Bournemouth, including the arrival of the railway, was a great economic force that affected the whole area, including Hengistbury. Under the Christchurch Inclosure Act 1802, there was an award in 1805 for the Liberty of Westover. Some 5,100 acres of common land were allocated to a limited number of owners: most of it to just three, Tapps, Dean and Malmesbury. The theory, from the middle of the eighteenth century, was that as much land as possible should be used for improving food supplies to help the French wars.

In Bournemouth, however, the waste areas would never make adequate arable land. The new owners simply planted fir trees and in due course developed the town. One farmer who received an award actually failed in an attempt to use the poor soil for crops. There was a form of compensation for 86 cottagers, who were allocated 422 acres of land for turf cutting at what became Kings Park, Queens Park, Redhill, Meyrick Park and Seafield Gardens. The significance for Hengistbury Head, which was already privately owned and occupied, was the creation of an effective structure permitting the fast development of the town.

Numbers of residents from the census show an enormous speed of growth. To the nearest hundred, they indicate the following dates and populations in brackets: 1851 (700) 1871 (6500) 1891 (37,700) 1911 (78,700)! No doubt the fact that Bournemouth was by then "on the map" was one attraction for Gordon Selfridge, who purchased the Head in 1919. The scene was set for the pressures and controversies of the twentieth century.

Remarkable story of the summit of Warren Hill

What can we say of the superb outlook from the top of Hengistbury Head? Tremendous though the view now is (Fig.1), in times gone by it had perhaps even more charm, the area being less accessible and less developed. A substantially constructed two-storey summerhouse (Figs. 11, 12 and 13) existed on the very top, at least as far back as the eighteenth century. It is easy to imagine family gatherings for days out and picnics in such an idyllic spot. Many must have struggled to reach it, only to be caught out by a typical sudden change in Hengistbury's weather! Even earlier, it must have been regularly visited when invasion-warning beacons were sited on the headland.

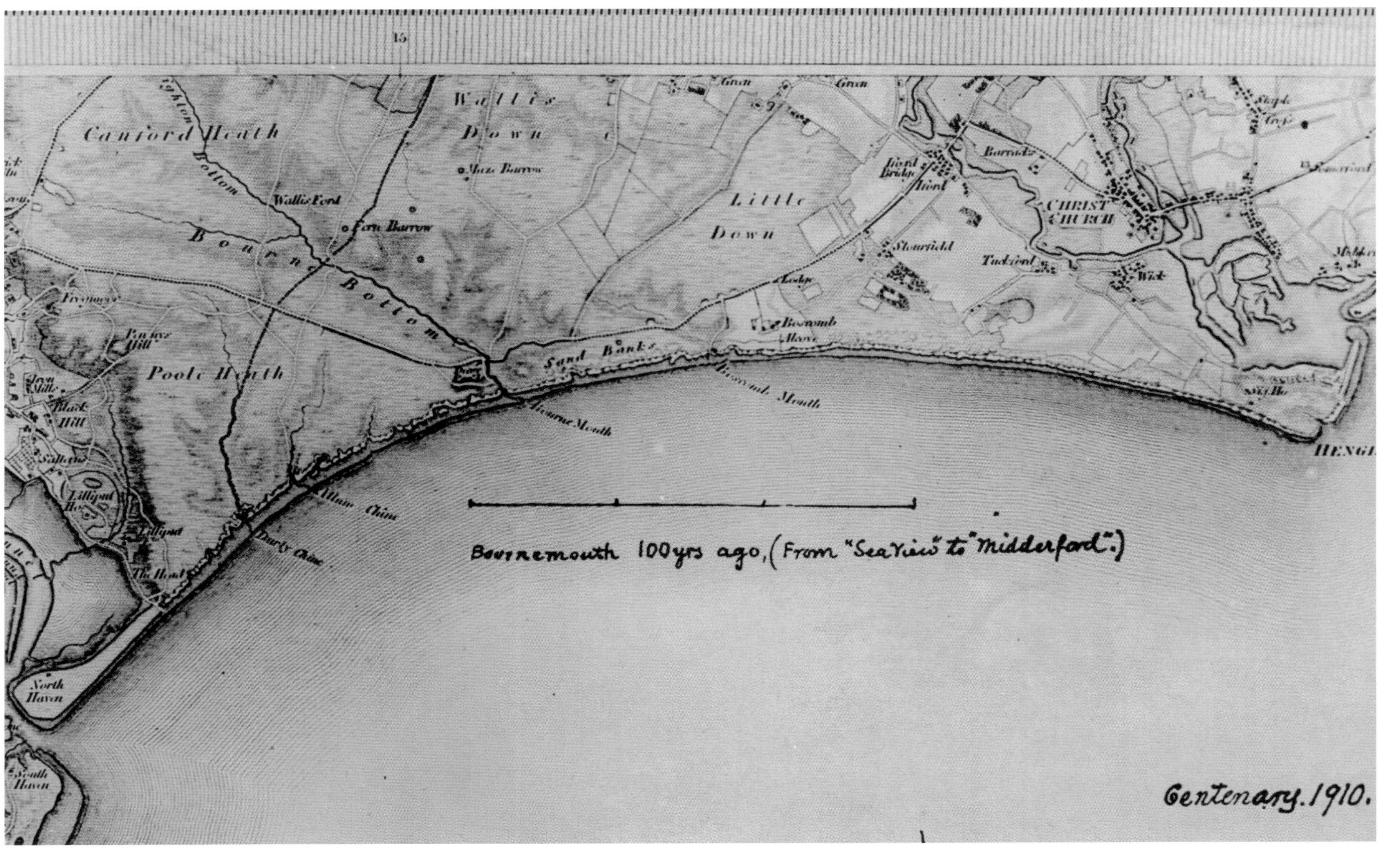

Fig.10 ***Bournemouth and Poole Bay, 1811***

(Reproduced from Ordnance Survey of that date © Crown Copyright and by consent of Classic Pictures)

Apparently taken for the centenary celebrations of 1910, the photograph makes clear that the town hardly existed at the earlier date. The illustration derives from a 1 inch to 1 mile scale OS map as engraved in the Drawing Room of the Tower and published on 10 April 1811. Wick Lane, Harbour Road and the shape of White Pits can still be identified. So can the position of the Dykes and the ranger's cottage. A track ran from the northern end of Harbour Road south-east towards the centre of the Dykes. The western part of this old road is now about the position of Thornbury Road.

However, looking initially at pre-history, there are the probable remains of a bowl barrow, not shown on Fig.5 with the other Bronze Age barrows, nor indeed on the Ordnance Survey. As first noted in Chapter Two, the 1969 county record indicates that it is at the highest point, being a mound nearly 100 feet diameter and about 4 feet 3 inches high. It states that not only was it "littered with building materials", but also that it was the site of the Warren Summerhouse described below. From Point House Café, the mound can be clearly seen between the top of the ascending footpath and the existing Coastguard Station. In view of the sheer size of the Summerhouse and the inconvenience of removing all the rubble after demolition, it is possible that the mound actually consists of this material.

Most of the history can be gleaned from the old maps. In 1759, Isaac Taylor (Fig.9) shows the Summer House, but accuracy is limited. In 1785, Mackenzie's naval map (Fig.11) shows Warren Summerhouse in the same place, but due to the small scale, this is still a little diagrammatic. One reason he shows it is to help ships steer clear of the Ledge, by "keeping Christ Church Tower just open to the westward of Warren Summer House." In 1791, a map by Milne shows the "Summer Ho." and indeed "Brander". The name on the map is indicative of ownership. Now, Gustavus Brander is known to have bought the subsidiary Manor of Christchurch, Twynham (the church property) in 1782 and to have died five years later. His family sold the Manor to the Meyrick family in 1830. We therefore have an intriguing pointer to Hengistbury Head forming part of the lands granted "as perpetual alms" to the church by the de Redvers family after the Norman Conquest.

As for who might have built the Summer House before it was shown on the 1759 map, there exists a complex recorded background of ownership and inheritance. Hoping that my sources make this an accurate account, the story now follows. Richard Fenn, a London alderman, who appears to have had a brother, Sir Robert Fenn, bought the Manor in 1630. Sir Robert was Lord Mayor of London in 1638. Richard's nephew, also Richard and doubtless the son of Sir Robert, inherited and died in 1683. The nephew's sister, Jane, inherited in turn. Now she was the widow of John Tregonwell (1598 to 1680). Jane conveyed the Manor to her beautiful daughter, Mary Luttrell, in 1690. After the death of her husband, Colonel Luttrell of Dunster Castle, Mary moved to London, where her house burnt down. Sir Jacob Banckes of Milton Abbas rescued her from the flames and became her second husband. His son, also Jacob, inherited in 1724 and sold on to Edward Lisle of Moyles Court, Ellingham in 1736. In 1754, James Willis of Ringwood purchased the Manor, passed it on to his son John, who in turn bequeathed it in his will, dated 1776, to his nephew, John Compton. The latter sold to Gustavus Brander in 1782. Assuming that the Summer House would not have been older than 1630, it might perhaps have been built by Richard Fenn, his nephew (also Richard Fenn), Jane Tregonwell, Mary Luttrell, Jacob Banckes, Edward Lisle or James Willis.

In 1797, an unpublished OS map shows a Signal House indicated as two structures. The northern one is in the same position as shown in the two maps above. The other one is about 400 feet to the south-south-east. In 1811, Elizabeth Fanshawe painted a watercolour showing a substantial building on Warren Hill together with what appears to be an even higher flagstaff, placed on lower ground to the east (Fig.12). In 1818, an unknown artist sketched a length of the south coast. Fig.13 is based on the artist's drawing, from the harbour, of what must have been the same building painted by Elizabeth Fanshawe and shown by Mackenzie in 1785. No separate flagstaff is shown on this sketch.

In 1826, Greenwood repeats the name as "Signal Ho.", again showing two structures on the summit in the same position as the 1797 map. As one overlooked the whole of the sea and the other the whole of the harbour, it may have been necessary to have two military lookouts to liaise with each other, at a time when the headland was so much wider. Another explanation could be that one was a beacon structure only. In 1836, the Signal House appears on Sylvester's report about harbour improvement.

The Summer House, Warren Summerhouse and Signal House are one and the same building, apparently used for a mixture of recreation and lookout purposes until demolished. The lookout or signal use would have been partly for the military to monitor invasion risks and partly for the coastguard service and its various functions. The building existed from before 1759 until at least 1836. It is fascinating to consider its design and size from all this information. Fig.13 is one interpretation. My view is that it was a substantial two-storey structure having a square plan with sides of 16 to 20 feet length. Each of the four sides appears to have had two windows at first floor level. The height to the top of the first floor would have been 40 to 50 feet and above this seems to have been an inset dome or cupola, having a central flagpole. Since it was inset, a walkway must have existed, approached by an internal staircase, allowing 360-degree views from the top. Were it still there, it is easy to imagine it now being classified as a typical early eighteenth century folly.

Part of Commander Sheringham's 1846 map is shown in Fig.38. Although this extract is limited, the original does extend to the summit. A small building is marked there as "**CoGd Watch Ho** *Built on the site of the old*

Warren Summer House". The map does not extend far enough to the south to show whether or not the southern structure remained in 1846. There was only one building on the top of the Head by 1870, described on the OS (Fig.29) as the Watch House (Coastguard Service). By 1870, the southern structure appearing in 1797 would have been on the cliff edge and probably long since removed. Indeed, by 1932, its location was below the current low water mark! There is a flagstaff shown in 1870 about 100 feet to the south-east in a nearby enclosure 140 feet by 40 feet.

In 1935, a Mrs. E.A. Jones, born 1851, was reported as remembering (from the time she was a small girl) the blasting operations of the mining company. Her father, Coastguard Captain Dowling, was stationed there at the "Old Watch House", which was described by Mrs. Jones as "one great room with four windows". Many happy days were spent there by the family and their pet jackdaw, "who stole anything". We could reasonably place this woman's recollection at about 1860 and deduce that this Watch House on the 1846 naval map and the 1870 OS map was single storey and much smaller than the Summer House, which it replaced. Indeed, scaling of the 1870 map shows it to have been about 18 feet by 13 feet average, and this is consistent with the 1846 map

By the time of the 1932 OS (Fig.2) a Coastguard lookout hut, erected in 1926, had replaced the Watch House. I believe that it was on the same site because the distance north to the bottom of the Batters is about the same as in 1870. It follows that the Summer House was replaced by the Watch House between 1836 and 1846 and the latter replaced by a Coastguard lookout hut in 1926. It seems that there was a period between demolition of the Watch House and erection of the 1926 hut, because the 1924 OS shows no building, only the nearby triangulation point.

Reverting to the county council record of 1969, this mentioned the lookout station on the summit of the apparent barrow. Because the current Coastguard building (Fig.37) was only erected in 1975, the record must refer to the 1926 lookout. The 1975 building is 100 yards to the east of the old one, which is now a bare site. To be clear, it is this bare site, currently of gravel and grass, which has probably seen a Bronze Age barrow and certainly the dramatic Summer House, the Watch House, the lookout hut and now has, on its northern edge, merely a viewing tablet for the visitor.

The Old Barn, oldest house in Bournemouth?

Apart from the coastguard station and the structures on Mudeford Sandbank, this is the only building of significance east of the Dykes. It is a substantial thatched barn and attached cottage, constructed in English Bond brickwork. This is the strongest type of bonding, with alternate courses of headers and stretchers, showing all brick ends on one course and all brick sides on the next. The ranger's cottage has four small bedrooms on the first floor, a living room, kitchen and bathroom/WC on the ground floor, and an attractively screened garden. A previous owner originally converted it from the barn area into a cottage for his gamekeeper. Over the years, it has also been known as Keeper's Cottage and Brewer's Cottage, after the name of the gamekeeper.

The remaining barn is now divided to give a store and office on the side of Barn Field and a much larger workshop and store on the side of the land train compound. Originally, the barn was probably used for threshing with the help of through draughts from the large open doors at each end. Before 1939, the ranger and his wife operated a café from the barn. Now it is needed for maintenance of the land train, including painting the coaches out of season. The small windows in the wall facing the road were for public toilets that have long since been converted into a store.

In 1947, after a councillor called for preservation of the Old Barn, a local paper published a picture of the ranger, Robert Brewer, pointing to a rafter inscribed W.J.B. 1537. Even then, these old timbers were affected by woodworm, which were steadily destroying the inscription. I have heard that the rafters may have been salvaged from elsewhere and could therefore be much older than the house, although the former ranger's son, Herbert Brewer, pointed out that it could simply have been an old timber batch number! It still remains a possibility, albeit remote, that this inscription was the work of a builder in the days of Henry VIII. Certainly, a local paper had stated before the war that it was of such an age, whilst claiming for good measure that it was "an old smuggler's haunt." From a brief inspection of some rafters from ground level, I think that they must have been renewed since 1947.

The earliest definite map showing the barn appears to be the unpublished 3 inches to 1-mile 1797 Ordnance Survey, but previous ones were so diagrammatic that many features like this would simply not be shown anyway. An exception is the Grose map of 1777 (Fig.52). Hence, we can say that it dates back at least to the eighteenth century.

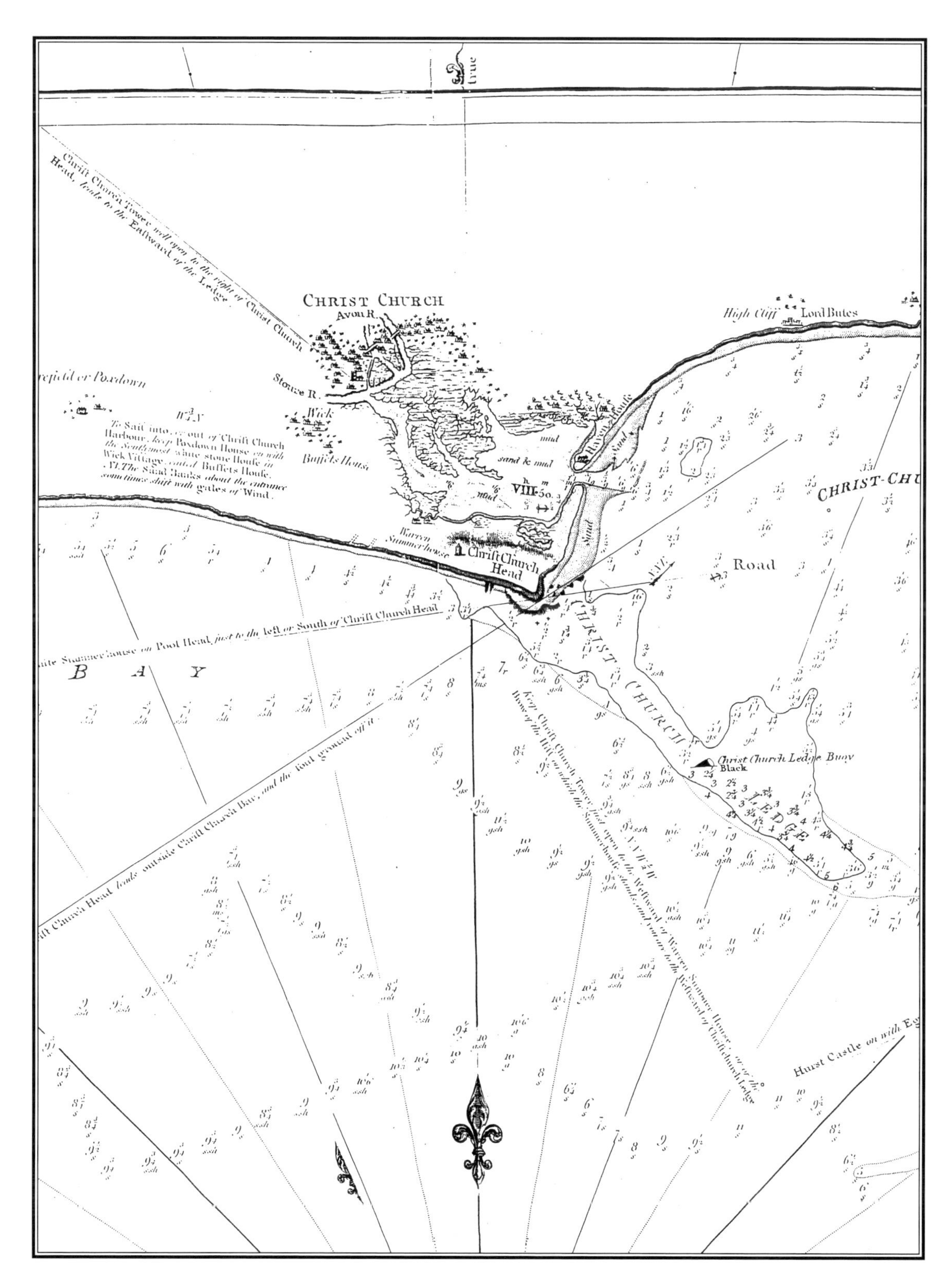

Fig.11 ***Naval navigation map showing Christchurch Ledge, 1785***

(Lieut. M. Mackenzie. Reproduced by permission of the Controller of Her Majesty's Stationery Office and the UK Hydrographic Office.)

An extract print from the superbly professional original drawing, which is about eight feet long and held at UKHO, Taunton. The ironstone Ledge, which extends nearly three miles, was originally part of a land bridge to the Isle of Wight. Erosion has since removed about half of Warren Hill. The ill-fated first castle or mansion, shown at High Cliff, had been built from 1773 to the 1780s.

Fig.12 ***Watercolour of Hengistbury Head and Warren Summer House from High Cliff 1811***
(Elizabeth Fanshawe 1779-1856. © Ian Stevenson Collection)
The viewpoint for this intriguing painting was the grounds of High Cliff mansion, which appears in Fig.39. It shows the cliff scene down to and across the Run with Warren Hill and its high Summer House in the background. The artist was noted for accuracy in her work and assuming this, the very top of the Signal House is about 45 feet high, some three times its width. What appears to be a Flagstaff of even greater height is located on lower ground to the east. Otherwise, certain other features can be made out: Haven House (now Haven Cottages), public wheeled bathing machines and the circular drawing room located on the east side of Sandhills, built in 1790. The west side of the headland shows as a natural gentle slope, in contrast to its later status as the aptly-named Batters following Holloway's open-cast mining operation.

There is a Tithe Map of 1844 referring to the Old Barn as item 3248 "House Garden and Barn" of area 1 rood and 28 perches. Nearby, to the west of the Dykes, is another building, item 3249 (which had been removed by the time of the 1870 large scale OS) described as a barn of 26 perches. They were lumped together for this purpose at a rateable value of £8.8s.0d, or eight guineas (£8.40), and gross rental value of £13.8s.0d. (£13.40). The owner was Sir George Gervis and the occupier the same as for Wick Farm, Mr. Levi Groves. By contrast, the "House Lookout" on the top of the Head was only 1 perch (30.25 square yards area) but given a gross rental of £2.17s.6d (£2.875). It may have had a much higher value per perch due to its position.

The ranger's cottage was historically a damp house. When conditions were extreme, water was even noted to be within two inches of the floorboards. In a very bad storm in 1953, it was surrounded in a lake of water for a time. A well is shown on the 1870 map (Fig.29) near the edge of the building. I am told that this was used in living memory for gardening purposes only, until filled in around 1962. About the same date as the map, the resident gamekeeper noticed that a post-hole was wet after the removal of a rabbit fence on the other side of the Dykes from his cottage. A well was dug in this position near to what is now the north-west side of the turning circle of Broadway. It proved most successful, providing drinking quality water, as monitored by the council, through to the 1950s. After drought and thunderstorm, it remained drinkable, although tasting of iron. Perhaps the water supply sounds a little primitive by today's standards, involving hand-pumping from the other side of the Dykes to the cottage's kitchen. But it was a big improvement at the time. Before then, a regular pony and trap brought a milk churn full of water from Wick!

Fig.13 ***Warren Summer House existing from before 1759 until 1836/1846***

(Reproduced by consent of Christopher Hollick)

In 1818, an unknown artist made a number of pencil sketches of the south coast, including a view of the headland from within Christchurch Harbour. Whilst the scale of the original is small and the detail limited, it has been possible to make an interpretation. This drawing, by Christopher Hollick, is based on the artist's depiction of the dramatic Summer House. The building appears to have been 40 to 50 feet in height up to the top of the first floor. Figs. 11 and 12 are consistent with this illustration, which shows what appears to have been a cupola and flagstaff.

Fig.14 ***Ranger's Cottage***
(Author 2005)

Originally known as the Old Barn, the Keeper's Cottage or Brewer's Cottage, after the name of the owner's gamekeeper, this is one of the few permanent buildings east of the Dykes. Only the rendered section south of the barn is residential, most of the building now being used as a workshop and store. Use, by the section nearest the road as public toilets and the barn as a café, has long since ceased. Claims that it dates back to the days of Henry VIII are far from proven.

By 1975, the Old Barn was less admired by some, with one councillor suggesting a "bonfire party" to get rid of it, due to poor condition and mildew. A sale was discouraged on the grounds that no one would live there. It was later occupied as the ranger's cottage, and the whole property was re-thatched in 1980. The Old Barn has proved to be the only permanent building on Hengistbury Head. It has always been occupied in connection with the headland and shows every sign of continuing in this way. Of the others, only the 1975 Coastguard building remains, and that will not last for ever, being about twice as close to the cliff edge as when built.

FOUR

THE TWENTIETH CENTURY AND ONWARDS

Democracy means government by discussion, but it is only effective if you can stop people talking

Clement Atlee 1957

The struggle for local authority boundaries

BEFORE 1894, Hengistbury fell within the large Christchurch parish. In that year, however, the one parish was split into six, one of which was Southbourne, including the Head. By 1901, the headland had been transferred to Highcliffe parish, which covered the coastal strip from Milton to the west.

In 1911 there was much local excitement about which borough council should have Hengistbury within its responsibility. Solicitors for the owner, Sir George Meyrick, wrote to the Christchurch Town Clerk saying that if it had to go into Christchurch or Bournemouth, he would prefer Bournemouth. The previous few years had seen increasing concern in Christchurch at the erosion problem, which was not being addressed.

The Christchurch Borough Extension Committee met on many occasions in order to push the case for the town against its larger neighbour. It met on 19 June 1911 to consider a petition presented by Bournemouth Corporation and Sir George Meyrick to oppose the Provisional Order to include the Head within Christchurch, and resolved to oppose it on the grounds that Bournemouth had no *locus standi*. This piece of Latin, meaning "legal standing," seems to have won the day for Christchurch. The Court of Referees of the House of Commons decided on 26 June that Bournemouth was indeed lacking in *locus standi*. When this was reported back to the Extension Committee on 6 July, it was also known that Sir George had withdrawn his opposition to the Bill. Accordingly, with great ongoing speed of meetings, which seemed to be possible in those days, the Committee resolved to go ahead with the confirmation Bill as soon as possible. In this way, the Head, east of the Dykes, came into Christchurch Borough in 1911.

In 1919, Sir George Meyrick sold the Head to Gordon Selfridge. When the time came for Selfridge to find a buyer in 1930, Christchurch Council was worried about development taking place following its sale at the time of a boom in house building. In order to secure its continuation as a wonderful public open space, the council decided to make the purchase of it as attractive as possible to Bournemouth Council. One difference between the councils was that Christchurch could not afford to buy, whilst Bournemouth obtained a loan sanction from the Minister of Health to finance the purchase. The local paper reported in May 1930 that co-operation between the councils before the purchase by Bournemouth deserved the thanks of the public, and "all danger of the spoilation of the Head by speculators has been averted." A major attraction to Bournemouth (in stark contrast to the battle about *locus standi* in 1911) was the offer that local authority responsibility for the Head should be transferred from Christchurch if the deal went through. The transfer duly took place in 1932. It was a timely change from private to local authority hands for the protection of the Head and the benefit of the public.

Christchurch secured a lease with effect from 25 March 1931, on concessionary terms (99 years at only £50 p.a. rent), for part of the beach hut land at the sandspit. Hence, to this day, Christchurch leases most of the

Sandbank from Bournemouth, and the rest of it, up to the Run, from the Meyrick Estate on similar terms, but with expiry in 2061. It remains the local authority for the isolated peninsula of the Meyrick land (Fig.27) but not for the Bournemouth land. I cannot explain the anomaly of why this section was originally excluded from the 1919 sale to Selfridge.

The extension of Bournemouth's borough boundary in 1932 to include Hengistbury Head was the latest in a long line. The original 1856 district of the Bournemouth Commissioners was the shape of a half circle centred on the Pier and with a radius only as far as the Central Station. Extensions happened in 1876, 1884, 1895, 1901, 1914, 1931 and 1932. Travelling east from the centre, part of Boscombe was added in 1876 and the remainder of it, together with Southbourne as far as the Dykes, in 1901. It is a measure of the speed of the town's expansion, and the consequent pressure on the headland, that its acreage in 1932 at 11,628 (about 18 square miles) was more than ten times greater than in 1856.

Military Review, 1915

In an early stage of World War I, there was a ceremonial review of the 74th Infantry Brigade east of the Dykes. Several thousand people, including the mayor, saw Major General Ventris inspect the troops. All those taking part were billeted in Boscombe and Southbourne. Such a sight today would seem incongruous, but that was a very different era.

Extension of Broadway in 1935

I have never regarded politics as the arena of morals. It is the arena of interests.

Aneurin Bevan

There is quite an argument against the wisdom of building Broadway. Before the sale to the council by Selfridge in 1930, there was only a narrow road or track from Wick Lane to the Dykes which was quite unsuitable for full public access. The line of this old road can be seen clearly on the extract of the 1932 map in Fig.46 as the continuation of Thornbury Road, then called Thornbury Avenue. As mentioned later in the section about drainage, a major reason appears to have been the need at the time to provide the eastern part of the town with a large foul water sewage upgrade. In other words, the council may have felt it most practical to put in the road to give good cover for the piping.

In the event, although a sensible compromise has been made over the years, it remains the case that the provision of the Broadway extension caused, and continues to cause, strong pressure for development. Its existence allowed the construction of the big wartime facility, the large headland car park in the 1970s, and indeed all the leisure development west of the Dykes. It has greatly promoted "tourist erosion."

Agricultural use

Before World War II, the land from the Dykes to Solent Road was used for growing barley. During the war, it was partly sprouts and cabbages, and partly barley. After the war, for a short period, the land was used for mangolds for cattle feed and cow cabbages at the eastern end. Later, it was just grass and hay.

Before the war the Head was virtually overrun with rabbits. About half the time of the gamekeeper was spent keeping them in check, typically delivering to the estate 25 to 30 dead rabbits in a day's work. Ferrets were used to drive the rabbits into nets, because shooting was far too expensive a method. Although there was a policy of "live and let live" between gamekeeper and poacher, it had to be discreet. On one occasion, a poacher scared the gamekeeper's son, Herbert Brewer, by shouting "Your father's cost me ten bob!" This was because, despite being warned to keep quiet, the poacher had continued to brag of his exploits in the pub, and was duly brought to book and fined! During the outbreak of myxomatosis in the 1950s, the grass grew long on the Head for the first time.

In recent years, the council has carried on landscape management as necessary, with some fields set aside for cattle.

Idyllic inter-war period and the tea boats

In those far-off days between two world wars, life must have seemed so much simpler. The Great War was over, and many thought it was indeed "the war to end wars." Most people did not even see Hitler as a real threat until the late 1930s. Hengistbury had not been opened up to large numbers of tourists, and Broadway would have created only a fraction of its current traffic. It was a truly unspoilt, little-used wilderness with access limited to a relatively few hardy souls. In pre-war times, most of the existing residential area, known as Hengistbury by estate agents, was open land. When housing began to be built in the 1920s and 1930s, it was a slow process, starting from Belle Vue Road eastwards. For those happy to undertake the walk, teas were available at the end of it (Fig.15). As such, the present Hengistbury residential area would have had more affinity to the headland than the town.

To give a feel for the place at that time, I can do no better than repeat some local recollections from the 1930s. They follow in no particular order. Blackberry bushes were very extensive on the largely undeveloped land in Harland and Baring Roads. Since there were enough for everyone, they were only picked when fully ripe. A common sight was a lady in a coach with four horses, driven by a top-hatted coachman and having two Dalmatians running at the back axle. A dead sheep was washed up at Southbourne about once a year. A prep school, known as Mount Pleasant, with half the boys being boarders, existed between Dalmeny and Hengistbury Roads. The partly developed Harland Road was gravel only, and so potholed that cyclists would use the footpaths. A beach café on stilts existed near the site of the old pier, but was wrecked by the sea and its timber salvaged by local people. Around 20 beach huts were placed literally on the beach in the region of Solent Road, but removed by handcart for the winters. The Batters on the north slopes of the Head were not then so overgrown and the children who cycled up there christened this quarry spoil the White Elephants.

The Brightlands Estate owned part of Broadway and the first roads including Brightlands, Broadlands, Springfield, Sunnylands and Southlands. The South Coast Land Society bought the area from there to Harbour Road. These estates would have been effective in controlling the type and density of residential development. Street lighting was initially by gas lamps. The large building, now flats, at the top of Wildown Road, was St. Katherine's Home for children. The girls of St. Cuthbert's School, Foxholes Road, in their green uniform, were

Fig.15 ***Lobster and crab teas served at the Margaret tea boat, 1925***

(Reproduced by consent of Vic Derham)

Ten years before Broadway was extended, it was possible to hike through the natural countryside right up to the south side of Christchurch Harbour and have tea. Notice the claws on the plate of seafood! The family's catering business started here and has continued to this day at Avon Beach.

Fig.16 ***Barge Tea Boat, Mudeford, 1930s***

(Reproduced by consent of Classic Pictures)

Probably taken between 1935 and 1939, this picture may be evidence of a more civilised era. The boat, run by Frank Croucher, was one of three pre-war tea boats. The others included one nearby, also with a jetty to the harbour side of the Sandbank and one to the west of Holloway's Dock.

great rivals with those at Grassendale (now part of St. Peter's) high-class Boarding School for Young Ladies, who wore blue. The Grassendale girls kept chickens, a milking cow, and horses for riding in the lower field. This school was bought by the Jesuits for educating Catholic boys, mainly boarders, and later the by the De La Salle brothers; hence the naming of the theatre at St. Peter's. The teachers could often be seen in their long black robes. One resident, who was among the first to own a television, suffered complaints about the unsightly roof aerial!

I am trying to paint a picture of the sparsely occupied western approach to Hengistbury. It was then possible to take a horse from the riding stables at Tuckton over the fields to a training circle near to the Dykes. Mr. Curling Hunter, who lived at Carbery (now Belle Vue Close) and owned the Brightlands Estate, also owned what was named locally as Southbourne Park. This was simply inaccessible water meadow and swamp from Tuckton to Wick. There was always a swan's nest in the reeds at the bottom of Broadlands Avenue each year, but no riverside walk. The tearoom and café, with its waitress service at Tuckton, was very popular. I gather that there was an initial layout for chalet sites to be provided at Southbourne Park, including some canal digging and creation of spoil banks. The plan came to nothing, however, and the land was made over to the council in lieu of rates.

Trams ran over the toll bridge nearby at a cost of one old penny including the toll from Tuckton to Christchurch. Pedestrians could cross for just half this amount, whilst a vehicle driver would be charged two pennies! After council tipping, Southbourne Park was grassed over and now provides a most attractively laid-out area, giving little sign of its former state. Many of its trees were brought in by crane fully-grown. Fortunately, a post-war council plan to permit a row of houses from the car park to Wick Ferry did not survive local opposition. The nearest Southbourne shopping centre at Crossroads was very good, including two butchers, a bakery, and greengrocers. The rear outlook from the attractive villa style maisonettes (over the shops) was simply across dunes to the cliffs.

There were three tea boats and five houseboats on the harbour edge. Two of the tea boats were located near the present sandspit jetty, whilst the remainder were on the south side of the harbour near Holloway's Dock. Transport of people and materials was by boat from 1930 onwards, because at that time Broadway had not been extended and there was merely a track past what is now the ranger's cottage. Most supplies came from Christchurch Quay by passenger boats.

The "Barge" Tea Boat (Fig.16) was opened on 21st May 1930, offering "special teas and refreshments at popular prices, daintily served in delightful surroundings." Visitors approached from Christchurch Quay on the United Services Motor Boats to the tea boat stage on the Sandbank. Frank Croucher ran this until 1939.

Derham's Tea Boat, alongside, also continued until the outbreak of war. Derham is a long established local name, usually connected with lifesaving and fishing. From about 1936, Ken Derham kept a small boat on Avon Beach for this purpose and in 1959 carried out a particularly dangerous rescue. The following year, there was a royal presentation of the RNLI silver medal for gallantry. An award for fund-raising was also made by Queen Elizabeth the Queen Mother (Fig.32) in May 1984 at the Festival Hall.

The floating café on the sandspit had started due to three lads asking for a drink of water from Mrs. Derham, when the family had a houseboat, the *Margaret*, on the south side of the harbour. Having been given tea and scones, they pointed out that it could work as a business venture. The idea was taken up, tables and chairs were set out, and teas served. Fig.15 is a snapshot of lobster and crab teas being prepared by the family in 1925. How delightful to hike through the unspoilt beauty of the western approach to the headland and be rewarded with such a tea on the harbour's edge! The *Margaret* had been built in 1911 and occupied in 1912. During the winter, the houseboat was relocated to what is now the Highcliffe Sailing Club's dinghy park on Mudeford Quay.

I must mention the imaginative way in which one of the children on the *Margaret* dealt with an irritating sibling, Sidney, in about 1918. Having reached the end of her tether, his older sister, aged only four or five years, hit on a most effective solution. She placed Sidney in a tin bath, which floated right up to the Run before a fisherman rescued him!

Derham's Tea Boat on the sandspit was converted from an icebreaker. Around 1920, the family bought it and had the houseboat and café built on top of the original hull. It was even possible to use it for tea dances, with a band. In 1940, it was towed to Wick and later sunk. Before then, it had been sold to allow the purchase of Avon Beach in 1934. The family still runs the bookshop and café there. Fig.17 is a pre-war photograph of the Sandbank including both tea boats. The *Delsia* Tea Boat by Holloway's Cut, run by the Strides, operated rather longer, from 1926 to 1940, in its last year providing food for troops on the Head. For the first four years, before the council provided a pipe, water supplies for this boat were rowed over from Stanpit in galvanised steel tanks.

An idea of the nature of the times can be gleaned from a council decision in 1931. Some 18 bathing cubicles were to be bought for £3.2s.0d. (£3.10) each, with bathing restricted to them after 9am, except from a place especially set aside. 108 costumes and 72 towels were to be purchased by the council. Charges were laid down for tents (10s. (50p) a week) and fishermen's stores sites (10s. a year). The Beach Superintendent, the former police constable of Highcliffe, was to have a uniform, oil coat and sou'wester. In 1937, the council were letting their huts at £1 per week in high season and still offering sites at a minimum of one guinea p.a., albeit that 20 huts had been washed away in 1936!

The houseboats had to be vacated during the war and were wrecked by the Army, apparently in order to prevent use by invading Germans. Looking back, it seems an illogical move. There was no compensation, although no rent was paid to the council in the first place. One of the houseboats had been a 50-foot American motor launch, originally ordered by the Admiralty during World War I. By the 1930s, it was used for camping by the Sea Scouts. After it had been wrecked, some wag painted the name "Dunerbit" on the side!

Planning applications

I felt it worthwhile to set out a brief summary of the main consents and refusals, as culled form the council's public planning record. A local planning authority is supposed to treat applications by itself to itself on its own land exactly the same as normal applications. Rather a superhuman requirement, I would say!

Apart from those identified in the table below, there have been a number of minor applications, including temporary public conveniences (1949); alterations to ranger's cottage (1959); diesel tank for Mr. Faris, who ran the land train (1969); a public shelter at the Sandbank (1969); alterations to barn to make it a workshop in connection with the land train (1982), and a cattle shed (1993).

Fig.17 ***Mudeford Sandbank, 1930s***

(Reproduced by consent of Classic Pictures)

A photograph, probably dated 1935 to 1939 as for Fig.16. The tea boats are clearly visible on a wide version of the sandspit, which then had the benefit of a lot of sand. The tea boat of oval appearance was originally Derham's. By 1940, in different ownership, it had been towed to Wick and later sunk.

DATE	EVENT
1949	Consent for construction of café for 1 year, later extended to 3 years.
1954	Use granted of part of thatched barn as public conveniences.
1962	Application for Marine Training Centre: granted.
1963	Refuse tipping in ironstone quarry approved in principle, but it had to be deferred for Minister's consent, which (thank goodness) was refused in 1965.
1966	Extension approved to Marine Training Centre.
1969	Yacht marina and adjoining buildings approved in principle on south side of harbour. (The council later reversed this decision, resulting in a planning inquiry in 1973 that upheld the reversal.)
1971	Full application made for dinghy park, slipway, car park, club buildings and caretaker's flat.
1972	Refusal issued since against development plan, not appropriate for public open space, prejudicial to conservation, loss of visual amenity and would create noise and general disturbance.
1972	Application for public conveniences, café, pump room, refreshment kiosk and ticket office: granted.
1975	Property Services Agency applied for consent to resite the Coastguard lookout station: granted.
1983	Hengistbury Head noted on planning record as included under Section 1 of Ancient Monuments and Archaeological Areas Act 1979. County Monument 824.
1984	Christchurch Council obtained consent to replace the water main from terminus buildings to the Black House, subject to oversight by Oxford University.
1986	Property Services Agency applied for consent to re-position existing wreck post to the west of the Dykes.

1987 Application for 31 feet high aerial mast.

2002 Application on 10 December for Field Studies and Interpretation Centre, granted in 2003. Please see next section.

2004 Consent given on 21 April for challenge course apparatus and ramps on an area partly occupied by two existing classrooms at the Hengistbury Head Centre, meaning that they would need to be removed first, in order to implement the consent.

Redevelopment proposals for the Hengistbury Head Centre

I'll not listen to reason... reason always means what someone else has to say
Elizabeth Gaskell, *Cranford* (1853)

This section may be read together with the description appearing in Chapter Twelve.

The 1960s-built Marine Training Centre has expanded its functions over the years and become known as the Hengistbury Head Outdoor Education and Field Studies Centre.

For conservation reasons to do with reducing impact from tourists, the 1997 Management Plan controversially wanted to move facilities west towards Southbourne Coast Road. A later plan, to rebuild the café and erect a new visitor centre, together with part of the Hengistbury Head Centre and Classroom of the Future, on the pitch and putt course by the Dykes, was also opposed. English Heritage said that it was "destructive" because it would be a bad setting for the Dykes, which are an Ancient Monument. Wessex Archaeology then found internationally important archaeological remains, which had to be preserved. People from a wide area and all three local councillors felt that it was inappropriate in this position. Another name for the scheme has been "E-Learning Centre."

On 18 July 2003, at a planning committee meeting "in the community" at St. Peter's School, a full consent was granted for a £2.4 million revised scheme to be sited in the Hengistbury car park. Most of the car park would have been lost and access greatly restricted along a much-narrowed Broadway. After major opposition and a £1.1 million shortfall in funding, the plans were eventually dropped in 2005. Despite the main reason relating to inadequate capital funding, it cannot have helped that cutbacks on outdoor educational trips were anticipated, with schools having greater control of their budgets. Although this was an educationally exciting project with special government support, most felt that it did not need to be in this sensitive Green Belt location, which is also subject to flood risk from the sea. "Alternative ways of developing a facility at the heritage site," presumably a modest visitor centre, were reportedly being explored in 2005. Much "interpretation" work had been done, including animations of breaching the chalk ridge, and camp life in the Iron Age. Rather than lose this to the public, other ways of getting the message across will doubtless be pursued.

The whole business is a good instance of high feelings concerning Hengistbury Head. Both the Southbourne Forum, attended by about 500 people in January 2003, and the public planning committee meeting in July that year, showed the strong public feeling against the scheme. Whilst some councillors were apparently "heartbroken" at its loss, others were delighted. Most of the public attending the planning meeting were unhappy with a drawn vote, followed by the chairman voting in favour for the second time, but supporters felt that this was fair. Although the proposers considered the scheme so good that it justified infringing high quality Green Belt, the opponents were convinced no case whatsoever had been made. Both the Ombudsman and MP became involved. Debate ranged widely from the safety of children at a joint educational and public building to the merit of providing public access via the internet to archaeological information concerning French sites.

At the time of publication, we can say that the existing centre and café are likely to be retained and refurbished for now, with a new, cheaper E-Learning Centre to be placed on an existing school site. Options, for converting existing buildings, may also be considered.

Drainage

I can remember swimming in the sea at Southbourne as a child in the 1950s and having to evade floating raw sewage. This does not happen any more. It appears that a main reason for the construction of Broadway in 1935 was to include piping for the town's sewage from the higher ground to the west and well out to sea near the Dykes. Another gravity system existed with an outfall near Bournemouth Pier. Clearly, some improvement was needed.

Bournemouth has a combined system of surface and foul water drainage, meaning that both flow in the same pipes. In the 1960s, an east to west Coastal Interceptor Sewer (CIS) was installed, consisting of a pipe of nearly six feet diameter with about ten vertical access shafts, which takes the drainage from the town's coastal area. Before this upgrade, sewer pipes were up to nine inches diameter only. Pumping stations from east and west send the sewage to a relatively high point at Woodland Walk, Boscombe, where it can run purely by gravity via Kings Park to Holdenhurst sewage works, and into the Stour, fully treated. This is a big improvement, because it means no sewage will normally go out to sea directly, although there is a safety overflow within the design to deal with any excessive load. The design also has a system of valves, which allows the old system to operate as before if need be, to allow maintenance of the CIS.

One main pumping station is located near Bournemouth Pier to pump from the west. The main pumping station for the water from the east is in a disguised house at the corner of Broadway and Clowes Avenue. Other smaller pumping facilities exist such as one in the Hungry Hiker building at Hengistbury. Sewage passes down the Broadway drain to the Clowes Avenue pumping station. Pumping stations in Wick Lane and Iford Lane send the sewage uphill to the CIS.

The design allows for sewage to be held, if necessary, in enormous attenuation tanks, one of which is buried under the Solent Beach car park. Should there be overload, sewage can flow out to sea by gravity from that tank in a pipe over 30 inches wide and nearly 400 yards long. Once the emergency is over, pumps will automatically restart in order to reverse the flow and take the waste on its normal route to Holdenhurst. As a result, the only occasions when raw sewage is likely to find its way into the sea are at times of extremely heavy and exceptionally prolonged rainfall. This well-engineered system means that sewage does not flow into the sea more than about once a year, whereas it did every day with the old system.

Land train

Against the usual local opposition, 1968 saw the introduction of this tourist facility, which allowed people to avoid walking from the Dykes to Mudeford.

It is another example of the mixture of opinions the Head tends to generate: "If people can't be bothered to walk, why go there?"; "Let's give the town an extra attraction to the benefit of the holiday trade"; "Why damage the Head with more tourist pollution, trampling and generally set back conservation needs?"; "This town should make the most of its assets and allow enjoyment by the less mobile."

The original contract from the council was to a local family, which included four sons, all of whom worked on the train. It is said that during interviews for the job, the question was asked: "When do pedestrians have priority over the land train?" Anyone who did not answer "Always" would not get the job! It appears that on at least one occasion at night in those early days, the train was actually driven up Warren Hill. Indeed, I have even heard that an opponent, who felt particularly strongly, took the train to the top and sent it over the cliff edge! If this is true, presumably the council had to rescue it from the beach.

Property development and market

In the interests of telling the whole story, I felt that some aspects at least of this major subject had to be covered. Being rather specialist, they are included in the Appendix.

The Human Impact on Hengistbury

FIVE

IRONSTONE MINING CATASTROPHE

The removal of the Headland is an evil in itself as destroying a good Landmark, and a certain amount of good shelter for small craft, but also as causing the dispersion of the loose soil, of which it is chiefly composed, into a tideway..,and it may be safely averred that whatever value the stones carried away may possess, it will entail a cost 100 times greater to compensate for the evil done, and to arrest further mischief.

Captain Vetch R.E. 1854

THE MOST NOTORIOUS part of the story of Hengistbury Head is the nineteenth century mining of ironstones, otherwise known as ironstone nodules or doggers. Natural erosion is to be regretted, but there is something altogether worse about serious, unnecessary man-made damage, compounded by the absence of any effective action to put it right, when such action is easily available and the need for it is plain.

Even before the removal of the doggers, the area was at risk from both nature and man. In other words, just when the development pressures of modern times were beginning in the nineteenth century, and protection became more important, the headland was abandoned to the forces of commerce.

We know that there has been great natural erosion of the Head ever since the end of the last Ice Age and the flooding of land in the valley of the old River Solent. However, it is likely that the erosion, which caused the ironstones to form the Christchurch Ledge, took place over more than the current interglacial period. This means that not all of it necessarily happened in the last 10,000 years or so, but some of it perhaps occurred before the last Ice Age, when sea levels may have been higher than now.

Over the centuries, many nodules have fallen from the cliffs, thereby providing a protective apron against coastal erosion. The Christchurch Ledge (Fig.11) and Beer Pan Rocks are made from them, so indicating the extent of erosion. Despite this, the resistance of the ironstones has provided an eastern headland to Poole Bay. The future protection of the town now requires some continuity of the headland by coastal defence measures, but more of this later.

Even Clarendon's Rocks were made from doggers. Hence their removal, before 1848, may have had an effect on the coastline. Fortunately, Charles II did not implement the Yarranton Report of 1676, which proposed that the Hengistbury ironstones be used for the large-scale manufacture of cannon. Had he done so, it is possible that the headland would have been just a tiny island now in front of a coast set back as a single bay from Poole to Hurst Castle.

Although Holloway's mining activity, from 1848 to 1870, certainly caused a disastrous increase in coastal erosion, the impact of previous mining is not at all obvious. For example, there was a large Iron Age settlement, and the Romans would have been aware of the easily accessible nodules. Much later, from the seventeenth century onwards, ironstone was needed for the Sowley ironworks, located about three miles east of Lymington. The hammer pond of 100 acres was used to beat out the slag as part of the smelting process. The Sowley Pond can still be seen on the OS map, marked on the other side of Sowley Lane from the old ironworks. A specimen from there has been analysed and almost certainly came from Hengistbury. In addition to the Hengistbury ironstone, the process used charcoal from the forest, and limestone from the Isle of Wight as a flux.

Things were to prove very different in 1848, when Mr. J. E. Holloway, then aged 27, formed a mining company and gained a lease or concession from the Head's owner, Sir George Gervis. At various times Holloway, one of thirteen siblings, was a coal merchant, architect, and councillor, and was mayor of Christchurch in 1865, 1866 and 1887. The lease allowed the company to take ironstone nodules from the Head. They were found to be of siderite (ferrous carbonate), with sand and clay content. There was also some vegetable matter, which Mr. Holloway found helped the reduction of the iron ore.

From 1848 to 1856, they were removed from the beach at the base of the cliff, so affecting the stability of Poole Bay. The doggers had formed an essential headland, which tended to keep the sand in Poole Bay and protect the Head from sea erosion. The 1846 map at Fig.38 and the 1830 painting at Fig.18 both show the mass of ironstones. Once they were removed, the sea attacked the cliff base with vigour, carrying away the sand. It is believed that in 1848 the Head extended to Beer Pan Rocks. In 1926, it was reported that "the grandfathers of elderly Christchurch men used to be able to walk out to the Beer Pan Rocks." By 1851, Sir George Rose of Sandhills was writing about the heavy wastage and the increasing speed at which the cliff was foundering. He drew a contrast with the fact that there had been no great erosion within the lives of men then aged 70. It was noticed that by 1854, Old Harry Rocks became visible directly from previously sheltered anchorages in Christchurch Bay. Fig.19 shows the extent of loss by 1870 and the great gap between the coast and the Rocks.

Notes were made by a member of a local fishing family in about 1890: "Within the last 15 years, we have seen the astounding effects resulting from the removal of the Beer Pan Rocks by the Hengistbury Mining Company." Haven House was noted as at risk of being undermined. On 22 November 1881, a passage was opened opposite Sandhills. Five days later, the valleys of the Stour and Avon looked like an inland sea for miles. Another report, in 1903, refers to the sandbank being 50 yards wide and six feet high and being the cause of big floods in the town. These remarks refer to the extension of the Sandbank due to sand being transported around the Head.

Part of the operation was to take coal from South Wales to Southampton by ship and from there to Christchurch by coal lighter. An 1855 advertisement for J.E. Holloway refers to a steam tug and powerful barges constructed especially for the shallow waters of the harbour and with a tonnage of 600 in aggregate. The price was 24 shillings (£1.20) cash per ton, delivered. Doggers were used to provide ballast for the lighters on their return to Southampton and for the ships returning to South Wales from Southampton. Clearly, it was a good economic cycle because, apart from transporting the ironstones for smelting, ballast was needed for safety reasons, to prevent the vessels riding too high in the water.

A sight to be seen at Hengistbury, in those days, was the paddle steamer *Carrs* towing four shallow draught barges used for coal and ironstone. According to Holloway's stationery, each barge had a small sail. They came through the Run and into Holloway's Dock via the new short canal length he created, known as Holloway's Cut (Fig.46). The 1846 map (Fig.38) shows the natural inlet before the straight canal was cut to the new dock. It appears that after the ironstone mining had stopped, the town's subsequent need for coal was satisfied, at least in part, by a coal barge, the *Charlotte*. From 1872 to 1906, 1,000 tons per year were carried, in loads of 36 tons, direct from Portsmouth to Christchurch Quay.

It is likely that the Head appeared quite industrial from 1848 to the 1870 cessation of mining: regular noise from explosives; a tramway to ferry the ironstones from the beach under the Head round to Holloway's Dock; a loading quay with cranes, horses and large numbers of labourers. Although very short, this tramway had the distinction of being the town's first railway. What is now the Lily Pond was made to water the horses. Estimates of daily tonnage vary from 40 to 150. Such figures are consistent with Holloway's obituary notice of 1901, which referred to the employment of "hundreds of work people in the excavation of ironstone." The council would use the same route in 1938, but working in the opposite direction, in order to rectify the damage, with a railway transporting the heavy materials for constructing the Long Groyne around the headland.

The danger to the coast was always evident. The Admiralty received a crystal clear report in September 1854 from Captain Vetch, who had inspected on 26 August 1854 and taken evidence from 15 witnesses. He

Fig.18 ***Hengistbury Head with ironstone apron, c.1830***
(J. Brown of Avebury. Reproduced by consent of Red House Museum)
The earliest picture of the headland, which I have been able to find. Although the section of cliff shown has long since disappeared under the sea due to erosion, it is clear that it had developed, with some vegetation, at a relatively shallow and stable angle. There was also an enormous amount of ironstone as a protective apron, which skirted the base of the Head. The painting even shows two rows of ironstone nodules in the cliff face. In contrast, Warren Hill today is smaller, steeper and more vulnerable.

personally saw an estimated 4,000 tons, lately moved by tramway from the south cliff to the north cliff, waiting for shipment. "The accumulation of ages had been carried away by the lessees," he notes. Vetch strongly submitted that the solicitors for the Admiralty should stop any more removal of stones "eastwards of Double Ditches." It is hard to imagine a more firm report on the subject, but the fact is that the Admiralty took no action which proved effective, either before or after the failure of the 1856 court case mentioned below.

On 7 July 1855, the mining company withdrew an appeal to the Quarter Sessions against their rating assessment. Presumably this was because they felt, on investigation, that there was little chance of reducing the rateable value. This would have been based on the annual value of the property, as applies for all rating assessments. Moreover, as a "mineral hereditament," it was no doubt calculated on quantity extracted. It would certainly have not been open to Mr. Holloway to argue that his occupation should not be rated, because it was not lawful. Rating case law could be quite robust in ensuring liability on this sort of thing. In one case (R. v. Bell 1798) such an attempt to avoid liability by a trespasser had failed: although the trespasser was in unlawful occupation, he was gaining value from it and had to pay his rates.

After taking away the beach's natural barrier to erosion, the company proceeded in 1856 to dig a canyon down from Warren Hill to the low ground on the north-east. This was the same year that the Bournemouth Improvement Act was passed, setting up the Commissioners, whose district extended literally in a circular shape. The centre was the front door of the Belle Vue Hotel and the radius was one mile. Hence, the start of the first real local authority for the town coincided with a fresh attack on land as yet well beyond its eastern limits. One of the most vocal opponents, Sir George Rose of Sandhills, Mudeford, had died the previous year. It is speculated that the loss of the foreshore, clearly visible from Sandhills, hastened his death. Open-cast mining methods were also used to drag away the land on the north and west aspects of the Head. The steps carved in the hillside on these aspects were used for spoil dumping. They are now known most appropriately as The Batters. Captain Vetch re-inspected in 1860 and was entirely confirmed in his original opinion. The same year there were negotiations with the Admiralty for the sale of property interests in the Head, but although the owner might have come to terms, the Hengistbury Mining Company reportedly wanted too much money.

The 1870 Ordnance Survey map extract in Fig.19 shows the extent of the quarry as at the time of cessation, by a stippled area. The southern edge of the quarry land can be seen as a cut into the hillside and parts of the northern edge as steep-sided fingers of waste material pushed out over the lower ground. Fig.37 shows the quarry as now dammed in order to create a wildlife lake. Fig.12 is a watercolour of the Head from the grounds of the mansion at High Cliff in 1811. The western face of Warren Hill is rather jagged (as a result of the mining) when viewed from this position today, compared to the gentle slope in the painting.

It is commonly said that half of the Head has been eroded, as a consequence both of the work of the mining company and the lack of preventive action until 1938, when the Long Groyne was built. In the meantime, great quantities of sand drifted around to Mudeford Sandbank, which had reached a mile long by 1880. It was breached a number of times including 1895, 1911 and 1935. Each time, the long length of the Run proved untenable against high water conditions, when the extended sandbank was found vulnerable to a breakthrough. Lagoons were sometimes created until the remnant of the severed sandspit was washed ashore. An 1891 map by Staff Captain J. Parsons shows a "Dry Run" in 1886.

Whilst it was always clear that something should be done, it was hard for those genuinely concerned at the time to stop the company's operations. For example, the Admiralty was pressed by Sir George Rose to take court action for malicious trespass on the seashore. He had watched with despair the decimation of the Head from his excellent vantage point at Sandhills. The Solicitor of the Admiralty issued an impressive notice forbidding the taking of anything below High Water Mark on pain of prosecution. I have included it as a warning against misplaced optimism and to show that nothing really changes in this sort of case. Whilst many must have been delighted by the issue of this strong-sounding legal document, they found that the law failed them later. The text follows:

> *TAKE NOTICE that you and all others are forbidden to dig out, excavate, break, dredge up or otherwise disturb, take or remove any Stone, Shingle or other Soil or matter at or from the Shore below high water mark at Hengistbury Head, otherwise called Christchurch Head, or the water adjacent thereto, or at or from any part of the Bays called Poole Bay and Christchurch Bay, or the Shores thereof, the same being the property of Her Majesty. And that if contrary to this Notice you do on any pretence whatever dig out, excavate, break, dredge up or otherwise disturb, take or remove any such Stone, Shingle or other Soil or matter from the said Shore or Shores, Water or Bays, or any of them, you will be prosecuted according to Law.*
>
> Dated this 1st day of March, 1856.
> (Signed) WILLM. FROGETT ROBSON,
> Solicitor of the Admiralty

(Reproduced by permission of the UK Hydrographic Office)

The magistrates considered in 1856 whether there had been trespass. The Admiralty contended that the owner of the Head had had no legal right to grant the lease because the ironstones were placed beyond his ownership, which extended only to the High Water Mark. The court decided that it did not have jurisdiction, because it was satisfied that the tenant genuinely thought his right extended to the Low Water Mark. This meant that the court felt duty-bound to dismiss the complaint, which went beyond its powers to hear. The question never did come before a court of competent jurisdiction. Despite this, and although the 1856 hearing dismissed the complaint, the nature of the operation did change that year. Instead of taking the doggers from the beach, they were extracted by open-cast mining from the headland itself.

Eventually, the Board of Trade apparently succeeded in stopping the ironstone mining in 1870. There had been increasing opposition from the Bournemouth Commissioners, local churchmen and the Christchurch Town Clerk, James Druitt. However, I use the word "apparently," because it has been said that the real reason for cessation was that the operation was no longer profitable. Certainly, all previous attempts to stop the mining had failed, and the easy pickings must have gone by 1870. We probably owe the survival of the Head to the vagaries of the market stopping its deprivation in the nick of time.

The open-cast mining, which left such a scar across Warren Hill, was the most intensive use of the Head since the Iron Age. The 1870 OS sheet shows a building near to the south side of Holloway's Dock about 35

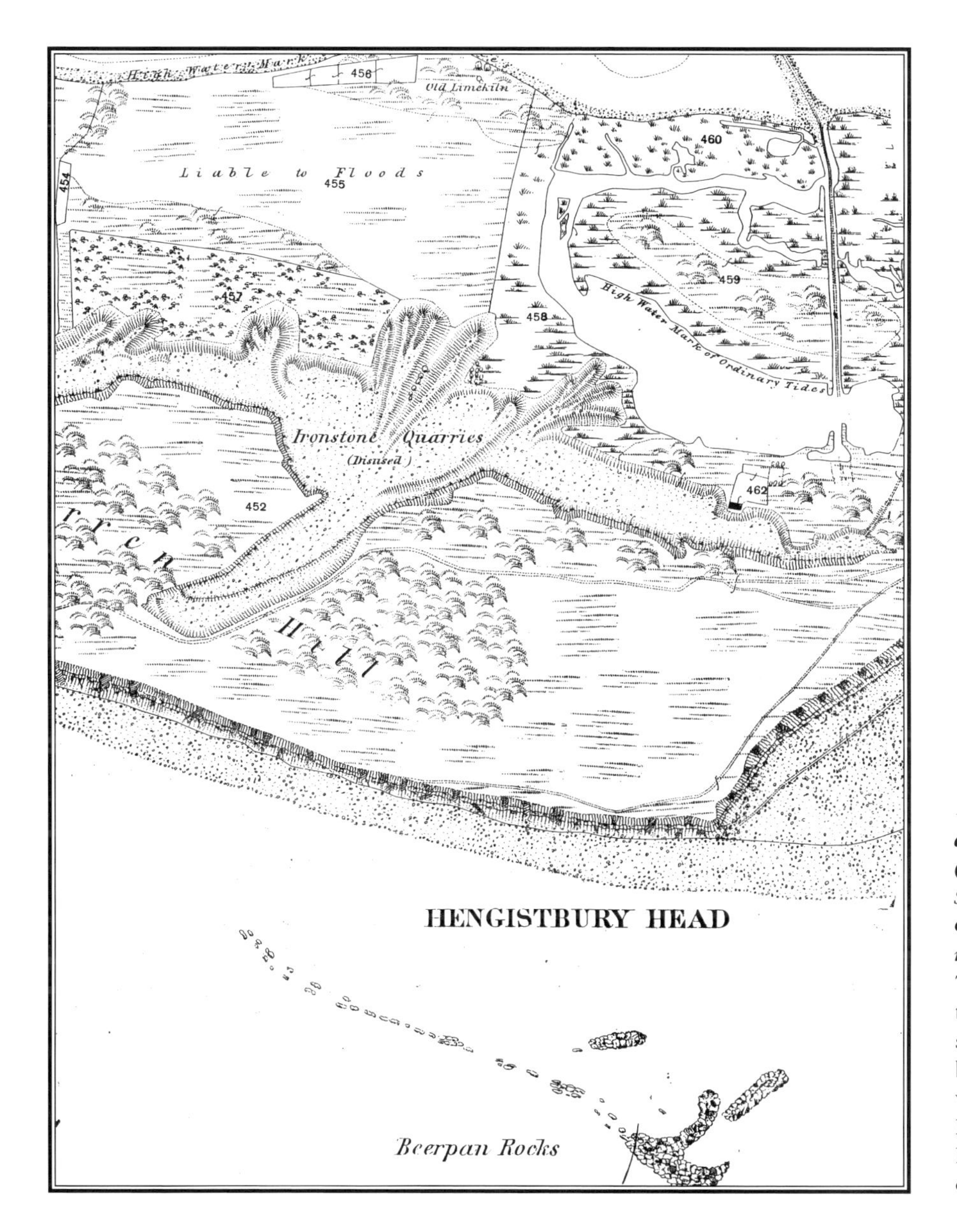

Fig.19 ***Ironstone quarry and Beer Pan Rocks, 1870***
(Reproduced from the Ordnance Survey map of that date. © Crown Copyright. 1/2,500 scale before reduction)
The map is dated around the time that mining ceased and shows what must have been a building connected with the works to the south of Holloway's Dock. Many authorities cite the Beer Pan Rocks as the eighteenth century coastline.

feet by 20 feet, together with an adjoining enclosure of nearly 0.2 acres, presumably needed for the mining operation, then just finishing. One can imagine the need for a workshop and store, and a reasonably secure yard for plant and equipment. The industrial scene would have included animals for heavy haulage and cranes for lifting ironstones on to barges in Holloway's Dock.

Mining accidents in the nineteenth century

The local paper reported in May 1857 "another sad accident" during blasting at the ironstone works. A piece of stone struck Frederick Dunn on the head causing the back of the skull to fracture and a portion of the brain to protrude. He was removed the same evening to the Union Workhouse, but did not survive beyond a few days.

A further report, in November 1857, was headed "Another Fatal Accident at Warren Head." It seems that as navvies were moving earth to extract the iron ore, there was a sudden slip of ground. Edward Budden had a pickaxe above his head when earth fell, driving the point of it into his skull, breaking his leg and otherwise injuring him. He lived for a day only, and it appears his widow and children did not have the benefit of an inquest, despite a plea for one from a correspondent to the paper a week later. The letter comments: "When so many accidents fatal and otherwise have occurred at Warren, it becomes all the more imperative that a case like poor Budden's should not be allowed to pass by without some proper investigation being made, the result of which should be made public."

Legacy of erosion

There are perhaps two positive aspects to the otherwise disastrous mining operation. Firstly, an unexpected benefit, of the quarry up to Warren Hill, is that an attractive landscape and wildlife feature has been created, by damming about half way in order to create a lake. Perhaps the idea for this1970s scheme was generated by the antics of the boys in the 1930s, whose dams were of lower engineering quality, but reportedly great fun anyway! Secondly, a geologist might say that the steady cliff erosion due to the mining is good for research.

For the most part, however, the mining was ruinous, and it remains crucial to an understanding the Head and its future. Any visitor today is confronted by many restrictions on access in order to protect Hengistbury. This is quite right, but it does contrast grossly with the negligence of the nineteenth century. So it is that nothing effective was done whilst half the headland disappeared, but now, we must keep to the paths!

There is an increased risk of a breakthrough by the sea near Double Dykes. Without the removal of ironstones from the beach, there would have been much less erosion by the Dykes. The cliff is only a few feet high there and made of river gravel, a very loose material. Moreover, once it happened, the breakthrough would be helped by the north-east slope of land, down towards the harbour. Apart from the headland becoming narrower on the low ground due to the mining, it has also eroded greatly on Warren Hill. Since it is only a matter of time before the Head is lost to the sea anyway, the significance of the mining is that this loss has been greatly brought forward.

SIX

OTHER MAN-MADE THREATS TO HENGISTBURY HEAD

We have always known that heedless self-interest was bad morals; we know now that it is bad economics.

F.D.Roosevelt

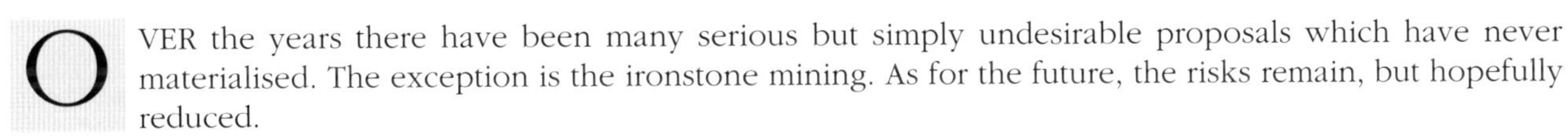

OVER the years there have been many serious but simply undesirable proposals which have never materialised. The exception is the ironstone mining. As for the future, the risks remain, but hopefully reduced.

Some of the mooted plans are probably little more than the work of the rumour mill, as when it had to be confirmed in 1939 that there were no plans for trolley buses east of the Dykes. In 1968, when the council was considering the idea of the Head being taken over by the National Trust, one councillor suggested banning visitors, whilst another took a totally different attitude: "I would sooner see football pitches than Double Dykes and that's flat!"

Salisbury Avon Navigation

The River Avon Navigation Act 1664 created this scheme to enable commercial vessels to travel from the harbour to Salisbury, which was to become a port, as it had been in medieval times.

Turfs were cut, locks built and parts of the Avon canalised. It is recorded that in 1684, two 25-ton barges actually made the journey from Christchurch to Salisbury. Tolls were imposed in 1687. Traffic proceeded to flow from 1684 to 1695, and then (after repairs in 1700) for a further 20 years at the start of the eighteenth century. Eventually, floods washed away the works and debris filled the dredged channel. Final abandonment was in 1730. It is possible that a legal right remains to navigate the Avon, but owing to the inconvenience of obstructions such as Christchurch waterworks, no one is now likely to pursue it.

In 1695, Lord Clarendon made a cut in Mudeford Sandbank, using the ironstone nodules to build a new breakwater out to sea. The sea end of the rocks is still marked by a pole to aid navigation. The 1846 naval map, an extract of which is at Fig.38, describes it as Yarranton's Pier. There had been a meeting between Clarendon and Yarranton in 1675, at which the latter had urged the "making of a harbour," which can only refer to diverting the Run to a new break in the Sandbank. Moreover, this is consistent with the sketch from his book published the next year and referred to below (Fig.21). The pier is generally now called Clarendon's Rocks or Long Rocks. They are clearly shown in Fig.2, jutting out on the eastern side of Mudeford Sandbank. Clarendon's Cut was silted up and closed by the sea after the Stour and Avon went back to their old channel at the Run.

A naval survey of ports on the south coast was carried out from Dover to Lands End in 1698. Fig.20 is a map showing the outlet of the Harbour running east-south-east. Since at point "a" on the map, the legend says "Pier now making" and the direction looks right for an outlet by Clarendon's Rocks, my view is that this implies that the Run was blocked and the Cut successful at the date of the survey. Although the map is not very accurate, it does support the Smeaton comment below that the Cut was formed to the south-west of the breakwater. Indeed, the harbour would look quite different today, had the Cut been made to the north-east of the breakwater in 1695. This is because the downdrift of sand would then have been unlikely to block it, and result in the reinstatement of the Run. I say "unlikely" because the storms hitting the country in November 1703 were so overwhelmingly destructive that we cannot be sure of their impact. As ever, much of the story of Hengistbury Head and its surroundings relates to pure chance: things are as they are due to historical accident more than any other reason.

Although Defoe recorded in 1727 that the improved Avon was still in use to within two miles of Salisbury, it appears to have failed within the next three years due to poor viability. Clarendon's Rocks remain (Fig.46) and can be seen still at low tide, the last vestige of the Navigation idea.

"England's improvement by sea and land ..."

Andrew Yarranton, 1676

After the River Avon Navigation Act and before tolls began to be collected under that Act, Yarranton's book sought to advise the king about many things, including Hengistbury. He promised a good method to have "all his iron made and guns cast at a very cheap rate." He suggested there was nowhere better than the harbour for building fifth and sixth rate frigates, the timber for this being floated down the Avon from the New Forest. Transport would have been only about 18% of the cost of sending timber to Portsmouth. Although the language is archaic, his meaning is clear, as some other extracts will show:

> "At last I found in the Sea great quantities of Iron Stones lye in a Ridge."
>
> "I found the Ridge of Iron Stones was the cause that forc't the ground Tide about the point, which had carried and lodged the sands so, as it had choaked up the Harbour: but the Stones near the Shore lay so great and thick that they were the occasion of lodging the Sands by them, near the Western Shore, and so of preserving a place which is very deep and good anchorage, and within one hundred Yards of the Shore, which gives unto that River the advantage of making there as good an Harbour, as to the depth of Water it will drain, as any is in *England*, where a Boy and a Cord two Inches Diameter will be sufficient to hold a ship; the Harbour being a great Inland Lake or Pool and well Defended from all Winds."
>
> "50 or 60 fifth and sixth rate frigates may safely ride."
>
> "... hill... which was an old camp, which will lodge 100,000 men and in three days made so defensible ..."
>
> "... entrenched by a vast ditch, yet very useful..."
>
> "And to me it is very strange, that notice long since had not been taken of it, and some Forts built there."
>
> "Thirdly, this place is and may be made by Art, with the laying out of two thousand pounds upon a Fort, a full defence against any Enemy landing and secure all His Majesty's Ships..."

The report suggests that the New Forest would be an excellent source of timber (for shipbuilding) and charcoal (for ironworks) whilst Hengistbury Head would be the best source of iron. Two docks could be installed there allowing three ships to be built at once. Two furnaces to cast guns and two forges to make iron were envisaged "about Ringwood." The cost of building the docks and ironworks was put at £8,000. Fig.21 is a copy of the plan from the original book. Although illustrative only, the general idea can be seen: an armed camp at the Head with a fort at the end, shipbuilding docks on the south side of the harbour, and ironstones to be taken up the Avon to forges, fuelled by New Forest charcoal, at Ringwood. Not least, it demonstrates a new break in the Sandbank (presumably at Yarranton's Pier, also known as Clarendon's Rocks) directly opposite the Avon, with a ship sailing through it.

Although Yarranton's suggestion was never implemented, it could have worked in whole or part. We must also remember that the harbour used to be much deeper.

Proposed harbour improvements

John Smeaton, 1762

Not for the first time, or the last, the purpose of the investigation was the feasibility of making the harbour commercially useful to the benefit of Christchurch.

Smeaton advised that great amounts of sand and rocks had been removed from the Head by violent storms. He painted a picture of heavy erosion and sand driven from the cliffs into the bottom of Christchurch Bay. The consequent sandspits narrowed the harbour mouth, which was then moved from the Head towards Mudeford

Fig.20 ***Survey of ports on SW coast, 1698***
(Dummer, Wiltshaw, Conaway & Cruft. Reproduced by consent of Red House Museum)

This survey cannot be reconciled with the Yarranton map in Fig.21. But it is more accurate and comparison is possible with the 1785 Mackenzie map in Fig.11. In 1695, Clarendon's Rocks had been installed as part of the improvement scheme to divert water from the Run. Legend "a.Pier now making" shows the diversion operating successfully, three years after the installation, whilst "b.Store-house" is probably Haven House (built around 1695 to 1698) on the Mackenzie map, or its predecessor. By 1785, the Run had resumed its normal route by Haven House, leaving the pier as it is today, i.e. merely an ironstone groyne. The narrative going with the 1698 map states:

Christ Church

River disembogues into the Sea in a Bay within the Shingles, and about 3 Leagues without the Needles Westward. The Town lyes about 2 Miles from the Mouth of it, and yet the Flood Tyde scarce Washes to it, And altho~ there falls into this Haven two Considerable Freshes, the one from Salisbury, the other from Blandford, yet 'tis no Port for other vessells than of 30 Tuns downwards.

Great Banks of land lye before it and not more than 2 ft. Water upon the Barr, nor Flowes on Spring Tydes more than 6 ft. upright, are insuperable impediments to those Offices, the Works of the Navy require, therefore utterly incapable of such improvements.

as part of the same process. The hummocks of Mudeford Sandbank were created by wind blown sand. Water depths and ground conditions were noted at various places. He further remarked that Christchurch would never have a harbour of any great depth or capacity. The reasons were the small tides, the double high tide (which caused a loss of power of the rivers) the flatness of the harbour bottom and the constant movement of sand.

As for the Clarendon Cut, he felt this was quite likely to have survived up to the time of his report, if only the breakwater had been placed on the windward side of the Cut. It would then have defended the channel from sands drifting into it from the south-west. When he inspected, sands were about a foot higher on this south-west or windward side of the pier. Water breaking over it from windward would also have had a useful deepening effect. In any case, the Cut had not been built to the original idea, which assumed two breakwaters. It did nonetheless take water to a depth of 15 to 16 feet for some time. Moreover, the height of the bar, just beyond the pier, was reduced by about two feet, "a very great improvement." However, the land water eventually found that the passage to the sea was "not sufficiently ready." A breakthrough followed in the old place, i.e. the Run, which had been blocked with piles at considerable expense. The sea proceeded to shut up the Cut with sand.

The first conclusion was that natural conditions certainly favoured an outlet in the position of the Run. But it would be a difficult operation to move the shoal and too expensive to make two very long breakwaters in such a location. The second conclusion therefore was to provide an improved construction at Yarranton's Pier, i.e. build another breakwater 240 feet to the south-west and lengthen the existing one, both to 1,500 feet. Then a cut could be made through the Sandbank (66 yards by 66 yards by a depth of 3 yards) at the same time blocking the Run with 4,200 tons of rough stones.

In view of what happened later with the mining company, it is surprising that this respected engineer planned to use 38,320 tons of ironstone for the breakwaters, as obtained from the beach at the Head. He even allowed for the possibility that there was not enough ironstone, saying that it would then be required to bring supplies from Portland. It seems likely that neither he, nor Armstrong in 1836 (below). appreciated the disastrous results which would follow. His total costing was £5,007 including 10% for incidentals. The calculations assumed getting an extra foot of depth for every 100-foot extension to the piers. Dredging would also be necessary in places to provide a six-foot channel from the harbour mouth to the town quay at mean tides.

Smeaton thought that vessels of eight-foot draught would be able to enter the harbour on a middling spring tide. He said that the improvement would have meant the harbour being very good for small merchant ships, and specifically mentioned armed cutters. The council took no action on the recommendations. One explanation is that few wanted to disrupt the popular smuggling trade by creating a harbour, which would be more accessible to the revenue men. The reference in the report to armed cutters may well have been significant in the decision to shelve it. Only 22 years later, the Battle of Mudeford took place, showing the huge importance of smuggling to the local economy.

First Harbour of Christchurch Report, 1836

William Armstrong, 25 July

"Several gentlemen" formed a private committee and commissioned a report in order to encourage an increase in trade for the benefit of the town. Yet again, harbour improvements allowing large merchant vessels were to be considered. The plan was to lay the matter before the inhabitants of the town, presumably in the hope that the council would fund any works recommended.

The report found that there would always be a limit to the chance of making this a "commodious harbour" arising from three natural obstacles: the flat land through which the river passes, the low tidal range and the double high tide in the harbour. However, Armstrong also said that the harbour would be good and secure if a sufficient depth of water could be obtained. The only way to get this would be to confine the river to a straight and narrow channel. Much of his opinion agrees with Smeaton, in particular the merit of cutting through the Sandbank again. One problem highlighted concerned the "gravel and other heavy matter" carried down by the rivers. Once the tides opposed the river currents, this was deposited immediately, so creating a shallow bar in front of the entrance.

The advice was to channel the water next to a straight new embankment in the harbour, through a fresh cut made in the sandspit and leading out to sea by the existing breakwater, Clarendon's Rocks. The other side of the channel would be marked by another breakwater 80 to 100 yards long and parallel to the existing one, as extended. There was also a need to dredge the shoals and provide a drain and flood hatch at the upper end of a breakwater for the Mude and another stream. The costing of £6,000 implied the use of "the immense quantity" of stones (32,000 tons in fact) at Hengistbury Head. "They may be taken up at low water from the channel upwards of a mile from the Head." Boats were envisaged equipped with cranes and "nippers," each to carry 30 to 40 tons.

Once again, we have the assumption that the ironstones were there for the taking, apparently without regard

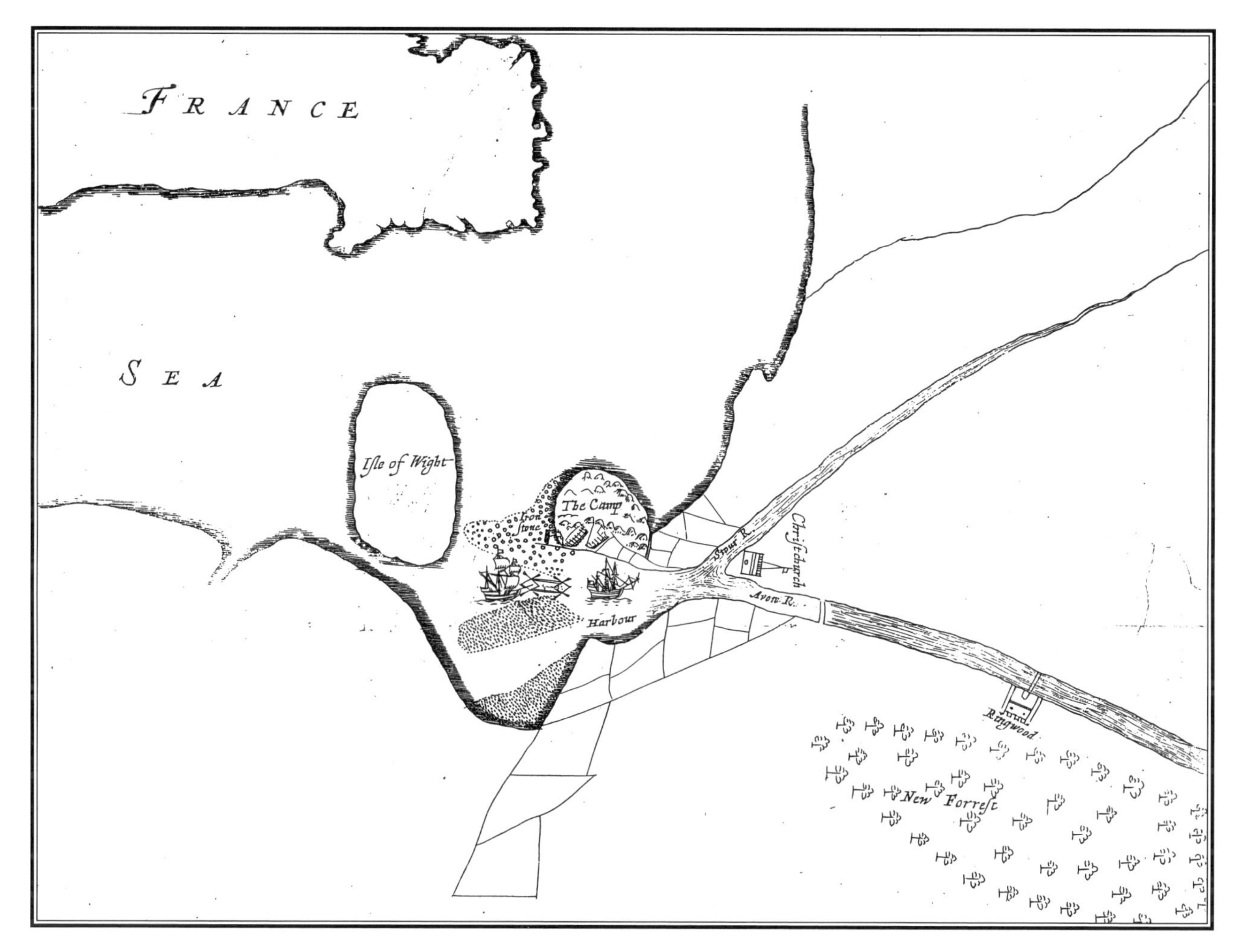

Fig.21 ***Military and development plans, 1676***

(Andrew Yarranton. Reproduced by consent of Christchurch Local History Society)

This is a very diagrammatic map. It shows a fort, an army camp suitable for up to 100,000 men and a dock in the lee of the headland, i.e. in the same place as the Iron Age port. The large quantity of ironstone is also prominent. Two large ships are making their way through a new gap in the Sandbank. The gap itself appears in the drawing to be lined with timber piles in the hope that the force of current would produce a good depth. Although never implemented, the object was to show King Charles II how he could have cheap ships and guns by using the ironstones at Hengistbury together with charcoal and timber from the New Forest.

to either the consequences or the ownership. I suppose that the consequential enormous erosion of the headland was only visible with hindsight, but one does wonder. As for ownership, all this would have needed the agreement of the estate owner (the Gervis family) and probably the Crown. Another item, which could have been usefully included, was an opinion about the draught of vessels that would be able to reach Christchurch Quay. At all events, this report also was shelved.

Second Harbour of Christchurch Report, 1836

John Sylvester, 23 September

The corporation requested this review of the "present state of the Harbour" in the same year as the private one just described. Soundings were taken, shoals were marked on a map and bars to the harbour investigated. Water depth was found to be barely nine feet half a mile out, and not four fathoms, three miles out. Much of the report dwelt on such description of the harbour conditions. Sylvester concluded that it was evident upon observation, as it was to Smeaton, that "very little could be hoped for in the way of a permanent improvement." He pointed out that there would always be a sand bar where land waters from the rivers met sea currents. To provide a harbour of general utility would involve piers above water level, enclosing the land stream and extending right out to sea. In short, the work would be so formidable that "the idea could not for a moment be entertained." So much for the fresh look at relocating the Run again by Clarendon's Rocks.

The report went on to consider what might be possible if the existing entrance were to be retained. Having decided that the outlet is only kept open by the strong force of the land stream, Sylvester explained that the unusual double high tide of the harbour (arising from the tidal interruption of the Isle of Wight) would always prevent this force from forming a deep channel to sea. Indeed, when water was "penned up" in the harbour at these times, there was much less force out to sea and a "facility to deposit in the Harbour road." To make matters worse, he felt that the bay was kept shallow by vast quantities of sand from Hengistbury Head and Long Ledge being driven there by the violent action of the sea. He thought that the land stream would have limited force and the bay would stay shallow as long as "any part of the high land remains." Inevitably, he decided: "Against natural opposition so strong, there is little that art can do."

The report finally suggested a limited, but simple and inexpensive solution, involving dredging the shoals from the main channel and providing about a mile of "fencing," defined as piling backed by rough stone. The position of the Run would remain. The idea was to ensure that there would always thereafter be an equal depth of water in the road of the rivers' channel to that over the bar. Sylvester evidently thought that his costing of "not more than £1,700" would be value for money, but that any greater scheme would not. According to a letter of 16 November 1836 from Sir George Rose to the mayor, Sir George Gervis offered a sum of £1,700 towards the expenses of harbour improvement. It seems that Rose took a dim view of this offer as he felt that he was supposed to make a similar one and this would be objectionable since he was MP.

It is remarkable that two reports about harbour improvement were produced in the same year, this one more pessimistic than Armstrong. J H Dunkin, one of the instigators of the Armstrong report, had a statement printed on 16 September 1836, exactly one week before the date of Sylvester's report. In it he endorses Armstrong's conclusions at the greater cost of £6,000, and anticipates laying the details before the public. Again, no action was taken.

Railway and docks scheme of 1885

This scheme arose in context with the nineteenth century railway building, which was needed to open up the region to improved transport:

- The London and South Western Railway completed the line from Waterloo to Southampton by 1840.
- The Southampton and Dorchester Railway, via Brockenhurst, Holmsley, Ringwood and Wimborne, was opened in 1847. It was christened The Snake due to its twists and turns to serve population centres and avoid hills. A bus then took passengers the seven miles from Holmsley to Christchurch three times a day. If they wanted to go on to the village of Bournemouth, there was only one bus a day.
- In 1856, a plan for a new 12.5-mile line from Ringwood to Christchurch and then Bournemouth was costed at £100,000. A saving of two hours was expected in the journey time to London from Bournemouth. It seems that the Bill was withdrawn in 1857 due to inadequate local financial support and a difficult money market.
- Eventually, an Act of Parliament obtained Royal Assent in 1859 for a more economical design, to Christchurch only, the line opening in 1862 and following roughly the current A338 Ringwood to Bournemouth road. The extension to Bournemouth, planned in 1863, finally opened in 1870 after something of a financial struggle, but had quadrupled gross receipts within three years.
- The final phase, in the attempt to give Bournemouth a good rail link to London, proved to be the 1888 connection from Brockenhurst to Christchurch, which was shorter and allowed faster trains. An upgraded station had been built in Bournemouth in 1885. The less convenient Ringwood line became a branch only, closing in 1935, whilst The Snake was axed by Dr. Beeching in 1963.

Application for the railway and docks scheme was planned for the Parliamentary session of 1885. The Somerset and Dorset Railway promoted it, based on the engineers' estimated cost of construction of £167,623 10s. 10d. It was expected that 109 acres, including any buildings, would have to be acquired at a cost, within this global figure, of £180 per acre. The total number of people with an interest (owners, occupiers and lessees) was 166, of which only 33 had assented to the scheme. The remainder had either dissented, were "neuter" or had given the promoters no answer: hence the need for compulsory powers. The detailed land schedules and

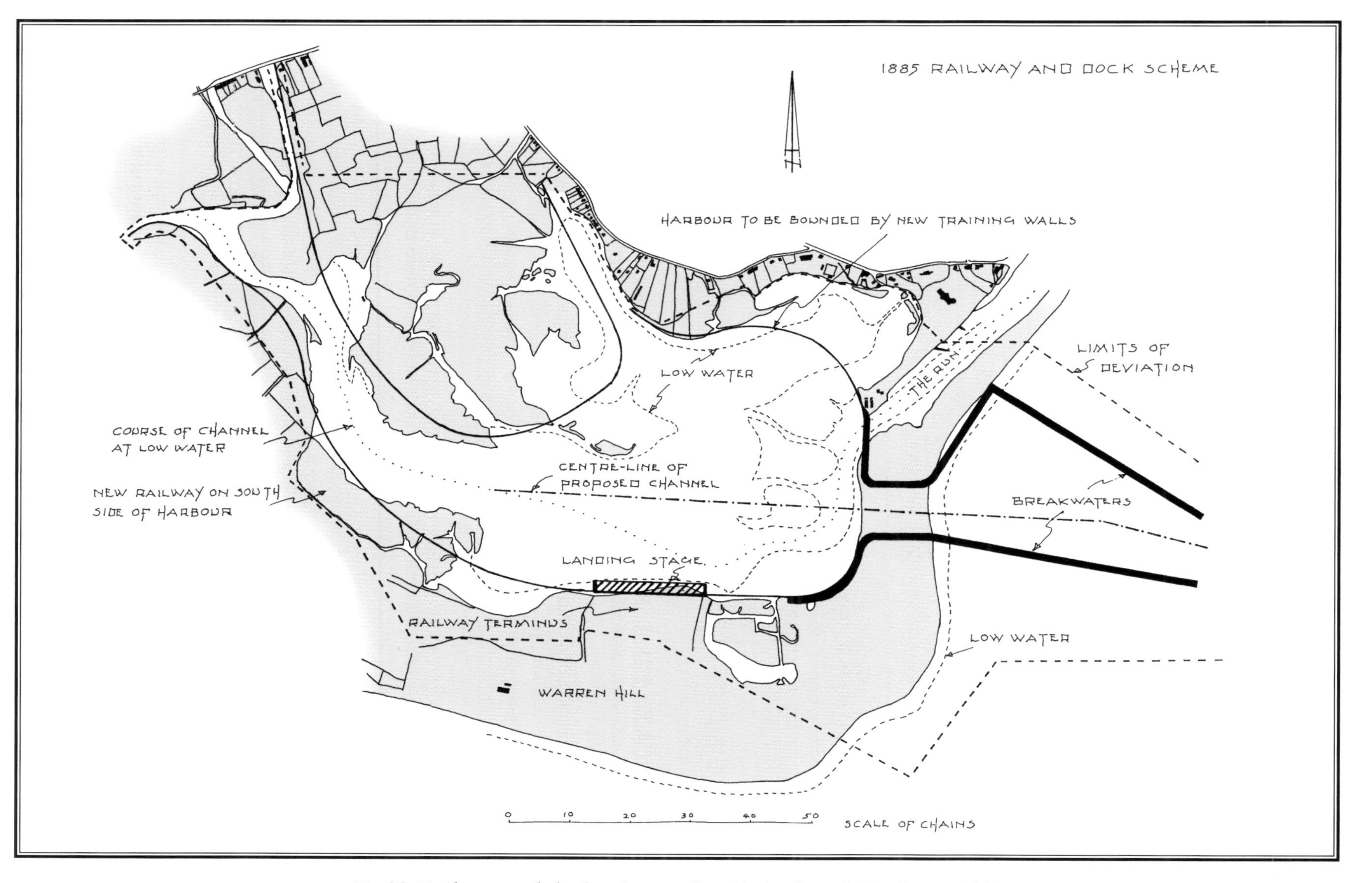

Fig.22 ***Railway and dock schemes for Christchurch Harbour, 1885***

(Drawing based on original engineer's plan. Reproduced by consent of Hampshire Record Office. Ref. DP/422)

This is the biggest "harbour improvement" ever promoted for Christchurch, with 1,000-yard breakwaters and a railway line via Wick and the south side of the harbour to a terminus and landing stage by Holloway's Dock. By spending a considerable amount on the infrastructure, the company plan was to ensure continuing deep water and therefore viability. The Southampton trade could perhaps have been gained, i.e. from ship owners anxious to avoid the Needles Channel. In the end, the promoters did not take the risk and withdrew the scheme.

plans give yet another indication of the large amount of preliminary work then needed for a new line. For instance, the Christchurch parish schedule covered 93 separate parcels of land, together with owners, lessees and occupiers.

The proposed line ran from Wimborne along the Stour valley to the south side of Christchurch Harbour near to the Head. The Avon and Stour were to be confined to a joint channel 500 feet wide, the harbour was to be dredged to a depth of 26 feet for nearly a mile to accommodate ocean going vessels, and a replacement outlet created for The Run in Mudeford Sandbank. It can be seen from Fig.22 that the intention was the same as for the seventeenth century plan, in that the changed harbour entrance coincides with Clarendon's Rocks.

There was to be a 2,000-yard channel starting from the new eight-chain width entrance in the sandspit. There were to be 1,000-yard breakwaters out to sea, a railway terminus at the site of the lime kiln under the Head, and a landing stage nearly 400 yards long. Full details were included such as piloting, navigation, buoys, compulsory purchase, bye-laws, tolls and extinguishment of others' rights. In short, the company would have secured 100% control of the harbour and about half of the Head.

Such a major railway port was expected to steal trade from Southampton, which suffered from a difficult sea approach through the Needles Channel. Although the council seemed in favour, hoping that it would make Christchurch the favourite yachting station on the south coast, the scheme was withdrawn within a year following opposition from the London and South Western Railway. The acid test of intentions came when the Standing Orders Examiner of Parliament came to hear the proposal in January 1885: the promoters failed to attend.

It is perhaps a matter of luck that the market apparently changed, so preventing Christchurch Harbour becoming a mini-Southampton. On the other hand, it is surprising that the railway engineers even considered Christchurch as suitable for a deep-water dock. That idea must always have been problematic, not only due to the shallow estuary and bay, but also the potential silting up of dredged areas. Although the harbour was deeper in the nineteenth century, it could never have had the deep-water potential of Southampton.

Military hospital

According to the notes of a lecture by the famous local historian Herbert Druitt on 6 July 1921, a large hospital was planned for the Head in the latter part of the nineteenth century. Although this was a serious proposition, it did not proceed owing to the difficulties of bringing steamers into the harbour. The shallowness of the harbour has indeed proved a great protection for the headland. Eventually, the hospital was sited instead at Haslar, near Gosport. The Haslar site, containing the Royal Hospital, has taken casualties from all wars and battles since the middle of the eighteenth century. Presumably, therefore, the proposal for a new hospital at Hengistbury was changed into one for an upgrade of existing facilities at Haslar.

Eighty houses on the headland

When the owners of Hengistbury Head decided at the start of the twentieth century to sell, the local historian, Druitt, was very concerned at what might be lost, and persuaded them to have the site investigated professionally. Indeed, it seems that this was the impetus for the first main archaeological excavation. Although the rich finds by J.P. Bushe-Fox in 1911-1912 meant that it was no longer planned to build 80 houses, the intention remained to sell, and the next idea to emerge was a golf course.

Golf course

Hengistbury Golf Club Ltd. produced a brochure in 1913 to attract subscriptions to an enterprise called "Scotch Golf on the South Coast." It was an attempt first envisaged in 1911 by the owner, Sir George A. E. Tapps-Gervis-Meyrick, Bart. (who was also the President of the proposed club), to repeat the St. Andrews course at Hengistbury.

Proposals for the 18-hole course promised that "it will be possible to make use of many natural features and to obtain many striking effects." Golf architect James Hepburn "felt certain there is a grand opportunity of making a first class golf course, a course that could not be beaten anywhere." Normal subscriptions were to be £5 5s 0d (£5.25) p.a. for the 100 gentlemen members and £3 3s 0d (£3.15) p.a. for the 50 ladies allowed, although ladies could not play on Saturdays, Sundays or Bank Holidays, unless they paid £5 5s 0d and their handicap was below 12! Debentures were issued and paid for at £20 per new member, with further amounts due later, up to a total of £100. Such a debenture is really a loan to a company, and when this company folded, the money was simply lost.

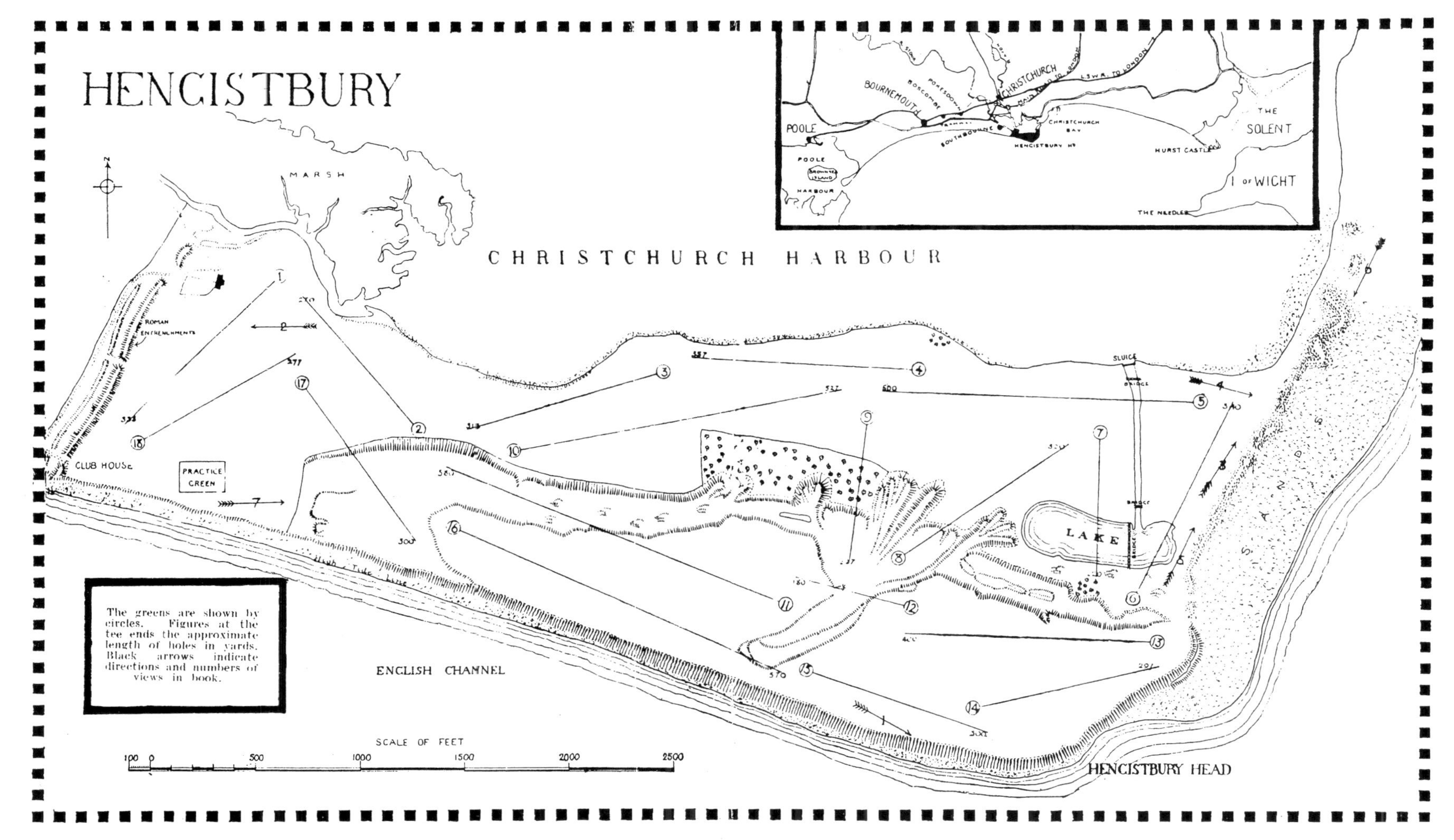

Fig.23 ***Golf course proposed, 1913***

(Hengistbury Golf Club Ltd. [in liquidation])

The Head was seen as an ideal site for a golf course to rival St. Andrews and was supported strongly by the local Who's Who. No doubt, the changes of level, challenging hazards and views would have been fantastic. The last eight holes of the design were the most spectacular. The scheme did not proceed ostensibly due to poor transport links, resulting in financial loss to the debenture holders. Another factor may have been the expectation of war.

Fig.24 ***Idea for bridge to connect Mudeford Quay and Sandbank, over the Run***
(Reproduced by consent of Tim Baber)
This illustration of a pedestrian footbridge was produced for Tim and kindly made available to me, following a talk to the Hengistbury Residents' Association. In 1930, there was a grand proposal by Councillor Seal to build a road bridge, so creating a marine drive from the New Forest around the headland and on to Poole. The idea of any sort of bridge over the Run was opposed at the time and would be today. Intriguingly, a bridge was built before the First World War. The Royal Engineers constructed it with pontoons, to a single vehicle width.

It must have seemed a perfectly feasible project at the time, with Meyrick as President, Lord Montagu of Beaulieu as Vice President, and Mr. L. Page Croft, the local MP, on the committee. Not only was a clubhouse planned for the east side of Double Dykes at the sea end, but life members were to have bungalows adjacent to the course, "details on request." The approximate location for these bungalows was to be between Holloway's Dock and the present-day land train terminus at Mudeford Sandbank. No planning permission would have been necessary since town planning, as we know it, did not exist for another 34 years.

That this was a serious plan is proved by the facts of large-scale ploughing in 1913 and the implements purchased. The plough turned up thousands of flints for the archaeologists, despite the uncouth nature of the dig, whilst the implements had to be sold by County Court Order on 27 February 1914. It has been said that the financial miscalculation which led to the collapse of the plan related to the poor train service from London to Dorset, and poor road access through the New Forest. Even in the 1980s, there was talk of whether a course could be put on the site.

Marine drive around the Head

In September 1930, an architect's plan was produced by ex-Councillor A.J. Seal for this drive, together with a bridge at Mudeford. It is of course very controversial to link the Sandbank with Mudeford Quay over the top of the Run, but the idea has come forward a number of times. Fig.24 shows one sketch produced, possibly tongue-in-cheek. Certainly, even a pedestrian bridge like this one would have to give a very high clearance for boat masts, whilst a vehicle bridge would be altogether too drastic to contemplate! Before World War I, the Royal Engineers temporarily bridged the Run using pontoons. This exercise was no doubt good practice on how to provide a vehicle crossing over a deep and fast flowing river.

Mr. Seal's plan was put forward in the year that the council acquired the Head from Selfridge. He said that "as this was the only undeveloped area adjacent to Bournemouth on the seafront, the future of the town would be marred or made according to the wise or otherwise handling of the situation." He evidently thought of the Head as the "coping stone to a finished Bournemouth and its possibilities are almost infinite."

Fig.25 ***Castle planned for Hengistbury Head by Gordon Selfridge, 1920s***
(P.Tilden. RIBA Library Drawings Collection. Reproduced by consent of RIBA)
The architect, for this grandiose proposal, produced hundreds of drawings. This one shows a view of the smaller of two castles. Others showed buildings of almost unbelievable proportions, including for instance a dome almost the size of the one at St. Paul's Cathedral. The irony is that when he sold the Head to Bournemouth in 1930, Selfridge was keen to ensure that the area east of the Dykes (which he had planned to cover in buildings) would remain public open space.

His idea was to provide a link to allow the motorist to proceed from the New Forest and Christchurch, over the proposed bridge, around the marine drive at Hengistbury, and on to Southbourne and Poole. I think it was impractical even then on grounds of cost, never mind amenity loss.

The largest house in the world and its aftermath

"An Englishman is a person who does things because they have been done before.
An American is a person who does things because they haven't been done before"
Mark Twain

"One day early in 1919, Martin Conway came down from London looking very pleased with the world. He plumped himself down in an armchair in the long gallery and burst out: 'You know Philip, Selfridge is going to build a castle'." Thus begins Philip Tilden's memoir as the architect of what could only have proved an immense folly. Philip Armstrong Tilden (1887-1956) also designed a tower for the store in Oxford Street.

Selfridge was already 63 when he bought Hengistbury from Meyrick, and immediately visualised a castle. According to the *Echo*, the purchase took place the year following the death of his wife, Rose. His mother survived Rose by about six years. He had achieved great success, causing something of a revolution in United Kingdom retailing by importing American methods. He felt the British were good at making things, but not at selling them, and was building his network of provincial stores at the time of the purchase of Hengistbury Head. It is Selfridge who is credited with the saying that "the customer is always right."

Fig.26 ***Gordon Selfridge in front of his store in Oxford Street, London, 1912***

(Vanity Fair "Man of the Day" illustration. Reproduced by consent of Selfridges)

Selfridge was completely successful in bringing his ground breaking retailing ideas from Chicago to his enormous new store in Oxford Street. Perhaps it was simply in character to "think big" at Hengistbury Head and have "more of the same"! It certainly takes an unusual man to visualise it as the site for two castles, four miles of walls, 250 bedroom suites and so forth.

Harry Gordon Selfridge came to this country from Chicago in 1906, founded the Oxford Street store in 1909, and was generally regarded as a man of great aspirations and imagination. If proof were needed of this, it is amply provided by the scheme for Hengistbury Head. Fig.26 gives an early twentieth century idea of Gordon Selfridge "in his setting" as seen by *Vanity Fair.*

Like many Americans, he certainly thought big. His architect produced hundreds of drawings for him, when he resided at Highcliffe Castle. An extract of one is shown at Fig.25. The plan was to occupy first the "little castle," a building the size of Highcliffe Castle, to be constructed on the very tip of the headland. There were to be four miles of walls punctuated by towers, a "1,000 foot vista," a theatre, galleries, tennis courts, baths, a winter garden and a nursery. Dining rooms were planned "for many hundreds." A dome was to be built, with a diameter only ten feet less than the dome of St. Paul's Cathedral. As for the bedrooms, there were to be 250 suites, each with bedroom, dressing room, sitting room and bathroom. Perhaps the easiest way to imagine the scheme is to visualise Warren Hill completely covered by castle-like buildings dropping sheer to the sea, together with stacks of other buildings right up to Double Dykes. When financial difficulties forced the cancellation of the entire project, Selfridge sold to Bournemouth Council in 1930, stipulating open space use only to the east of the Dykes, a paradox indeed.

Curiously, the nursery land was fenced in, as it still is, being used as a protected wildlife area, bird ringing station and screened open storage (Fig.46). It is almost the only visible evidence that is left of the Selfridge ownership. I do not know whether it was ever used as intended, to supply the restaurant of his Oxford Street store. His other legacy is the rhododendron display on the north side of the headland. Although their restriction by the rangers is locally unpopular, there are good management reasons for this, as explained in the chapter on wildlife.

An exhibition of the Selfridge plans was organised in Washington DC from drawings gathered by the curator of the Royal Institute of British Architects. With stunning understatement, the organisers called it an "imaginative exercise"! They also put the cost at £2 million to £2.5 million and suggested the reason it was never built was the 1929 stock market crash. Selfridge himself died in poor circumstances at the age of 91 in 1947, surviving his wife Rose by 29 years.

There had been much controversy about the sale to Bournemouth in 1930. Councillor Druitt particularly wanted his authority, Christchurch, to purchase it, and in 1939 was saying it should be with the National Trust. Auction particulars were produced for 6 August 1930, but the council were successful in acquiring it by agreement the previous May. The particulars referred to a total of 700 acres including the Head and Stanpit Marsh. It also appears that there was a late amendment to the proposed restrictive covenants to permit the buyers to develop residentially west of Double Dykes. By the time the auction particulars were available, an addendum in red ink had been affixed concerning the contracts already in place for the sale to the council. This stated that Lot 1 (the Dykes and land east) was to be for public recreation only and Lot 2 (from what is now Harbour Road up to the Dykes) for the same use, or for building, subject to restrictions. Despite this, the council claimed that there was no such intention, the only plans being for "a few seats dotted about." The addendum also referred to the other sale, prior to auction, of Lot 4, Stanpit Marsh, to Christchurch Council for public open space use. The price for this area of 146.857 acres was £4,000. A copy of the conveyance is held in Red House Museum, Christchurch.

As for the price, the agents apparently required and received a commission based on a much higher offer of 50,000 guineas, which was rejected by the vendor. This was in order to safeguard the headland from total development: in those days there was no need for planning consent. It appears that the offer was from a syndicate of three Christchurch businessmen, who wished to build extensively on both sides of the Dykes. It was reported in 1930 that the council paid only £25,250, to reflect the lack of full development potential. It is often said that Selfridge sold on a purely "open space basis" to the council, who were therefore quite wrong to sell off parts for development, but this is not correct.

What actually happened was that the vendor sold on the basis of partial residential development potential, which was much better in his eyes than the alternative of bungalows all over the Head. Hence, in 1930, it was reported that of the 400 acres, "some 80 to 90 acres could be utilised for building purposes." Perhaps it was a compromise to enable the vendor to secure a reasonable sum of money in hand at a very difficult financial time, whilst trusting the council (much more than a private buyer at auction) to keep it mainly as a public park. Certainly, the monthly meeting of the council had no doubts in accepting the advice of the negotiating committee, because its decision reportedly took between only one and two minutes. To use the vernacular, "it was a steal," and I think the ratifying committee knew that.

Seaside Park

Once the council had ownership of the Head, many felt it imperative that it should be saved.

In 1930, it was suggested that the continental model should be applied, where a ring of land, a mile wide, should exist for every five or six miles of existing residential development. This public recreation area was called the "parkway system." As applied to Hengistbury, a number of sports could be set up, including cricket, tennis, bowling, boating and golf, as a true seaside park.

The ideas evidently developed further, since within two weeks, the same publication was saying that a national playground, or sports centre, or municipal aerodrome, were all excellent schemes to pursue. In the case of the latter, seaplanes were envisaged using the Stour. The *Graphic* was concerned enough about Hengistbury to exhort: "let every care be taken in the council chamber!"

Aerodrome

By March 1931, people were concerned about what would happen after the sale of the headland to Bournemouth Council. One idea mooted had been a major aerodrome, which was denied at this time. It was probably remembered that the brochure of the 1910 flying display, to commemorate the town's centenary, had described the site as Southbourne Aerodrome. There must also have been ongoing debate arising from the comments of the *Graphic*, mentioned above. Certainly, it is possible that this could have happened, but eventually the space would have been too limited compared to Hurn, not to mention the risks arising from the extreme winds of Hengistbury.

One of the most exciting public tours of the pre-war era was Sir Alan Cobham's Flying Circus. This event, using some 15 planes, travelled the country, drawing huge crowds. There were not only aerobatics, parachutists and wing-walking stunts, but also "flips" were provided at five shillings each! Although facilities were probably minimal, there seems to have been a landing strip for the Circus to use on its visits in the early 1930s. There is also local recollection from this time that light planes were sometimes forced to make a landing due to bad weather. The airstrip may have been on the line of the current Broadway, which was extended in 1935 as a public road.

New café by Keeper's Cottage

There was great local controversy in 1939 about the council's plan to place a new café on the east side of Double Dykes and close to the Bronze Age tumulus. At that time, three tea boats and a café run from the barn by the keeper's cottage, then also called Brewer's Cottage, catered for visitors. A main contribution came from Herbert Druitt, ex-chairman of Christchurch Planning Committee. He wrote to the local press saying: "Will not a modern café be utterly incongruous in such a place, like taking tea in a cemetery?" And, "One cannot but regret that Hengistbury is not the property of the National Trust." He also quoted Lord Melbourne's question to his cabinet: "Can't we let it alone?"

Certainly, Druitt thought his council had been short sighted in letting the Head be included in Bournemouth Borough, despite assurances at the time that Bournemouth would "prevent building and other vandalism." He concluded: "The man who destroys the beauty of England is the enemy of England." Such is the interest and commitment, which Hengistbury generates. As for the café, which was run from the barn by the ranger and his wife, this continued for the benefit of the military after 1939.

The main reason for the council proposal not going forward must have been the onset of war, which required a self-contained military establishment on the Head, extending back to Solent Road.

Bournemouth marina plans

Peter Ashworth planned a yacht marina about 1965 on the south side of the harbour at Wick Hams. Having originally been favourable to the proposal, the council in the end decided to refuse planning consent. The matter dragged on until 1973. A planning inspector upheld the refusal on appeal, mainly on the grounds that the water was not deep enough. In addition, he was concerned about the area's character and the introduction of many more people into the vicinity. He did not feel it would have been unduly intrusive. Nor was he concerned about overcrowding in the harbour, saying that this was more relevant to the Run and the river well above the appeal site.

At an early stage in its development, a 1966 proposal by Mr. J. Macklin and Mr. K. Lander for a modern boat basin, for all types of recreational craft, was deemed impractical. The idea for the Bournemouth Marina was to excavate 400 feet by 350 feet, or 3.21 acres, and then simply connect to the sea. Apart from moorings for 200 boats and a car park, the scheme included servicing, provisions, slipways, winter boat storage, changing rooms, showers, a bar and a restaurant. Since it was to be connected to the sea, I assume the excavation was to be in the highly sensitive Green Belt west of the Dykes. That said, it should be noted that Hampshire County Council did produce a draft Christchurch Harbour Plan (approved in principle by Bournemouth Council) showing dinghy sailing and a speedboat launching place to the sea, just west of the Dykes.

Reclamation of Christchurch Bay

Scheme One, enclosing 3,000 acres

In 1966, at the instigation of John Arlott, an expert on marina developments suggested "Project Oceanus". The intention was both to protect the coast and to reclaim land for development purposes, including the largest marina in Europe, moorings, reservoir, nature reserve and residential development. Breakwaters were to be built out both from Hengistbury Head and from a point close to the harbour entrance, east, all the way past Milford, joining land at the north end of the Hurst Castle peninsula. In support, it was stressed that there was continuing serious erosion, which was very expensive to combat without trying to reclaim from the sea. If such schemes worked at the Wash, with an 18-foot tidal range, perhaps they would at Christchurch with only six feet. The idea was to use spoil from dredging the area for the reservoir to create building land to expand Highcliffe and Barton to the south. The author felt the scheme could be viable as a public/private partnership and was much better than spending millions on supporting the crumbling cliffs.

I suppose this was indeed a crazy idea, reliant as it was on taming the sea with the main breakwater. It would have been an enormous investment to risk. Sooner or later, an engineer would have had to sign his name to it and hope for the best. In the event, despite considerable commercial interest, it was rejected at a public meeting and fell by the wayside.

Scheme Two

Under the sub-heading "An exciting pipe dream lives again," the idea was resurrected in 1981. The same point was made about unrewarding and costly sea defences, compared to the ambition of creating a national asset with an updated "Project Oceanus." This time the layout was different, showing a road-topped caisson breakwater extending over three miles from the Head along the Ledge and another about twice as long above Dolphin Bank and Shingles Bank, connecting with a bridge to the Hurst Castle peninsula. Enclosed within the newly protected waters of the bay were two marinas, a reservoir, a fresh water fish lagoon, two car parks each at least a mile long, a fishing boat harbour, offshore moorings on "star" pontoons and salt water fish lagoons. A letter followed to the *Hampshire Chronicle* raising the possibility of an airport in Christchurch Bay with a nine-mile runway.

Arguments in favour included coast protection, safe bathing, protection from oil slicks, promotion of fish farming, reversion to the state of a national asset after a 99 year development lease, water storage needs in view of the 1976 drought (as pumped to the right level with wind power) and short term and long term employment creation. Comparison was drawn with Brighton Marina, which had turned into a big commercial success despite being scoffed at by supposedly informed opinion.

I really do not know if this whole concept, or something like it, is practicable. Certainly, it never seems to have been given serious consideration by the powers-that-be and as such may be regarded by most as maverick.

Bournemouth University adjoining Double Dykes

In November 1963, Bournemouth was thinking about a site for the proposed university and suggested the area close to Double Dykes as a possibility. At that time, the council thought of the area as the "empty lands."

Fortunately, the plan came to nothing, but it does give an instance of the sheer power of words to get any controversial scheme through a council committee. Firstly, everyone is concerned about a plan, which simply sounds to be unacceptable; secondly, it is modified slightly; thirdly, it is pushed forward for acceptance on the grounds that "the concerns have been addressed." In fact, no concerns have been addressed, because those objecting never wanted a slight modification of the unacceptable scheme. They were actually trying to secure

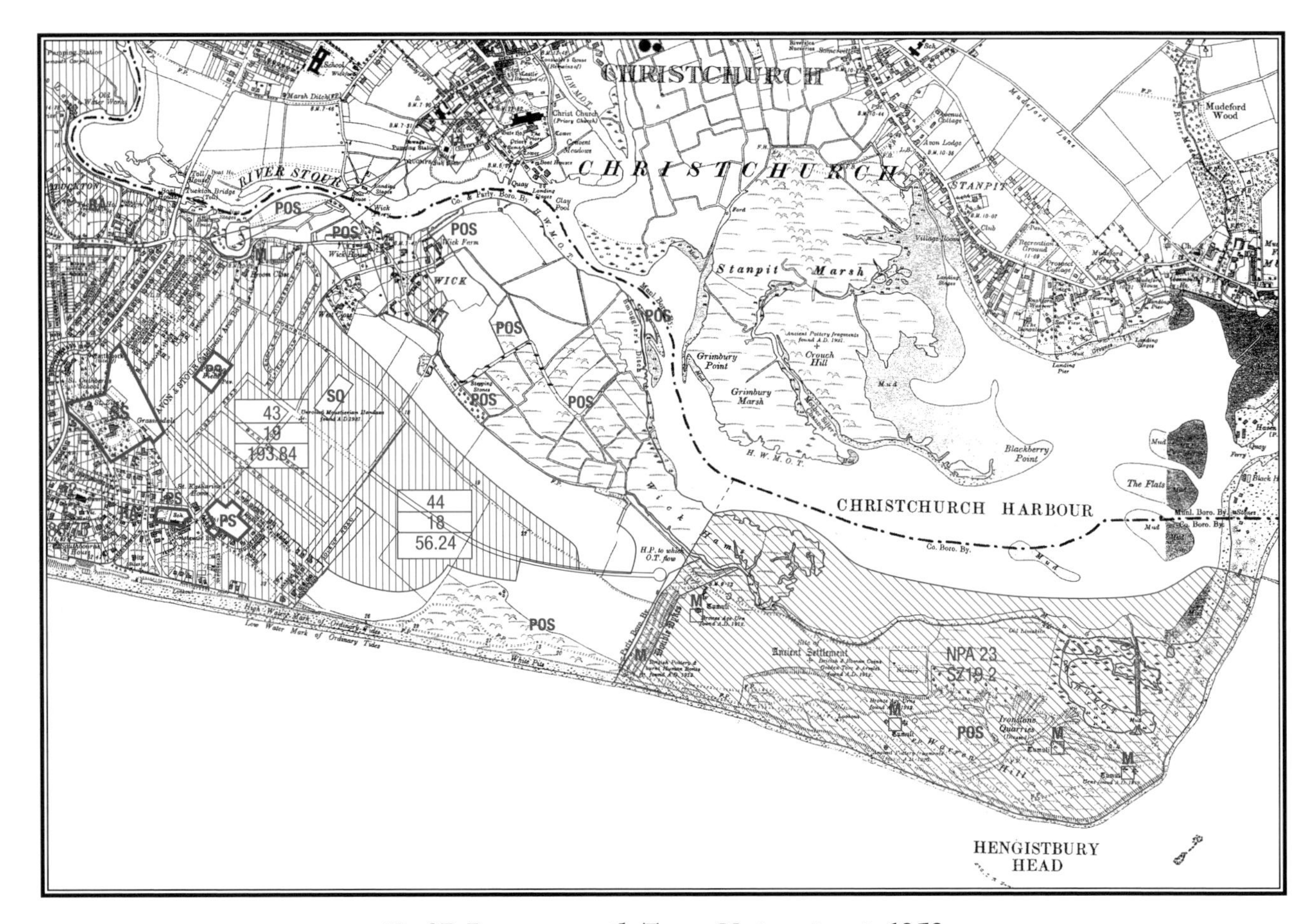

Fig.27 ***Bournemouth Town Map extract, 1952***

(Reproduced courtesy of Bournemouth Borough Council and from the 1932 Ordnance Survey map. © Crown Copyright. 1/10,560 scale before reduction)

The first post-war Town Plan was submitted by the council in October 1952 under the Town and Country Planning Act 1947. It showed most of Hengistbury as Public Open Space (POS) but a considerable area had the vertical hatching denoting land for residential development. In the event, the part south of Wick was built upon, but fortunately, building stopped much further to the west of the Dykes than shown. The diagonal hatching on the map means an area of scientific interest under the National Parks and Access to the Countryside Act 1949.

its rejection. Members are also vulnerable to claims that the developer is well financed and likely to win any planning appeal, so landing the council with heavy costs not within budget. By the time objectors have been classified as "militant" and misquoted as to their real concerns, they may have very little chance left. Local democracy has been further compromised by the recent shift of power from committees to officers, with councillors often reduced to the status of "consultants."

I have included this digression because it is relevant to most local decisions, including those affecting Hengistbury Head. It is a matter of good fortune, in my view, that council policy is fairly enlightened at present, because if it were not, there would be little chance of changing it. We have, in essence, a good management plan based on coast protection, limiting tourist damage and conservation. This last is actively developing to the benefit of the Head. Despite this, the sheer development potential of the headland means that complacency would be foolish. In 2004, there were real concerns that the large new building proposed by the Dykes would prove the thin end of the wedge.

Bungalow development

It is commonly thought that the basis of the purchase from Selfridge was for open space, but this is not correct. The whole area west of the Dykes was shown for potential development in the sale documents. By

1939, 112 acres of land owned by the council to the west of the Dykes were under consideration for low-density development of four houses to the acre. We must credit Hitler for the demise of this idea.

A plan was duly produced by the council in 1952, (Fig.27) under the Town & Country Planning Act, 1947, suggesting only some of this land for residential development. It also showed the Head as an area of scientific interest to the east of Double Dykes. The plan showed "residential" some 1,300 feet closer to the Head along Broadway on its north side than Rolls Drive as now built. This part is now a golf course. On the south side, where the Solent Meads car park is situated now, it was again planned to sell for residential development.

Local press reports in 1954 referred to bungalows right up to Double Dykes, a scheme so controversial that the Hengistbury Residents' Association (HENRA) was formed to fight it. There was no dissent to the strong representations planned at the meeting: to urge the council to keep as open space forever land to the east of Harbour Road. A resolution was passed opposing any residential development east of the Saxon King public house on Broadway. It was couched in terms referring to such housing being to the "everlasting shame and detriment of Bournemouth"! A loudspeaker van was organised with the slogan "Hands off Hengistbury"! The Association, with a membership of over 300, still meets with a monthly programme of talks and social events. Despite HENRA being non-political from the start, each meeting has an update from a ward councillor.

The *Bournemouth Echo* reported on 7 April 1954 that a petition of 4,250 signatures was presented to the council. However, it was criticised in committee on the grounds that people had signed without reading it. Whilst the petition talked of a "disaster of the first magnitude," another written submission from a local resident claimed that one reason people had signed was being told of the longer-term plan to build houses on the Head itself. Eventually, the Town Clerk confirmed that the plan was not against the terms of purchase and the vote went in favour. A consequence the following year was the auction of 23 building plots, mainly in Broadway, at an average price of £750. In spite of the strength of local feeling the previous year, there was no adverse comment at the auction.

In summary, although the council was able under the terms of purchase to sell for residential development right up to the Dykes, the town plan showed much less than this as residentially zoned, and the eventual land sold was much less again. That said, there is now more intensity of use west of the Dykes, including the golf course, kite flying area and two car parks of 1,350 total capacity.

Landfill site in the ironstone quarry

The Housing Ministry rejected this unwelcome plan by Bournemouth Council in 1965. Perhaps "unwelcome" is not the right word: after all, it was reported that the Southbourne Residents' and Ratepayers' Association would be "happy to see this ugly gap filled in"! But that was before the Ironstone Canyon was dammed and turned into a wildlife pond and tourist attraction. The council said that the ratepayers would be saved £10,000, but the Inspector rejected the claim, commenting that this amount would possibly have to be spent anyway, but earlier than expected. The quarry would have taken the town's refuse output in 1965 for only three months.

The Inspector decided that the charm and serenity of the headland would be adversely affected by the screening round the site and the filling process. He was also rightly concerned about the likely damage to undiscovered archaeological remains from Stone Age Man, and the possible loss to geological science. I like his understated comment: "The filling of the quarries would not necessarily improve the place for public enjoyment"!

Solent Meads policy proposals

In November 1969, a sketch plan was produced about how best to open up the Head to more visitors and development. Some of the scheme was realised, including the two big car parks, the golf course and residential extensions east of Thornbury Road and at Southbourne Coast Road.

The parts, which "might have been," are now covered. A boat park and public slipway were to be built at the closest point of Southbourne Coast Road to the cliff. A much larger golf course was planned, right up to the harbour edge. The Solent Beach car park was to include a café and beach office, whilst the ranger's cottage was to be partly converted into a café. Of particular interest is the fact that the promenade was to be extended up to the Dykes. I believe that such an extension has never been suggested since and would not be now on grounds of cost. A yacht basin was envisaged west of the Marine Training Centre together with unrestricted public access to the bank alongside.

Work had already started on the "proposed" golf course in November 1969 (when it was still strictly a proposal only). Vacant possession of the land south of Broadway was expected from the farmer by September 1970, and the promenade was to be extended between 1971 and 1973. But this was not the end of the story. Local protests caused a refusal in July 1975 for an 18-hole course up to, but not including, the reed beds. In April 1976, a 9-hole golf course was given planning approval on the former tip land, only to be bitterly contested when a formal scheme was planned the following year. The local branch of the Ramblers Association, the Southbourne Ratepayers' and Residents' Association, the Hengistbury Residents' Association and the Marine Training Centre were all opposed. The old tip had become grassland, which was a very popular piece of open country that people did not wish to see lost to golf. It was felt that the existing course was ample for golfers, who were much fewer than walkers. Concerns were also forcefully expressed about loss of wildlife habitats and risks to reed beds.

The scheme was dropped. After a reasonable interval, it was resurrected. In September 1989, the Christchurch Harbour Ornithological Group and the Friends of Stanpit Marsh were calling for rejection of new plans to extend the golf facility. It was seen as disastrous for bird migrations. David Atkinson, MP, was closely involved. A new pressure group, CHASM (Campaign for Hengistbury and Solent Meads), RSPB, NCC, CPRE, joined together and saw the whole idea shelved again by the Amenities Committee of 1 November 1989. A newsletter of the same date, from the Hengistbury and St. Katherine's Protest Group, remarked that although the matter was "on ice" it remained also firmly on the council's agenda and continued vigilance was needed. The decision was officially postponed, pending a report from the management group for the Head. The latest concerns revolve around the leasing of the existing course to a private operator, who may apply to the council to extend it to the north.

Iron Age village

A five-year plan was put out to public consultation in 1990 by the council, involving a new Iron Age Village, a redesigned golf course and a new visitor centre.

It was intended to close down and return to grass most of the car park by the Dykes, close off Broadway near to Rolls Drive, remove the existing building by the Dykes and erect a new visitor centre and Iron Age Village at Solent Meads car park. Those not wanting to walk or cycle to the Head could go on the land train, whose new terminus would be where Broadway was closed. Moreover, it was planned to relocate the geological terrace from the Russell-Cotes Museum to the new site.

This scheme attracted enormous local objections including a letter to the National Lottery by the residents' association asking that the necessary money would not be made available to the council.

Despite the success of the objections, a version of the plan appeared in the Management Plan of 1997, described as "the move west." It was now intended to locate a new Iron Age Village adjoining the Hengistbury Head Centre and integral with it. The visitor centre was shown just east of an expanded Solent Meads car park. By 2005, the latest scheme, without an Iron Age Village, but including the E-Learning Centre, had been dropped.

Recent conservation policies

Having seen the proposals by man since the seventeenth century, one could be forgiven for being a little negative. They generally amount to an unacceptable exploitation of a unique and beautiful site. However, they did not come to pass, whilst the actual development of the Head has proved reasonable, except of course for the ironstone mining.

Now that we have a large number of interested parties and protective bodies, which are committed (nominally at least) to conservation and sustainability, have the threats disappeared? I am optimistic, on balance, because there are a lot of forces operating to oppose any real exploitation. Significant budgets are spent on enhancing wildlife and reducing tourist erosion. My only reservation here is whether adequate coast protection measures will secure funding in order to prevent for as long as possible the headland becoming an island.

SEVEN

TRAGEDIES, DISASTERS AND MYSTERIES

It often happens that the real tragedies of life occur in such an inartistic manner that they hurt us by their crude violence, their absolute incoherence, their absurd want of meaning, their entire lack of style.

Oscar Wilde

NE OF THE MOST captivating facets of this story is the sheer number of misadventures that have happened at Hengistbury. They sit in stark contrast to more academic features, such as its geology. Here we can see the human dramas played out against the timeless backdrop of the headland.

Woman found dead below Warren Hill

A lady of 84 gave an account of this from living memory in July 1935. It seems that as a small girl, she often went up to the Watch House with her family, including her father, the Coastguard. One of her most vivid memories is of him coming into the Watch House and saying that the woman had been found dead "on the rocks below." Presumably, this was before the removal of ironstones on that part of the shore.

Gun accident at Mudeford

I wonder whether we have the full story behind this tragedy. The preventive men had the job of acting against smugglers, a somewhat dangerous occupation, which could give rise to grudges. It is likely that they were trained and careful in the proper use of firearms. Despite this, in November 1858, a local preventive man, Thomas Sherrick, was helping men into a boat at the quay near Haven House. He was accidentally killed in doing so by a duck gun. Fig.12 shows Haven House as it was in 1811.

Firearm accident and the monument on Double Dykes

Charles Edmund Smith, the 16 year-old youngest son of Mr. H.J. Smith of Stourcliff House, Southbourne, ventured alone to shoot rabbits on 30 August 1861. It is believed that his death was due simply to shooting himself accidentally, by taking up a loaded gun while sitting on the cliff. In May 1862, a broken column on a plinth was erected near the spot, at the sea end of the Dykes, as a monument. Fig.28 shows that it was enclosed by an iron-railing fence.

At that time, the whole area was very remote. An 1872 map, at 6 inches to 1 mile, shows both the monument and Stourcliff House. From the house to the sea was mainly heath and to the Dykes, mainly fields. To the north-east of the house was Foxholes wood and further up, Tuckton Farm by the Stour. Nearly half a mile to the west was Carbery, but the only habitation between Stourcliff and the Dykes was Cellarfield Farm.

This monument provided a good measurement of sea erosion. Fig.29 shows its first position on the Ordnance Survey map of 1870 about 100 feet from the edge. Having been moved twice, due to the erosion, a total distance of 160 feet, it was finally relocated elsewhere. It can now be seen in the churchyard of St. James's, Christchurch Road, Pokesdown to the east of the church. Its inscription referring to a "gun accident" is hardly legible.

Fig.28 ***Double Dykes monument to tragic gun accident of 1861***
(Reproduced by consent of Red House Museum)
The place where a local 16 year old boy, Charles Smith, lost his life was marked by this broken column monument, surrounded by iron railings. Its three positions are shown on the 1870 OS extract in Fig.29. All this part of the dyke shown in the photograph has long since been lost to the sea.

The position after the first move (of about 60 feet) was shown on the 1898 OS map. By then, the cliff had eroded up to the monument's original location. This meant that over half of the Dykes, south of their southern opening, had been lost to the sea. The 1898 location was again on the inner dyke but now directly overlooking to the north this southern opening, and about 60 feet from the cliff edge. To prevent being swamped, a second move, of about 100 feet, had occurred before the 1924 OS, which shows the monument just to the north of the opening. It was now about 90 feet from the cliff edge, and the Dykes south of the opening had virtually disappeared.

The removal to St. James's seems to have been between 1924 and 1933, because the 1933 OS map no longer shows it. Although the local paper dated the removal rather later, in 1936, I prefer the evidence of the OS. The gabion sea defences now in place seem to have stopped the erosion short of the monument's last position on the inner dyke, north of the existing footpath. However, a comparison with the latest OS shows there was more erosion before the gabions were installed. I consider that position of the monument's last location at Hengistbury is now on the footpath, between the fencing of the inner Dyke and the gabion edge above the beach. Fig.29 shows the relocations and cliff losses.

Fatality on Western Shore

In October 1874, a boating accident took place at Lymington, when a Mr. Upson drowned. Eleven days later, on 14 October, a young man's body was found on the Western Shore by Tuckton Coastguard and removed to the Preventive Station. The next day, it was identified as him, and the day after, a verdict of accidental drowning was recorded at the inquest. It might be surprising that a body, swept out to sea at Lymington, can appear to travel against prevailing winds and currents and be washed up about ten miles to the west. Although the prevailing winds are south-west, tides change from east to west flowing at different times. This is a more probable explanation than the only other one, of false identification.

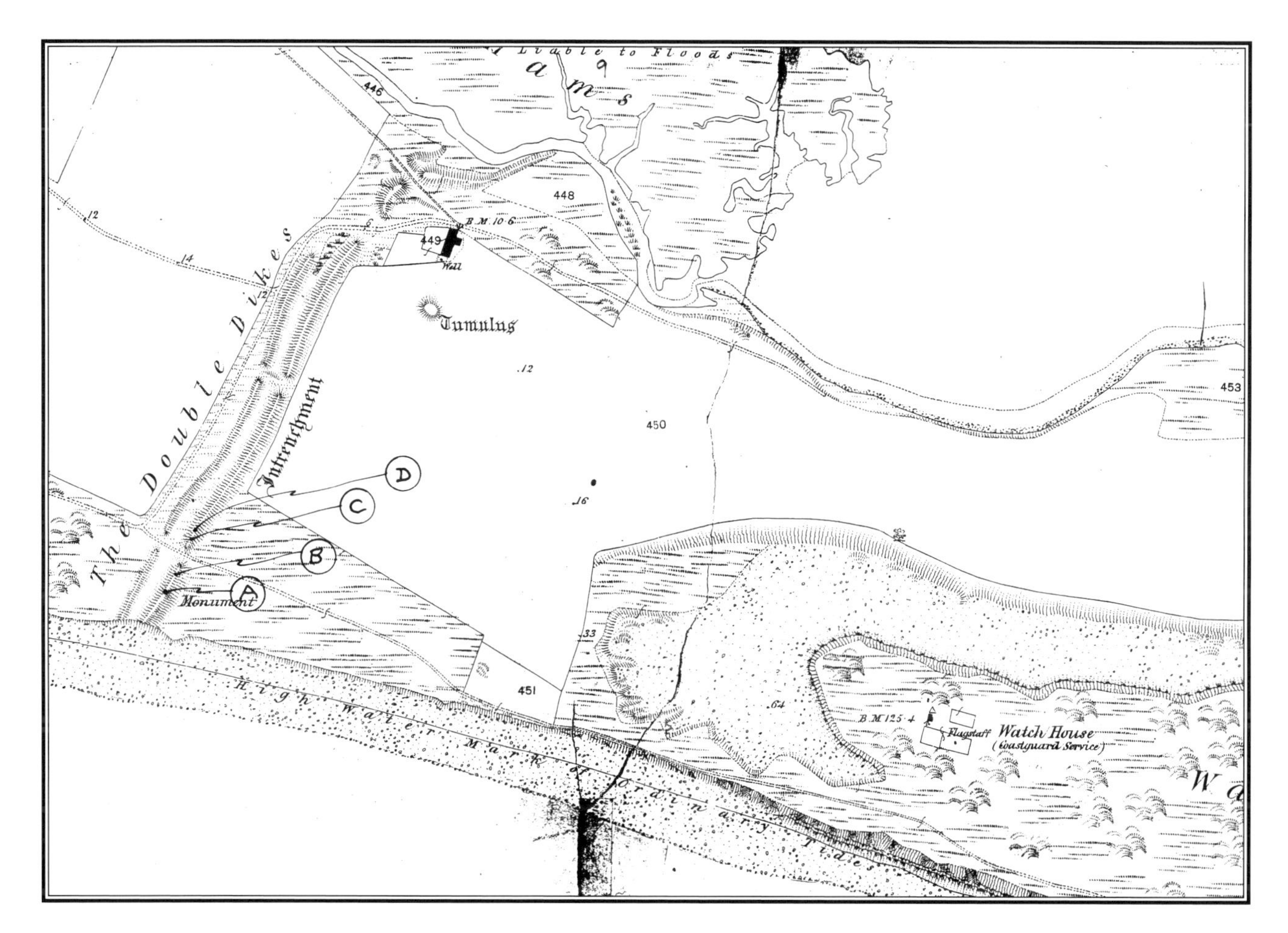

Fig.29 ***"Double Dikes Intrenchment", monument to gun accident, open cast mining damage and Watch House 1870***

(Reproduced from the Ordnance Survey map of that date. © Crown Copyright. 1/2,500 scale before reduction)

This extract is from the earliest published OS map at the scale. The open cast mining, which dragged away a lot of the Head from 1856 to 1870, can be clearly seen as a stippled area north and west of the Watch House. The monument was erected after the 1861 shooting accident, but it had to be moved along the top of the Inner Dyke on two occasions, due to erosion. The total distance was about 160 feet, before the final relocation at St. James's, Pokesdown. The existing coastline is slightly north of the footpath shown running through the south break in the Dykes. The legend is as follows:

"A" Monument in 1870.
"B" Monument in 1898.
"C" Monument in 1924, but moved to Pokesdown by 1933.
"D" Current (2004) end point of inner Dyke.

Drowning at Wick Ferry

In July 1876, James Maidment had been out drinking porter ale with friends on a Saturday night at the Dolphin in Christchurch. When they arrived back at Wick Ferry for the return trip to Southbourne at 10.30pm, he was reportedly still sober. The night was very dark and Fig.48 gives some idea of how remote the ferry approach would feel on their return. Since there was no boat available, he stripped and entered the water in order to get one. When told that he had mistaken a tree for a boat in the dark, he pressed forward anyway saying that he would get hold of another if need be. The evidence was that he then called out loudly twice "Come in!" but another member of the party, on wading in, could find nothing. The ferryman was duly awoken and a boat taken out onto the water with a net. The body was found on the first cast of the net some 30 yards from shore. The verdict of the inquest was "accidental drowning."

Death at Regatta

In September 1877, four men were in a race and rounding a buoy at Christchurch Ledge. The boat shipped water on the turn and sank instantly. They all nearly drowned, but fortunately were picked up within minutes. Stephen Gossling, aged 48, the proprietor of a Staffordshire company of boilermakers, did not survive. The shore was two or three miles away and it took an hour for the rescue boat to get there. By then he was exhausted and unconscious. Although they tried to give him liquor and wrapped him in a sail, it was no use. The inquest accepted the medical evidence of death due to the effects of cold and exposure on a weak heart.

Cast up by Beer Pan Rocks

On 27 December 1898, a 327 net tonnage three-masted sailing barque, the Norwegian registered Marie Theresa, went aground just off the Head, on only her third voyage, whilst carrying a cargo of coal brickettes to Poole (Fig.30). The route was from Le Havre to Martinique. Bad weather had managed to blow away the sails, forcing the ship to run before the wind. She was seen from Southbourne Pier to be in difficulty. It seems that the ship went above Christchurch Ledge at a high tide and then ran aground on a sandy bottom near Beer Pan Rocks. The position made it very hazardous to reach the open sea again. When she was found to be badly leaking two days later, the Coastguard took charge. Coastguards rescued all twelve crew, including Captain Beven, who left last of all and with reluctance.

It was a textbook use of rocket apparatus, a skilled procedure involving a block with instructions in French and English, a hawser, a travelling block, and a life-belt paid out from the cliff top fixing. The Coastguard practised the procedure every quarter. The right tension had to be achieved on the hawser before attempting to bring the men ashore, direct to the top of Warren Hill, a somewhat scary journey. When the third rocket line was made secure and the crew transferred safely, there was much cheering from the crowds of spectators on Southbourne Pier and promenade. The pier itself was smashed by storms just two years later.

The Royal Engineers blew up the wreck the following June, witnessed by large crowds, with Lady Meyrick setting off the detonation. Although very dramatic, the explosion was only partly successful, and the sea cleared the remains over several years. The purchase for £40 of the rescued cargo sounds like good value to the buyer. Many timbers were salvaged for the interior of a house in Springbourne, the site of which has been redeveloped in recent years.

Other local wrecks and disasters

There are no roses on sailors' graves,
Nor wreaths upon the storm tossed waves,
No last post from the Royals' band,
So far away from their native land,
No heartbroken words carved on stone,
Just shipmates bodies there alone,
The only tributes are the seagulls' sweeps,
And the teardrop when a loved one weeps.

Hundreds of ships were wrecked around the British coast every year in those far-off days. A sailing vessel was unable to move directly into the wind, navigation aids were poor, and communication was primitive. No wonder seamen then were much more at the mercy of wind and tide. It was a high-risk occupation, with only two-thirds of all seamen likely to avoid death at sea in the nineteenth century. There were cases of the elements simply preventing the escape of a ship to the open sea, because wind and tide could stop it being able to round a headland. Tacking to starboard and port, at around 45 degrees to the direction of the wind, was not enough in an unfavourable tide. The men would work against the odds to try and avoid being swept ashore, but sometimes it was inevitable. If the shore was rocky, survival was unlikely.

In October 1870, a large brig reportedly escaped by a hairsbreadth. Owing to a lack of canvas the ship miss-stayed, which means that she failed to turn properly into and across the wind to make a fresh tack. The attempt at tacking having failed, she fell back on to the old course. During heavy weather, the captain was stem on for shore opposite the Haven, with breakers close under his lee. He just managed to clear the Head, but it was considered that destruction, and probably death to the crew, would have been inevitable a few inches further to leeward.

Fig.30 ***Wreck of Marie Theresa at Hengistbury, 1898***
(Reproduced by consent of Red House Museum)
The stranding of this fairly new sailing ship was spectacular, including the rescue of crew in a Bosun's Chair to the top of Warren Hill. Later, the Army wired it with high explosive and a large crowd at Hengistbury watched and cheered, when Lady Meyrick set off the charge. Even that did not complete its destruction, which was mainly left to the elements over time. Indeed, its heavy timbers were salvaged for building a house in Boscombe.

Fig.31 shows the positions of only some of the local wrecks described below. These are not necessarily accurate, but indeed the same may be said regarding some of the stories. Generally, I have left out details altogether where there are greatly conflicting accounts about the same event from differing sources. The same illustration includes World War II items.

There follows, in date order, particulars of many of the wrecks of the Hengistbury region.

There were auctions advertised in Mudeford for 11 February 1779 of ships' cargoes, ships' boats and wrecks of two Spanish brigs: *Nostra Sinora dil Carmen* and *Saint Juan Baptista.* The second auction was to be held where she lay on shore. The auction notice continued "Also to be sold some very good Spanish nuts"!

The sailing ship *Chesapeake*, under Captain Edwards voyaging from le Havre to Baltimore, was stranded and lost near Christchurch on 29 January 1796. On the same date and in the same place, the sailing ship *John*, under Captain Owers, also voyaging from Le Havre, was beached in a gale and feared lost.

In 1804, an open boat from the *Fox*, a revenue lugger, was going over the Christchurch Ledge. The sail jibed – the wind must have passed round the stern of the boat, caught the sail and whipped it across very quickly, so upsetting the boat. All four crew were drowned.

The *Good Intent*, a transport ship with about 130 sick and wounded including women and children from the Battle of Corunna "got on shore" at White Pit reef at 9pm on 31 January 1809. The position of the stranding in Fig.31 may not be quite right because no reef is shown on the maps at White Pits, nor is there knowledge of one by local fishermen. The explanation could be that an ironstone reef was removed by later mining operations or, more likely, that the stranding was at or close to Beer Pan Rocks.

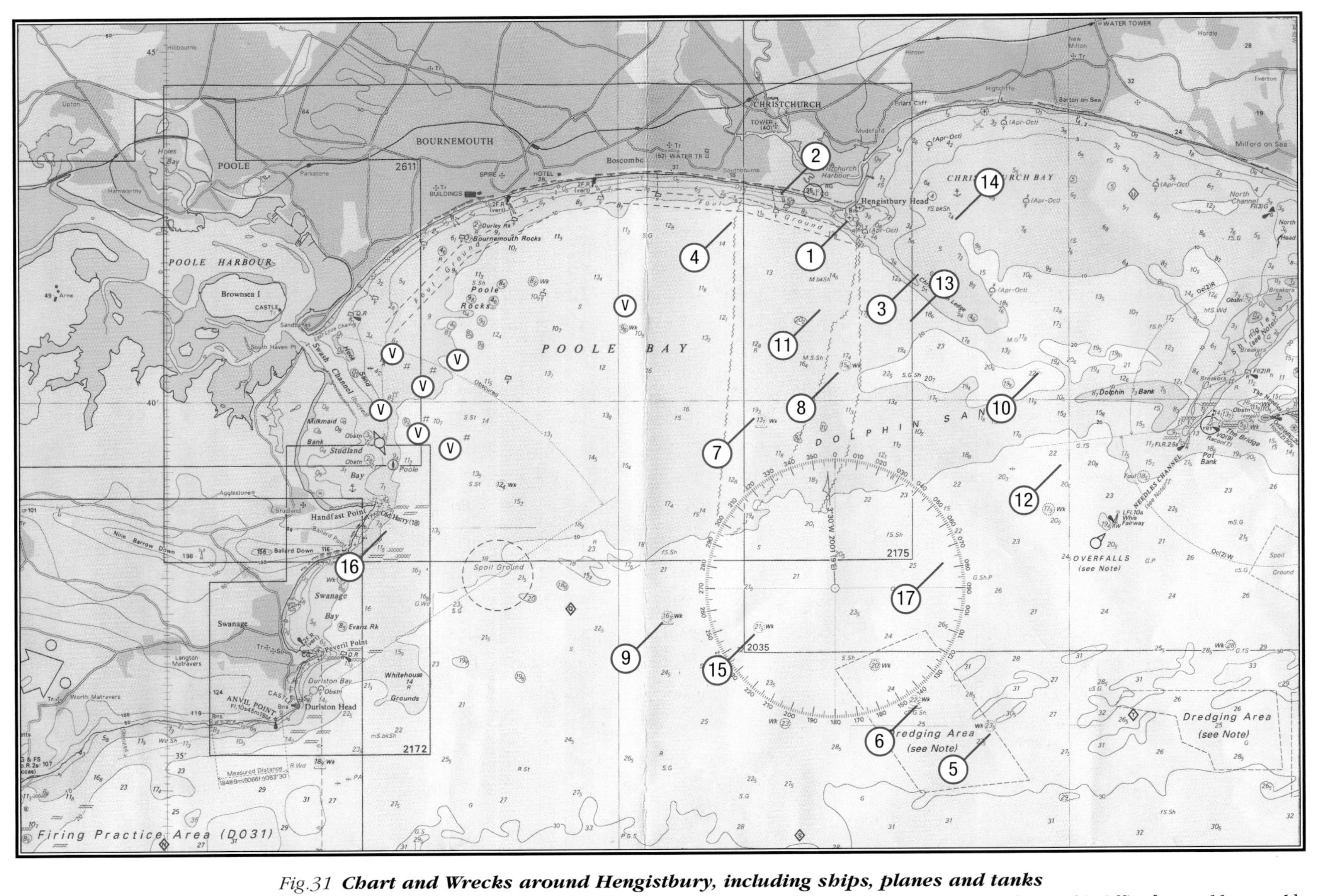

Fig.31 **Chart and Wrecks around Hengistbury, including ships, planes and tanks**

(Chart: Reproduced from Admiralty chart 2615 by permission of the Controller of Her Majesty's Stationery Office and the UK Hydrographic Office [www.ukho.gov.uk]
Wrecks: © Crown Copyright 2002. Published by permission as above. Scale 1/75,000 before reduction)

Extract from the edition of 27 September 2001. Not to be used for navigation.

KEY TO SOME OF THE LOCAL WRECKS, i.e. TO THOSE PLOTTED ON CHART

REF.	DATE	ITEM	LOCATION	COMMENT
1	27 Dec 1898	Marie Theresa	Beer Pan Rocks	Came to rest on sandy bottom near to the rocks.
1	Not Known	Spitfire	Beer Pan Rocks	Remains noted in Dive Dorset (see Bibliography); nothing else known!
2	31 Jan 1809	Good Intent	White Pits	Location assumed from report, i.e. ""got on shore at White Pit reef.""
3	23 Nov 1824	Hero	Christchurch Ledge	Stranded in the Great Gale and crew lost.
4	Mar 1876	Speculation	1.5 miles WSW of Head	46-ton sloop foundered in terrific storm. Three lost. Wreck buoy placed.
5	26 Feb 1918	Borgny	50 35.44N; 01 41.64W	Dangerous wreck. Much looted. Various positions reported.
6	14 Mar 1918	Venezuela	50 35.73N; 01 43.35W	"Argentinian steamship torpedoed, the day after leaving Falmouth."
7	8 Aug 1918	Clan Macvey	50 39.69N; 01 46.71W	400-foot ship on maiden voyage sunk after U boat attack.
8	5 Sep 1924	Excelsior	50 40.48N; 01 44.88W	Dangerous wreck. Fishing drifter with cargo of scrap iron.
9	Oct 1926	Betsy Anna	50 36.91N; 01 48.88W	Dangerous wreck. 880-ton ship originally mistaken for the Dagmar.
10	13 Jun 1940	Caroline Susan	50 40.40N; 01 40.67W	23-ton yacht either foundered or blown up. Cargo of ballast.
11	14 Aug 1940	Hurricane P3310	50 41.40N; 01 45.60W	"Sgt. G. Atkinson baled out at 0700, after aerial combat."
11	23 Aug 1943	Spitfire BS115 "V"	50 41.40N; 01 45.60W	Flt. Sgt. R.T.Wright went into sea on shipping recce. Rescued.
12	1 Oct 1940	Unidentified aircraft	6 miles @ 140°	One of two aircraft downed in sea after air battle; the other further south.
13	1 Oct 1940	Unidentified aircraft	50 41.70N; 01 43.50W	Firing heard just before sea crash at 1055; no-one baled out.
14	1 Dec 1940	German aircraft	50 42.60N; 01 42.60W	"One report of crash due to AA gunfire, the other to attack by Hurricane."
14	28 Apr 1941	Fairey Battle K9230	50 42.60N; 01 42.60W	Lt. A. Watson awarded George Medal for extraordinary rescue attempt.
15	Not Known	Whitley bomber	50 36.75N; 01 46.80W	Dangerous wreck. Close to telecom cable.
16	12 Jun 1944	Typhoon MN115 1b	50 38.20N; 01 55.08W	"Ft.Lt. J.G.Gohl baled out after running into flak, but did not survive."
17	1993	Capped oil well	50 37.68N; 01 42.78W	"This platform type trial oil well, known as MENROD 85, capped in 1993"
V	4 Apr 1944	Valentine tank	50 40.08N; 01 54.86W	"Valentine tanks were converted into amphibious vehicles for the purpose of the D-Day landings. Trials were carried out in Poole Bay to the satisfaction of the military, although seven were lost, as plotted here and six men drowned. The problem was overtopping by waves. Presumably, enough reached shore to make the design viable. They were fitted with canvas sides to keep out the water and a drive which allowed a speed of 4 knots. The Navy has blown up the remains of five of the tanks."
V	4 Apr 1944	Valentine tank	50 40.23N; 01 54.75W	
V	4 Apr 1944	Valentine tank	50 40 48N; 01 54.62W	
V	4 Apr 1944	Valentine tank	50 39.74N; 01 54.19W	
V	4 Apr 1944	Valentine tank	50 40.44N; 01 53.91W	
V	4 Apr 1944	Valentine tank	50 39.47N; 01 53.41W	
V	4 Apr 1944	Valentine tank	50 41.50N; 01 50.28W	

Despite tremendous surf, the Royal Horse Artillery saved everyone from drowning by the next morning. After great help from local people, sick and wounded soldiers were accommodated at the old Tudor Hurst Castle within the day.

The hardship for those rescued is difficult to imagine. The troops harried Napoleon's supply lines in Spain with a smaller force, and then had to beat a fighting retreat in bad weather over 250 miles of mountainous terrain to the coast. The French attacked whilst they were in poor condition from the journey. They fought a successful battle at Corunna before being able to board the *Good Intent.* Finally, they were at risk of drowning during a long winter night of heavy surf. That same year, a soldier wrecked on the west shore "from the Expedition to Spain" was buried, having died from a fever.

In the 1820s, a wreck was reported on the beach by Haven House, Mudeford. It was believed to be the remains of a boat from Napoleon's flotilla.

On 14 January 1823, the sailing vessel the *Mary* was upset by the sea at Christchurch Head, which was a common alternative name for Hengistbury Head at that time. The captain was Jacob Long and the cargo was brandy. It is said that the Coastguard arrived on hearing the desperate cries of the smugglers and went on to recover 80 tubs, for transferring to the Poole warehouse. Another report claims that the crew drowned whilst trying to bring these smuggled goods ashore. Were the revenue men more interested in the goods and their share of them, than the saving of life? In the face of conflicting accounts, we shall perhaps never know what really happened.

On 23 November 1824, the coast suffered such severe conditions that they passed into folklore as the Great Gale. The 100-ton *Hero* under Captain Hanna was lost on the Christchurch Ledge, with a cargo of stone from Swanage for London. Sources vary between four and six as to the number of crew, who lost their lives when the ship stranded.

On 14 July 1824, a sloop with six men foundered off the Head: none were rescued.

On 11 December 1839, a barque, *Wemyss*, based in Aberdeen, was wrecked on Hengistbury Head, although it is also reported as wrecked at St. Alban's Head. A cargo of 800 quarters of wheat was lost. In the same year, two men from a party of four were drowned when their boat capsized one night off Blackberry Point in the harbour.

In 1842, a jury reached a verdict of accidental drowning for John Blizard, whose fishing smack the *Unity* foundered near Christchurch beach and was lost at sea. The body came ashore at Highcliffe and was taken to the Preventive Station at Mudeford for identification. It was thought that he had been blown overboard by a sudden gust of wind.

In February 1866, several ships were wrecked in a storm at Christchurch Ledge and in Poole Bay. In a remarkable operation, eight local men in a fishing boat saved four men, but found three others, dying of exhaustion. Eight seamen were buried at Christchurch following that storm and others taken away for burial elsewhere. Rocket apparatus was appealed for and provided after this tragedy.

On the south side of Church Road, Southbourne, and at its eastern end, is a small brick shed, facing down Wildown Road. This contained such apparatus, always ready for use on a cart. When a maroon sounded, volunteers would rush to the shed and take the cart to a local farm to attach to a horse. The party would then make all haste to the site of distress, but often the process proved too slow.

In March 1873, two men out yachting in Christchurch Bay saw a boat, apparently unmanageable, and bore down upon her. A man was seen clinging to a line from the boat and the body was taken to Lymington. He was later identified as Philip Cartridge, the late mate of the *Enchantress,* on his way to Poole.

In May 1875, the ketch *Eliza* came to grief on Christchurch bar. She was in the roads, parted her cable, came broadside to the bar and was rendered helpless. Her cargo of coal was retrieved from the hold and the hull of the ship was then to be "auctioned on the spot" on the instructions of owner James Lawrence.

In March 1876, a terrific storm drove the *Speculation*, a sloop of 46 net tons, towards the Christchurch Ledge. Realising the danger, the crew put down an anchor, but the vessel was not buoyant enough and foundered 1.5 miles WSW of Hengistbury Head. All three crew were lost. Swanage lifeboatmen were called out from a Sunday church service to search, but found no trace. The ship was bound for Southampton from Plymouth, with a 73-ton cargo of limestone and superphosphate. A few days later, on 16 March, when the sea was calmer, a masthead was spotted. The Board of Trade placed a wreck buoy to mark the spot and warned shipping to give it a wide berth. The jury at an inquest in July returned "found drowned" in respect of a badly decomposed body of a man of about 40 discovered on Christchurch Ledge by two fishermen. It was thought to have been in the water about three or four months, and may well have been one of the crew of the *Speculation.*

A famous rescue took place from the Black House at the Run on 1 February 1886 by Mrs. Emily Stride, who was awarded a bronze life-saving medal. Two men were collecting seaweed, but their boat capsized, drowning one of them and leaving the other holding on to the upturned boat. She waded into the Run, at great personal risk in very cold water, managing to bring him to shore.

The *Bournemouth* was a fine "state-of-the-art" paddle steamer, which could take about 200 passengers, but had lifeboats for only a quarter of this number. Her first excursion from the pier was in 1884. Returning from a day trip to Torquay on 27 August 1886, she ran directly into the rocks near Pulpit Rock at Portland Bill at a good speed, possibly as high as16 knots, in dense fog. Another steamer, the *Empress*, was on the same route that day, so raising a query at the subsequent inquiry as to whether there was a race. The much-criticised captain blamed compass error.

There were distressing scenes when families were separated to allow women and children into the lifeboats. Some men were taken with the help of a rocket line to the headland, whilst other small boats gathered round to remove the remainder. Luckily, all 197 passengers were rescued and not one person was killed or injured. This was however due to the benign sea conditions. As ever in such things, it took the tragedy of the *Titanic* in 1912 to make the provision of adequate lifeboats compulsory. The *Bournemouth* broke its back becoming a total loss. Unfortunately, she had been insured for only half the original cost new of £14,000. She was a fine ship indeed, prompting the following poem from local man Robert Otter:

But the beautiful 'Bournemouth' has parted in two;
Her work is now done; her years have been few;
She's a wreck on the rocks, for already the bell
Of the once splendid boat has tolled her death knell.

The following story shows the sheer horror, which often had to be faced by seamen in those far-off times. On the morning of 23 November 1898, the *Ernst*, a three-masted schooner, was in difficulty in a Channel gale. The mainly German crew had survived a very rough run with a cargo of salt from Liverpool (destined for Danzig), culminating in the loss of all the canvas, so making the ship impossible to sail. The captain had nearly reached the relative calm of the Solent when control was lost. The storm then made short work of dragging the anchor and ship on to the Shingles, where she was seriously battered. Waves were so great that a lifeboat was unable to get alongside or anchor.

By about 6am the next day, the ship began to break up, gave out a loud crashing noise and then disappeared within minutes. The heroic crew of the lifeboat saved the captain and two others, but could not find a man last seen hanging on to the rungs of a ladder. Information about a makeshift raft, expected to fetch up at Mudeford, was telegraphed to the Coastguard, who manned the beach in some strength. Four men used a galley roof as a raft and were close to the end of their tether after two days of exposure without food. On its arrival, Coastguards carried out a dangerous rescue to save the lives of all four, who were then cared for by the wives of the rescuers. A body, entwined in a ladder, was later spotted by men fishing in the Run and found to be from the same ship. Presumably, this was the body of the ship's carpenter.

A ketch, the *Diver*, sprung a leak and was wrecked off the Head in November 1903. Fishermen and Coastguards carried out a successful rescue. Although the captain went down with the ship, he resurfaced and was helped into the ship's boat to await rescue.

In 1907, the body of a 20-year-old fisherman was found near the Long Rocks after capsizing due to a huge wave at the Beer Pan Rocks.

During World War I, it was said that a German submarine ran aground off Hengistbury and their officers rowed ashore to have dinner at the Royal Bath Hotel, but I cannot vouch for the accuracy of this tale!

The 230-foot, 1,149 gross tonnage Norwegian *SS Borgny* was sunk on 26 February 1918. Although the master thought he had been torpedoed, there was no claim by a U-boat. It is therefore likely to have been a mine. The cargo was coal from Newport to Rouen. This 1909-built ship was reported as much looted in 1993 and difficult to identify. The Diver Magazine of September 2002 said that it was inverted and mainly collapsed, apart from bow and stern. Identification was by brass letters on the stern.

The 225-foot *Venezuela*, an Argentinian registered steamship of 733 gross tons, built in Paisley in 1907, was torpedoed by the German submarine UB 59 on 14 March 1918. The previous day, according to Lloyds War Losses, she left Falmouth with coal for Rouen. The wreck lies upright in about 85 feet of water with the highest

Fig.32 ***Presentation by Queen Elizabeth the Queen Mother to Ken Derham, May 1984***
(Reproduced by consent of Vic Derham and photograph courtesy of RNLI)
A number of lives were saved over the years from Avon Beach. On 30 March 1959, Kenneth Derham carried out a difficult rescue in his 11-foot dinghy, in a very heavy breaking sea. A fishing boat had capsized, throwing a 15-year-old girl and her friend into the cold water. The body of the girl's father was washed up nearby a few minutes after the rescue. Eyewitnesses had not even expected the dinghy to make it safely back to shore. Although the rescue earned him a silver medal from the RNLI at the time, the presentation in this photograph was of a gold badge in recognition of fund-raising efforts.

part, a boiler, found in 1975 to be about 13 feet above the seabed. It had been misidentified as the *Empire Crusader*, which was bombed and sunk by German aircraft on 6 August 1940. A diver retrieved a gun from the wreck in 1984, claiming that this proved it to be the *Venezuela.* A dive in 1987 found the name *Venezuela* in brass letters under concretion on the stern of the wreck. This identification was confirmed in 1993.

On 8 August 1918, the 400-foot steamship *Clan Macvey* was torpedoed on her maiden voyage, by the crack Commander Lohs in UB 57. She had been built to 5,818 gross tons in Newcastle that year and was on her way to Port Said via Falmouth with a cargo of coals from Newcastle, when attacked 3.25 miles SSW of Hengistbury Head. The previous day had already seen action with a submarine, which Captain Jones claimed had been destroyed with his four-inch gun, although the Admiralty demurred, possibly due to some reluctance to pay the £1,000 prize money.

Seven were killed in the explosion, but 48 crewmembers were saved by a warship and landed at Poole. Having been towed some distance, the ship broke in two, taking four hours to sink. The Navy had to remove the superstructure, because it was too near the surface. Lohs' body was washed up near the mouth of the River Scheldt later that month, probably as a result of the UB 57 striking a mine.

The *Excelsior* foundered 2.25 miles south of the Head on 5 September 1924 due to a leak. The possible identification, by the United Kingdom Hydrographic Office, of a dangerous wreck as the *Excelsior*, is marked on Fig.31. Apparently, she sank in only ten minutes. This fishing drifter, with a wooden hull and triple expansion engine, was carrying a cargo of scrap metal from Portsmouth to Newport. Since part of the cargo, comprising metal pipes, was still visible to divers, she was known for some time as the "pipe wreck."

The 206-foot, 880-ton *Betsy Anna* went aground at Prawle Point, was patched up at Salcombe and then towed towards Cowes for engine repairs. The original name of this ship, built in 1892 on the Tyne, was the *Ashington.* South-westerly gales made the tow rope part from the tug *Trustee* and undid the temporary hull repairs, causing the ship to leak as she drifted across Poole Bay. The men on board were taken off before she sank in October 1926. She lies in 79 feet of water, seven miles south of Bournemouth. The UKHO classify it as a dangerous wreck as marked on Fig.31, noting that it is upright, intact but collapsing. In 1983, the bow was standing 20 feet high.

There must usually be quite a story which lies behind the bare facts of most disasters and remains unknown. For example, the *Caroline Susan,* a 23 gross ton motorised yacht, sank with a cargo of ballast on 13 June 1940, 3.5 miles SE of the Head. The UKHO position (quality given as unreliable) is plotted on Fig.31. The Lloyds' report refers to it either foundering or being lost through an explosion. Why was it in such a location with such an unlikely cargo at such a critical early stage of the war?

There have continued to be many rescues and disasters around Hengistbury Head since these earlier times, eventually resulting in the RNLI lifeboat station at Mudeford Quay. For example, Kenneth Derham received the RNLI Silver Medal for gallantry, after carrying out a very skilful and brave rescue on 30 March 1959, when a 30-foot fishing boat capsized in a very heavy breaking sea and showery weather. Although others tried and failed to reach the three in danger, he managed to prevail with an 11-foot dinghy. One 15 year-old girl was dragged aboard and her friend held on to the transom of the tiny rescue boat. Not only was the boat push-rowed to sea from a standing position, but also, he brought it back to shore stern first and landed the two survivors safely. Sadly, the girl's father was drowned and washed up nearby just later. The dinghy is on display in the RNLI station. The family has continued to be prominent in local rescues. Fig.32 shows a presentation by Queen Elizabeth the Queen Mother to Ken Derham of a gold badge in 1984, in recognition of RNLI fund-raising efforts over many years.

Loss of Southbourne Pier

The story of this pier, built some way from the Head at Southbourne-on-Sea, as it was then known, shows the sheer potential of winter weather at this end of Poole Bay.

Fig.33 shows a substantial structure in 1894, but it was not good enough to withstand the storms. Built at a cost of £4,000, it was 300 feet long and 30 feet wide. When opened on 6 August 1888, 1,200 went through the turnstiles, but the daily figure had dropped to only 50 within the month. Moreover, the paddle steamers did not like its landing stage, so greatly reducing profitability. It was usable until the gales of 28 December 1900 and 3 January 1901. The first caused serious damage and the second partially demolished the pier. The second photograph in Fig.33 shows the loss of its main structural supports and a smashed promenade. Public safety needs prompted the council to remove the remains in 1907. The third picture in Fig.33 is a dramatic shot of the wrecked pier abutment to the promenade. The buttresses have been smashed and a temporary link made from the toll office. It is sobering to imagine the effect of such a storm today near the Dykes. The dog in the foreground belonged to Mr. Saul, a chemist and photographer in Southbourne.

Fig.34 is an illustration of how it was planned to develop Southbourne-on-Sea in those optimistic early days. Dr. Thomas Compton was the driving force behind various efforts to promote the town, including the pier company, the company which constructed the toll bridge at Tuckton, and the building of Belle Vue Road. He genuinely believed in the health-giving aspects of the area and for a time lived in one of six new houses adjoining the new promenade leading to the pier. The houses had to be demolished. They proved to be totally unsuitable close to an aggressive winter sea. One local resident told me that her grandmother was planning to buy one of these houses in the 1890s, but during her second inspection she was completely soaked by the sea. Although the story as told to the granddaughter involved a wave, she thinks it was more likely to have been only sea spray. Whatever it was proved enough to put her off and buy a house at cliff height instead.

The sea wall to the promenade suffered a major collapse in 1902. The remnants were locally christened the Southbourne Rocks until largely removed by the council when the new promenade was built many years later. There remains a cautionary notice to bathers even now opposite the Bistro on the Beach, referring to the remains of the old promenade and the need to be careful at low water. The other houses, planned to extend all along the promenade to east and west, will remain forever on the drawing board.

Fig.33

Southbourne Pier in 1894 and after wrecked by storm in 1900

(Reproduced by consent of Red House Museum, Daily Echo and David Reeves)

There is no denying the substantial nature of the structure, 300 feet long by 30 feet wide, as erected in 1888. However, both the pier and the promenade proved quite inadequate when faced with an "extreme event", in December 1900. This fatal damage meant that the council had to remove it a few years later for safety reasons. The six houses adjacent to the promenade did not survive for very long either. A major significance of the disaster is the power of the sea and the risk of a future breakthrough near to the Dykes. The old promenade and pier were located a little way out to sea opposite the Bistro on the Beach.

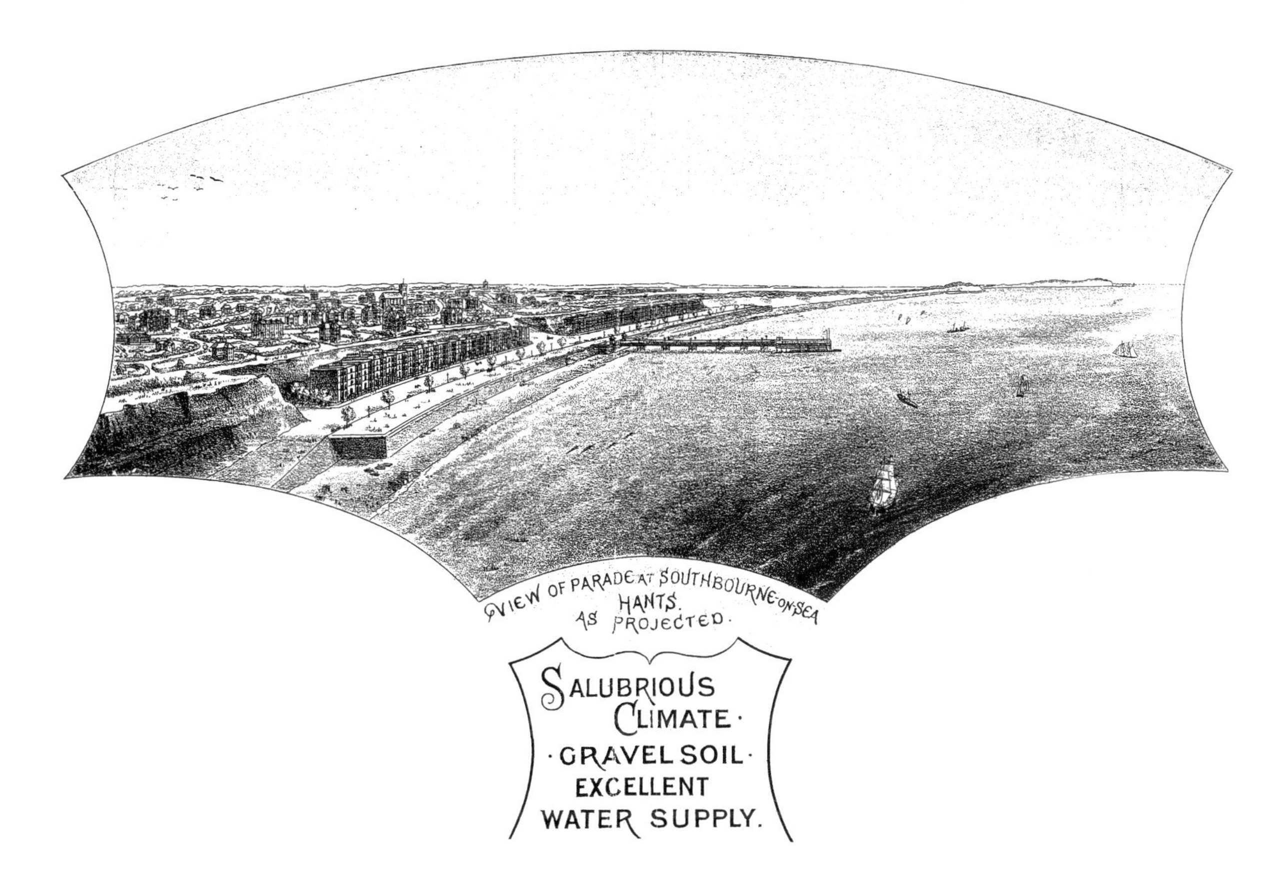

Fig.34 ***Proposed parade and Southbourne Pier, late 19th Century***

(Reproduced by consent of Bournemouth Central Library)

When Doctor Thomas Compton was planning Southbourne-on-Sea as a separate health resort in the late nineteenth century, the pier and promenade was built as part of his grand design. The first six of the villa houses shown here were also built, one of them occupied for a time by the doctor personally. Unfortunately, all the building works were misconceived and found to be inadequate against the elements.

As a footnote to this story, we suffered the complete loss of our family beach hut one winter, around 1955 as far as I can recall. All the huts, along the section of promenade east of Fisherman's Walk, had been shifted by the heavy seas of the previous night and most had been damaged. The breakers had had to climb the slope, cross the prom, climb three steep steps, get between the huts, run against the cliff-retaining wall and rebound from that wall in order to take our hut out to sea!

Crash at 1910 Bournemouth Centenary Air Show

Bournemouth is a very new town, as shown by the date of this centenary event. In 1810 Captain L. D. G. Tregonwell bought land to build a home near to the sea at the behest of his second wife, who fell in love with the place. His own knowledge of the area (then aptly known as Bourne Heath or Pool Heath) had been gained from his job: pursuing smugglers on horseback for the Crown. Fig.10 shows how undeveloped the town was in 1811.

The council felt justly proud of the success of the development of Bournemouth in its first 100 years. The festivities were bound to be loss-making (expenses of £18,461 compared to receipts of £7,286), but these were heady days before the First World War. Although "heavier than air machines," as they were then described, were known to be very risky, this would simply have added to the excitement. Powered flight, which began with the Wright Brothers in 1903, had already claimed a number of lives. There was a sense of strong competition between the contestants, with prizes for longest flight, about 90 miles, greatest altitude, 4,170 feet, and top speed, 56 mph.

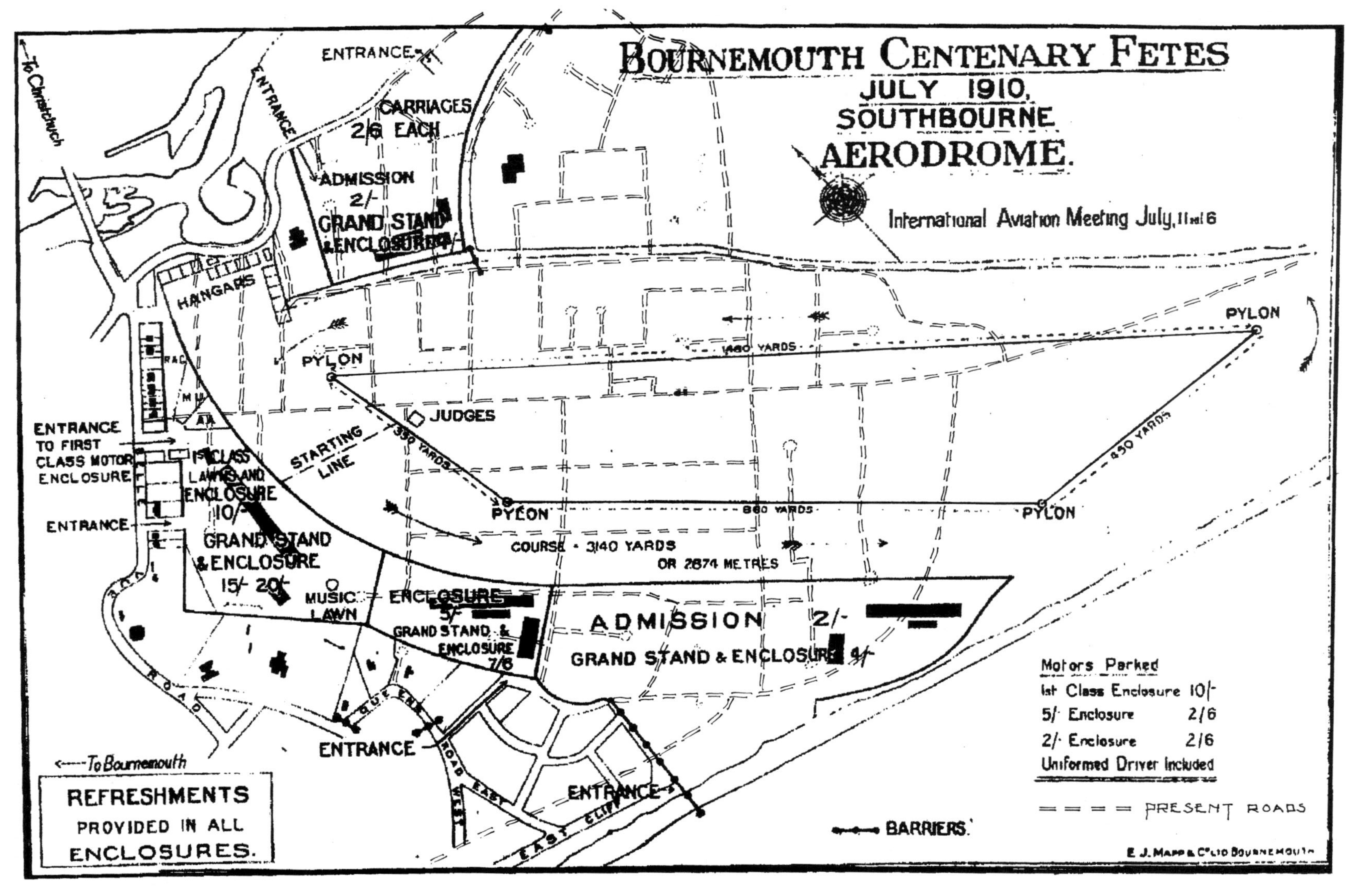

Fig.35 ***Southbourne Aerodrome for Bournemouth Centenary, 1910***

(E.J. Mapp & Co. [no longer existing])

The 1910 fete publication had this layout plan, showing the anti-clockwise course around four pylons, judges' box, grandstands, enclosure prices etc. It was a prestige although loss-making enterprise for the town. The approximate location of Rolls' fatal crash is at the "S" of Starting Line on the plan and of his memorial a little to the north-east in the corner of St. Peter's playing fields. For any readers living at Hengistbury and interested in their position on the course, I have shown the approximate position of the residential roads since built.

Fig.36 ***C.S.Rolls, co-founder of Rolls-Royce and fatal biplane crash scene, 1910***
(Reproduced by consent of Rolls-Royce Heritage Trust)
The portrait of Charlie Rolls is the family's favourite, its composure in stark contrast to the horror of the crash site in the second photograph. The cordon of friends holding hands (many in tears) was to prevent photographs being taken as far as possible, as was the advancing policeman with hand outstretched towards the camera.

Fig.35 shows the course layout, which ran between Belle Vue Road and Double Dykes. High hessian fencing surrounded the site to prevent anyone having a free look at ground level events. For those interested in the relative position of the residential roads since built, I have shown the roads superimposed on the layout. A comparison of this with a local map will allow road identification, although the road positions are necessarily approximate.

On the second day of the competitions, 12 July, at about 1 o'clock, Charles Stewart Rolls, joint founder of the Rolls-Royce motor company, crashed in his French-built Wright aircraft. He was attempting to land as close as possible to the centre of a marked circle. According to one commentator, the fatal crash was exactly similar to another one at Rheims nine days earlier. It seems that, at an altitude of 50 feet, the pilot gave a rather violent pull on a lever attached to a tail plane (fixed on only two days previously) the left side of which broke away together with part of the left rudder. According to Mr. D. Reeves, whose family are longstanding Southbourne residents, Rolls had replaced the aileron equipment in a workshop at Iford in order to make it more effective. The horror of the sight made the crowd silent as the machine turned a complete somersault and fell to the ground from a height of 30 to 40 feet. After the crash, the motor exploded. According to the doctor in attendance, death occurred within minutes due to concussion and laceration of the brain. Flying was cancelled for the day.

Only the previous month, Rolls had been the first to fly the English Channel in both directions. This tragedy also made him the first Englishman to die in an air crash. His funeral took place in Monmouth on the last day of the air show.

There are few photographs, because the crowd reportedly smashed cameras and beat up photographers. Fig.36 shows a picture of the aviator, who was only 33 at the time of his death, and one surviving photograph of the crash site. More than 50 owners of Rolls-Royce cars were present at the unveiling of a memorial in 1978. After much discussion with an official from the Victoria and Albert Museum, it was placed in the corner of the lower playing field of St. Peter's School, just behind the houses in Broadway and those in Sunnylands Road.

The crash site was said by some to be in Springfield Avenue close to the corner of Broadway: it was even rumoured to be in the position of someone's lounge. With great variation in eyewitness accounts and the passage of time, the true location is not clear. However, no one has done more work on this than the author of a book published by the Rolls-Royce Heritage Trust (*Charlie Rolls – Pioneer Aviator,* Gordon Bruce 1990.) After six pages of analysis, he concludes that the site is actually a little to the south of the memorial in the playing field.

In other incidents during the same week Major Alfred Rawlinson was badly injured, Mr. A. Boyle's monoplane overturned, and Mr. R. Loraine was blown 30 to 40 miles off course before managing to land on a golf course on the Isle of Wight.

Murder near the Dykes

On 20 February 1908, Emma Sherriff, a Boscombe dressmaker aged 36, was found strangled to death on the cliffs between Southbourne and the Dykes. Boys from a local private school came upon the tragic scene in a lonely area noted as a clifftop "lovers' lane." Miss Sherriff was known to be religious and in good health. When the police and Coastguard arrived, the body was face down with a handkerchief gag, torn fur around the neck and a mark on the neck. The inquest was told that there were no love affairs or men friends to anyone's knowledge. Several hundred mourners attended the funeral.

An ex-lifeguard, Frank Maguire, was arrested and put on trial. The prosecution said that he was the son of a friend of the victim. He had borrowed money from her, and when she wanted it back, he arranged the outing and killed her, having prepared an alibi claiming he was in London. He was acquitted when the jury could not agree on a verdict. At the retrial, no evidence was offered by the prosecution and Frank Maguire was released.

The same spot was subsequently used for a gun emplacement for artillery practice. Its remains had fallen to the beach by 1939, as a result of cliff erosion.

Suicide of the Town Clerk

Albert Harley opened a poll for the Purewell by-election of Monday 18 June 1928, after going into work at the weekend to prepare and post off an agenda to councillors for a meeting. After not turning up at home for lunch or tea as usual that day, the alarm was raised and two policemen began enquiries. That morning, at 9.30 am, he had bought a bathing costume for two shillings from a gent's outfitters. At 10 am, he had given some papers to PC Elkins at the polling station and the next thing discovered was a pile of his clothes, without a towel, at 7.40 p.m. at Mudeford Beach. Foreshore and cliffs were searched and the infamous lagoon at Steamer Point was dragged, but all to no avail. On 21 June, the previous Town Clerk, John Druitt, was appointed on a temporary basis. Next day, Albert Harley's body was discovered and identified at Lee-on-Solent.

He was a conscientious man known to be under some strain from the increasing workload, arising from what was supposed to be a part-time post. Moreover, he was not in the best of health and there were worries about a recent accident where the injured party was seeking damages. A note was left for his wife, but its contents were never disclosed. At that time, he had been responsible for an audit, which was found to be satisfactory. The verdict was "suicide by drowning while temporarily insane". On re-advertisement, the council made it a full-time post.

Tregonwell's roof plunge

In a lighter vein, we now have a story of a "near-disaster" only! This particular John Tregonwell, of the many John Tregonwells, is referred to in the chapter dealing with the summit of Warren Hill. When only five years old in 1603, the future spouse of the owner of the headland was on the roof of Milton Abbey. When the attention of his nurse minder was diverted, he climbed the parapet of the south transept in order to grab a wild rose growing in the wall. Having lost his balance, he plunged sixty feet to the ground in a single fall. The distraught nurse rushed down to ground level to find him completely unhurt and picking daisies. The child's full dress, made of nankeen, had billowed out in the strong wind and acted as a parachute! He went on to become High Sheriff of Dorset and lived to be 82. His widow Jane had a tablet put up at the Abbey to commemorate such a remarkable deliverance. Had he died in the fall, it would have changed the ownership history of Hengistbury Head.

Seven boys die near Steamer Point

In May 1868, perhaps the worst local tragedy of the nineteenth century took place. Eight boys, aged from 11 to 15, were bathing in the sea under the supervision of their German tutor between Highcliffe and the Old Steamer, now called Steamer Point. The sea was very calm, the boys all within their depth, and the tutor swimming on the seaward side of them to ensure that they did not venture too far.

A sudden inflow of the ocean swept towards them, probably at the turning of the tide, putting them all in deep water. The one lad who escaped, a non-swimmer, had been closer to the shore, but still had to fight for his life, arriving there almost senseless. The tutor had been unaware of the wave. He was alerted by a cry, only to see extended hands just sinking below the surface. He seized the nearest lad who so pinioned his arms in a dying grasp that they sunk together, so that only on its relaxing, he reached the shore with difficulty.

Within two hours of the group starting to bathe, there were six bodies laid out side by side in the inn parlour of the Sandford Hotel. The seventh was added during the night. James Druitt, the coroner, held an inquest the next day, with the jury inspecting all the bodies and returning the inevitable verdict of accidental drowning. A letter to the local paper pressed for warning notices to be placed and commented: "Another melancholy accident has again warned us of the danger of bathing inside the spit of sand, which extends so far along the eastern shore and is continually advancing in that direction."

However unfair this may seem, some perhaps blamed Mr. Holloway for the accident, since it would not have occurred without his mining operation. Holloway was mayor in 1865 and 1866, but his third term of office was not until 1887.

Disasters of the Mudeford lagoon

This tragedy, like the previous one, resulted indirectly from commercial exploitation of ironstone at the Head during the 19th century. Mudeford lagoon was formed when the waters cut through the extended sandspit direct to the sea, rather than flow through a much longer Run. Hence, a long, narrow, enclosed and dangerous strip of water was established from Mudeford to Highcliffe. Apparently, it was sometimes free of water, as shown by Captain Parsons' map of the "Dry Run" in 1886. Eventually, the elements drove the exposed sand bar on to the shore, so leaving the short Run as it is today.

Whilst the immediate shore of the lagoon was shallow, the steep slope meant that it swiftly became up to 20 feet deep in places. Weeds could trap the legs, and the water could be too murky for rescuers to see the drowning person. At first, no warning notices existed for this deceptively attractive bathing area. One rescued bather in 1926 said that he had thought the whole area was shallow. The same year, a man of twenty tragically drowned, watched by his fiancée. He had gone in to cool down on a hot day. Attempts to find the body by 53 men from the Royal Engineers failed, and it was eventually retrieved by a fisherman's net.

In 1936, a visitor carried out his fourth rescue from the lagoon, this time of a small boy. It appears that one of a number of suicides in the lagoon occurred the following year, when the body of a 60-year-old woman was found floating. In 1937, two boys swimming next to the warning notices, which were being ignored by a number of bathers, got into difficulty. Several people failed to save them, including one man who nearly drowned when his legs were trapped. Again, a net was needed to drag up the bodies.

Land mines cause death at Double Dykes

During World War II, Hengistbury was protected by large anti-tank mines and small but very lethal anti-personnel mines, which required a pressure of only seven pounds to set them off. They killed several dogs, although it seems that rabbits were quite safe.

In 1943, despite danger warnings, two soldiers took a short cut through a minefield on the cliff top about 200 yards east of the Dykes. One of them was blown up and killed. The other one was so shocked that it was an hour before he could be persuaded to move.

In about 1947, two soldiers were checking for mine clearance in the sands of White Pits on the other side of the Dykes. Their equipment was supposed to identify at a depth of 15 inches, but it is thought the sands may have shifted in the wind, making the operation even more dangerous. Both were killed instantly. A boot was found later with the foot still inside it.

Sea mine and drowning tragedies

In around 1940, soldiers spotted a sea mine drifting just off the coast. It had the usual "horns," which would cause an explosion if hit. Sadly, two were killed as a result of throwing stones at it. In another incident, a soldier's body was deposited at the Dykes on 27 November 1941. He was Sergeant James Croft, who had been washed off some rocks on the coast, whilst trying to retrieve army equipment.

Broom Close fatality

During the war, the house, which is now the Tuckton Library, was taken over as a military HQ. In 1944, it seems that one of the troops climbed a tree with a loaded gun and accidentally shot himself. I do not know why he climbed up, but as with anything mentioned in this book, I would welcome further information from any reader via the publisher.

Falls from Warren Hill

There have been a number of falls over the years resulting in death or injury. Council policy is to provide fencing in more populated areas such as the East Cliff, but not where the danger is fairly obvious. Having been at the cliff edge Mesolithic site when two very small children were too close to the edge for my liking, but the mother was oblivious, I am not convinced. At the very least, I think the danger notices should be made more prominent.

A gifted musician of eighteen received multiple injuries from a fall in 2001, the cause of which could not be established. Either he jumped or simply had an accident. The family agreed to transplants of his liver, heart and kidneys. He was known to be suffering from depression.

Earlier in the same year, a black Labrador, called Morgan, was with four children quite close to the cliff edge, when it apparently gave way. The dog fell from the highest point, reportedly inches away from the children, but had only minor injuries. A Coastguard and three vets were on the scene as quickly as possible. The vet treating him remarked that it was quite amazing the dog was not badly hurt.

Death in the harbour

A body was noticed in the harbour at 7a.m. one morning in September 2002. Many tributes were paid to this lady of 85 years, who had apparently dedicated her life to helping others. This included work at both hospital and church as well as the Regent Centre, Christchurch. Two years previously, after 20 years of voluntary work at the hospital, the League of Friends presented her with a Certificate of Merit. Police had no reason to treat her death as suspicious.

The ghostly horseman

Three people were convinced about this haunting, as reported by a local paper in February 1985. Only a disbelieving cynic would draw any conclusion from the fact that one witness was a manager with the newspaper, which printed the story and the other two, his parents!

"I'm absolutely certain he wasn't flesh and blood because he vanished in seconds," said Clive, the son. Both sightings are said to have occurred in 1982 at about 6 a.m.

Peggy and Stan were walking along the track by the harbour. The horseman galloped towards them, but had vanished when they turned round to look at him. There was no obvious route that he could have taken. A month later, all three were walking the same way, and Clive too saw the ghostly rider, although this time the horse was walking. As before, the rider did not appear to see the walkers and had vanished when they turned round to look at him. They rushed to a vantage-point, but there was no sign. "There was no way an ordinary rider could have vanished like that. There was nowhere for him to hide."

The rider was described as having a young face and with unkempt, collar-length hair. He wore scruffy looking clothes, and the white sleeves protruding from his jacket were flared in seventeenth century style. The final word to Clive: "I've heard of workmen working on the erosion at the Head who've seen him too, but I'd be fascinated to confirm this or hear from others who've had any ghostly experiences there."

Coastguard Service

The Coastguard, which is now part of the Maritime and Coastguard Agency, has a considerable history of its own, covering smuggling, life saving, and maritime safety.

It originated as an anti-smuggling force, the Preventive Water Guard, formed in 1809 by the Board of Customs and expanded to 151 stations under the Treasury in 1816. By 1822, the service was back under the Customs and renamed the Coast Guard, becoming the Coastguard, one word, in the twentieth century. By 1921, the service was involved with a number of additional coastal matters: signalling, telegraphy, reporting movements of ships, making sea-mines safe, reporting changes in navigation marks, searching and collecting dues from vessels, patrolling the coast, helping ships in distress, providing statistics to the Fishery Department, enforcing quarantine, sending on distress calls to RNLI, reporting faulty navigation aids and making meteorological reports.

Fig.37 ***Lake at ironstone quarry and Coastguard station on Warren Hill***
(Author 2005)

The upper quarry was dammed with ironstones to allow it to fill with water as a wildlife habitat and provide a culverted footpath. The scar on the hillside has thus been made into thing of beauty, which is of particular attraction to dragonflies. Although boarded up due to risk of vandalism, the generally unmanned Coastguard station is still in use and performing a valuable function, being remote-controlled from Weymouth. Easter Sunday brought out the crowds, including some in this picture walking close to the lethal cliff edge.

In 1923 the Coastguard, by now under the Board of Trade, became dedicated to life saving, wreck salvage and foreshore administration. Rough terrain vehicles, helicopters, access to RNLI lifeboats and to fixed wing aircraft have all enhanced the life saving ability of this emergency service. This is a far cry even from pre-war times, when the Coastguard practised with the breeches buoy life saving apparatus, using a post near the Dykes and a rocket line from the top to the beach.

Hengistbury is covered from the Portland Station, although there is co-ordination as required with Lee-on-the-Solent Coastguard, which covers up to Chewton Bunny. The two stations were the busiest in the UK in 2004. Here is an example of how the Coastguard co-ordinates other services. About 9.30pm on 27 May 2002, there was a loud and heavy rumble, which brought a number Southbourne residents out on to the street and created a deluge of calls to the police. A Brixham trawler, *Goldfinder*, had dredged up at 4.20pm a cylindrical object some two feet wide and three feet long. When reported by the captain to the Coastguard, it was referred to the Royal Navy explosives team. The vessel was asked to stop about one mile offshore, the object was sunk to the seabed and exploded after the enforcement of a one-mile exclusion zone. It was an English World War II submarine-laid buoyant mine. It is quite common for the Coastguard to deal with old ordnance, which can even get stuck in groynes. Live unexploded shells, hand grenades etc. have all been found within the last 20 years.

In 1975, an increasing need to co-ordinate rescues at sea resulted in a new Coastguard lookout in a better position (Fig.37). It was felt vital to install the latest life-saving equipment and increase the manning level from bad weather to full-time. West of this 1975 building, the area of raised grass by the sightseeing obelisk is the site of the old lookout hut of 1926. This hut was lit by a table lamp fed from a 12 volt battery and had a paraffin heater. Nonetheless, these arrangements were effective enough, if a rescue in August 1962 is considered. The lookout officer spotted red distress flares in the early hours of a Saturday morning. A 20-foot hired yacht, *Fair Lady Judith*, had run aground on the Long Rocks after developing engine trouble. Although two official boats were launched, including a lifeboat from Yarmouth, the rescue was carried out, as it so often has been, by local fishermen. Since it was difficult to enter the harbour in the dark, a fisherman's wife, Mrs. M. Stride, stayed at the quay illuminating the entrance with car headlamps!

Now that the lookout is remote controlled and boarded-up, this appears to reflect today's better methods of communication, but with one exception: the need to have someone there on 5th November to distinguish fireworks from flares! It seems it is the best lookout point to guard against false alarms. In view of the increasing number of fireworks let off on other nights, there must be some remaining risk of mistake.

The National Coastwatch Institution is a charity dedicated to reopening such unmanned lookouts to improve lifesaving. It seems there is evidence to prove that a pair of trained eyes can be more effective on occasion than radar and similar aids. In other words, some people are alive today thanks to Coastwatch volunteers, many of whom are ex-Coastguard staff, who never agreed with lookouts being unmanned. Despite the interest of the NCI in manning the Warren Hill station, it has not yet been possible to agree this. Whilst on a clear day, surprisingly good images can be seen through the NCI Peveril Point telescope, they would be much better from Hengistbury, which could also cover Christchurch Bay.

The Coastguard premises covering Hengistbury Head are in Admiralty Road, Southbourne. Some 150 to 200 incidents are dealt with each year, including on average at least one suicide from the top of the Head. Members of the auxiliary Coastal Rescue Team (CRT) are notified of an incident by pagers, prompting them to phone in to get instructions before rushing to the station. There is a station officer, plus a deputy station officer and ten other members of the CRT. Although there are always two men on standby, the whole CRT is called upon for a major search. Equipment in the four-wheel drive vehicle includes an abseiling kit including quad-pod, life saving apparatus, stretcher, torches, and a generator.

In one incident some 20 years ago, a gentleman in his seventies had fallen from Warren Hill but surprisingly was not badly hurt. Following standard procedure, a check was made by the Coastguard to see whether there had been a cliff fall, which would imply it was probably an accident, rather than a suicide attempt. No cliff fall had taken place but a bottle full of aspirin was found at the top. It had a childproof screw top and had not been opened. He was successfully treated in hospital for the minor physical injuries but eventually found to need long term mental care.

Much of the work involves liaison with the other emergency services and frequently, the RNLI rescue boat at Mudeford is called out to attend. Searches may take place for lost or missing persons, suicide cases or body recoveries. Dog rescues from the steep cliffs are not uncommon, one factor being that owners who attempt a rescue may place themselves in danger, making the situation much worse. Some years ago, abseiling equipment was needed to rescue geologists who got stuck about three-quarters of the way up. Helicopters are available at both Lee-on-Solent and Portland. One can sometimes arrive in about ten minutes, even quicker than the local response.

Requests for assistance to ships arise from red flares, orange smoke, Channel 16 reports and mobile phone reports. The station on the Head is still very useful, because it is remotely controlled from the Portland Station, together with another radar point at the Needles, to provide co-ordinates of ships in distress. It will one day have to be demolished as unsafe, due to the loss of cliffs through erosion. If it is not replaced, there will be a "dead area" east of the Head, where it will not be possible to fix co-ordinates. However, by 2010, the crew of a ship in distress will only need to press a single button for her position to be relayed immediately by satellite to the Coastguard.

The daily round of Coastguard work includes great variety. Propellers need freeing from mooring ropes, boats need towing to shore, boys regularly need rescue from the cliff face at the Head, a number of boats have been stranded on Long Rocks and Beer Pan Rocks and then refloated at high tide, small boats need safety inspections, divers with the bends are often taken to a decompression chamber at Poole, while safety rules need constant publicity.

Between them, Solent and Portland responded to 2,577 incidents in 2004, 558 lives were saved, but there were 59 fatalities and 63 hoax calls.

Royal National Lifeboat Institution

Many will be familiar with this charity, which is entirely supported by voluntary contributions. Early lifesaving at Mudeford was carried out by Ken Derham, who operated an 11-foot clinker built rowing dinghy at Avon Beach from 1936. Clearly, this was a limited facility, and Mr. Derham was involved in the provision of a better one by the RNLI. His son became Operations Manager of the lifeboat station and his grandson one of the crew.

The service is available 24 hours a day and typically succeeds in launching within five to ten minutes of being notified. Much work arises from a notification from the Coastguard, with people in difficulty and needing to be towed ashore. A daily public log is kept on display at the lifeboat house, which was rebuilt for operational reasons in 2003.

The worth of the service is evident in the national figures, which show around 5,000 calls to 260 boats and 1,500 lives saved. The heavily used Mudeford boat currently averages about 60 launches every year and had already achieved that figure in 2004 by Christmas. From the time the Mudeford station was established in 1963 up to 2003, there were 1,440 launches and 404 lives were saved. A notice in the building commemorates the heroic rescue by Ken Derham in 1959, described in the section about wrecks and disasters.

The boat itself is an Atlantic 21 of 1,750 lbs. displacement, a type introduced in 1972. It is of rigid inflatable construction 23 feet long and with an 8-foot beam. Navigation lights, radio, compass and other equipment are on board. The two outboard engines supply 70 horse power, allowing a speed of 29 to 34 knots (the fastest in the fleet) and radius of operation of 45 nautical miles. The crew of three are equipped to right the boat in the event of capsize, by swiftly inflating a self-righting bag. The engines are inversion-proofed to deal with such a situation.

Mount Misery

The zigzag opposite Clifton Road, Southbourne, used to be a track used by smugglers. The cliff top at this point was christened Mount Misery following the tragic death of a young woman in love. Reportedly, there was a sand dune above a headland, which fell steeply to rocks below. Although coastal engineers cannot confirm the existence of any rocks, W. Tucker, writing in 1921 (see Bibliography), states that Mount Misery was indeed a large sand dune on the cliff top.

The captain of a smuggler's lugger was thinking about the risks from these rocks, of coming into shore one stormy winter night. When the young woman, who was betrothed to the captain, stood away from the rest of the shore party and waved so that he could see her, he rashly took the boat forward. It broached, capsized and was smashed, all crew lost. Determined to be united in death, if it was now impossible in life, she threw herself with a terrible scream on to the rocks below. It is said that for years afterwards her ghost could be seen and heard leaping over the cliff on the anniversary of the tragedy.

Another mooted explanation for the name is the laborious nature of the ascent from the beach to the cliff top. Although less exciting, perhaps this one is more likely to be true!

Dragon of Christchurch

I include this legend or fable because it involves a flying dragon arising out of the sea, presumably near Hengistbury Head!

In 1113, nine brethren, including five canons from the church at Laon in France, travelled through Wessex on a fund raising expedition. The result was the publication of The Miracles of Our Lady of Laon. A need for money had arisen from a fire at the church the previous year. The portable shrine of Our Lady included miracle-working relics, which were claimed to be capable of healing people, thereby hopefully raising cash to rebuild the church. Although there were occasional disputes between local and foreign clergy as to who was entitled to the money, many miracles were reported on the journey.

A pirate was killed and his ship driven back, through the power of prayer and one of the relics, even before the Channel had been crossed. A peasant's daughter, who had been crippled from birth, was healed in gratitude for his employer taking in the monks.

There is an eyewitness account of a five-headed, flame-breathing dragon in Christchurch. It seems that the Dean of the local church, then being built, did not make the travelling clergy welcome at a time of torrential rain. As a result, there was heavenly vengeance, causing the town to be set ablaze after the brethren left. A flying dragon emerged from the sea, and set light to the church by breathing fire from its nostrils. Even the largest stones of the church were reduced to dust and ashes, likewise the altars. It was flying around setting fire to houses one by one. The Dean fared no better, suffering the complete loss of the ship in which he was trying to escape. It had been beached in Christchurch Harbour and loaded with all his clothing and furniture. Meanwhile, the kindly host who had looked after the canons was untouched, as were his outbuildings and cattle. Finally, the Dean was moved to repentance, prostrating himself before the shrine of Our Lady.

The history of Christchurch Priory is consistent to an extent with the story. Building was going on in 1113 under the supervision of the Dean, Peter de Oglandres, who, according to the Victoria County History, misappropriated the canons' stipends. Since he was relying on pilgrims' offerings to pay for the building, he would not have been keen to see a rival shrine set up in his own church. As for flying dragons, there are many reported from early times in Europe, and many explanations mooted, from "phantoms imposed on phantasies," to the aerial lights of southwest Hampshire; from meteors to ball lightning. This is more likely to be a mythological explanation of the destruction of the original thatched Saxon church.

Alternative Hengistbury

> *....It is force against daintiness. To visit here is to turn your back on the present and walk into antiquity. Everything about the traveller is remote and strange....there is the smell of the sea in the material air and there is the ghostly something in the air of imagination. There seem to be prophesying voices all over the Head of an evening. The raven that flits across your path is a wicked thing – mayhap, by the spell of some strong enchantress, a human soul is balefully imprisoned in the hearse-like carcass...*
>
> Southbourne 3rd Edition 1913 Souvenir.

This book is overtly factual for the most part, and what follows is not necessarily to scientifically verified standards of proof: but my opinion is that some sort of spiritual dimension does exist.

An Internet report, about Unidentified Flying Objects, referred to Hengistbury as being the location of a fourth sighting on 28 February 2002, in respect of an object travelling east:

> "Fourth report from Hengistbury Head area, Dorset. 23.05hours. Four separate witnesses walking and walking their dogs. Height estimated at about 500 to 600 feet over the sea, this description of height was confirmed by a fisherman out "dropping his crab pots." Once again no noise reported, the navigation lights?? were pulsating like a "rope light." Only seen for a maximum of two minutes by witnesses. The craft departed this time by climbing vertically very quickly until it became about the size of a star and then "blinked out," the witnesses stated. The interesting thing at this location was that very soon after the craft started to ascend two jet fighters screamed overhead, the witnesses said. There were a total of 18 witnesses that saw the craft during its flight path over the South Coast."

This is only one example of a reported UFO sighting, but it seems there are a number of others, although not by the ranger. I have been told for instance about a "cigar shaped U.F.O" seen from the bottom of Dalmeny

Road in the direction of St. Peter's playing fields, where Rolls had his fatal crash. The son of another local witness referred me to a stationary cigar-shaped object seen offshore from the headland, by several people in the 1970s. His father, an Evening Echo reporter who had witnessed the object, suffered considerable leg-pulling at his place of work!

I am informed that there is a dark figure, which haunts the Point House café and does not like building alterations. One person has all the lights on if he is alone there at night.

Water dowsing, which is considered important for energy lines, is commonly practised at Hengistbury. The Dykes are considered particularly significant. For those interested, a local society exists in Bournemouth. Anyone tempted to think that dowsing is nonsense should bear in mind that architects have been known to use it. Dowsing can be tried as a method of last resort to research uncertain ground conditions.

Nineteen ley lines are said to converge at the end of the Long Groyne. Before erosion, Beer Pan Rocks would have been part of the headland, which some believe used to have a henge. Unfortunately, the loss of land to the sea means that such opinions must remain speculation only. There are several competing theories to explain ley lines, including astrology, the farming calendar, cross-country routes for the poor, death routes, lines of focus points, e.g. hill forts, henges, long barrows and churches. In this region, lines go through many locations such as the headland, St. Catherine's Chapel, the Saxon Minster, the New Forest and the Isle of Wight. More specifically, certain Hengistbury lines appear to cut through Christchurch Priory, Worth Matravers, Peveril Point and Drinking Barrow on the Isle of Purbeck, and Ludgershall in Wiltshire. Stone Age and Bronze Age settlement sites can feature on ley lines. Indeed, it is believed that many church sites are on these alignments because the early Christians felt it best to place a church where pagan rituals had been carried out. Some feel that Hengistbury maintains to this day a somewhat dark spiritual nature. It might not be too fanciful to comment (consistent with the 1913 quote above) that this nature may never have been subdued, because a church or chapel has never been built here.

EIGHT

SMUGGLING

"A little tea, one leaf I did not steal,
For guiltless bloodshed I to God appeal:
Put tea in one scale human blood in t'other,
And think what 'tis to slay a harmless brother."

Churchyard epitaph of Robert Trotman, shot
on the shore near to Poole, in an encounter
in 1765 with Excise Officers.

WHAT a misleading piece of poetry! To set the scene, it is best to be clear that smuggling, however one may wish to justify or romanticise it, was a ruthless business as a matter of course, involving many offences up to and including murder.

The eighteenth century, and the first half of the following one, saw enormous amounts of smuggling along the south coast. Reductions in duty and the establishment of an effective Coastguard Service eventually put paid to "The Gentlemen" or "Free Traders," but not before much conflict with "The King's Men" or "Preventives." Some smugglers operated with an unopposed army of 200 people. Many people, including the likes of magistrates, were sympathetic or involved. For example, in 1682, cloth was transferred (on behalf of magistrate John Carter) from a ship off Hengistbury Head to Poole. It is even said that the Carter gang were armed and terrorised the whole area.

The prevalence of smuggling has always depended on the amount of duty that can be avoided, and therefore the level of profits available. When in 1789, many duties were reduced by more than half, profitability was greatly reduced. Another instance, which made the attraction of smuggling wax and wane, concerns tea: Pitt reduced duty from 119% to 12.5% in 1784, but had to increase it again to 96% in 1793 with the start of the Napoleonic Wars.

Turning points were reached at Trafalgar in 1805 and Waterloo in 1815, because the Royal Navy took over the Revenue Cutters, so improving enforcement. They later used their own ships to blockade the English coast instead of the French coast. With many more seizures, smugglers had to be much more ingenious at hiding the contraband. Probably the biggest blow to the trade was the large-scale removal of duty by the mid- nineteenth century.

When we lament the current politics or incompetence of governments of all persuasions, it may help to realise how true this has always been. Large sums were raised for the military by import duty. This led to an enormous industry being formed to evade the law. In this fashion, the worst of all worlds was created for about 150 years: not enough duty was raised, corruption was rife, enforcement was expensive and ineffective, carriage of goods was costly and many were killed or injured in the process.

Although you can set against this the way smuggling "kept the wolf from the door" for many poor people, this was merely an accidental benefit. It must have been frustrating to be a committed person in the front line against the smugglers, with a good knowledge of how to do the job, but no proper support from the Board of Customs, which tended to suggest that the best solution would be more spending on administrators!

It was profitable to operate on a large scale. Typical figures for brandy were £1.60 for a legal tub duty-paid in England, 80p to the smuggler in France, and £1.125 to the smuggler's customer. Napoleon financed his wars partly with British gold smuggled into France. A sovereign would sell in France for 30 shillings, or be paid for in kind with brandy. As referred to later, it seems that Napoleon's suppliers often preferred to be paid in gold.

The "guinea boats" were fast low rowing boats, which could also be sailed, but most important, were difficult to see at night with the sails down.

Many were tempted to regard it as a legitimate trade, in the same way as people regard the present-day "black economy" as an attractive form of tax evasion. There was much hypocrisy or ambivalence. Seemingly honest, upright, law-abiding members of society, such as lords of the manor and parsons, were said to have benefited from smuggling. A good indication of this has been reported from 1776. The Parish Clerk, on being told by the vicar that smuggling was a sin, apparently responded: "Then may the Lord have mercy on the poor town of Christchurch, your Reverence, for who is here who has not had a tub?"

Some avoid taking a moral line about the wickedness of the times. Economic conditions were pretty desperate for many people, who faced grim choices, such as between poaching and starvation. A labourer could earn ten shillings for a night's work, which was more than his normal weekly wage. It can be argued that the workhouse, poor relief, high unemployment, the practice of reducing agricultural wages, and the inclosure system, which helped the better off, all happened for good reasons in keeping with the times.

Quite apart from natural sympathy for a romantic figure, defying the government of the day, many genuinely felt the smuggler should be supported because he was defying a bad law. And why not, they reasoned, if it meant cheap tea and brandy? The more truly law-abiding were variously threatened or bribed into turning a blind eye and keeping quiet. Techniques to "encourage the others" included beatings and deporting a miscreant on a smuggler's lugger into France – where, in the time of Napoleon, any unexpected Englishman got extremely short shrift. Although it took place before the heyday of smuggling and there is no local connection to my knowledge, Stephen Haynes provides an example of the extremity of the times. A pirate of the late sixteenth century, he was greatly feared for cruelty. A crewmember of a vessel captured by him could expect to be disembowelled and his entrails nailed to the mast. He would then have to leap around the mast, so winding the entrails in the process. Lighted papers were apparently applied to the bare buttocks of the victim to force him into this horrifying circular dance.

Not all the populace was corrupt. William Arnold was an honest Collector of Customs based in the Isle of Wight. He not only spent his own money to fit out a boat, but also submitted many original ideas to his superiors about how to combat the trade. They included limiting the length and therefore speed of the smugglers' fast rowing boats and increasing from three to nine miles the distance from shore within which luggers could not "hover." The first would mean a chance to catch up with them and the second would mean a big increase in costs due to the Lander's party having to wait in a state of uncertainty. Arnold was an effective crusader and generally well regarded. His tombstone makes clear that he was held in the "warmest esteem and affection of all." His remarkable personality gained him friends everywhere, despite his success at breaking up smuggling gangs.

Smuggling techniques

Considerable planning was needed. The *Venturer* would arrange capital and organisation. He needed to be a wealthy local man who could use gold to finance the operation, and was happy to do so on trust and by word of mouth only. His *Agent* would collect shares or contributions to capital, from local well-off people, and cross the Channel, with the *Captain*, to buy the contraband. The *Clerk*, again employed by the Venturer, would keep the books. The Captain would ensure the collection from France and delivery to the south coast at the right time and place. The *Lander* was responsible for the shore party, who would collect the goods from the lugger and distribute them inland.

"Spout lanterns" were often used by lookouts on land to answer the lugger's blue flash with a "flink." The point of the long spout was security, as it was aimed at the vessel, so preventing anyone else seeing it to right or left. The light told the captain that he was indeed on the spot, meaning the coast was clear and he was in the right place at the right time. Both expressions have passed into the language. Being on the spot must have been an exciting moment in the "run." An immediate decision or response was called for without prevarication. As for the smugglers' security, when the blue flash was visible to those on land, this does seem quite a risk but was probably unavoidable. But when the Riding Officers were in the pocket of the gang or unable to raise an effective opposing force, runs were made in broad daylight.

Timing was important for the Lander. He would not want to arrive too early as his party might get drunk before the landing! To inform them of time and place, it is said that a milkmaid went through the streets of Christchurch with certain numbers of small wooden balls in two milk pails on a shoulder yoke – quite an unusual code!

Here are some more definitions of smuggling jargon:

Creepers. Grapnels with small flukes for catching on to the lines connecting underwater tubs.

Rump stool. A one-legged stool used by coastguards on watch: as it had only the one leg, they could not go to sleep.

Dark. Noun for a moonless night, which was preferred for smuggling.

Stinkibus. Brandy tub hidden underwater for too long.

Hollands. Another name for gin.

Flaskers. Those smuggling liquor.

Laggan. Buoy-marked sunken contraband for later collection.

Half-anker. Standard size container of spirits amounting to 4.167 gallons also simply called a "tub."

Flashing off the lugger. The Lander's party would strike steel against flint a number of times to warn off the lugger from landing, due to a waiting party of revenue officers.

The smuggling business was affected by the "letters of marque" system. These were official government authorisations of privately owned vessels, permitting them to become privateers. Smugglers could thus be turned into legitimate naval armed forces for the Crown. The French also used the same method to capture cargo vessels of the enemy.

The local scene

Smuggling was very active from Poole through to Christchurch.

The Napoleonic Wars seemed to create some curious results. Before the French were defeated, local defences were strengthened in ways that helped the Preventives, such as the new Christchurch barracks, built in 1795, and later enlarged in 1812 and 1875. This is because they were entitled to call on the military for assistance to intercept the Free Traders. Improved defences against the French thus worked against the smugglers. On the other hand, when the wars were over, some ex-servicemen became excellent defenders of a Lander's party, so helping the Venturer.

Napoleon's use of gold smuggled from England to finance his wars was good business for the smuggler, who was paid well over face value. It seems that many of Napoleon's suppliers were paid in gold because they were not happy to receive payment in an unstable currency, whilst the smuggler was probably paid in brandy, anyway.

Isaac Gulliver, a major smuggler, reputedly led a charmed existence. He was known as the "gentle smuggler" from his claim of never having killed anyone! The trade made him rich, with a farm near Dorchester and property in Wimborne, where he ended his days. He had a base in a large house (long since demolished) with various hiding places in Kinson, Bournemouth. The story is that the government valued his inside information from France so highly that he was left alone by the Customs men. If, as claimed, he correctly and patriotically revealed a French plot to kill George III, perhaps this was reasonable!

As an example of the scale of some "runs," when smuggling was at its height, there is a popular account from a writer of the time. Richard Warner was a pupil at Christchurch Grammar School, in its premises above the Lady Chapel of Christchurch Priory, from 1776 to 1780, before a distinguished career including the post of official historian to the City of Bath. He wrote:

"I have myself, more than once, seen a procession of twenty or thirty wagons, loaded with kegs of spirit; an armed man sitting at the front and tail of each; and surrounded by a troop of two or three hundred horse-men, every one carrying on his enormous saddle, from two to four tubs of spirits; winding deliberately and with most picturesque and imposing effect along the skirts of *Hengistbury Head* in their way towards the wild country to the north-west of Christchurch, the point of their separation."

This tends to contradict accounts of the enormous value to the smugglers of being able to hide the Lander's party, together with horses and wagons, in the Dykes. However, both may be accurate, since the smuggler could operate much more freely before the barracks were established in Barrack Road. Thereafter, discretion became necessary. Prisoners' cells at the barracks were probably a deterrent to any carelessness, being six feet by six feet, with a block of wood for a pillow.

There are a number of reports of a local decoy system. Either by dint of a false tip-off or misleading fires on Bourne Heath – now Bournemouth – the revenue men would be in the wrong place. A lugger off

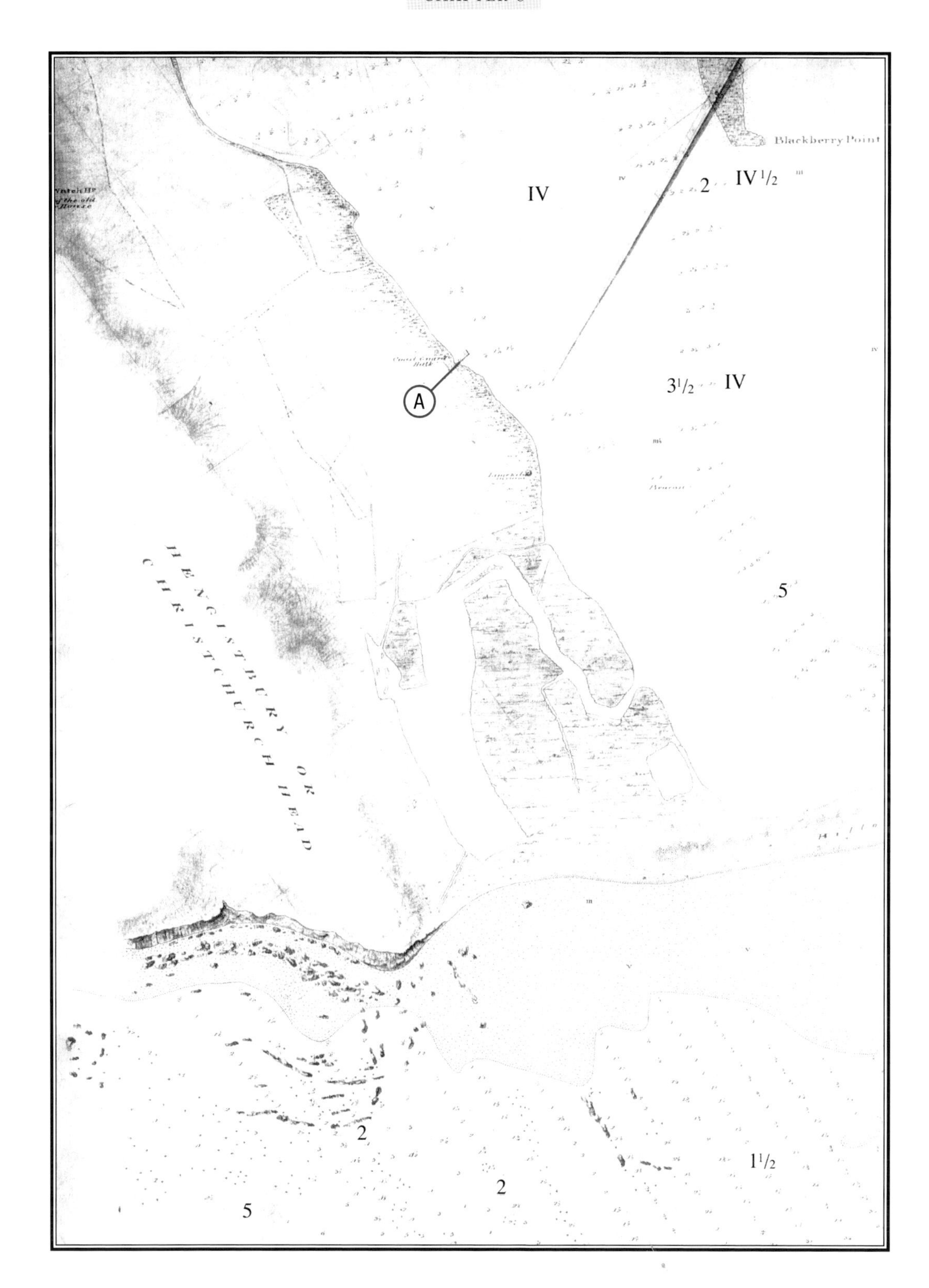

Fig.38 ***Ironstones, Coastguard hulk (at 'A' above) and inlet before the creation of Holloway's Dock, 1846*** ***(Christchurch by Commander Sheringham. Reproduced by permission of the Controller of Her Majesty's Stationery Office and the UK Hydrographic Office Scale 300 feet to 1 inch before reduction)***

The Roman numerals give the cover in feet at high Spring tides and the other figures the soundings at the lows. The great majority of the harbour was then exposed sand and mud only. The hulk was a lookout comprising part of an upturned boat, as an open-sided shelter. The original shape of the inlet made into Holloway's Dock is apparent as are the large quantity of ironstones before the mining started in 1848.

Hengistbury would know the code and run in to a beach around Highcliffe. If the officers attempted to ride all the way to the east, the run would be completed before they were able to get there.

It is well known locally that Wick Lane, Southbourne, is a smugglers' track leading to the old ford, which adjoined the existing ferry. It was approached by a track that led directly from the Dykes to the south end of the Lane, across what is now the golf course. When decisions had to be taken about siting Coastguard stations, the level of smuggling activity was an important factor. As testament to its importance locally, a Coastguard station was built at Admiralty Road, Southbourne.

Legends around Hengistbury

As might be expected, there is much doubtful folklore. For example, it is said that a legend about gold being buried in the tumuli at the Head, attracted the "Wicked Man of Wick," the notorious smuggler Sam Hookey. He and his gang began digging into a mound, but his helpers abandoned the tunnelling one by one, through fear. In the end, the capstone is said to have given way, trapping Sam inside the grave. The gang fled in terror, but his cries for help were heard by a passer-by, who rescued him.

In another story, which is likely to be more truthful, Hookey decoyed the revenue men to the mouth of the Bourne with a planted tip-off involving a single lugger. They duly seized the cargo after a skirmish with the "smugglers," who fled, but they found the kegs were filled with seawater! By the time they arrived on horseback at the true landing point in Wick, the run had been completed on a big scale, said to be 12,033 tubs of brandy, two tons of tea and five bales of silk.

Hookey is said to have perished in 1796 through losing his footing whilst crossing the Stour at Wick Ford. He was supposed to have been unduly weighed down by a heavy belt of smuggled gold, which caused him to be swept into a pit in the riverbed and drowned at the age of 71. "Hookey's Hole" is marked on certain maps, encouraging divers in 1954 to see if they could find his gold, but they did not succeed.

But had he decided to become "missing, presumed drowned" and change his identity, in order to retire in peace? Then I came across a confession letter from R. Ede England dated 26 February 1962, to the Curator of the Red House Museum: the tale of Hookey's Hole was "based on no facts whatever"! It arose purely from a story he had written at the request of W.G. Warner of Wick Ferry Holiday Camp in 1954. This found its way into a pamphlet and was repeated in the book *History of Christchurch* by T. Dyson (1954). The original purpose was simply to have a suitable story to go with the building of a club at the holiday camp!

In 1799, a Riding Officer arranged for his men to be hidden in the sand from Mudeford to Chewton Bunny. They kept watch from under "seaweed head-dresses" and succeeded in capturing a consignment of brandy. When they arose from the sand, the Lander's party fled in terror!

On the Ordnance Survey maps, Mother Siller's Channel is still to be seen on the north side of Christchurch Harbour. As the landlady of the Ship in Distress, which is located beyond the end of the channel, Widow Siller became engaged to Billy Coombs, the captain of a 100-ton lugger and privateer. He was to give up smuggling for good after one last run, in order to marry her and become landlord of the pub. As an earnest of intent, he left various private papers to her safekeeping, but she could not resist opening them, only to find he was also betrothed to a girl in his home port of Hamble! This resulted in a tip-off to Customs, and a battle on his return to Christchurch Bay. His luck then got even worse. It is said that he was only brought to trial due to a breach of battle rules with the revenue cutter, i.e., the mistaken surrender of his ship, followed by continued firing from it. The sentence of the court was death by hanging.

I wonder if Widow Siller felt any guilt? But according to Oakley (see Bibliography), Billy Coombs never existed in the flesh, being merely a character in a novel by W.H.G. Kingston, who has been elaborated into theatre plays and folklore ever since. It may be no coincidence that George Coombes, a noted philanderer, was actually executed following the Battle of Mudeford dealt with below. He was reportedly carrying on a romance with Widow Sellers of the Haven House Inn. So was there some truth in the legend after all?

Abe Coakes is famed for swimming with submerged tubs of brandy through the Run, right up to Place Mill at Christchurch Quay. By that time, a Coastguard station existed at the entrance to the harbour. Having swum into position in the bay, the brandy would be dropped to him from the boat, just within the tidal stream. He would take his raft of 20 kegs, all strung together by rope, with the strong incoming tide under the very noses of those on watch. It was a skilled operation requiring great strength, negotiating the changing sandbars within the harbour, and the point where Stour and Avon meet. He was eventually arrested through betrayal.

It is said that the Black House was so called because it was burnt black by revenue men setting fires to smoke out smugglers hiding there. Even if that is true, it is now black purely due to the use of paint. It has also been reported as the site of a shipyard, perhaps for the smuggling trade. A 94-foot brig of 253 tons called the *Enterprize* was built and launched there in August 1848. The 1846 map shows this end of the Sandbank as Holloway's Building Sheds, but this is beyond the extract in Fig.38. Included however, is a Coast Guard Hulk, which has long since disappeared. A common method of providing a sheltered observation point was to cut a ship in half and use one half turned over, with its open side facing the water. Evidently it served as a simple but substantial lookout (approximately 60 feet by 20 feet) from the south side of the harbour.

Battle of Mudeford 1784

This is probably the most famous local smugglers' story, and one fully substantiated.

It started with a 73-ton lugger, the *Civil Usage*, loaded with contraband, being chased back across to Cherbourg by a revenue cutter, the *Rose*. In fact, Captain May was so concerned about capture, he unloaded fully in France and returned to Christchurch with ballast only, as reported by the *Rose*'s boarding party before dawn on 12 July 1784.

A conference was held at the Haven Inn between the owner, John Streeter, and the captain, together with Captain Parrott from another of his luggers, the 96-ton *Phoenix*. Streeter was a respected local man, albeit a known smuggler, who bought the *Phoenix* back from Customs following a previous seizure of contraband. The outcome was the return to France of both ships to pick up a full load, so that each had four tons of tea and a total of 42,000 gallons of spirits. By increasing the size of the operation, Streeter was trying to recoup his costs from the wasted trip by gambling "double or quits." Some idea of scale can be got from the report of about 300 men, 400 horses and 100 wagons being used by the Lander's party. The tension and stakes were high.

The lookout on Hengistbury Head sighted the distant sails of the luggers, prompting the final assembly of the shore party by John Streeter. Before they could unload, however, the revenue cutter *Resolution* was spotted approaching the harbour. It seems that the *Resolution* had just chanced along. Being outgunned, the cutter could only observe from a distance whilst planning to call for reinforcements. The corrupt Riding Officers proceeded to arrange with Streeter their usual limited seizure and personal cut, amounting to 100 tubs. It appears however that there was one honest Riding Officer, James Noyce, who had gone to Lymington to get military assistance. Troops rode through the night to Christchurch, but failed to intercept any contraband. It had been fully distributed as planned.

The *Resolution* contacted *H.M.S. Orestes* (commanded by the experienced and successful naval officer, James Ellis) by guessing that a moving light in the darkness was that particular ship, and dispatching a small boat to intercept. The *Orestes* was a brig-rigged sloop-of-war of 395 tons, being more than twice the combined tonnage of the two luggers. It also had nine-pounder guns to set against the smugglers' six-pounders. Contact was also made with the patrolling cutter, the *Swan*, enabling a conference at sea between all three captains. George Sarman and his brother James Sarman captained the *Swan* and the *Resolution* respectively. By the time the three ships got back to Christchurch, Streeter had re-ballasted each lugger with 50 tons of gravel, and made ready for sea, but he was trapped and knew his ships would be forfeit. His long-suffering men were then ordered to remove as much gear as possible, including masts and sails. Fig.45 is an early photograph of The Haven, probably giving a very good idea of the scene of action. Even better possibly is Fig.39, a painting dated just six years after the battle.

Six rowing boats from the King's squadron pulled up to the luggers and those still on board were called to "Surrender in the name of the King!" A fusillade of shots was the response. The sailing-master, William Allen, aged only twenty-five, who had called for the surrender, was fatally wounded. An alternative version says Allen was wounded by an unprovoked shot from behind the luggers when he stepped out of his boat to push it off a sandbank. There were many tears at his funeral in Cowes, because he was a fine and well-loved officer. The report by Arnold to the Board of Customs stressed that the smugglers were the first to open fire. The luggers were captured by marines, but at the cost of other injuries, and in the face of fire from the Haven House windows. The Haven House Inn appears to have been the southern half of the building known as the Dutch Houses erected about 1695 to 1698. The smaller parallel terrace had not been built, nor had the current Haven House Inn to the north-east.

The inquest decided Allen's death was wilful murder by an unknown assailant, aided and abetted by the two captains, May and Parrott. The Supervisor of the Riding Officers, Jeans, tipped off May, Parrott and Streeter, who escaped to the Channel Islands. Various warrants were issued but proved ineffective, except for three smugglers, including George Coombes, who were sent for trial to the Old Bailey. Two were acquitted through lack of evidence, but Coombes was sentenced to death by hanging at Wapping. Although no one said he fired the fatal shot, he was found guilty of aiding and abetting. The body was brought back and hung in an iron cage from a gibbet by the Haven House. That night, his friends cut him down, and probably secured a Christian burial with the aid of a sympathetic parson.

Just two months after the Battle of Mudeford, the *Orestes* was in action again off Hengistbury Head against a heavily armed smugglers' lugger, the *British Lion.* Only 13 crew of the lugger survived to be taken prisoner, all wounded. The *Orestes* had two dead and nine wounded. After the July action, I doubt that the revenue men felt too benign towards smugglers.

A postscript is the dismissal after investigation in 1786 of the Supervisor of Riding Officers based in the town, Joshua Jeans. He died a broken man about six months later. His house and office can still be seen at 10 Bridge Street. He was found to be implicated and to have actively dissuaded his junior officers from taking action, both generally and when they reported the Lander's party taking wagons through the night for the rendezvous. Within two weeks, his replacement had arrested Streeter for smuggling. It is rumoured that the gaoler at Winchester assisted in his subsequent escape to Guernsey. He returned to Christchurch once he felt a free man with the 1804 amnesty, which quashed any existing warrants, and lived to be seventy-four. William Arnold, on the other hand, only lived to be 55, whilst Commander Ellis died aged 79 in 1824, a few weeks before Streeter. The *Orestes* was lost with all hands in the East Indies in 1799.

Provided the reader is convinced of the rightness of the law, this can be seen as something of a morality tale. The hard work of William Arnold resulted in the availability of the *Orestes* and the courage of the preventive men had enabled the enforcement. To achieve justice, one fine officer died and many were wounded, albeit that the two captains of the luggers went free, as did the Venturer. One smuggler was found guilty and executed. Although the price of justice was high, a lesson had been taught. Or had it? An enormous amount of goods escaped the law, as did those who made most money. The risk of losing a lugger was merely an operational expense: they would be more careful next time. How right was the court to send Coombes to his death when there were clearly plenty of others "aiding and abetting" in the heat of battle? And how just is all this if you decide that the corruption in the application of the law (customs men turning a blind eye, the general public buying cheap brandy, etc.) was not acceptable in the first place? Difficult questions.

Fig.39 ***Mudeford Sandbank, the Quay and Christchurch Bay, c.1790***

(*Nicholas Pocock, ex naval Captain. Reproduced by consent of Red House Museum*)

The harbour entrance, Haven Inn and the mansion, High Cliff are depicted from the top of Warren Hill. The sand dunes were much more substantial then. The mansion shown is the first one built from 1773 by Lord Bute, on land since partly lost to the sea through erosion. The present Highcliffe Castle was erected in the 1830's well back from the cliff. A land projection may be noted just past the Run, indicating that the smooth curve of the bay had still to develop.

NINE

WORLD WAR II AND ITS AFTERMATH

The enjoyment of rights depends upon the acceptance of duties by the individual as well as the State. Liberty and law have a price, in terms of both taxation and behaviour.

Michael Hodges

Bournemouth at war

ALTHOUGH some town centre damage is known about, in particular to Beales' department store, it is not always realised that Bournemouth suffered significantly from German bombs. The *Bournemouth Times* of 8 December 1944 gives some figures: between 3 July 1940 and 29 February 1944, there were 219 killed, 507 injured, 401 dealt with at rest centres, 75 buildings totally destroyed, 171 buildings which had to be demolished, 675 repairable, 9,413 slightly damaged and 3,256 with broken glass only. The worst incident was on 23 May 1943, involving 25 enemy planes, ten areas of the town, 77 dead and 3,481 buildings damaged.

The German invasion plan, Operation Sea Lion, assumed their Sixth Army would invade between Portland and Hurst. Defences included shoreline scaffolding equipped with contact mines, holes blown in the piers, mines in the beaches and barbed wire at beach exits. The gun emplacements installed at the Dykes (Fig.42) pay respect to the Iron Age work in building the original promontory defence. I believe opinion is fairly evenly divided on the likely success of a German invasion. The date of "indefinite postponement" was 17 September 1940, although this information, obtained by code breaking, was not given to defending troops at the time.

The Central Reference Library contains a street plan named "Stadtplan Von Bournemouth" dated 1 August 1941. Key installations such as barracks, hospitals, bridges and sewage pumping stations are marked, presumably for the benefit of German bombers. It is clearly based on the latest available 6 inch to 1 mile Ordnance Survey, although I doubt that bombing accuracy was adequate to make the map of much real use. The Civil Defence Controller for Christchurch gave a record of enemy action including bombs on 21 December 1940 in Cedar Avenue. He believed that they were aimed at Iford Bridge. Fortuitously for the Head perhaps, that particular OS map stopped short of Hengistbury, where the important military facilities were.

Military operations at Hengistbury and in the surrounding region

It has not been possible to identify precisely all the many military facilities installed after the Head was requisitioned. Some idea (for identification purposes only) can be gained from Fig.40 and the numbered key to the installations: they are much more extensive than would be realised from Fig.41. The whole site was under full military control and security to the east of the defence wire boundary near Solent Road. The newly-built

Saxon King public house, with its trademark shiny blue tiled roof, was taken over for military use, including headquarters for the Home Guard. It had been provided with an air raid shelter as a building condition, due to the imminence of war. The Celtic House Hotel, Warren Edge Road, was also taken over by the military. It has long since been redeveloped as low rise housing for the elderly. Although I have been unable to trace this on plans or photographs, one resident recalls that a wide and deep tank trap was dug from the river to the sea through the spot where the church now stands. Fig.42 shows the use of the Double Dykes, including dragons' teeth, weapons pits on the higher dyke, etc. The 1947 aerial photograph at Fig.44 shows a very different landscape from that of today. In particular, seven towers can be seen of various heights up to about 250 feet. Fig.41 shows three of the towers more clearly. American troops were extensively camped and billeted in Southbourne as D-Day, 6 June 1944, approached. Just before that day, Poole Bay was crammed with many ships of the invasion fleet. The view from Warren Hill must have been incredible.

There were a number of different operations. Hengistbury was a Chain Home Radar Station, set up to track enemy aircraft and alert RAF fighters. It first went on air, according to the Operations Record Book (Public Records Office, Kew), at 00.15 hours on 8 April 1942, and operated until September 1945. The plotting of aircraft was carried out in buildings partly in the present-day car park by the Dykes, and partly on the edge of Roebury Lane. The pillboxes, beach mines, dragon's teeth and weapons pits were placed to counter an invasion from the sea. Scaffolding defences ran along the sandspit, instead of huts, with poles bolted together and sunk in the sand in a way that would at least delay an invasion force. The full coastal battery comprised more than 100 personnel, including the ATS and Royal Navy to identify shipping. To the west of Sea Road, Southbourne, a dummy battery of 4.5 inch howitzers was installed.

PLUTO (see Fig.40 and Fig.42) stands for Pipeline Under the Ocean. An 11-mile loop of pipe carrying petrol was successfully tested in Poole Bay in 1944, in order to ensure that troops could be supplied on D-Day, from Shanklin. It is thought that huts by the Dykes were part of this trial. Although it has been said that Hengistbury beach was the site for the real PLUTO, it was probably used for trials only, and not in the invasion of mainland Europe. PLUTO was also developed from Poole. Piping was laid and joined from drums by a boat plying between Brownsea Island and Ballast Quay. Eventually, using the large type of drum (known as a Tweedledrum) 12 miles of pipe were run across the bay to the Isle of Wight. I believe it was all part of "Operation Conundrum".

Hengistbury Head was also a base for secret radio listening. Enemy signals were monitored in a search for the Lorenz VHF navigation beams that helped German bombers find targets on night raids. The bomber would follow one beam and unload when it intersected with another. The devastation of Coventry is witness to their effectiveness. Fortunately, it was possible to design jamming equipment, following a study of the device in a German bomber forced to land on a Dorset beach. A truck was fitted with a mobile listening system, so that it could patrol from Mudeford to Poole, searching for enemy transmissions. Thirty men from 80 Wing RAF were based at the Head. The operation was a success, because the Germans failed with several types of beam system. When the beams were jammed, they became unusable, finally causing the enemy to abandon the method.

The Valentine tanks

Although Fig.31 may be mainly of interest as it is an Admiralty chart extract, I have plotted as closely as possible the remains of wrecks, tanks and aircraft crashes. Preparations for D-Day on 6 June 1944 involved testing the Valentine, a new amphibious tank in Poole Bay. The name was probably a manufacturer's code name, rather than the most common explanation that it was offered to the War Ministry by Vickers on St. Valentine's Day 1939.

The tank was used with pneumatically raised canvas sides to keep out the sea. The propulsion method was known as a duplex drive, giving a speed of four knots. The tank's engine was connected to a propeller. The idea was to "launch" the tank from an offshore ship, so that it could be "sailed" right into shore and climb the beach. Unfortunately, once waves splashed above the canvas, the tank would ride lower in the water (despite a hull pump) and could then sink. The method devised of having everyone, except the driver, on top of the tank did not remove the risk of overtopping and the canvas sides collapsing on the crew. Experiments were successful in that most got to shore and the military decision was taken to go ahead, although one lesson was learnt, i.e. they were launched closer to shore on D-Day, allowing them to "wade" rather than sail.

In the trial forming part of Exercise Smash on 4 April 1944, the tanks left their landing craft just before dawn after a night at sea, two miles from shore. Sadly, the weather worsened shortly after they set off, six men drowned and the remains of seven sunken tanks are on the seabed to this day. Of the six men lost, only one has a known grave, at Highcliffe. Six tank wrecks have been reported in Studland Bay and one in Poole Bay.

All have been plotted on Fig.31 from published co-ordinates. One eye witness account talks of a bow strut breaking and then a wave approaching three or four feet above the height of the canvas screen, the men being trapped by the rest of the broken framework and sinking to about 25 feet depth. The Navy blew up five of them, having taken a dim view of a diver retrieving live ammunition in 1989, but the others may still be intact. Since the remains are on flat sand, they attract conger eels, crabs and lobsters. Nonetheless, divers have brought up many finds such as half a goggle, a shaving brush, a razor and shoe brushes.

There was a memorial stone to the six men unveiled at a well-attended Studland Remembrance Service on the sixtieth anniversary of the tragedy, 4 April 2004. The unveiling was performed by General Sir Robert Ford, who, as Lieutenant Ford managed to free his legs (initially trapped by the canvas screen) and rise to the surface in 1944. A Mark IX DD tank was offloaded at Studland beach as part of the event. Bovington Tank Museum had this only known surviving Valentine temporarily on display in June 2004. It had been restored by an enthusiast and now travels the country to various exhibitions.

Aircraft crashes and other disasters

It is both little known and surprising how many aircraft disasters took place. Reports of incidents in the Hengistbury general area are available from various logs etc:

- On 22 June 1940, a parachute flare was reported falling in the direction of Hengistbury Head and an explosion heard.
- On 14 August 1940, a Hurricane, P3310, came down when Sgt. G. Atkinson baled out after combat with Do17s at 0700 hours. Some of these reports (including this one) are acknowledged from *Franks N.L.R.: RAF Fighter Command Losses of the Second World War. Volume 1-3. Operational Losses. 1997-2000.*
- On 24 September 1940, an unknown aircraft crashed into the sea 10 to 12 miles @ 165° due to an air battle.
- On 1 October 1940, two unknown aircraft went into the sea due to an air battle: one six miles @ 140° and one nine miles @ 190°.
- On 1 October 1940, a plane is reported down in sea at 1055 hours east of south of Hengistbury Head, firing heard just before. No one baled out.
- It is reported that anti-aircraft guns on the cliffs brought down two German planes, including one, which crashed into the sea off Hengistbury on 1 December 1940. Another report for the same date confirms that AA guns shot down two planes, but also says Hurricanes shot down four other planes, of which three fell inland and one "in the sea off Hengistbury."
- On 10 March 1941, two explosions were heard and bombs reported as dropping in the sea off Hengistbury Head.
- On 13 March 1941, an unknown aircraft believed to be a German bomber crashed into the sea four to five miles @ 120° in flames after being in action with a night fighter.
- On 11 April 1941, an unknown aircraft believed to be a German bomber crashed into the sea four miles @ 200° in flames.
- The George Medal was awarded to Lieutenant Andrew Watson for an attempted rescue on 28 April 1941 of RAF Pilot Officer James. His Fairey Battle aircraft crashed into the sea off the Head after he had been forced to bale out. Sadly, Lieutenant Watson had to give up his rescue attempt due to exhaustion in the cold water and the impossibility of freeing the pilot from his parachute. Moreover, he had to be rescued himself on the swim back to shore. On the basis of the reported position alone, this must have been an extraordinary and dangerous rescue attempt.
- The remains of a bomber, thought by divers to be probably a Halifax, were found in 1975. As the co-ordinates are so similar, it may well be a different type of aircraft, mentioned next. Wreckage of a World War II Whitley bomber was found in 1981. The position of the wreck *believed* to be a Halifax was 50 36.70N; 01 46.79W. That for the wreck *identified* as a Whitley was 50 36.75N; 01 46.80W. I have used the latter for the Fig.31 schedule. It is classified as a dangerous wreck by UKHO. Little of the main fuselage then remained, the largest pieces being the engine nacelles and wings. It was reported as being "close west of telecom cable". Fig.31 shows cables as "vvvvvvvv" up to the 20-metre depth line running towards the plot of this wreck.
- The remains of a Spitfire have been found on Christchurch Ledge near the Beer Pan Rocks.
- On 23 August 1943, a Spitfire Mark BS115 "V" from 616 Squadron went into the sea when on an early

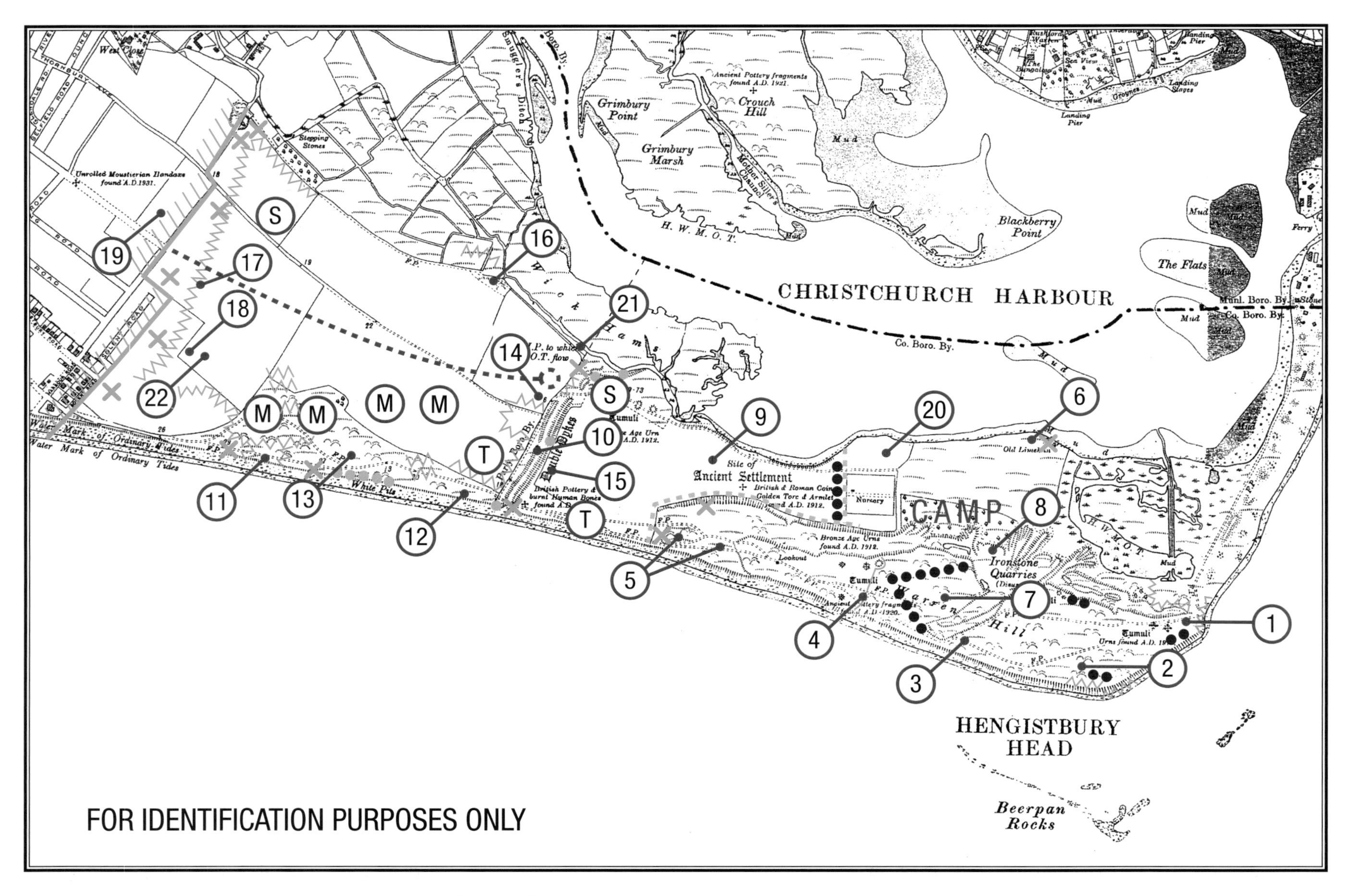

Fig.40 ***World War II installations at Hengistbury Head***

(Reproduced from the Ordnance Survey map of 1932. © Crown Copyright. 1/10,560 scale before reduction. Also by agreement of RAF Museum and M. A. Edgington)

After the war, there was a big programme of reinstatement at Hengistbury. The use had been very extensive, including a lot of smaller installations not even shown here.

Key to World War II Military Installations to be removed Schedule of Dilapidations and layout Plan dated 12 April 1948

1	12 weapons' pits and brick building with 13 1/2 inch thick walls	11	Searchlight emplacement
2	10 weapons' pits	12	Camouflaged radar enclosure
3	2 Bofors' gun sites	13	Fire control building, 2 gun emplacements, brick sheds, nissen huts at White Pits
4	570 foot irregular communicating trench	14	Standby set
5	2 Vickers' gun sites	15	PLUTO base including R.C. engine bases
6	2 weapons' pits	16	2 Vickers' gun sites and radar enclosure
7	Trenches and 20 weapons' pits at Warren Hill	17	Guard huts
8	Dugouts and 12 weapons' pits at Batters	18	Signals enclosure
9	Practice trenches and 5 weapons' pits at Long Field	19	Saxon King public house site
10	3 railway rails, 13 weapons' pits, trenches, at the Dykes	20	Septic tank for Officers' Mess
		21	Brick ammunition store
		22	Vickers' gun site

(T)	Wooden tower
(M)	Steel mast (250 feet)
×	Pillbox
(S)	Squatters
WWWW	Defence wire
CAMP	14 buildings served by foul and surface water sewers draining into harbour and 4 buildings including Officers' Mess to the north
········	Anti-tank ditching
●●●●●	Mine craters
●●●●●	Dragons' teeth

This sort of plan and schedule is simply a list of instructions to a contractor, i.e. a specification for reinstating Hengistbury to its peacetime use of public open space. Although the schedule is stated to be approximate only, the surprisingly large military presence is made clear. I am providing merely a summary of the 274 instructions. There were for instance 86 weapons pits, only some of which are mentioned here. In addition, there are indications that certain decommissioning work had already been done, e.g. the mast in Barn Field is not included.

morning shipping recce. Flight Sergeant R.T. Wright was rescued. Location reported was the same as the Hurricane P3310 mentioned above.

- On 26 January 1944, a line of flares @ 270° and three miles was seen. The crashed aircraft was later identified as a Halifax bomber, with a crew of six. Three bodies were recovered and taken away by RAF Hurn.
- On 12 June 1944, a Typhoon MN 115 1b aircraft came down. Flight Lieutenant J.G. Gohl of the RCAF encountered flak, his engine failed but he did not survive after baling out. As for many wrecks, it is not possible to be absolutely sure about the facts. For example, UKHO information is not quite definitive with a query on the date as "1945?" and the position quality as "unreliable". Nonetheless, this is plotted on Fig.31 as near to Old Harry. In a dive in 1970, the only recognisable part was the engine.

From Fig.41, large radar towers can be seen on both sides of the Dykes. Another installation was a large circular petrol storage tank. This item arises from local recollection only, since it does not appear on the sketch, possibly because it was only in place for about two years up to 1944.

The Head was used as an army training area. Fig.43 shows infantry scaling the sandy slope in a mock attack on the coast defence battery at the top, operated by 554 Coast Regiment Royal Artillery. On 19 April 1941, the coastal battery opened up on E-boats, as they laid magnetic mines. French Canadian forces used the Head as a

Fig.41 ***Radar towers at Double Dykes, 1940s***
(Reproduced by consent of Red House Museum)
An aerial photograph showing also the general military occupation including, for example, even the dragons' teeth in the inner dyke, which also appear as item 127 in Fig.42.

"battle inoculation" ground, including mortar practice and a field firing range. The 7th (Boscombe) Battalion of the Home Guard, including a total of 80 men, was trained to man the coastal guns to relieve the regular crews.

On a different note, Stanpit Marsh and Wick Fields were both municipal rubbish tips before and during the War. Exercises were held by the respective Home Guards of Bournemouth and Christchurch, rehearsing the responses to a German invasion. For this purpose, firing was not allowed, with the participants shouting "bang" and a nominated umpire on each side of the water deciding just who had been shot. For one special policeman, it was a big enough joke to be put on the "rubbish tip beat", quite apart from the inevitable hilarity of repelling invaders or otherwise by determining which shouted "bangs" were fatal! Consistent with this lack of ammunition, is another local recollection about a company of the regular army, which used to muster at the corner of Dalmeny and Harbour Roads. It was very noticeable that post Dunkirk in 1940 they were ill equipped for several months, implying that small arms would have been initially too scarce to supply the Home Guard.

Two large guns (presumably part of reference 13 from Fig.40) protected the low ground, from Solent Road to the Dykes. According to a resident in the road, the one time they were fired, most of the windows of the houses were blown out or cracked! From another source, I gather that these may have been two of the 5.5-inch guns from the aircraft carrier *HMS Furious*. This ship had three major re-constructions such that the ten 5.5-inch guns fitted in 1917 had been replaced with different armament by 1932. It is still extraordinary to think that White Pits (whose shape has stayed unchanged since 1811, Fig.10) has probably seen the deployment of 1917 era heavy naval guns from what was originally a 31.5 knot carrier of 19,513 tons. For some time, a Tuckton butcher in the Home Guard commanded the battery. Whether he was personally responsible for firing the shells of some 85 lbs. that may have caused the window damage, I do not know!

Ammunition was assembled and dismantled for the gun shells at the site of what is now the Hengistbury Head Centre. Restrictions were in place on this parcel of land until decontamination had been completed after the War. I understand, from different sources, that the Point House Café at the end of Harbour Road was either a NAAFI or the HQ of military security. Perhaps it was both. A metalled road ran from here past the Dykes right up to the base of the Head. Anti-aircraft guns on the Head itself were removed, but their bases remained until they slid over the cliff edge.

The only war damage close to the Head, to my knowledge, is a fractured water main caused by a high explosive bomb at Broadway and some craters in fields near to Wicklea Road. There was however an accident at Mudeford. One local report, from November 1944, is a little enigmatic: "The largest number of casualties occurred as a result of an accident in the Mudeford area in June 1944, when 16 persons lost their lives, 23 were injured and 130 properties were damaged. Among the killed was one air raid warden on duty." It may be the same event as reported by the *Christchurch Times* on 1,8,15 July 1944 and 9 September 1944. A pilot over-shot the runway, when failing to take off, and ran into a bungalow. Fuel tanks and bombs on board exploded, bringing down a Thunderbolt. A fireman and civilians in the bungalow were killed. The final casualty list given was 16 dead as above and 18 injured. A separate report explains that on 29 June 1944, Lt. James was flying a Thunderbolt carrying a full war-load on two occasions and both times failed to rise at the end of his take-off. At midday, he crashed into one bungalow in Foxwood Avenue and one hour later, in a different Thunderbolt crashed into another. At one point, an unstable bomb, lying in the road exploded, killing many rescuers. It has been surmised that the accidents were caused by excessive throttle, which caused detonation and loss of power.

Christchurch Airfield, which had a fairly short life from 1934 to 1968, made a big contribution to the war effort. There was an air force base and radar research facility. The factory made 550 Oxfords for the RAF and 670 Horsa gliders and converted 160 Spitfires to Seafires for the Fleet Air Arm. It was never bombed, perhaps because the camouflaged extensions of local roads prevented the Germans from identifying it.

The Mudeford huts had to be vacated for the duration. Indeed, at least six of the vacant huts were taken by the servicemen to the top of the Head to provide accommodation with easy access to the Watch House. Two others were bought by a local family for ten shillings each and relocated by boat to Christchurch itself. At the time of Dunkirk, there was a clear sense of urgency, panic even, due to the expectation of invasion. One local illustration here is that the Derhams were living in a timber bungalow built in 1936 on Avon Beach. Since it obstructed an army lookout point, they were given 72 hours to move out before it was demolished!

As part of wartime security, not only were the public excluded, but whole areas were mined. In the race against time with imminent expectation of invasion, it was not possible to do everything correctly, such as always having plans of mined areas, on-site safety precautions etc. At all events, on one occasion, a lorry strayed off-road on to a landmine. It was a contractor bringing materials for pillbox construction. The explosion blew the driver out of the vehicle, but luckily he did recover from concussion in a few days and without lasting damage. However, the nearside front tyre was apparently blown right over the roof of the ranger's cottage!

Aftermath and restoration

There was a continuing safety problem after the war from mines and explosives still in place. RAF sentries were withdrawn by 1946, i.e. before the land was even de-requisitioned. Children wanted to climb the masts, whilst the public was told they "visit at their own risk". What a fantastic temptation it must have been for boys wanting to tackle a mast of 250 feet - and there was a choice of four! They are shown as "M" at White Pits and West Field on Fig.40 and can be seen on the photograph at Fig.44. Eventually, a military unit swept the whole area and declared it safe. Since the anti-personnel mines were too dangerous to handle, a number of craters exist where located mines were blown up on the spot. Indeed, even after the area was declared safe, another sweep proved necessary, because of local knowledge of mines still in place. There was one occasion in about 1948 when the council's ranger Robert Brewer found two boys playing "catch" with a rusted hand grenade. Fortunately, he was able to stop the game before it was dropped to the ground! A number of Nissen huts remained and were soon occupied by nine families. The ranger collected for the council 7s.9d. per week rent from each family, until they were removed.

Up to 1939, the ranger and his wife had operated a café from the barn adjoining the cottage (Fig.14). Although, just after Dunkirk, there was some question of them having to move out to allow military occupation, the Army decided that the ranger's proficiency with a Lee Enfield 303 rifle meant they should stay! The café then proceeded to cater under licence for the troops. Mr. Brewer, the gamekeeper's son, purchased and had erected an asbestos-type Nissen hut shortly after the war for use as a café, together with toilets and cesspool. It can be seen on Fig.41 west of the Dykes, in what is now the car park. Although it was only on a three-year licence from the council, it remained for about 22 years until the new café was built in 1973. It had been thatched by then. Unsurprisingly, business was very brisk indeed. One point of contention with the council was

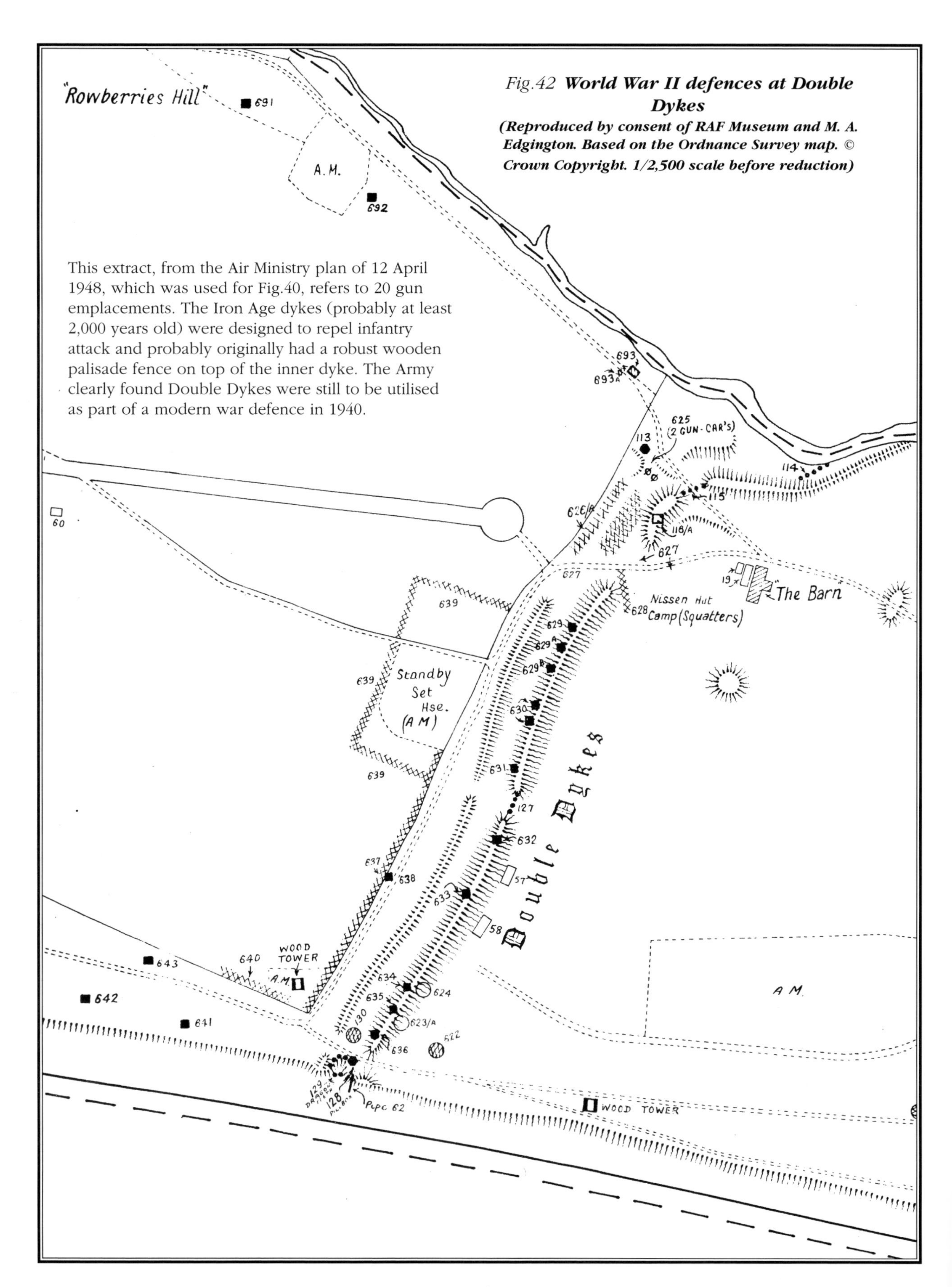

Fig.42 ***World War II defences at Double Dykes***

(Reproduced by consent of RAF Museum and M. A. Edgington. Based on the Ordnance Survey map. © Crown Copyright. 1/2,500 scale before reduction)

This extract, from the Air Ministry plan of 12 April 1948, which was used for Fig.40, refers to 20 gun emplacements. The Iron Age dykes (probably at least 2,000 years old) were designed to repel infantry attack and probably originally had a robust wooden palisade fence on top of the inner dyke. The Army clearly found Double Dykes were still to be utilised as part of a modern war defence in 1940.

KEY TO EXTRACT PLAN FOR WARTIME DEFENCES AT THE DYKES

The following information is taken from the schedule, working down from the north to the south, rather than in number order. In cases where the meaning is unclear, e.g. item 624, the specification for reinstatement is simply repeated.

690	Dugout	15' x 9'
691	Vickers mounting	9' diameter
692	Radar enclosure and Vickers emplacement	
693	Ammunition shed. Brick.	9' x 6'6"
693A	Barb entanglement	
625	2 gun carriages	
113	Pillbox	
114	5 Dragon's teeth	each 6' x 4' x 4'
115	2 Dragon's teeth	each 6' x 4' x 4'
116A	Dugout	
626	Dannert stack	10 tipper loads
626A	Loose dannert	10 tipper loads
627	Railway rails	3
60	Coal yard	50' x 60'
19	Nissen hut C.I. shed	36' x 17' 27' x 9'
628	Defence wire	1 row dannert and double dannert apron
629	2 Weapons pits	each 6' x 5'
629A	Weapons pit	
629B	Weapons pit	
630	2 Weapons pits	each 6' x 5'
639	Double barb defence wire	
127	4 Dragon's teeth	each 6' x 4' x 4'
632	2 Trenches	39' x 3' x 3'
57	PLUTO general base 15 loose PCC blocks	39' x 27' x 1'6"(?) each 7' x 1'6" x 1'6"
633	Weapon pit	9' x 6'
637	Defence wire	3 rows dannert and loose barb double apron
638	Weapon pit	30' x 9'

58	PLUTO general base 2 RC engine bases 4 RC engine bases P.C.C.	33' x 27' x 1'6"(?) each 12' x 5'6 x 1'2" each 4' x 14' x 8" 30' x 3'6" x 6"
634	2 Weapons pits	each 6' x 3'
624	Cutting (now with seat in it) revetting subsided, return to toe of bank, by bulldozer	40 cubic yards
635	2 Weapons pits	each 6' x 3'
623A	Weapon pit	6' x 3'
636	3 Weapons pits	each 6' x 6'
130	Dannert wire stack	20 tipper loads
622	Dannert wire stack	40 tipper loads
640	50 yards loose dannert wire	1 tipper load
643	Irregular trench	75' x 4' x 4'
642	A.M. will extend trench to include 2 drainage pits and Vickers gun mounting	
641	On cliff, half octagonal trench	bulldoze 111' x 3' x 2'6"
129	8 Dragon's teeth on cliff (low place)	each 6' x 4' x 4'
128	Pillbox.	Soon going to collapsc.
62	Pipeline	Two 4" pipes, each 60' long
621	Dannert wire stack	20 tipper loads

Fig.43
Royal Artillery defence battery Warren Hill and mock attack by 12th Battalion, Hampshire Regiment, 1940s
(Dorset's War Diary by Rodney Legg [Dorset Publishing Company])
Troops are scaling the sandy cliffs of Warren Hill, to practice taking the battery at the top.

that the cesspool took waste from the general public as well as from patrons of the café, but the cost of emptying up to twice a week was fully borne by the proprietor. No doubt this factor was mentioned at every rent review!

Despite the 1948 schedule of works in Fig.40, there were still wartime relics to be removed in 1953, such as the anti-tank blocks by the Dykes. From around that time, I can also recall pillboxes, which had clearly been used as latrines. But virtually all signs of the war (with one possible exception) have now gone. An exception is the huge quantity of scaffold poles set into the beach below Warren Hill. This anti-invasion measure was never removed. They might be visible again in the event of a very low tide and sand level, but it is unlikely in view of the effectiveness of both the Long Groyne as a retainer of sand and the beach replenishment programmes.

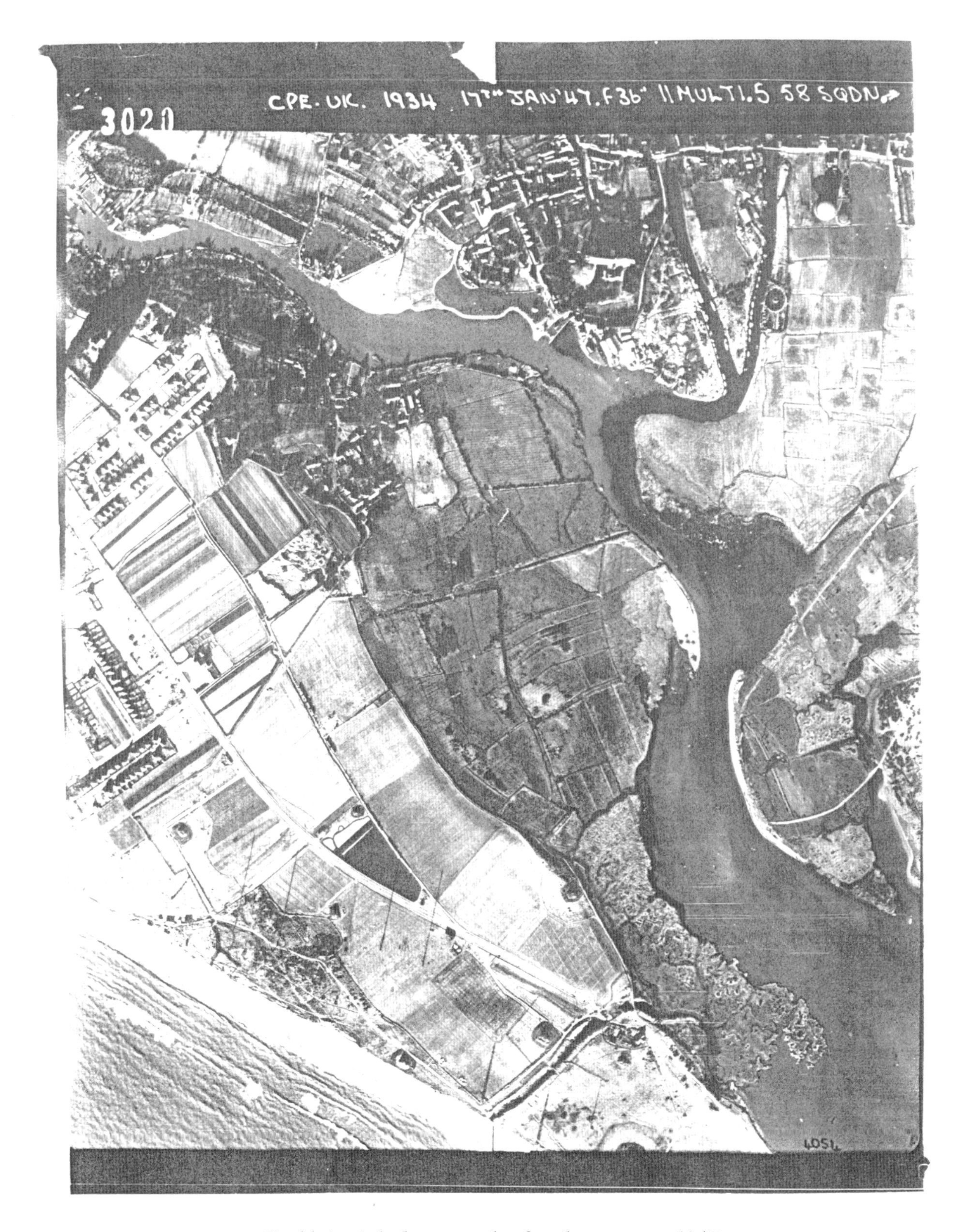

Fig.44 ***Aerial photograph of radar towers, 1947***

(Reproduced by consent of English Heritage [NMR] RAF Photography)

Apart from the two wooden towers either side of the Dykes (shown more clearly in Fig.41) the four tall radar masts can be seen. RAF Southbourne was a major installation, used both as a Chain Home Radar Station and to prevent the Germans using radio beams to help navigate their bombers to the West Midlands.

TEN

WILDLIFE

In all things of nature, there is something of the marvellous

Aristotle

HENGISTBURY is a natural migration spot for birds and insects both for arrival and departure. It is also notable for having a great variety of habitats. Some enthusiasts think of it as a great out-door biological laboratory.

Part of the management job is to promote wildlife and conserve it. A dramatic instance was the 1976 damming of the old quarry to create Quarry Pond (Fig.37), an attractive new freshwater habitat. The acidic run-off prevents pond weed from thriving, but algae will change the colour from blue to green in the Spring.

Birds

To give an idea of the variety of birds, which can be spotted, in the area, I have included a list in the Appendix, although it is unlikely to be exhaustive.

There are over 300 birds at Hengistbury, amounting to more than half of the United Kingdom list. The local bird-watching group (web site address in the Appendix) is well organised and very keen. The web site identifies the nine best sites for bird watching around the harbour, and explains how to obtain its annual report, which includes sections on both bird ringing and butterflies. In 2001, it noted that 217 bird species were spotted. There is also an excellent illustrated council publication *Birds of Hengistbury Head*, available from the ranger's office.

As an indication of the way in which information is available to an enthusiast with Internet access, I set out below a typical day's report from the Head:

> *October 17th*
>
> A fairly settled day with a good selection of birds. There are now 4 Bearded Tit in the HHC reedbed and a Short-eared Owl was quartering the same area this morning. A Little Owl has also been seen around Wick Fields over the last couple of days. 2 Firecrest are still present in the Wood along with 35 Chiffchaff, but Goldcrest numbers are reduced. Easterly visible migration was recorded as 800 Goldfinch, 600 Linnet, 500 Chaffinch, 350 Meadow Pipit, 300 Greenfinch, 300 alba Wagtail, 180 Siskin, 76 Swallow, 45 Reed Bunting, 25 Brambling, 23 Rook, 11 Golden Plover, 11 House Martin and 7 Jackdaw. Moving north-west were 163 Skylark, 50 Song Thrush, 11 Redwing, 5 Mistle Thrush and 1 Ring Ouzel.

A few examples of the bird-life follow. Herons fish in the creek north-east of the ranger's cottage. Reed Warblers and Reed Buntings nest in the reeds during the summer fringing the nearby saltmarsh, which is also home to the Kingfisher. Mudflats are sites for the Black-headed and Herring Gulls and waders such as the Redshank, Curlew and Oystercatcher to rest and feed. Cormorants are regularly fishing for eels and flatfish. Walking on by the south harbour edge, Swans, Coot and Mallard may be seen, and Terns in the summer, visiting from Africa's west coast. Entering the woods, Green Woodpeckers may be seen nesting by making deep holes in White Poplars. Magpies and Chaffinches may be seen or heard, as well as Blue Tits and Great Tits. Sparrowhawks attack other birds, even Woodpigeons, in the woods. Sand Martins, which live in the yellow sand at the top of Warren Hill cliff, may be seen feeding on dragonflies at the Quarry Pond.

Barn Field has many ground nesting skylarks, with their distinctive song. The Meadow Pipit and kestrel may also be seen. Linnets will forage in groups. Brent Geese, which breed in Siberia, visit Stanpit in the winter. Some birds, like the Swift, migrate here from central Africa to raise their young and then return before the winter becomes too cold for them and lacking in food. Others, such as the Teal will come here in the winter to escape the harsh climate of Russia. Ringing the birds will mean that their migration can be established, wherever they are subsequently found in the world.

Plants

If anything, this is an even more specialist field than birds. Much of the Management Plan is rightly concerned to maximise conservation of different species. For example, cattle grazing of salt-marsh habitats will encourage flowering plants and insects. The same applies to the Plan for Stanpit Marsh. I have found a list of the Latin names of over 900 local plants but felt it would be excessive to repeat it here. Moreover, vegetation keeps changing. Anyone interested would be best advised to go on the ranger-led wildlife walks and look at specialist publications.

Again, I should like to give just a few examples. Sea Aster, Sea Lavender and Scurvy Grass are able to withstand the salt water flooding in the harbour. The saltings include Sea Club-rush, Red Fescue, Sea Plantain, Thrift and Strawberry Clover. Reed beds fringe the salt marshes and were historically used for thatching. Near to the south harbour edge, Brambles, White Bryony, Woody Nightshade and Goosegrass co-exist. Areas of spiny scrubland, which include gorse and blackthorn, are important here to give protection and shelter to insects, wood-lice etc. This is because the migrating birds need such small animals. Ling, Bell Heather, Heath Bedstraw and Sheep's Sorrel favour the acid soil east of the Dykes. Birdsfoot-trefoil and Stitchwort can also be found in Barn Field.

In the main woodland area, just east of the Nursery Garden, are trees, which provide a home for birds and insects. They include English Oak, Holm Oak, White Poplar, Silver Birch, Sallow, Spindle, Pine and Alder. The Garden, which is closed to the public, is important both for the feeding and shelter of the migrating birds and for other wildlife. It is shielded by being in the lee of the headland and by tall conifers. Honeysuckle grows on oak and gives out a strong scent, which attracts moths at night. Ivy also climbs these trees, giving shelter to some small animals as it does so. Foxglove, Speedwell and Violet thrive in woodland clearings. The fairly level area at the top of Warren Hill is heathland, which features dwarf scrub dominated by different heathers. These include Ling, Bell Heather, Cross-leaved Heath and Gorse. Bracken can be seen back from the cliff. Due to water percolating through the north cliff face of Warren Hill, the land changes from dry heath, to wet heath, to bog as you move from top to bottom. Hence the bog area has Sphagnum and Cotton Grass, whilst the dry slopes support, for example, Wavy Hair-grass. The deep-rooting sand dune plant, Marram Grass, helps the stability of the sandy face of Warren Hill. The same applies to the base of the cliff west of Long Groyne. Trampling of dune grasses will always inhibit such creation of "new land."

Insects

There are almost endless varieties of aphids, beetles, bugs, spiders, and flies. As above, a few examples will have to suffice.

Butterflies include the three common Whites, Brimstone, Skippers, Peacock, Grayling, Comma, Speckled Wood, Common Blue, Green Hairstreak, Meadow Brown, Small Heath, Small Tortoiseshell and Hedge Brown. The Red Admiral, Painted Lady and Clouded Yellow generally migrate across the Channel in spring, but die out in the winter. The Meadow Grasshopper and Field Grasshopper frequent the grasslands of Hengistbury, whilst the Lesser Marsh Grasshopper lives on the saltmarshes. There are also bush-crickets and cockroaches (although not the domestic pest variety).

Dragonflies and Mosquitoes are common, particularly at Quarry Pond and Lily Pond. Quarry Pond is a freshwater, acidic habitat since the water running down from the heath is acidic. As such, it does not encourage pond weeds. Lily Pond is especially suited to insects such as the Greater Water Boatman, Pond Skater and Whirligig, a type of beetle. Different Damselflies, including the dramatic Common Blue, are common. Incidentally, the Damselfly is much smaller than the various types of Hawker and Darter Dragonflies, being only a little over one inch in length and less bulky. The other two species can be up to three inches and the Hawker can have a wingspan of four inches. Many creatures hibernate in the pond mud over winter.

Moths and their larvae are very important to other animals, like birds, bats, lizards, spiders and dragonflies, which feed on them. There are hundreds of species including Pale Tussock, Lackey Moth, Puss Moth, Large Emerald, Gold Swift, Drinker, Cream-spot Tiger and Six-spot Burnet. Some are resident and some migrant. This is a study in its own right.

The Bloody-nosed Beetle, so called as it emits red droplets, is common during spring and summer. The carnivorous Green Tiger Beetle occupies the heathland, the one-inch Violet Ground-beetle lives in bushes, the Sexton Beetle scavenges under carcasses, the Black-tipped Soldier favours the flower of the Ragwort: and so it goes on. Others found at the Head include the Great Diving Beetle, Minotaur, Cockchafer, Spotted Longhorn and Black Burying Beetle. There are countless more for the naturalist to study.

Reptiles and snakes

Sun-basking Adders frequent the heath, but are unlikely to be seen if you keep to the footpaths. Recognition of this poisonous snake, generally less than 18 inches long, is by a zigzag on the back. It should not bite unless you step on it. The well camouflaged, tail-shedding Common Lizard is often visible in the heather and can grow to six inches. Although it is shaped like a snake, the Slow-worm is actually a lizard that likes to get under stones or pieces of wood and can live over 30 years. The harmless, swimming Grass-Snake is less commonly found.

Seashore habitat

Although many creatures are very small indeed, it remains a fact that there is a greater variety on the shore than on land. Seaweed gives essential shelter to most of them. Various wracks, such as the Spiralled Wrack and Knotted Wrack, grow in the area between low and high tide lines. Other seaweeds are Sea Lettuce, red seaweeds and Bootlace Weed.

Breadcrumb Sponge spreads over rocks and Sea-squirt has been seen on the Long Groyne. Lug Worm and Rag Worm are dug from the sands as fishing bait. Sea Mouse, Keel Worm and the carnivorous Bootlace Worm, which can get to 13 feet in length, have also been found. Jellyfish, sea-anemones and starfish live near the shore. The Coat-of-mail Shell, which is similar to a woodlouse, clings to the ironstones at low tide. Mussels and the yellow eggs of Dog Whelk exist on the Long Groyne. Univalves found include Limpets, Winkles and Whelks. Bivalves, where the shell is in two parts, include Mussels, Oysters, Scallops, Cockles and Razors. Cuttlebones, the internal shells of Cuttlefish, are a common sight on the beach. Sometimes, what looks like a bunch of black grapes appears after a storm. These are the eggs, which opened up reveal fully formed Cuttlefish complete with tentacles.

As for other forms of sea life, crustaceans are well represented. The Acorn Barnacle attaches to rocks and the Goose Barnacle is found on driftwood. The Sand Hopper and Common Shrimp can be seen, together with lobsters and quite a variety of crabs. Different species of fish come to this area including Sharks, Dogfish, Skate, Sting Ray, Plaice, Red Mullet, Wrasse, Salmon and many, many more. The more unusual include the Sea Horse and Greater Pipe Fish. The Lesser Weever often lies buried in sand and has been known to sting anyone unfortunate enough to step on to its poisonous spine.

Other animals

Water voles live in the banks on the harbour edge. Woodmice, shrews, rabbits, and moles are not uncommon. Hedgehogs, brown rats, voles and bats have been seen at Hengistbury. The Weasel and Stoat are known to breed here. In Barn Field, the scent of the fox can sometimes be recognised early in the morning. There have been reports of the Grey Seal and the Common Seal at Barn Bight.

A particularly important feature is the successful reintroduction in 1989 of the endangered Natterjack Toad, which disappeared from the harbour in the 1950s and was thought to be extinct. It has been provided with two fenced habitats, one at White Pits, the other on the south side of the track, which ascends Warren Hill from the west. Established populations have thereby been created for this threatened species and, for good measure, spawn provided to three artificial nursery pools at Stanpit Marsh.

Leatherback turtle

These creatures, which are the largest of the seven types of turtle worldwide, can have a flipper span of ten feet and weigh up to 18 cwt. They migrate annually from the Caribbean. Only five types visit the United Kingdom. In August 2002, a crab fisherman thought he had spotted an upturned dinghy a mile out from Hengistbury. This is not surprising as the shell looks like ship lap boarding. It was happily among a swarm of its favourite prey, the large Rhizo-stoma jellyfish. The Marine Conservation Society published a new UK Turtle Code in 2002, which encourages us to report all sightings. Although they go back 23 million years, this is a critically endangered species, with a world population of nesting females estimated at only 26,000. They often die from entanglement in buoy ropes, from eating marine litter such as plastic bags (which they mistake for jellyfish) from being unlawfully fished for their meat and eggs, and from pollution.

Christchurch Ledge

In 1985, a SCUBA survey was carried out for the government. It identified the Ledge as running for three miles SW of the Head and separating Poole Bay (up to 66 feet deep) from Christchurch Bay (up to 33 feet deep). This general point that Christchurch Bay is about half the depth of Poole Bay is evident from the depths shown on the Admiralty Chart extract Fig.31. The same can be said of the length of the Ledge at three miles. A great variety of fauna were mentioned, including crab, lobster, mussel, anemone, barnacle, starfish, tube worm, etc.

Pilot whale at White Pits

During the war, there was a practice of securing specimens or portions of fish, such as whales and porpoises, for the Natural History Museum in London. When a whale was discovered, a telegram was duly sent in December 1943. Condition was fair and no examples of damage or injuries were found. It was white lower half, dark grey upper half, 11 feet in length, several teeth 1/2 inch wide in lower jaw and emitting a high smell. On Christmas Eve, the Museum sent a telegram asking to be sent the lower jaw, and this was done.

The whale was found on the beach about 3/4 mile west of the Hengistbury Head lookout. It was buried the same distance west of the lookout and 100 yards inland on top of the cliff. I make this about 100 yards east of the south-eastern corner of Solent Beach car park, within White Pits.

ELEVEN

CHRISTCHURCH HARBOUR AND VICINITY

EXCELLENT SEA BATHING may be obtained at this
Delightful Watering-place
HOT BATHS AT A SHORT NOTICE
Visitors are also supplied with hot water and tea services at
very reasonable charges, by
JANE WEST, Conductor of the Baths, MUDEFORD

Christchurch Times 1855

BY any standards, the view from the top of Warren Hill across the harbour is quite superb. One can see from the White Bear at the Needles, out to sea and round to the Isle of Purbeck, the conurbation of Poole and Bournemouth, St. Catherine's Hill, the town of Christchurch and the Priory, the harbour itself with sandbanks, small boats and Stanpit Marsh, and finally, still turning clockwise, Mudeford Sandbank, Mudeford Quay and the sweep of Christchurch Bay out to Highcliffe. Historically, as we shall see, none of this has restrained those anxious to "improve" the harbour since the seventeenth century.

Over the greater part of the harbour, depth does not exceed some four feet, as might be expected perhaps of a drowned shallow river valley. At low tides, the gulls are seen walking over great mud flats, the main one being in a crescent shape just inside the harbour entrance. The exceptions to the rule about depth are the deep-water channel marked by red and green buoys, and the Run. Even the smallest boats risk grounding if they stray from this channel at low tides and the sailing clubs race dinghies only at high tides. Even at high tides, a dinghy can easily ground in places, such as approaching Blackberry Point. If there is a combination of high barometric pressure and reduced flow from the rivers due to an absence of rain, water level can be much less than shown in the tide tables. River alluvium, which is a deposit of silty mud, has created Wick Hams, Salt Hurns and Stanpit Marsh since the end of the Ice Age. The mud is deposited simply because the speed of the water has slowed down, so preventing it staying in suspension.

The Run should be treated with great caution due to its fast water. Anyone entering the harbour needs to know the state of tide in relation to the boat's ability to contest it. For instance, a sailing dinghy is generally unable to get in against a strong ebb tide. One curious result of a low sea tide is that the harbour cannot clear itself fast enough, causing the water level to be higher at the Haven compared to the entrance further east: a true case of sloping water!

A lot of works have been carried out over the years, with various effects. Dredging the main channel has slowed the water from around eight knots to five in the Run. Raising the height of the banks, due to the rubbish tips on both sides, has increased flood risk due to the loss of some flood plain area. In turn, more defence has been installed, such as bunding, particularly since the big flood of the 1979/1980 winter. I understand that in the nineteenth century the Run was several feet deeper, and the harbour generally was deeper. Although hard to imagine, it has even been reported in more recent times that people have been able to walk across to the Sandbank in only twelve inches of water at a low spring tide.

Jane West, from the advertisement above, claimed to be greatly concerned about public decency, but some said that she was simply trying to secure her one-shilling hire charge for each changing hut. She pressed Sir George Rose to be a "constable" of the shore at Mudeford. This he did most willingly. However, a "very stout agricultural couple" took against her on being required to hire two huts at a shilling each, instead of just one. They declined, undressed close to the cliff and were later spotted in a state of nature disporting themselves amongst the billows! Presumably, the huts had superseded the bathing machines shown around this location in the Fanshawe painting of 1811 (Fig.12).

Management of the Harbour

The harbour can be thought of as roughly divided into four quarters:

- NE owned by the Crown and within Christchurch borough.
- SE owned by the Crown and within Bournemouth borough.
- NW owned by Bournemouth and West Hampshire Water Company and within Christchurch borough.
- SW owned by Bournemouth and West Hampshire Water Company and within Bournemouth borough.

The boundary between the boroughs is clear from the Ordnance Survey maps, e.g. Fig.27, and that between east and west by the yellow buoys, which also mark the eastern end of the Royalty Fishery. They run from Holloway's Cut to Inveravon on the north side. Crown ownership always applies to land below Low Water Mark. It has meant that Christchurch has had to lease from the Meyrick Estate that land between High and Low Water Marks.

In the future, there may be a formal management plan for the harbour itself. Dorset Coast Forum meets regularly to plan management action. A Christchurch Harbour sub-group has been considering the idea of such a management plan for the harbour bed, at the request of the Environment Agency. For example, they would like the Water Company, which owns the freehold of this Site of Special Scientific Interest (SSSI) to manage the moorings to cause minimum environmental impact, by the development of a harbour management plan.

As applies to Hengistbury, the biggest single problem relates to resolving the conflict between public use and conservation, recreational use and the natural environment. English Nature maintain strict control of a SSSI, meaning for example that old trailers and boats have to be cleared away from the harbour edge gravel in front of beach huts. That SSSI extends as far as the edge of the tarmac access road. The water company has agreed with English Nature not to increase the number of moorings in the harbour.

Christchurch Council polices the harbour speed limit of four knots from a boat based at the Civic Offices. As users of powered watercraft are in touch with each other by mobile phone, the boat turns up for enforcement purposes somewhat at random. A recent prosecution involved a fine of £650 plus costs for a jetski rider, who came through the Run at about 35 knots. The owner of a rigid inflatable doing 37 knots through the channel by the Hengistbury Head Centre was fined £500 plus £100 costs.

There are always jobs to be done to keep up standards. For instance, underwater small boat wrecks need to be removed from time to time and silt needs to be removed from beneath the moorings. There is also the deep-water channel to monitor for location and against silting up. Despite local concern, it currently tends to clear itself naturally every March to an adequate depth for craft, albeit in a somewhat different position. Although not completely accurate, the red and green marker buoys are generally kept in place. The channel was last dredged in 1983, but there have been plans for a dredging scheme that would deepen the mid-harbour bar near the Hengistbury Head Centre by about four inches, and widen the navigation channel to something over 100 feet. There was successful opposition to the planning application for the consequent spoil deposit at Grimbury, with the committee apparently swayed by talk of the harbour channel being used by Brittany Ferries.

Management of Mudeford Sandbank

The Sandbank is now designated as a Site of Nature Conservation Interest (SNCI) on a voluntary basis. However, if English Nature felt it was needed, it could easily be upgraded to a full SSSI and a much greater measure of control. Management must for example be sympathetic to Seaknot Grass, a South African species of international importance. I am told that it came from ships arriving in Christchurch from South Africa that dumped sand ballast containing the grass.

Certain relevant historical background is given in the Management Plan of 2001, which exists to protect the coast, restrict development and maintain the character of the Sandbank. The harbour had a deltaic mouth in the sixteenth century and Hengistbury Head was twice the current size. The Sandbank was created from the downdrift of Bournemouth beaches, with dunes developing more than twenty feet high. An idea of this can be gathered from the 1790 painting (Fig.39) which is consistent with the description in the Smeaton Report of 1762.

Ironstone removal from 1848 to 1856 greatly increased the downdrift, which was only reduced again by the Long Groyne of 1938. Breaches occurred in 1883, 1896, 1911, 1935, 1951, 1960, 1966 and 1976, so causing a temporary island next to the Run. Fig.17 (late 1930s) shows a wide sandspit, owing to sand drifting around the Head, whilst Fig.2 shows it with a long tail, which proved unsustainable. The difficulty of access is shown by a letter from the secretary of Christchurch Sailing Club in January 1911. He explained that the committee wished to obtain a permanent entrance to the harbour. This would assist fishermen, local boat owners and yachtsmen, who would visit the harbour "if only they could get there!"

Apart from the maximum permitted number of 346 privately licensed huts, there are five toilet blocks, the Black House (now holiday flats) and four fishermen's huts. The café, formerly called the Hut, has been upgraded and is now known as the Beach House. A host of management matters have to be in place for the proper enjoyment of the area: restrictions on vehicle movements to the Hut and Black House, allowance of two dinghies per hut, no electricity supply or WC (except a chemical toilet) allowed in any hut, hot showers key-controlled for hut users only, provision of water supply, refuse collection and toilets by council, provision of bottled gas from café, habitat database, ecology survey, crime awareness strategy, phone boxes, mains sewage via a tunnel under the Run to a pumping station on the quay, etc. Since the improved sewage facility was installed in 1999, there is no need for septic tanks and visits by sewage tankers.

The capital spend of £1.5 million in 1999/2000 brought the Sandbank up to the 1 in 200 years storm standard. Although between March and October typically some 1,000 people sleep there, it is not really a safety risk, because the storms and breaches tend to happen in winter. The 200 feet wide beaches on the sea side are designed to be sacrificed in a storm, so exposing the gravel underneath as a sort of rearguard protection. Sand can also be regularly recycled from the tip to the Head, so artificial updrift counters the natural downdrift.

Most of the huts (over 80%) are in the Bournemouth council owned section of the Sandbank. As they provide a considerable income to the tenant, Christchurch council, there will probably be some pressure to increase the head rent paid by Christchurch at lease expiry in 2029, perhaps to a percentage of site profits. Christchurch had a "gross surplus" of £164,810 in 2000/2001. The other 20% of huts, whose occupiers seem to be more local to Hampshire and Dorset, are in the Meyrick-owned section where the head lease to Christchurch does not expire until 2061.

Some say that Bournemouth gets a poor deal here with its low fixed rental income, but this is not fair comment. Christchurch fully supported Bournemouth's purchase from Selfridge in 1930 of Hengistbury Head in a joint negotiation. The risk was that it would be sold off privately for development at a much higher price. The auction particulars were produced and an offer made by local businessmen to Selfridge, well above the price he eventually agreed with Bournemouth. Christchurch pragmatically sacrificed its own ambition to purchase the headland in the expectation of seeing the other council protect it in the future. At least, it was able to buy Stanpit Marsh from Selfridge at the same time. A broad *quid pro quo* for its valuable help to Bournemouth was the lease of the Sandbank, albeit including a clause giving the very costly coastal protection responsibility to Christchurch.

History and management of Mudeford Quay

The name of Mudeford may derive from the need to "ford the Mudie." which could still be difficult at the start of the nineteenth century. A second theory maintains that the name pre-dated the name of the river. On this basis, the real explanation may be that a ford was needed over a muddy place.

Originally, the quay was more of a sandspit than the present car park and buildings, which have since been developed and heavily fortified against the sea. The first building seems to have been erected about 1695 to 1698 and remains to this day as the larger of the two residential terraces. First called the Dutch Houses, it became known later as Haven House and the southern half of it was the Haven House Inn. Together with the second terrace, from the nineteenth century, they became Haven Cottages and are now privately owned. A separate building to the north-east was built in 1830 as a public house, known as Haven House Inn and clearly the trade transferred. It was extended by the present café in 1969. The auction particulars of 1855 (sale by the executors of the late Sir G. Rose) show just two buildings as the Preventive Station and the third one, as the Haven House Inn. The 1846 map (extract in Fig.38 does not extend this far) shows the same situation, with what appears to be a minor sea wall only along the south side. Fig.45 is an early photograph showing just a few buildings at the end of a simple sandbank. Fig.49, a photograph from around 1900, tells the same story, with no sign of the millions since spent on sea defences, car parking and leisure facilities.

Fig.45 ***The Haven, Mudeford, c.1800***

(Reproduced by consent of Classic Pictures)

This was the sort of scene, which probably greeted the revenue men during the Battle of Mudeford in 1784. The still water and land, in the foreground, may imply, consistent with Fig.39, that much erosion of Christchurch Bay was still awaited. At this time, the great shelter, provided by the Head, meant no need for the extensive sea defences of today's quay.

The quay was initially sheltered from the sea by the large mass of the headland and after the erosion, to an extent by the downdrift of sand feeding Mudeford Sandbank. Conditions appeared to impose no need for protection when the Dutch Houses were built. However, sea attack reached a stage in 1935 when the owner, a brewery, had to put in the first piled sea defences. The Long Groyne of 1938 increased vulnerability by greatly restricting the downdrift. By 1951, when the council bought the quay, the 1935 quay wall was no longer adequate and some of Mudeford beach was reclaimed by sheet piling and providing a continuation of the wall. When arrangements were finally in place for the £1.8 million quay reconstruction in 1995, defences had deteriorated to a critical extent. Steel piling was again used, this time silently driven hydraulically, with a reinforced concrete capping beam, tied back and filled, the whole built around existing defences and given an expected life of 64 years.

I have seen the sea come in over the car park from the Run on a number of occasions, as indeed is planned in the design of the latest works. The 2001 Management Plan is reassuring about this slightly unnerving situation, referring to the quay's compliance with 1 in 200 years' events. It also points out the increasing rate of sea level rise (now at over 1.5 feet per century) and the consequent increase in the number of times water will over-wash the quay head in the future.

The Plan for the quay gives a short history. The land was a natural sand and gravel spit, protecting saltings at the end of the seventeenth century. A big section has been reclaimed from the saltings for the dinghy park and picnic area and the old crabbers' quay was built between 1952 and 1964. Other developments are much more recent, such as the Highcliffe Sailing Club (1970), the large fish stall (1979) and the RNLI (1980). The latest development is the new RNLI station, rebuilt in 2003. It also gives details about litter control, general bylaws, restrictions on planning permissions, parking permits, protection of flora and swans, the 28-boat local fishing industry, harbour speed limits, grounds maintenance, and special arrangements for items from seat cleaning and

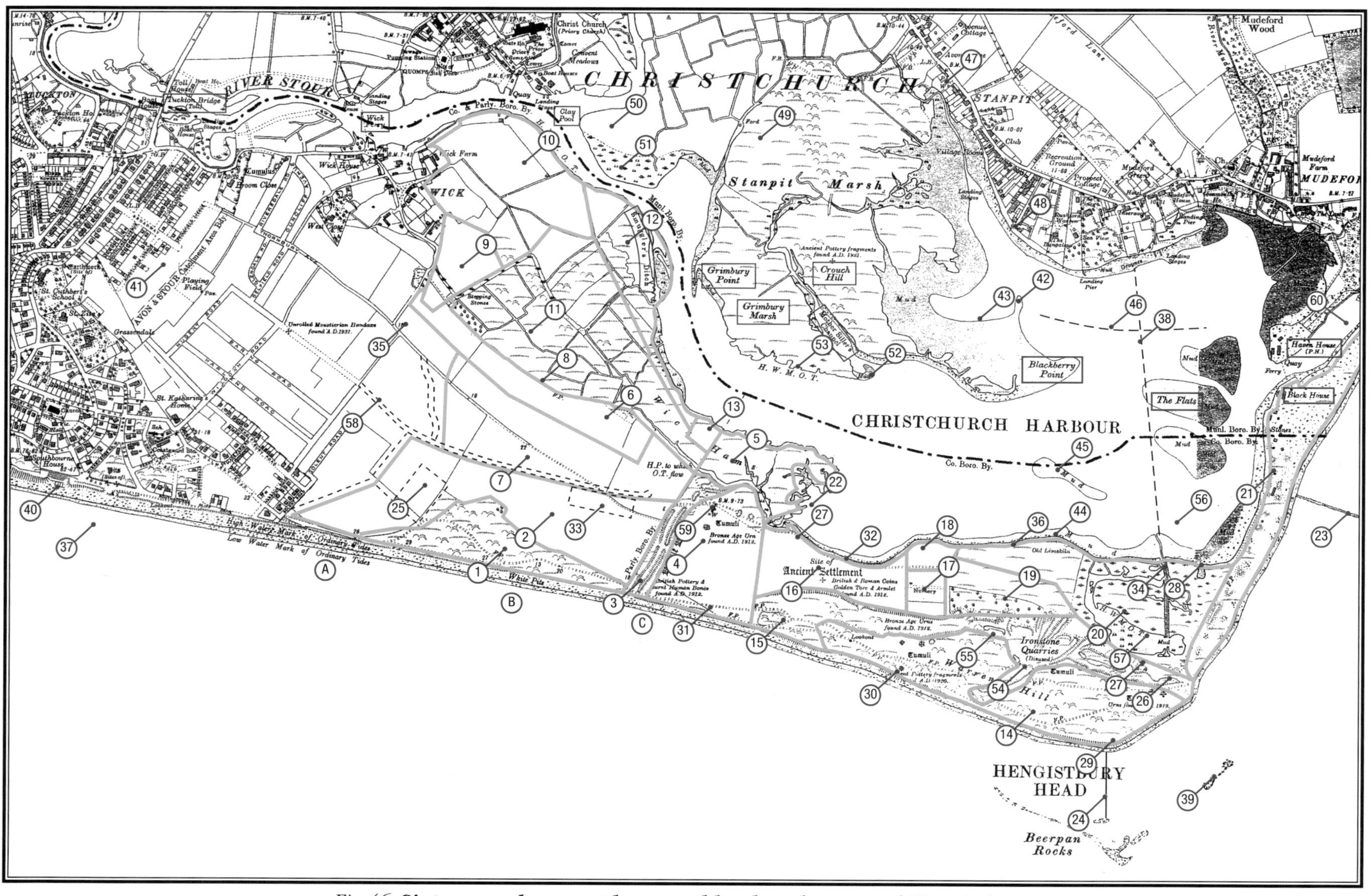

Fig.46 ***Sixty named areas, places and landmarks around Hengistbury***

(Reproduced from the 1932 Ordnance Survey map. © Crown Copyright. 1/10,560 scale before reduction)

Although not all of the names are now common, they are included for completeness and historic interest. Where the printed map gives a name, this has been enclosed in a red box. Those named areas (or land compartments) with heavy borders, such as 2 and 20, coincide with detailed policies in the Management Plan.

Sixty named areas, places and landmarks around Hengistbury

1 WHITE PITS
2 WEST FIELD
3 DOUBLE DYKES
4 BARN FIELD
5 WICK HAMS
6 ROEBURY MEADOW
7 GOLF COURSE
8 ROEBURY LANE
9 DRIVING RANGE
10 WICK FARM MEADOWS
11 WICK FIELDS
12 WICK SPIRES
13 HENGISTBURY HEAD CENTRE
14 WARREN HILL
15 THE BATTERS
16 LONG FIELD
17 NURSERY GARDEN
18 RUSHY PIECE
19 WITHYBED WOOD
20 SALT HURNS
21 MUDEFORD SANDSPIT
22 BARN BIGHT
23 CLARENDON'S OR LONG ROCKS
24 LONG GROYNE
25 SOLENT BEACH CAR PARK
26 STEPS DOWN FROM THE HEAD
27 TARMAC ROAD
28 HARBOUR EDGE FOOTPATH
29 OLD STONE AGE SITE
30 MIDDLE STONE AGE SITE
31 SECONDARY DYKE AND DITCH
32 OLD HOLM OAK SITE
33 HENGISTBURY HEAD CAR PARK
34 HOLLOWAY'S CUT
35 ST. KATHERINE'S SCHOOL
36 COASTGUARD HULK SITE
37 SOUTHBOURNE PIER SITE
38 CROWN - WATER CO. BOUNDARY
39 DANIEL ROCKS
40 SITE OF 6 HOUSES ON FORMER PROMENADE
41 ROLLS' APPROX. CRASH SITE
42 ROCKY BANK
43 SHAG BED
44 OLD LIME KILN
45 FRISCOMB MUD REMAINS
46 HERN CHANNEL
47 TUTTON'S WELL
48 OLD COASTGUARD STATION S.E. OF FISHERMAN'S BANK
49 IRON BOAT
50 PRIORY MARSH
51 GREAT SPIRES
52 SPELLERS POINT
53 BRANDERS BANK
54 QUARRY LAKE
55 LILY POND
56 LOB'S HOLE
57 HOLLOWAY'S DOCK
58 BROADWAY
59 OLD BARN
60 THE RUN

The locations marked 'A', 'B' & 'C' are posts used for measuring cliff and seabed erosion.

woodland management to access to fuel tanks for the Mudeford and District Fishermen's Association. Such unsung work does stop this place of great character becoming messy and unattractive.

The quay is also a Site of Nature Conservation Interest, with the same implications as the Sandbank for greater control by English Nature in the future. Care has therefore to be taken with the Suffocated Clover, which lives in the gravel area of the car park on the quay's SNCI. The 430-space car park is very heavily used (and profitable), creating a need for good management.

Stanpit Marsh

The marsh has been a Local Nature Reserve since 1964 and a Site of Special Scientific Interest, because of its wildlife value, since 1986. It is also a Site of Nature Conservation Interest. The LNR includes Priory Marsh, giving a total area of about 160 acres or 0.25 square miles. It has formed mainly from alluvial mud during the last 4,000 years. In practice, management and conservation are carried out by co-operation between the rangers working for the Christchurch Countryside Service (part of the council) and English Nature. In addition, there is a Stanpit Marsh Warden, partly financed by the Friends of Stanpit Marsh. A strong group of local volunteers are also employed about three times a week. There is the East Dorset Local Group of the RSPB and the Christchurch Conservation Volunteers, who in effect act as assistant wardens. Their conservation events are published on the Greenlink web site (see Appendix).

Compared to Hengistbury Head, Stanpit Marsh is much quieter, feels much more off the beaten track, and there are no plans to carry out any significant form of tourist development.

It is possible to park free by the Scouts' hut in Stanpit and take a very pleasant circular walk around the marsh, of about two miles. The land is generally very low-lying, with somewhat higher sections such as Crouch Hill, which are useful retreats for the horses and cattle. The marsh is regularly flooded, apart from the high ground, at high spring tides, when it is simply not possible to walk the circuit with the water at knee-height in places. I gather that someone has actually rowed from Fisherman's Bank (Fig.46) direct to the Priory at such a tide.

The reason for grazing both New Forest ponies and cattle is that wildlife need a mixture of grazing methods and different types of dung, which have different nutrients. The ponies will eat both gorse and brambles, and crop the grass low, whilst cattle will rip out the more lush grasses with their tongues, leaving some bare patches. A greater variety of species becomes possible, because those needing sunlight are not "shaded out" by high grass. Another useful result is the need for fewer working parties to keep the scrub down, because horses are doing it to some extent already.

Stanpit Marsh has vegetation and mudflats, exposed at low tide, which allow the survival of many bird species. Visitors and dogs are discouraged from walking too far east towards these areas at the harbour's edge, in the direction of Blackberry Point. A main part of the rangers' work is to help the survival of wildlife by protecting it from disturbance, including scrub firing and illegal hunting. Blackberry Point may also be of archaeological interest because of the remains of a burnt Roman ship found in 1910, although there are doubts about its location. Some iron, bronze and pottery were noted together with a small Roman incense cup.

Apart from the bird-life, the marsh supports many invertebrate fauna such as dragonflies and butterflies, together with over 300 species of plant, of which 14 are endangered. A recent project has been to establish the Natterjack Toad by collecting spawn from the established population on Hengistbury Head, so helping to prevent its extinction.

A new oak-framed information centre on stilts has been proposed to replace the existing converted caravan. This building, costed at about £35,000, with an environmentally friendly solar panel and wind turbine, has been funded by the work of the Friends of Stanpit Marsh. A good wildlife leaflet and map is currently available from the caravan.

Another feature on the circular path is the "iron boat," now surrounded for safety reasons by a fence. The boat is known to have "arrived" after World War II, perhaps between 1947 and 1963, because it does not appear on pre-war aerial photographs, but I have not been able to prove how it got to its final resting-place. It may have been a lifeboat from a much larger vessel, such as an American Liberty Ship from World War Two. It might have been given to a scout troop based upriver on the Avon and then floated down during a high spring tide and abandoned. Alternatively, it may have broken moorings in bad weather and floated downstream of its own accord. I would welcome hearing via the publisher of any further and better information.

Priory Marsh is different from the main part, because it is a freshwater, rather than salt type of marsh. Turf-cutting used to take place here, both for fuel and to help drainage. It has been so dry, that cricket was played upon it, as evidenced by a photograph of such a match, now kept at Lords. There is a need for areas to be dug in order to promote more species, but this, like so many desirable plans, must be a matter of competing financial priorities.

Owing to the low-lying nature of the marsh, the rising sea level, at a rate of about 2.5 inches every ten years, is quite serious. The increasing frequency of flooding will kill off many species in the future. Curiously, it is likely that the parts justifying protection will be those higher areas of land in Stanpit, the golf course and recreation ground. The reason is that they were tips at one time, and it is undesirable to allow water to disturb toxic waste material. The marsh itself may get a sea wall, but if it were left alone, more reed beds would develop.

Tutton's Well

The significance of the well to Hengistbury is the possibility that it provided water for the Iron Age settlement as described below. The location, which has been described as Christchurch's oldest link to antiquity, is marked on Fig.46. Although strict historical evidence of the well itself begins only in the nineteenth century, there are indications that use of the spring which supplied it, may date back to the Iron Age or even earlier. There have been finds of Bronze Age pottery in the vicinity, but this does not prove use at that time.

It has attracted a lot of attention from local enthusiasts, who set up the Friends of Tutton's Well, under the patronage of Mr. Tom Tutton. The origin of the well's name is not known. Following restoration, including a new wellhead, benches, and a plaque on a separate plinth, a grand reopening was held on 10 July 2004. Committee members were decked out in authentic period costume, including milkmaid, smuggler, fisherman, monk, doctor and leper with bell. Mike Parker, a retired fisherman, told the assembly that Tutton's was a meeting place for many years for the people of Stanpit and Mudeford. Before World War II, the fishermen were still using the brook or stream at the harbour edge for their boats. In the 1960s, the council said that boats could no longer be pulled up there. Tests show that a strong flow of 5,000 to 10,000 gallons of clear water an hour can be extracted by pump. The water can be seen through a locked steel mesh standing at about two feet below ground level.

The original spring may have been located on the edge of the plot near to the south-east corner of the new Guide Hut, built in 2001/2, although excavation there did not produce a great deal of water. If it had not been restricted due to the presence of the hut, a full rush of water might have been found at a greater depth. Signs of a buried brick wall, likely to be part of the "dipping place" for local people, were found there. As the water flowed south to the harbour, animals could drink, before it fed into watercress beds near to the harbour edge. The second excavation, which was not limited in any way, revealed the high supply rate mentioned above in the centre of the plot. Hence, the original spring may be at the centre of the plot, where the old and the restored wellhead are located. We do not yet know if the edge of the site fed the centre or *vice versa*.

Tutton's Well may have been visited by people from the Iron Age town at Hengistbury Head, via a causeway from the Dykes. A ford or causeway usable at low tide is thought to have existed from the Dykes to Grimbury. It is a theory supported by finding wood and stones in this location. The stones were reported in 1928 to be like a submerged trackway and removed as a danger to navigation. It makes sense that a people living in the lee of the Head would construct such a crossing to secure a substantial pure water supply. The closest known spring to them would have been Lob's Hole, near the entrance of what is now Holloway's Dock, but this has always been inaccessible, due to being covered by the water of the harbour. It is said to have been named after Lud or Lug the Celtic god.

The source of water is understood to be the same as Pure Well nearby, the latter being more important and giving its name to the street. Some consider that the spring may originate from the New Forest and erupt here due to the Christchurch Fault running underneath. Ground radar has shown that there has been a shift in strata here. Both wells were said in bygone times to be good for healing the eyes. A stone wharf and slipway, now covered over by reeds, were built there, known as Stanpit Docks, Stanpit Creek. A large lagoon, about three feet deep, existed in front of the small quay, but was silted up when a stream to it from Purewell was diverted due to tipping on the marsh. Smugglers' equipment is known to have been stored close to Tutton's Well.

The first historical mention of the "mineral spring in the centre of the plot" seems to be the sale by auction in 1809 of the Manor of Somerford. An 1837 guide to Christchurch refers to a constant and never-failing stream of water of uncommon purity and transparency. Indeed, it was sold as the Christchurch Elixir. In 1859, a public subscription provided for a well structure to prevent contamination and a drinking trough for cattle. In 1868, the well was noted to be covered every high tide, but still to provide beautiful sparkling water. A resident born in 1883 recalled a traditional well (with two-foot shaft, bucket and chain and roofed roller) in the middle of the land. Another remembered the village pump and stone sink below in the early years of the twentieth century.

The well, pump and surrounding land were given to the town of Christchurch (the present owners) by Sir William Rose of Sandhills in 1885 and it became the Town Pump. The gift followed a complaint to the M.P., Horace Davey, about the need to stop "contamination of all kinds." It was pointed out that the well was almost the only source of drinking water for the inhabitants of Stanpit. By 1899, the dipping place was approached by steps and surrounded by iron railings over a raised stone border. That year, the water was found to be faintly chalybeate, due to iron content. Since this site was both noted for its water supply and as a landing point for fishermen and smugglers, it would have been central to village life. In the early decades of the twentieth century, when piped water became available, harbour access was restricted due to tipping causing the stream diversion, and the well fell into disuse and disrepair. It was noted in 1933 to be sadly neglected. The well was fitted with a pump but was capped in 1941 at the time of a diphtheria scare and the pump removed thereafter.

In 1957, Christchurch Council made the site available to the Guides for a temporary building only. A prefabricated hut was built, but disputes arose in 1982 about the site's status as public open space. Due to confusion between Tutton's and Purewell in 1999, the council gave permission for a permanent guide hut to be erected, thereby hindering a full archaeological excavation. Construction started in late 2001, with a watching brief by Wessex Archaeology. Eventually, with much compromise and enthusiasm, the investigation was completed as far as possible and an attractive heritage site secured for the town.

Fisherman's Bank

The harbour bank (Fig.47), approached from the end of Argyle Road, was traditionally used for the drying

Fig.47 ***Fisherman's Bank, c.1900***

(Illustration courtesy of Chris Austin)

We see here the traditional fishing scene on the harbour's north edge at the end of Argyle Road. For generations, local fishermen used the bank as of right for the drying and mending of nets. Despite some history of obstruction, a public right of way, of varying width, has been established. An old community meeting place is further up the same inlet at the site of Tutton's Well.

and mending of nets. The date around 1900 is the same as for the picture of the Run in Fig.49. It extends to Coastguard Way in one direction and a similar distance in the other. Fig.47 shows the scene including the jetties, some boats and houses, mainly occupied by fishing families. As depicted in the old photograph, it is still the case that the Bank comprises the land between the rear garden boundaries of the harbour-edge houses and the water. It is a short distance by boat along the inlet, from here to the historic community meeting place at Tutton's Well.

The custom was that established fishermen such as the Strides, Parkers, Edgells and Derhams had the right to use the land in this way. It is safe to say that such rights, which were included in property covenants, go back to the eighteenth century, although by about the 1960s they were no longer exercised. Unfortunately, during the following decade, a legal dispute arose concerning the status of Fisherman's Bank. Gates and notices were erected impeding free pedestrian movement. Eventually, it was held to be common land with a public right of way, which varied from three to eight feet wide in different parts. This is not the place to provide a legal opinion, but there does appear to be at least a pedestrian public right of way, which should be upheld against any future obstruction.

Wick Ferry

If the possible ford from the Dykes to Grimbury in Roman times is ignored, Wick has always been the lowest crossing place of the Stour. For a long time, a ford ran alongside the ferry and both allowed access between Christchurch and what is now Southbourne. The gravel base of the ford was dredged out and deposited near Christchurch Quay. Although this was a great help to the increasing post-war river traffic, it gave a river crossing monopoly to the ferry. There is photographic evidence of a piled timber structure above the river level, which I am told crossed about two thirds of the Stour, east of Wick Ferry. The route (shown on the 1872 OS) changed direction across the ferry line and sloped into shallow water for the rest of the crossing.

Fig.48 ***Wick Ferry, from Southbourne c.1900***

(Illustration courtesy of Chris Austin)

A ford, adjoining the ferry, was then available, giving some choice about how to cross the Stour. However, its stone base was removed to assist boat navigation, leaving the toll ferry as the only option. In 1900, passengers were rowed or punted across amidst a most attractive scene of rural peace. The crossing remains a most enjoyable experience.

The toll in 2004 was 50 pence adult single by motor boat. Fig.48, a photograph believed to date from about 1900, was taken from the Southbourne side of the river before a tented campsite was developed on the Christchurch side. This successful facility was eventually expanded and made into a holiday camp in 1954, run by Warners, and later by Pontins. The recent residential redevelopment of most of the site and the proposed 34-bed Captain's Club Hotel facing the river will only go some way to replacing the trade of the ferry, lost when Pontins closed.

Steamer Point

This name derives from a paddle steamer which was wedged into an enlarged opening in the cliff, near what is now the south end of Seaway Avenue, Friars Cliff, in about 1829. Some 30 years later, Steamer Cottage was built on the cliff edge above. In 1964, this part of the cliff was removed when a new sea wall was constructed. Steamer Point is frequently quoted as the position to which the sandspit extended, following the ironstone mining at Hengistbury.

Lord Stuart de Rothesay had acquired the *Arrow*, which was built in 1823, a ship of 94 tons having a length of 92 feet 7 inches. During the building of the replacement Highcliffe Castle, the steamer was first used as a temporary site office, when stone for the castle was being unloaded on the beach. Later it was used as a fishing lodge and then to provide accommodation for an estate worker. It is known to have survived until at least 1870, but had gone by 1925.

The name continues with the Steamer Point Nature Reserve. In March 2004, the last section of coastal path was opened to allow public access all the way from Highcliffe Castle to Mudeford. It runs from the castle grounds through woodland, past the ranger's cottage and the Steamer Point Information Centre, to the Highcliffe Training Centre of the Maritime and Coastguard Agency at the bottom of Seaway Avenue. The

Information Centre is a small single storey building used for public education and child-centred learning about wildlife. The Christchurch Council Countryside Service, which arranges volunteer events to help look after local nature reserves and wildlife areas, has a full programme including many events based at Steamer Point. For example, a morning might be spent digging up sand dune stabilising plants from the Sandbank and transplanting them at Steamer Point beach in the afternoon.

St. Catherine's Hill

There are some surprising links between the Hill and the Head. St. Catherine's Hill is often said to be "the twin" of Hengistbury Head and perhaps appeared very similar to it before the separation of the Isle of Wight. It has some similarity of geology and even supplies the area including Hengistbury with water.

Catherine achieved sainthood due to her legendary courage as she approached beheading, still proclaiming her faith, at the age of only eighteen. She is associated with the Catherine Wheel because the Roman emperor, Maxentius, ordered her to die on a spiked wheel, following her conversion of many (including the Empress) to Christianity. The emperor had not been converted, nor had she allowed him to seduce her. The legend is that she was beheaded because the wheel shattered, sending spikes flying into the crowd, just before she was due to be executed.

The first record of St Catherine's Chapel on this hill is 1302, and the last 1539. Excavations have not explained the unusual earthworks surrounding the chapel, but do show it was rebuilt on several occasions. It is a Site of Special Scientific Interest, due to its rare heathland wildlife and geology. The Hill contains a gravel quarry of geological interest with fossil plants in the Hengistbury Beds from a river delta some 40 million years ago. Since iron is also present, we have another link with the Head.

Hunter-gatherers occupied the Hill in the Stone Age and 11 barrows have been found from the Bronze Age. Iron Age settlers may have built the earthworks enclosure, located near a 100-foot mobile phone mast. It is believed to have been a beacon point and lookout from prehistoric times. Up to the Napoleonic Wars, the site of St. Catherine's Chapel was used as an intermediate beacon to help muster defences. The chapel was destroyed at the Reformation. From the nineteenth century, the Hill has been used as a military training ground, including trench warfare, grenade practice and a rifle range. It also contains two large concrete reservoirs (fed with water pumped from the Avon) to supply both Christchurch and Southbourne including the Hengistbury area.

Navigation and boating

Admiralty advice for sailors in 1963 suggested that, from westwards, the Head should be rounded at a distance of not less than three-quarters of a mile (Chart for Yachtsmen No. 5636 Admiralty Chart 2219). This is to avoid Beer Pan Rocks and other off-lying dangers. It is also wise to be well away from Christchurch Ledge, which has many floats attached by rope to the pots of lobster fishermen. These floats vary greatly and are not all easy to see. The Run is described as having very strong tidal streams attaining a rate of nine knots when outgoing. As a further caution it is stressed that not only is the entrance channel subject to frequent change due to the sandbanks moving every year, but also the buoys sometimes drag in bad weather. Local knowledge is recommended. As if this were not enough, a warning is given about foul ground about one cable (608 feet) either side of a line parallel with the shore from Hengistbury to Southbourne where the depth is about 35 feet. By the time you stay 608 feet out to sea at a depth of 35 feet, you will be wondering what kind of underwater obstruction exists! In addition, a wide swathe of water, south of the eastern end of Warren Hill, is a prohibited anchorage due to underwater cables.

Christchurch Ledge is the continuation under water of the ironstone nodules or "doggers." Some idea of the extent of historic erosion can be gained if you say that in 1962, the Ledge was only 14 feet deep at a considerable distance out from the end of the Long Groyne. The distance here is the same roughly as from the end of the Long Groyne to Mudeford Quay.

All this adds up to the need for good seamanship when negotiating the harbour and its entrance. To expect to sail in through the Run, without a motor, during a strong ebb tide, is almost always foolish. If winds are light when there is such a tide, dinghies should be careful to keep on the harbour side of the bar inside the entrance itself, to avoid being swept out of the Run.

One reason for the attraction to wind-surfers is the shallow water. The same applies to dinghy sailors. But small motor boats should keep to the deep-water channel as used by the ferry from Christchurch Quay. Dinghy sailors have challenging racing and cruising conditions due to the constant changes to weather, wind and water flows. The wind can actually be fairly constant but appears to change as the westward-bound boat comes clear of the lee or shelter of the Head. The quick way in which the general weather changes at Hengistbury Head is particularly evident in a dinghy. The speed and depth of water varies with river flows and tides. Sailors need to operate between the two high tides when the water is high enough. To disregard this basic advice is to court trouble in a fresh wind. At low tide, a dinghy will ground on the mud over most of the harbour. A capsize is possible if the centreboard gets stuck, so preventing the helmsman getting head to wind.

Lobster fishing

The nineteenth century ironstone removal caused a much-extended sandspit. When the Run became up to a mile long, fishermen found it better to row across the harbour in salmon punts, and walk over the south end of Mudeford Sandbank to the lobster boats, hauled up on to the beach. Fig.49, a photograph taken around 1900, shows a typical fishing scene at the Run. The small open lobster boats must have needed considerable skill to sail.

As long ago as 1970, the craft of making lobster pots from willow was dying out. It was found that galvanised wire pots were ten times quicker to construct and could be made at any time of the year in a small space. The traditional pot is made from 64 withies (slender willow shoots, eight feet long) in the winter, when the sap is low, needing a working area of 16 feet. There was an annual pollarding of trees to secure shoots of the right length and thickness. Each pot takes one man a day, involving an oak base (eight inches in diameter and two inches thick), an oak crown or "hake" (six inches diameter, removed after the pot is finished), immersion in tar to seal it, a rope fender to protect it, and weighting with ironstones to about 40lbs. Much of the skill relates to weaving the withies. Such a pot, which will last only two seasons, is too expensive to make now, except for the tourist industry as an ornament. Ironically, it seems that the more expensive withy pot was better at catching lobsters. They are put off the stale fish bait by vibrations from the wire mesh type.

Mudeford Quay now has a number of different types of pot on display. The wire type may be the square Parlour type or the round Inkwell type made with welded steel rods.

About a dozen men fish for lobster in summer, mainly on the ironstones of the Christchurch Ledge, and less than half that number in winter, when crabs are more common. One man may work up to 250 pots, identified by his personal floats; a float may be connected to about 20 pots. In the days of the withy pots, a man would typically tend only 40 pots and get to them by rowing out in a 20-foot clinker boat. Once a week, a lorry with saltwater tanks collects the lobsters and crabs, which have been kept in large store pots out to sea. The shellfish are disabled by nicking a tendon, before being weighed and loaded. Many are exported via Poole to France and Spain. A particular conservation rule is to return to the sea any undersized lobsters. The carapace as measured from the eye socket must exceed 85mm (3.35 inches).

Salmon fishing

Before there was an official ferry, some fishermen had an extra source of income from rowing people across the Run. Passengers paid what pleased them for the service, with Gordon Selfridge apparently tendering a sovereign on one occasion! There was some opposition to a motor ferry on grounds of safety. Before 1970, a salmon punt, the *Nimbus* – now in the Red House Museum – would be used to row up to 12 passengers across. Norman Derham built *Nimbus* in 1948 at Fisherman's Bank. Such punts had sturdy platforms for nets, which were very popular with children for diving purposes.

Monks are believed to have started salmon fishing in the eleventh century. Until fairly recently, the netting season used to run for about six months from January to July. Various licensees took it in turns to work the Run for some four hours at night on the fast ebb tide. A man stood on the bank with one end of a drift net, the other end being with two or three men in a punt. They made a semi-circular sweep of the net whilst the bank man walked down to keep pace and fixed his end to a post. Only three-quarters of the width of the Run were netted, to allow some salmon to escape upriver to spawn. In 1949, there was much upset at low catches of typically 300 fish only; there had been 1,413 fish in 1934, when the Run was very long.

Now the season is limited to only June and July for netting. There are six licensees, who can take it in turns to work a collective total of five days and two nights only each week during the season. Except for any damaged ones, the fish are all released as a conservation measure, and the men are paid up to £5 per lb. In 2002, more fish were caught than in 2001, which is encouraging for conservation. The system began about ten years ago, when Tesco Stores paid the fishermen. Since then, the costs have been borne by the Avon and Stour Rivers Association, and the Wessex Salmon and Rivers Trust. Both are charities.

Fig.49 ***Trading and fishing at the Run, c. 1900***

(Reproduced by consent of Red House Museum)

Looking towards the quay from the Sandbank, this photograph shows a trading barge of Dutch design, with keels lifted in order to enter the shallow water of the harbour. The other small vessel in the Run is a pot boat, as is the one beached in the foreground. These small open boats were used for lobster fishing in Christchurch Bay. Two to four men would use the net barrow on the gravel like a stretcher, in order to transport a cotton seine-net. Such nets, when wet and containing seaweed, could weigh well over 300 lbs.

The same six salmon licensees also fish for sea trout, again only during June and July. There is a rigorous inspection regime to ensure that the rules are being kept. In the case of sea trout, there are plastic ties and clips, which prove any particular fish is genuine and not poached. About 1,000 were caught in 2002, a very good year. For economic reasons, trawling has virtually finished, with only one part time trawler still operating. This is a great reduction compared to 1945, when there were ten, with the same number again coming into Christchurch Bay from Poole.

Angling for salmon by rod and line is another story. The owners of most of the harbour bed are Bournemouth and West Hampshire Water Company, who have leased fishing rights to the Christchurch Angling Club. The eastern boundary of both the ownership and the Royalty Fishery is a line approximately from Inveravon to Holloway's Cut. However, no salmon fishing is allowed downstream of Bridge Pool by the town bridges, and the day tickets are mainly for sea trout.

The main salmon fishery is beyond the Bargates tackle shop up to Great Weir. The catch and release scheme allows a £20 Tesco voucher to each angler who catches and returns a salmon. A maximum of five vouchers is possible per angler per season, which for rod and line runs from 1 February to 31 August. The Environment Agency keeps records of catches and has responsibility for taking action against poachers.

The salmon make their way upstream to oxygenated gravel beds such as at Fordingbridge, to spawn. Some survive, but some die of exhaustion. Despite conservation, salmon unfortunately remain at risk from seals, which are hard to control, and – for the young migrating fish – cormorants in much greater numbers. It may be that licensed culling of cormorants will be re-introduced. Fishermen have never been keen on this efficient bird, whose numbers and appetite can decimate the numbers of flat fish and eels in the harbour. They regularly used to shoot cormorants and in the 1950s, boys would be paid for each beak they could hand in to the police station.

Other fishing stories from Mudeford

Every year, the Rogation Sunday blessing is conducted at Mudeford Quay, in order to pray both for a good harvest for the coming year, and the safety of fishermen. Local fisherman Mike Parker has been taking vicars across the Run for 40 years in his rowing boat. In May 2003, the Reverend Andrew Saunders took the service from the boat and hymns were sung at the water's edge. The collection was divided between the church and the RNLI.

Livelihoods, in the Mudeford fishing industry, are affected by all sorts of things. Indeed, there are many stories from the old families who have fished from the quay for generations. In bygone times, oysters are believed to have flourished in the harbour, including the site of the Priory, before it was built. Shellfish could no longer survive there now. More recently, oyster beds were fished in Poole Bay but it appears that the beach replenishment of 1989 destroyed them. Special pots are used for cuttlefish from April to June. They are about 4 feet by 4 feet, with entrances made from soft plastic fingers. For bait, a female cuttlefish is placed inside. Much of the industry runs small boats at night, setting nets for bass, sole, plaice and wrays in Christchurch and Poole Bays.

A Royal sturgeon, measuring 9 ft 11 ins and weighing 300 lbs., was caught in the Run in June 1872. A much smaller one (6ft 9ins and 50 lbs.) was netted in 1912 and sent to the king. In 1874, a boy fought a 3ft 6ins shark near the Old Boathouse, when he saw it chasing some ducks. After a battle, which must have been hazardous to say the least, he captured the shark, saving the lives of many fish in the harbour. A dead whale came ashore at Boscombe in 1913. It re-floated and came through the Run during a storm, fetching up at the Haven. The stench was enormous and the council had to have the carcass burned with the aid of tar.

One story concerns a 12ft 7ins sturgeon carried from Mudeford to Christchurch, by a fisherman and the Haven House Inn landlord, in order to display it for all to see. It was a hot day and the fish seemed to get heavier. Having stopped to have a pint at the Star on the way, they left it outside, protected by bags found nearby. Duly refreshed, they emerged from the pub and were furious to find the fish with the bags removed and covered in road dust! It seems that the bags were the property of Mr. Hicks, the draper opposite. In no mood for shilly-shallying, the men raided the shop for anything they could find to provide a covering. There must have been great astonishment, when the long fish was duly carried into town resplendent in corsets and underwear more usually worn by Victorian ladies!

Fishermen may occasionally have different and unexpected duties these days, such as helping with sediment sampling. Both Bournemouth and Southampton Universities need assistance to collect batches of around 40 samples for heat analysis to monitor sediment movements.

Last word to Herbert the turbot

In November 2002 angler Mike Reeves caught a 1lb. turbot, wrapped it in a blue plastic bag, and put it in a domestic fridge. On removing it from the fridge in order to grill it, he was seriously shocked to find the turbot flapping, 15 hours after being caught at night off the Head. He felt unable to eat it for lunch. An aquarium in Portsmouth accepted Herbert, who made a good recovery. A marine expert commented that the slowed metabolic rate, caused by the fridge temperature, together with the moist environment of the plastic bag, helped it to survive.

TWELVE

CARE OF THE HEADLAND AND AMENITIES

The human use of the headland's natural and cultural resources should not in overall terms, diminish or destroy them. By effectively managing Hengistbury Head, we can hand down to our descendants something of great value, which has been enhanced and not harmed in terms of its beauty and scientific richness.

Management Plan 1997

A LOT OF EFFORT is needed to manage and improve the Head. Grass cutting, litter picking and fencing are contracted, whilst volunteers help with cutting back gorse and willow. In order to help insects and birds, there is a plan to plant 10,000 trees including birch, willow, hawthorn and dog rose. When trampling damaged new dune areas, they were fenced off to protect them. When research showed that there were too few aquatic insects in Lily Pond, it was drained and partially cleared with the aid of school groups, who also monitored the consequent wildlife. Bracken clearing has resulted in a large increase in insects, sycamore removal has allowed native species such as oaks to thrive, and trampled areas have been helped by aeration. Conflicts between dog owners and conservation issues, such as degrading habitats and wildlife disturbance, are managed as sensitively as possible.

English Nature (EN) has big influence on how Hengistbury is managed. It administers Sites of Special Scientific Importance (SSSIs) and Local Nature Reserves (LNRs) as part of its remit to protect the natural environment. The 1991 LNR broadly covers Hengistbury east of the residential development, excluding car parks and golf facilities. The SSSI was notified in 1964 and later amended. The 1986 version depicts roughly the same area as the LNR except West Field, but including the harbour and Stanpit Marsh. For certain matters, the council needs to get the approval of EN, who also advises the council concerning management. Examples are the balance between saltmarsh and reedbed, livestock management (where grants are made by EN) and the removal of gaultheria shallon. This alien species is extremely invasive and capable of spreading, by underground stems, to the extent that it has become known locally as the "creeping paralysis." Its dense, thicket-like ground cover, which can be up to six feet high, bristly branches and leathery leaves have to be controlled to prevent habitat degradation. There is also a high degree of involvement by EN in coastal defence.

English Heritage (EH) cares for the historic environment, including Ancient Monuments such as Double Dykes and other nationally important sites. Through a variety of name and function changes, the current body's history can be traced back to 1066. There are enormous records from battlefields to listed buildings to the Dorset Coastal Survey. Funds are available to EH for research and conservation purposes. Education packs are produced for schools. At one stage, EH were effectively preventing the E-Learning Centre from being sited close to the Dykes due to its remit to protect the setting of such ancient monuments.

Management Plan

This is one of main publications about the Head. Fig.46 shows historic and current names of the different areas for identification and management purposes. An area shown will often have its own section of the

Management Plan devoted to it. Although it sets out the council's thinking at that time, it has been overtaken by events and in 2004 was being updated by a new Draft Plan. The benefit of such a plan is that it gives a public framework of action proposed over five years. It is required reading for anyone wanting a full knowledge of the existing headland management. The new plan continues the same themes as the 1997 one including maintaining the flora, minimising visitor impact and extending grazing areas. One controversial aspect, to fence and graze White Pits, resulted in a lively public meeting called by the Hengistbury Residents' Association in February 2005. The council representatives spoke about trampling and loss of biodiversity, whilst contributions from the floor mainly wanted to keep it open with full access.

There existed a Technical Advisory Group (TAG) of up to 12 people, which met about twice a year to minute progress and decide how best to continue to implement the Plan. English Nature and English Heritage were closely involved. Follow-up research was arranged to establish that an objective had been met. In 2003, the Bournemouth Environmental Advisory Team, (BEAT), superseded TAG. BEAT performs the same function as TAG, but also reports on other open areas such as Turbary Common and the Stour Valley.

It may help to give a few examples of the thinking behind the Plan. Barn Field is managed as a buffer zone between the peace of the Head and the noise of the town. With the road, car park and café on one side of the Dykes and the quiet area on the other, there is an immediate sense of tranquillity. Better behaviour, in keeping with the place, is also evident. This major success was achieved by a combination of stopping public access to the Dykes (fenced off in 1992), and partially restricting access to Barn Field, so promoting wildlife on it. What an improvement compared to its previous state as an "over-used dust-bowl hinterland" to the Head.

Gravel footpaths may be attractive but the walking is less comfortable, so causing people to stray on to the grass and to cause areas of bare ground. Hence it is planned to replace the footpaths in tarmac at Warren Hill. The new draft plan refers to fencing around White Pits, the introduction of cattle and public access only under supervision. Due to this land having a long history of unrestricted public access and the recent designation as "open country" by the Countryside Agency, there is local opposition.

Another objective of the Plan is to protect the coast and the Warren Hill cliffs as a matter of urgency. Unfortunately, this is a good example of how such a good idea requires a lot of administrative effort and therefore expense to make it happen. For example, there need to be negotiations with English Nature about managed retreat, contributions to the Shoreline Management Plan involving annual appraisals and monitoring, definitions of working policies to overcome conflicts of interest between English Nature and English Heritage, etc. Day to day arrangements for coastal protection, are many and various, e.g. modifications to the drainage cascade to promote vegetative cover and maintain the filtering of water flows from heathland above.

The Plan lays down certain environmental policies. In biologically important areas, the hope is to ensure that any wear and tear is repaired by regeneration. Ecosystems are maintained at their existing size so that there is no detriment to the ecosystems of adjoining habitats. Grazing is used to promote biological richness. Public access is restricted in particularly sensitive areas such as the Nursery and sand dunes. There are also detailed objectives and policies concerning the archaeology, e.g. to conserve and interpret the features and artefacts. The same applies to educational and recreational matters.

The Plan details the 35 coast protection measures carried out from 1937 to 1993, the perceived need to investigate reed-bed management on Wick Spires, clear certain ditches at Salt Hurns, eradicate gaultheria in Long Field, etc. It demonstrates that the council operates a sophisticated type of land management. Unfortunately, the rhododendrons imported by Selfridge, which give a most attractive appearance to a footpath along the north side of the Head, are bad for wildlife and tend to sterilise the ground. The need to reduce them was explained by the ranger to a meeting of Hengistbury Residents' Association. I think this was accepted by the audience to some extent, which shows the merit of communication about management tasks.

Conservation

What is conservation, and does it really matter? It means looking after wildlife habitats in order to prevent injury to them. It also involves proper management and protection of natural resources. This is enormously important to Hengistbury, because good conservation delivers a string of solid benefits. Wildlife will be preserved for the future and examples of extinction reduced. Public enjoyment will be increased. The tranquillity of Barn Field is a major improvement due to conservation measures. Helping habitats will tend to preserve both geology and archaeology for the future.

The habitat list is quite exceptional: grass, heath, scrub, saltmarsh, freshwater marsh, freshwater pond, reeds, sand dune, shingle and rocky shore. Since these ten types are very close and need their own individual management, Hengistbury is an ideal centre for study. Examples of ongoing conservation include pond clearing, tree and hedge planting, enforcing Bylaws, creating wildflower meadows, path repairs, sign making, wildlife and erosion monitoring, promoting circular walks and nature trail, repairing the Dykes, and scrub clearing.

A good system exists to manage the Head, in terms of wildlife, paths, fencing, clearance, and some cattle. Regular meetings and tasks are put in hand, resulting in a steady improvement. Although there will always be some dissent, the main impact has been extremely good. It is to be hoped that this will continue indefinitely. The Head is now looked after by many different organisations, which have generally beneficial plans for it. This was not always true in the past.

Hengistbury Head Outdoor Education and Field Studies Centre

Formerly known as the Marine Training Centre, which received planning consent in 1962, this substantial educational resource is approached from the end of Broadway and has run courses for many years. It was built on Wick Hams, most of which used to be a landfill site. Before tipping started in 1953, the area from the Centre to Wick was beautiful green meadowland similar to the horse paddocks to the north of Wicklea Road today. But it was then unsuitable for building, as spring tides would cover it in up to two feet of water. In 1974, it was transferred to Dorset County Council as education authority, but returned to Bournemouth when it became a Unitary Authority in 1997.

There are three classrooms and a large boat shed for canoes, kayaks and sailing dinghies. Some 12,000 students are catered for all year round. The students undertake original research, e.g. archaeological investigations, and a report to Oxford University about the impact of trampling on Hengistbury. Although the Centre is keen to ensure that all its work respects the Head, there are a further 20,000 student visits unconnected with the Centre. Sadly, these sometimes reflect a lack of care and add to tourist erosion.

The main subjects are water activities and the environment. Royal Yachting Association courses are held for adults as well as children. Conservation, wildlife, archaeology, geology and coastal protection are dealt with in an original fashion. Specific topics include navigation and orienteering, dinghy sailing and dinghy racing, meteorology and safety at sea, citizenship, food chains and decomposition studies, interdependence of species, bird watching, Iron Age investigations, powerboat courses, first aid, kayaking and Canadian canoeing. The existing premises allow the children to be close to the boardwalk, open classroom and pond-life facilities, but with some access to computer facilities in the building.

In 2004, it was proposed that the building would be partly demolished, with the rest being refurbished. The boat shed and one classroom would have remained, with access to the harbour. Three classrooms would have been rebuilt in the car park near to the Dykes, together with a community centre. But with the plans for the new centre being dropped in 2005, it is expected that the existing one will simply be refurbished. It is very important for this unusual educational resource to be properly sustained for the future.

Leisure facilities

There are many things to do and see for the visitor, tourist or nearby resident. Walking with or without dogs is probably the most popular use of all. Archaeological and Nature Trail booklets are available from the Ranger's Office. The north side of Christchurch Harbour supports three sailing clubs, all of which have racing programmes. There are sea races in Christchurch Bay as well as harbour races. Christchurch Council let spaces on a yearly basis to the public in their own dinghy park, which adjoins Highcliffe Sailing Club's park on Mudeford Quay. Many moorings within the harbour and along the rivers provide for motor boats. The land train to Mudeford Sandbank café runs through most of the year.

Ferries run from pontoons opposite Wick Village via Christchurch Quay along the deep-water channel to the Sandbank jetty. The summer sees the annual Mudeford Fishermen's Trawler Race at the Run, where all spectator boats are advised to keep clear. The 10-day Christchurch Regatta ends in August with major rowing races along the Stour near to Town Quay. Every March, there is the Head of the Stour competition for rowing between the Head and Christchurch Sailing Club. Ringwood Canoe Club meets weekly at Mudeford Quay. Sea angling is popular along the shingle beach towards the Long Groyne, which is a particularly favoured spot, although unsafe in rough weather. A long cast to Beer Pan Rocks should give the best sport. Wrasse, mackerel, bass, garfish and at night conger eel, pouting and shore rockling have been caught.

The Hungry Hiker at the end of Broadway is a popular café, particularly as a refuge from the suddenly changing weather of the Head. The kite flying area west of the Dykes is one of the most popular venues for the sport. The Festival of Wind, held on 14 September 2003, attracted more than 1,000 people. One kite was in the shape of a biplane with RAF markings.

The Rangers run regular guided wildlife walks, which are free and open to all. They also run Hengistbury Head Astronomy Club, including "sunset and moonrise" events, where the public can see certain planets through an eight-inch telescope from the top of the Head. The club caters for beginners and those already interested in the night sky, with both outside and indoor meetings.

For many, a main attraction of the Sandbank is the chance of owning a beach hut, but it can be an expensive business. The first consideration is the remaining life of such a temporary structure, bearing in mind that the 2005 cost of replacement is about £22,500. The second might be the average purchase price, which roughly doubled to around £140,000 between 2002 and 2004. However, by March 2005, 22 huts were for sale, with one hut failing to reach an auction reserve of £80,000 and the market becoming more selective. The annual site fee for 2005/06 has been reported at £1,748, with a typical transfer fee (based on £1,033 per square metre) being about £20,900. But having spent a lot on sea defences, which have greatly increased the width of the sands, Christchurch Council has plans for a greatly increased fee for the licence to assign. Owners may eventually have to pay a fee of half the difference between original purchase price and the sale price. Consistent with these high figures, it is evident that the Sandbank and café have moved well upmarket, no doubt with its increasing popularity as an escape from modern life, despite some vulnerability to vandalism. The hut community has many debates with the council concerning such matters as licence fees, access arrangements and periods of occupancy. Most owners are not local and even television's *Changing Rooms* has produced a lifestyle programme about a hut.

THIRTEEN

EROSION OF LAND AND COASTAL PROTECTION

Your foe Oceanus does not sleep by day or night
But comes suddenly like a roaring lion
Seeking to devour the whole land.
God has given us the materials to fight the sea
And we must use them intelligently and subtly.
Andries Verlingh, Dutch engineer, *circa* 1580.

ALTHOUGH we may have known the Hengistbury area for a long time, and erosion appears to be only a gradual or insignificant event, this is somewhat misleading, and one day we may yet wake up to a disaster. For example, the first castle (or more strictly mansion) High Cliff, shown in the 1790 painting at Fig.39, was located much too close to the cliff edge. The second and current one was sensibly set well back.

Memories fade and risk awareness drops. Hengistbury Head has stood as a bastion of sea defence for hundreds of years. Without the headland, formed firstly by the ironstones and secondly by Long Groyne, there would be a single bay instead of Poole and Christchurch Bays. By the middle of the nineteenth century, many appreciated that the loss of the headland, due to ironstone mining, would be a disaster for Christchurch.

The chief means of coastal erosion is the "extreme event" and the key factor in creating more of these, and greater storminess in general, is global warming. After years of ordinary weather, we would find a 100-year storm to be a major shock. Fig.33, showing the wreckage of Southbourne Pier, is a dramatic illustration of the power of such an event.

Tourist erosion

This force is more potent than commonly realised. The trampling of many feet will enable the removal of the top surface. I am told that in the 1930s, before such trampling became excessive at Mudeford, the dunes were at least 25 feet high. Much of the Management Plan for the Head quite properly involves restricting visitors to limited areas. Apart from the fencing of certain parts to prevent public access, it is done by more subtle means, such as the placing of fences at right angles to the cliff face: this has been found to cause fewer footfalls, and therefore less damage, than putting one alongside it.

Walking by large numbers of people is not a harmless activity. Vegetation and loose sandy soil will disappear. "Panning" then develops on cliff-side areas, which have become at risk. This hard pan is the infertile soil directly above the old river gravel deposits. Trampling removes the vegetation, and the action of high winds and water removes levels of soil down to the hard clay pan, leading to gullies, which are a major erosion factor in their own right. Another example is the need for gabion protection for the harbour side, arising from speedboats and from visitors scrambling over the bank. The enormous growth in the numbers of visitors and dogs, estimated at around one million and 250,000 per year respectively, has certainly been detrimental to conservation of the Head. Nonetheless, proactive management means that a good balance is being struck between tourism and conservation. For example, although the Dykes are completely fenced off from the Old Barn to the footpath by the sea, there is still full public access over Warren Hill.

Wind and weather erosion

The southern wind
Doth play the trumpet to his purposes;
And by his hollow whistling in the leaves
Foretells a tempest and a blustering day
Shakespeare: *Henry IV Part I*

Hengistbury has more than its fair share of heavy weather. For example, the horizontal score lines in the top yellow sands of Warren Hill are the result of wind. It is a quite different situation from the main Bournemouth cliffs, which are in effect stable. Since the council has graded many of them back at 36 degrees and established vegetation, the rate of erosion is less than half an inch per year. Due to the narrow remaining width of Warren Hill, from north to south, it is not possible to grade back in this fashion. But for the sea, cliffs would reach their own stability over time, by weathering to a natural angle. This cannot happen at most of the headland due to cliff falls being washed away.

Gullies have been found to be a major cause of cliff erosion. They develop in soft sediments due to water run-off (made much worse by "panning") from the south face of the Head (Fig.59 and Fig.50). After heavy rain, a rivulet of water takes away loose material, widens and then cuts into the cliff. By the time a number of gullies are established, the cliff is much weaker resulting in slumping or falls.

Another process is the "splashback effect," where water will run off the exposed Barton Clay and splash back on to the Boscombe Sands, so widening gullies and forming unstable hollows. Then there is a "slip effect" which means the top sands lose adhesion when Warren Hill becomes saturated with rainwater. The top of the clay in the lower stratum becomes so slimy that the soft sands just slip off it. Such slips also happen between the strata, which used to be known as the Upper and Lower Hengistbury Beds. Unfortunately, these falls, which cause triangular taluses (Fig.50), get washed away by the sea, so preventing the chance of cliff stability through a more shallow angle of repose. On top of this, English Nature has a budget for removing taluses in order to assist geological studies. Although therefore a steep cliff can gain considerable stability by cliff falls, which become consolidated at a much lower angle and covered in vegetation, circumstances prevent this at the Head.

Where the cliff is very low near to the Dykes and composed purely of valley gravel, the face becomes less stable, tending to erode simply through expansion and contraction with changes in temperature. Frost action weakens the cliffs when trapped water freezes and expands. Even sand martin colonies, in the high section of yellow sands, can damage the cliffs with their burrows.

Harmful though these things may be, all the wind and weather attack on the cliff is much less significant than a wave-based extreme event.

Causes and history of sea erosion

The main background factor was global warming, or an "interglacial," causing the ice to retreat to the Poles and sea levels to rise. Britain was split from continental Europe, leaving what is now the Isle of Wight as still part of mainland Britain. But around 6,000 to 7,500 years ago, the Needles to Purbeck chalk ridge, protecting the River Solent, was dramatically breached, exposing the north side of the valley to the action of waves. One has to visualise a shallow valley of roughly 18 miles by 4 miles being swamped and filled by the sea. The swamping started vigorously from the south, with the sea fetching up against the far side of the valley to the north. Since then, there has been aggressive wave action combined with natural weathering of the soft deposits by the strong south-westerly winds. Vulnerability is high, compared to a rocky coastline. Fig.51 shows the low cliff of soft and crumbly valley gravel, which is unprotected against the waves. To the east, there are often cliff

Fig.50 ***Cliff fall at Warren Hill***
(Author 2002)
A typical cliff fall at Warren Hill creating a "talus," which will disappear fairly quickly. One reason would be the sea washing it away and another would be specific removal financed by English Nature, in order "to maintain the geological window." If a large number of ironstones still existed at the base of the Head, speed of erosion would be much less and the cliff would tend to be less steep and more resilient. The Eocene pebble strata can be seen just above the talus. Fig.59 refers.

falls on to the beach below Warren Hill, due to wave undercutting. Sometimes, a protective storm beach will develop, when gravel is thrown up against the soft cliff to a height of several feet. When this occurs, erosion is much reduced. Rising sea levels will increase the speed of ongoing erosion, because a storm will be more damaging starting from a higher level.

In heavy weather, it is common to see the Head drenched in sea spray. Erosion also comes from salt thrown on to the cliffs, which expands as it turns into crystals, causing some weakening. When sand is thrown up, it causes a form of scouring known as "corrasion." The waves shatter the cliffs due to trapped air pressure, and remove the shattered parts. Shingle is used for beach replenishment at Hengistbury to protect the cliff, both because it will brake an advancing wave much better than sand and not be scoured out as easily.

But for the headland, Poole Bay would have been a continuous sweep with Christchurch Bay. Its effectiveness has been due to the ironstones. Erosion caused them to fall to the beach, where they formed a natural defence from the sea for low-lying Christchurch.

About 65% of the time, the direction of prevailing winds in the English Channel is from the south to the west, causing beaches to be moved to the east. The statistics for the general direction of longshore drift are 62% to the east, 22% to the west, and the remainder indeterminate. A wave will generally wash out the sand on its return into the sea in a south or south-eastern direction. Therefore, not only does wave action take sand away from a beach, it also moves it along. With the provision of promenades in Bournemouth, this natural replenishment has been greatly reduced, as there are no longer any cliff sands to erode. Groynes from Poole to Southbourne, tending to retain the sand between them in compartments, have further diminished the supply, of sand and gravel from the west.

Fig.51 ***Coast erosion measuring post and low cliff near to Point House Café (Author 2002)***

These 30-foot long Greenheart timber posts are placed along the beach in several locations to keep track of seabed and cliff erosion. The sand and gravel cliff is vulnerable to extreme weather. If you just touch the cliff-face, a handful will come away at once. However, as seen here, the beach shingle greatly slows the waves in normal winter conditions.

Accordingly, It is wrong to think that all would be well if cliffs were protected by concrete. As indicated in Fig.55, the main thing is to keep sand volume in the bay above the critical level. The seabed is continually eroding and being monitored for several hundred yards from land. Regular sand replenishment in Poole Bay is an absolute necessity. Without it, the promenades would be undercut and fail. An illustration of this was the collapse of part of Southbourne promenade, by a narrow beach, in 1988. A 60-foot length was washed away and a 20-foot hole appeared, resulting in the pouring of 300 tonnes of concrete. Although this was an expensive disaster, it gave weight to the council's plans that year for replenishment, particularly as it did not follow an abnormal storm. A recharge of the western part Poole Bay will widen the beach there and feed the shore at Hengistbury. Without such a feed, the sea would attack the cliff base much more, resulting in annual erosion of over three feet.

The drift-based stability of Poole Bay, before Holloway's mining, was shown by the existence of the Sandbank and what is now Mudeford Quay to the north. The sand was steadily being moved from Sandbanks to and around Hengistbury Head, but with constant natural replenishment from the west. The removal of ironstone by Holloway took away the stability, as evidenced by both the accelerated erosion and the regular lengthening of the sandspit beyond Steamer Point.

Let us now turn to some specific features of the headland environment. Although cliff falls there provide some sediment feed, it is only about a tenth of that coming from central Poole Bay, and the Head suffers a net loss. Water from the Avon and Stour mainly reaches the sea at an ebb tide, because it is restricted to the harbour, or "penned up," when the sea is entering the Run during an incoming tide. River silt is deposited in the harbour because it falls out of suspension in slower water. The shape and extent of Mudeford Sandbank have varied greatly since the removal of the ironstones. Sand has drifted around the Head causing an enormous build-up, at times extending its length by a mile. Following such a build-up, the Sandbank became vulnerable to a breakthrough in bad weather, as happened in 1895, 1911 and 1935. The Run then resumed its old short course and the tail of sand was gradually washed ashore. Nonetheless, the two natural sandspits, which flank the Run, have the great historical importance of protecting Christchurch from the sea and helping the harbour to have a much smaller tidal range than the bay. With the loss of sand drifting around the Head and the great loss of shelter caused by its erosion, it became essential to preserve Mudeford Sandbank and Quay by artificial means.

A beach can build up when the forward wave (the "swash") is greater than the retreating one (the "backwash"). Generally, this occurs in the summer and is reversed in the winter, when beaches tend to disappear. Beach levels at the shoreline can easily mislead a casual observer. For instance, it is possible for massive onshore movement of sand to be swiftly followed by offshore movement. Within a week, at least a six-foot depth of sand appears to have gone! In fact, the volume in the bay is about the same, with these movements being merely local, i.e. moving the sand hump onshore and a little way offshore, but not affecting the general drift of about 10% p.a. eastwards. In the same way, it is not easy to see why there is any need to replenish, when the sand level is quite high, as now (2004), on the promenade's slope at Southbourne. However, the need arises from a much reduced seabed profile, which is not visible from the shore.

Halcrow reckons that from 1978 to 2002 there were about 3,900 cubic yards of cliff sediment falls each year in seven sectors from the Point House Café to a point beyond Long Groyne. This is about the cubic capacity of five medium-sized detached houses each year or 120 over the study period. The greatest cliff erosion occurred in Sector Five between the Coastguard Station and the western end of the dunes near to the Long Groyne, amounting to about 80 houses over the study period. Although therefore this 651-yard sector is only about one fifth of the cliff length, the erosion is around two thirds of the total. When a beach has to be renourished, there is another strong disadvantage to the use of sand: it has a "wave-modified angle of repose" of 1 in 40 compared to coarse gravel of up to 1 in 4. The result is that much less gravel will do the same job much more cheaply. Despite the benefits of shingle, a very heavy sea has no difficulty in removing a good storm beach made of shingle anyway! When this happens, the beach is much lower and the cliff can be attacked.

According to research by Christchurch Council published in 1993, the older methods of sea defence, including timber groynes, concrete seawalls and timber revetments, are being found to be less effective than the newer methods of rock armour or rubble groynes and shingle renourishment. The rubble groynes in particular have special advantages of cost, flexibility in construction, easier maintenance, greater dissipation of wave power, long term resilience and improved compartment shape. The general impact of the Long Groyne is referred to elsewhere. There is however a particular effect on the cliff immediately to the west. It has become "dead" rather than "active." It now lies well behind an expanse of dunes with no risk of sea erosion. Moreover, stability is helped by the invasion of heather from the clifftop above.

We can imagine a reasonably stable bay of sandy cliffs from the Iron Age onwards about 2,000 years ago, when the Dykes had been built. As a result of the fallen ironstone, there was a large build-up of sand on the doggers, which looked like a much larger natural version of the Long Groyne. This means that the taluses of fallen sand below the Head had not been washed away by the sea and had reinforced stability by making the cliffs much less steep and no doubt covered in vegetation. Fig.18 is very material, being a painting from about 1830, well before the mining operations started in 1848, showing a cliff at the Head of stable appearance. Moreover, Fig.6 gives a tentative indication that the Head is now half the size it was during the Iron Age. As mentioned elsewhere, I feel that it is much less than half.

The idyllic scene came to an abrupt end in 1848 when ironstones began to be taken from the base of the Head and the natural headland was largely lost. Colossal quantities of sand were scoured out from the bay and deposited to form an extension to Mudeford Sandbank. More than once, this was not sustainable, causing the rivers to form a break in the sandspit and create a narrow lagoon up to Highcliffe. Sea erosion continued at a greater rate after the removal of doggers from the beach, but was abated after the Long Groyne was built in 1938. Even here, there have been arguments about adverse consequences. A talk, given in 1951 to Bournemouth Rotary Club by a chartered surveyor, strongly contended that the new groyne had caused great erosion of Avon Beach.

In the early 1980s, some ironstone was "inadvertently" taken from the base of the cliff causing 115 feet of land to be lost within two years. This is probably the same event that the Borough Engineer was referring to in 1984 when he told the MP about erosion at the far end of the Head where over 15 yards of the Head itself have been lost in a year. The greater the research on Hengistbury Head, the more it seems to be at risk.

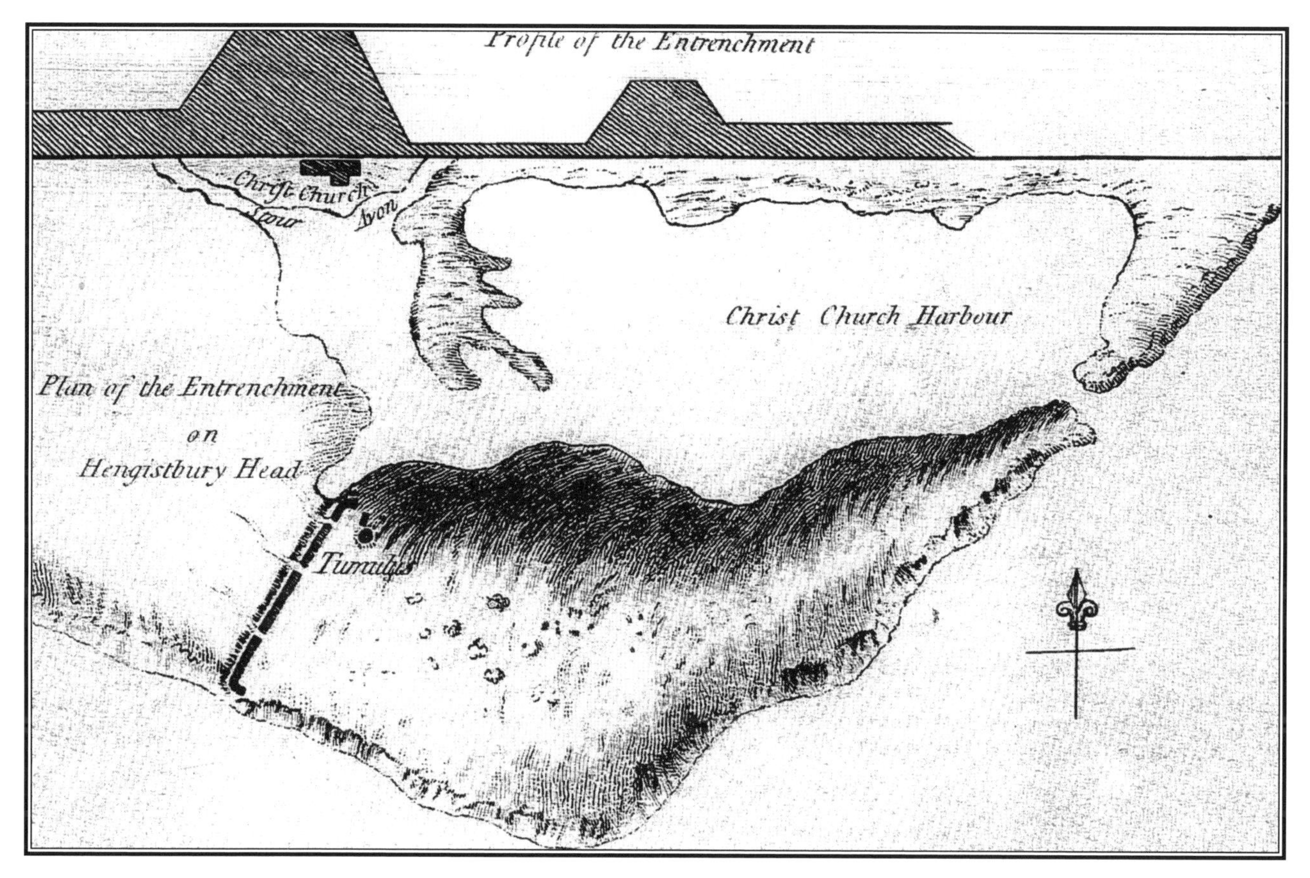

Fig.52 ***Hengistbury by Francis Grose, 1777***
(Reproduced by consent of Christchurch Local History Society)
A much-published map, produced without measuring aids, i.e. presumably by looking and pacing. Compared to an OS or naval map, it is diagrammatic only. It is nonetheless clear that the promontory was much wider than after the removal of the protective ironstones 1848 – 1856 from the beach. It is also evident that, before the erosion from the ironstone mining, the Dykes then "returned" at the south end, as well as the north end. The southern end of the Dykes, as existing now, is a little north of the position of the southern entrance, marked on Grose's map.

From building the Dykes to removing the ironstone

Erosion is generally thought to have been very limited indeed for nearly 2,000 years. In other words, it has been said that the bay was self-sustaining from the erection of Double Dykes, around the time of the birth of Christ, until removal of ironstone began in 1848. If you look at Fig.6 in relation to the sketch by Grose (Fig.52), the implication is that nearly all the loss of land since the Iron Age was post-1848. I am not convinced about this contention, however, in the absence of fully accurate maps before 1797. Although the 1777 report from Francis Grose gave various dimensions, it was not to the same standard as an Ordnance Survey, and the author himself referred to it as illustrative only. It is noteworthy in passing that Grose used no instrument to arrive at the figure of 500 yards: presumably the length of the dykes was paced only. Even if we think of the Grose report and map as reasonably accurate, it is quite a big step to conclude that there was virtually no erosion from AD 1 to AD 1848, but major erosion since.

This conclusion actually rests on the point that the Grose map shows a bend in the south end of Double Dykes matching a similar bend to the north. The theory contends that this is how it was built in the first place: no more, no less. Grose is said to have witnessed the full extent of the original Double Dykes in all its symmetry. Another theory, which I consider more plausible, is that the original Dykes were much longer but with a bend part way along, i.e., that in the Iron Age the Head was much bigger even than shown in Fig.6. I believe that this explanation also fits in better with the length of Christchurch Ledge, which consists merely of ironstones that fell to the shore from the eroding and retreating cliffs. The view that the Low Water Mark around the Head extended to Beer Pan Rocks from the Iron Age to the nineteenth century is far from proven. The Mackenzie map of 1785 (Fig.11) indicates a broad similarity with Grose and shows a considerable apron around the cliff base. The 1830 painting in Fig.18 tells the same story. So far, it is fair to say that about half the headland has been lost since around 1800.

Let us now consider the remains of the bank and ditch about 650 feet east of the Dykes (Fig.7). The bank was over 30-foot wide at the base with a 20-foot wide ditch some six feet deep. It is possible that this defence ran across to Barn Inlet and was part of a composite whole at a time during the Iron Age when the coast was much further out. Since we know that it was manually gravel-filled, it may have been the first defence before the Dykes were built, with the land being levelled thereafter. Certainly, the existence of this defence does not prove a lack of erosion before Grose.

An extra piece of evidence comes from the Smeaton Report of 1762, referred to elsewhere. He described the headland including the double heads, which then existed having a small bay between them. He stated that they formerly extended much further into the sea than now, but that storms had brought down sand in great quantities. This material reduced the width of the harbour mouth and moved it away from the Head towards Mudeford. In short, around the time of Grose, Smeaton spoke of great erosion of the headland in the past. Since we know that after the mining operation, erosion there meant erosion at the Dykes, the same can be assumed pre-Grose. Consistent with all this is the fact that there has been plenty of coastal erosion, even after the building of the Long Groyne in 1938.

The greatly respected local antiquarian Herbert Druitt, referring to the nineteenth century excavations in a general way, gave a lecture on 6 July 1921. The lecture notes say: "...Hengistbury Head, which, in former times, extended far out towards the Isle of Wight, as is evidenced by the dangerous reef of rocks which mariners are so wary of, and by the Beerpan rocks nearer the shore." He was referring to the Ledge beyond Beer Pan Rocks, as evidence of the headland's position before Holloway's mining operations.

The original Poole Bay, which formed after the separation of the Isle of Wight from the mainland around 6,000 to 7,500 years ago, was probably bounded by a very long Warren Hill, most of which has gone, leaving only the ironstone of Christchurch Ledge as evidence. Hence, if the Head coincided with the Ledge, say 6,500 years ago, it would then have been about three miles longer than today. This is the length from the existing cliff to the end of the Ledge shown on the chart in Fig.31. The average erosion speed of 2.4 feet p.a. (three miles divided by 6,500 years) hides the probability that it would have been much quicker initially. I consider that it was proceeding at anything from 6 to 12 inches p.a. from 1 AD to 1800 AD, probably closer to the higher figure. Even if we said erosion took place at only six inches p.a. from the erection of Double Dykes around AD 1 to the Grose inspection date of AD 1777, it would imply that they were originally built 800 yards long instead of the 500 yards in the Grose paper.

If this is correct, it is a shock to realise that Hengistbury Head is only a small percentage of its former glory and even that will disappear in the future. As for exactly when, that is for a later section.

Rising sea levels, subsidence of the coast and global warming

Many are concerned about the effect which global warming is going to have on sea levels everywhere. If the polar ice caps melt to a great extent, not only does sea level rise, but also coasts become at more risk from bad weather. There are two main reasons for the higher risk: storms are more destructive of existing defences when operating from a higher sea level, and global warming results in bigger storms.

Let us first look at the change to risks from "extreme events." Low atmospheric pressure, which automatically raises sea level, can combine with onshore winds to create a "storm surge" and a chance of flood. If this occurs at a high tide, then flooding is even more likely. In the harbour, we have yet another contributory cause: heavy rains can build up an abnormal flow of river water, which cannot swiftly escape. These factors, which can already come together to cause floods and storm damage, will be more drastic in the future. It follows that the low cliffs by the Dykes will become more vulnerable to overtopping.

Crustal Movement is also working to the disadvantage of the south coast. Gradual shifting of tectonic plates means that the United Kingdom is tilting down in the south and up in the north. As the local figure seems to be about 0.1 inch per year, or ten inches per century, perhaps it is not too serious? Probably not, but these shifts, on a world-wide basis, have not always been reflected in technical research papers about sea level predictions, thereby making them suspect and perhaps unduly conservative.

The individual effects of each aspect are very hard to isolate. Some relevant questions are far from fully answered. How much global warming is due to man-made greenhouse gases and how much would have happened during the current interglacial any way, i.e. how much of the increase in carbon dioxide, methane, nitrous oxide and even water vapour is natural and how much man-made? How much of the sea level rise is due to thermal expansion of the oceans and how much to melting of low glaciers such as at the Alps and Rockies? How much reported research is invalid due to not taking account of Post Glacial Rebound, the tendency for land buried under ice during the Ice Age to rebound upwards following melting? How useful are the tide gauge readings, currently taken every 15 minutes at 44 locations around the UK (including one at Bournemouth Pier), bearing in mind the problem of low frequency fluctuations in sea level? (This problem has led to the view that 50 years is the minimum period for the readings to be meaningful!) How much extra snow is expected over the polar ice caps due to climate change, and to what extent will this offset sea level rise for other reasons? The Intergovernmental Panel on Climate Change (IPCC) regularly reviews this matter. But, as if to show how uncertain things are, they say merely, "Most scientists agree that the balance of computer modelling evidence suggests discernible human influence on global climate". Not exactly clear proof including verified figures! Internationally, there is a massive research programme in an effort to answer questions of this type.

A serious warning about global warming was issued in 1998 by the World Wide Fund for Nature. A picture was produced showing the Head as an island by 2025. Not only did a sea channel replace the Dykes, but the Priory was accessed by gondolas! This "national wake-up call" described the future Christchurch as the "Atlantis of the south coast." One very fair comment was that the national coast protection budget was far too small. This was also the universal conclusion of a 2003 conference organised at the Hengistbury Head Centre by the University of East Anglia.

If there is a need for some healthy scepticism about the more dire predictions, what do we know for sure? There are local instances in living memory. A fisherman has remembered Blackberry Point in the harbour, Fig.2, simply as land with tufted grass and gorse, consistent with an 1846 Admiralty chart. From my observations, this is now either covered in water, or exposed at low tide as mud and gravel only. I could not say how much of this is caused by natural erosion and how much by rising sea levels. It is said that archaeological evidence in the Mediterranean shows a rise of only 16 inches in 2,000 years compared to four to eight inches in the last 100 years alone. Going back some 18,000 years, when the end phase of the last Ice Age began, sea levels were believed to be about 330 feet lower than now, implying a much faster rise in the early part of the current interglacial.

The predictions of the IPCC in 1990 were about seven inches by 2030 and 17 inches by 2070. Elsewhere, it is said that the next 100 years will see levels rising by 20 inches, with most of that rise in the second half of the century. Another prediction in 2001, again from IPCC, claims we can expect anything from 3.5 inches to 35 inches from 1990 to 2100, with the best estimate at 20 inches.

So far, these figures demonstrate nothing too disturbing in our lifetimes. They imply a gradual adjustment to coastal defences, whilst following a policy of "managed retreat." But it would be a very different matter in the event of a collapse of the inherently unstable West Antarctic Ice Sheet (WAIS), which contains about 13% of Antarctic ice. It would cause a global increase in sea level of 16 feet and flood estuaries and coastal areas worldwide.

It is amazing to reflect that although Antarctica has 90% of the world's ice and 70% of the world's fresh water, it is the driest continent, with about two inches of snow per year. Nonetheless, the immense weight of accumulated compacted snow has been enough to press the continent at least 3,000 feet into the Earth. It is still unclear how much impact global warming is having on the risk of such a catastrophe. Certainly, it cannot help that temperatures are rising in Antarctica at five times the average global rate, i.e. 2.5°C over the last 50 years compared to 0.5°C, generally. We also know that the WAIS is the only surviving marine-based sheet in the world, after the collapse of all others in the last 20,000 years, including the collapse of sections of the WAIS itself.

Fortunately, most of the Antarctic ice, equivalent to about 200 feet sea level rise, is on the stable eastern side. However, the WAIS is not land-based in the same fashion, leading to concerns about its long-term survival. Most of the WAIS is below sea level and able to slide over the marine sediments on which it is grounded. Floating ice shelves produce or "calve" icebergs every year without an increase in sea level, because they are already floating. Hence, recent collapses of shelf chunks (1995: 618 square miles; 1998: 425 square miles; 2002: 1235 square miles) are not of direct concern. But the consequences are. For example, a smaller shelf area means less of a brake on the glaciers feeding and forming the shelf. As a result, the glaciers have accelerated by up to eight times, so raising the melt rate.

A 1998 report suggested 100 to 1,000 years before collapse could occur, but the result would be so disastrous that international co-operation to limit global warming was needed now. The Third Scientific Assessment of the IPCC is very hopeful, implying about 500 to 600 years before melting. A tentative prediction in 2002 suggested that there was a only 5% risk of collapse, resulting in the 16-foot rise in sea level taking place over 500 years. Since then, new information is to hand, such as the discovery of a volcano under the ice and a 30-mile fold, indicating greater mobility than previously thought in the centre of the WAIS. The latter research from the British Antarctic Survey creates a need to reassess predictions. For those readers living, like me, close to sea level, there are two positive comments. Firstly, this marine ice shelf is on a deep, muddy basin-shaped bedrock floor, which has the geometry appropriate for hosting an unstable ice sheet. Secondly, there is general agreement that there is only a very small risk that the WAIS will collapse during the twenty-first century.

There are some Doomsday predictions, which would affect us all if proved right, not just Hengistbury Head. For instance, if the Gulf Stream is "turned off" through the impact of global warming, this country will get much colder, with icebergs around the coast. The Stream is a conveyor, whose existence depends upon salt density. The paradox is that the big increases in salt-free water, from rain and ice melting due to global warming, will dilute the salty water in the sinking zone of the conveyor, thereby slowing it. If it stops altogether, the warm waters from Mexico will no longer protect our climate. In short, the heating up of the planet may bring freezing conditions to Britain. Such major rapid climate change could happen without warning and within the short space of 50 years. The effects on us from much of Greenland melting could also be irreversible, although much more distant in time.

The sudden arrival of severe winters (including one like 1963 every few years) might or might not reduce storminess and therefore coastal erosion. We still do not have all the answers. However, I think we would be looking back with great nostalgia to the present day, when crops can be grown, the ports are accessible and there are no ice blizzards. Our local concerns about the finer points of managing Hengistbury Head would be replaced with more drastic national worries to do with physical and economic survival.

Impact of tides

We are fortunate in this area with tidal ranges of up to around six feet, because it means that much less coastal defence is required. At both ends of the Channel, it can at times be approaching 30 feet due to a phenomenon called "resonance," which operates like water swishing from end to end in a bath. The following table is an extract of predicted tides, comparing Bournemouth with both ends of the channel, but excluding meteorological effects. It shows that tidal range is much more benign here. Were this not so, the low cliffs by the Dykes would have long since been swept away.

LOCATION	DATE	TIDAL RANGE (feet)
DOVER	2 NOVEMBER 2002	17.25
NEWLYN	2 NOVEMBER 2002	14.73
BOURNEMOUTH	2 NOVEMBER 2002	4.43

We are in the relatively calm middle of the bath, compared to Dover and Newlyn at each end. But the existing regime at Hengistbury may not have obtained before the breakthrough, which created the Channel about 8,600 years ago. The chalk hills south of the River Solent were then on the north bank of a large inlet from the Atlantic. It is quite likely that there were enormous tides here, similar to the Severn Bore, which as an inlet, has even greater resonance than the existing Channel. Spring tides at Avonmouth are actually the second highest in the world at 40 feet. It has been argued therefore that the reason the chalk ridge disappeared so swiftly was the sheer resonance-induced violence of such a big tidal range.

Even "lunar and solar pull" is magnified by resonance within a sea basin. The gravity of the moon pulls up the water of the Earth, as it rotates beneath the tidal bulge. When this occurs, there is another equal high tide on the opposite side of the planet, whilst the parts in between have a low tide. When the moon, sun and Earth are all in line, we get the biggest highs and lows called the spring tides, whilst when the sun and moon are at right angles, they will tend to cancel out tidal effects, causing much more moderate highs and lows. Every 12 hours 25 minutes, a tidal wave (in the form of temporarily raised sea surface height) travels anti-clockwise around the North Atlantic. You might say, why not every 12 hours if there are two tidal bulges and the planet spins every 24 hours? The answer is that the moon has moved a bit more around its 28-day orbit of Earth. The wave will increase in height when it reaches the shallower water of the English Channel and cause considerable currents.

Fig.60 shows an opinion of an intermediate stage in the Flandrian Transgression: the existence of several islands between Purbeck and the Isle of Wight that were swiftly demolished by extremely violent sea action. It seems that normal conditions would be nothing like enough to explain the loss of the chalk ridge in such a short time. At least, the violence of resonance does provide an explanation. If this is right, it follows that the present coastal position results from the amount of difficulty the sea had in creating the Channel. In other words, if there had been more resistance to the Dover breakthrough, because of higher ground to the east, our coast would now be miles to the north, and vice versa. Put another way, it could be that the breakthrough from the North Sea (and consequent low tidal range at Hengistbury) occurred just in time for the preservation of the Head: much later and the tidal range violence could have proved too much for it to survive.

How much erosion over the years?

Hengistbury has always defended Christchurch from the sea. But there is a difference from the seventeenth onwards. The older maps, (Norden 1607, Speed 1611, Blaeu 1645, Blome 1673 and Morden 1695), all show a wide estuary without clear sandbanks either from Hengistbury or Mudeford. They do not indicate the present shape of Christchurch Bay. On the other hand, the more recent ones (Kitchin 1751, Taylor 1759, Mackenzie 1785, Milne 1791 and the unpublished OS 1797) all show both sandbanks and bay. It seems that the sandbanks and curved bay began to be formed towards the end of the seventeenth century. The heavy erosion, causing these changes, was probably continuing from previous centuries. Certainly, Mudeford Sandbank formation may have started by the time of the Yarranton Map of 1676 (Fig.21).

Many figures have been given in various sources about the speed of erosion. A 42-page document was sent in 1869 to Bournemouth Corporation by James Druitt, mentioning the loss of 66 feet of flatland by Double Dykes in seven years. Following an autumn storm, there was a lively correspondence in the local paper in 1877, involving two opposing views about encroachment risks. The first writer suggested that, at the current rate, the sea would burst through at double ditches in "only a few winters." He said the alarm only started when the ironstone was removed some 25 years previously, but that the whole area was at risk, including Christchurch and the "building estates at Southbourne." He wanted the council to get a technical report in order to inform the debate, but this did not happen. The second writer claimed that water level in the harbour was higher than sea level and, should a more direct route be made to the sea, this would act as a breakwater or protective bar together with the Christchurch Ledge. Indeed, the deeper water then possible in the harbour would allow much bigger ships. The first writer responded with figures about tide levels being up to two feet lower in the harbour than outside and the remark that if the two rivers flowed out at the Dykes they could not possibly hold their own against the sea. The result would be the Head and Sandbank would "melt away like sugar in hot water." Then it would be goodbye to Mudeford!

The 1921 Druitt lecture notes say: "On the foreshore, however, such quantities were removed that the natural protection of the headland was destroyed and erosion at the rate of about a yard per annum has followed." The respected Bushe-Fox report of 1915 mentioned erosion from 1907 to 1912 of 35 feet at the Dykes and 40 feet at the Head, an average of more than seven feet per year. A 1974 report referred to a loss of three feet a year and the possibility that without some form of conservation, the whole hill could disappear within 30 years. An archaeological report in 1983 by Barton and James referred to erosion of almost two feet per year over the previous 75 years at the cliff-top. In 1984, the local MP was told that the Head could become an island in just ten years.

The 1997 Management Plan refers to the retreat of the clifftop line from Solent Road to the eastern cliffs of Warren Hill at between 1m to 2m (3ft 3in to 6ft 6in) per year. It also mentions 120 metres loss from 1785 to 1996, which is about two feet per year. In stark contrast, the Halcrow report about a £20 million defence scheme for Poole Bay (exhibited at Bournemouth Town Hall on 12 November 2003) said that previous erosion measures were too high. The right average annual figure, for seven compartments for the same stretch from Solent Road mentioned above, was said to be about 6 inches for the period 1978 to 2002. A further instance of strong comment occurred in the *Echo* in January 1999: half a mile lost in 100 years. This speed of erosion of 26 feet per year is frightening indeed.

Certain historic events are undeniable however, such as the erosion of several feet per year from back gardens of modern houses in Southbourne Overcliff Drive. The *Echo* reported in 1949 that one was in danger of toppling over the cliff and had been vacated. This same report referred to the risk of the Head becoming an island. Four of these houses were demolished for safety reasons in 1957.

For a fairly accurate illustration of erosion at the Dykes, it is worth looking again at Fig.29, which shows the monument and the cliff edge in 1870. The existing coastline, being the edge of the gabions, is slightly north of the footpath shown running through of the south break in the Dykes.

My own view is that we can only hope to be fully accurate by looking in any one location over a stated period from the first official large scale (1:2500) Ordnance Survey map of 1870. The various old maps do not agree with one another and can only be regarded as diagrammatic for the most part. The 1676 Yarranton Map (Fig.21) is inaccurate beyond all reason. Even the famous Grose map was not based on measurements and is far from correct. For example, it shows the cliff towards the Run on a bearing of about north-east, when this should be much closer to north-north-east.

There does exist, however, an unpublished Ordnance Survey from 1797 to a scale of 3 inches to 1 mile. The scaled distance, from the cliff edge at the centre of the Dykes to the north side of the barn, can be compared to the same distance on the 1870 map extract (Fig.29). It shows a difference due to erosion of 115 feet: just over *1.5 feet per year.* Taking a following time period to a slightly better accuracy, we can measure the gap from the centre of the seaward break in the Dykes to the edge of the low cliff. In 1870, it was 225 feet and in 1932 (6 inches to 1 mile map, Fig.2) only 50 feet: nearly *three feet per year.* These two examples together show that the removal of ironstone, 1848 to 1856, greatly increased erosion of the Dykes by the sea. In addition, a comparison of the 1870 and 1898 maps indicates 225 feet as against 125 feet, a loss of 100 feet, or just over *3.5 feet per year.*

Going back with less accuracy, we know that Grose said the Dykes were 500 yards long including both returns in 1777. However, there is so much difference between the old maps as to the shape of the south side of the harbour, it is best to calculate from the seaward break in the Dykes shown on his map (Fig.52). I make this about 396 feet compared to the 1870 Ordnance Survey at 220 feet: a loss of 176 feet or nearly *two feet per year.* Although the 1777 map is not very accurate source material, it does give broad support to the figure mentioned above for a similar period, i.e. just over *1.5 feet per year.*

Another example is the reduction in size of Warren Hill. The 1870 map (Fig.19) shows a distance scaling 170 feet from the top edge of the quarry to the cliff face at its narrowest point. The 1932 map (Fig.2) shows only 50 feet, a loss of 120 feet: very nearly *2 feet per year.* Equivalent figures at the summit, based on erosion near to the Coastguard Lookout, are even higher: 350 feet from the edge in 1870 and only 140 feet in 1932, i.e. *nearly 3.5 feet per year.* In addition, the maps show that footpaths have been lost along with cliffs both at the higher levels and the lower levels near Double Dykes.

A map by Lieutenant Murdoch Mackenzie, dated 1785, has been used by the council (in the Management Plan of 1997) to demonstrate loss of land from 1785 to 1996. The conclusion reached is that over these 211 years, 120 metres have been lost, i.e., nearly *two feet per year.* Although there may still be questions about accuracy, we do find some consistency in most of these various estimates.

An archaeological report in 1983 by Barton and James mentioned 45 metres of land lost from the unstable cliff top in the previous 75 years, with the cliff face eroded to within two feet of the excavation site. This equates therefore to almost exactly *two feet per year,* from 1908 to 1983.

There follows a brief summary of the more reliable historic indications of erosion:

Double Dykes	1797 – 1870	Approx. 1.5 feet p.a.	(OS maps)
Double Dykes	1870 – 1898	Approx. 3.5 feet p.a.	(OS maps)
Double Dykes	1870 – 1932	Approx. 3.0 feet p.a.	(OS maps)
Double Dykes	1777 – 1870	Approx. 2.0 feet p.a.	(Grose/OS)
Warren Hill (quarry)	1870 – 1932	Approx. 2.0 feet p.a.	(OS maps)
Warren Hill (summit)	1870 – 1932	Approx. 3.5 feet p.a.	(OS maps)
Warren Hill	1908 – 1983	Approx. 2.0 feet p.a.	(Barton & James)
Average	1785 – 1996	Approx. 2.0 feet p.a.	(Management Plan)

It is tempting to project forward a rate of erosion to see when the Head will be cut off or disappear. This is much too simplistic and inaccurate. For example, if we take the narrowest part, at around 1,000 feet, we could decide that it would be 1,000 years before the sea encroaches to the harbour, assuming the rate is one foot per year. This takes no account of how a breakthrough, once achieved, can establish a tidal stream through remaining land. In addition, at the most vulnerable points, by the Dykes, the land slopes away to the north-east, making such a breakthrough easier for the sea each year. Other factors are rising sea levels and, more important still, increasing extreme weather events due to global warming. For example, a single 1 in 100-year event is expected to cause 36 feet of erosion at the Dykes.

As a brief but hopefully accessible record for the future, I measured (on three dates as below) with a surveyor's 100-foot tape, certain distances between timber piles and the cliff. Fig.46 shows the location (at points A, B, and C) of three of these piles, which are formed from strong and durable Greenheart timber, each approximately 30 feet long. Fig.51 is a photograph of one. The council installed them as points of reference for the production of regular sectional drawings giving the updated profile of land, cliff, beach and seabed. They were found to be much better than the scaffold poles previously used, as those tended to get washed away and were less safe for the public. The dimensions shown below were taken horizontally from the centre of the top of each post to the cliff side:

POSITION	28 DEC.2002	3 JAN.2004	23 DEC.2004
A	16'6"	16'10	16'9"
B	13'7"	16'8"	16'6"
C	14'7"	15'6"	16'0"

There is some difficulty in getting accurate measurements due to unevenness in the cliff face owing to gullies. It would therefore be best to look again in about ten years. Nonetheless, using the full two-year period, my measurements show that an average of nine inches p.a. had been lost, over a time without any extreme events. Although there is insufficient information here for full statistical validity, it may be indicative that point B suffered the greatest erosion by far at 35 inches. It was near this point that the sea broke through in the 1970s to flood the car park by the Dykes. Fig.54 shows the remains of the emergency repairs to the cliff done by the council at the time. Although the cliff height was then raised, there has been significant later erosion and the low cliff must be regarded as vulnerable to an extreme event on both sides of the Dykes. The large amount of erosion at the Dykes is very evident if you walk around them. Rough bays have been scoured away to the east and the west of the gabions.

Fig.53 is a photograph looking east on Warren Hill between the cliff and the footpath by the quarry edge. The dimensions measured on 2 June 2002 were 10ft.6in. from the centre of the footpath to the first post of the fence; 54ft 2in from the first post to the last, i.e. 9th post; 8ft 10in from the last post to the edge. Let us hope this total of 73ft 6in can be maintained as much as possible. In March 2005, I paced the distance from the coastguard station to the cliff edge at 75 feet. There is anecdotal evidence that this is only half the distance it was 30 years ago. Incidentally, I would consider it unsafe for anyone to measure to the cliff edge without special care and training.

Fig.53 ***Fence near cliff top at head of ironstone quarry, 2002***

(Author as measured 2 June that year)

For future reference, a nine-post fence existed near to the top of the ironstone quarry, running from the wide main gravel footpath almost to the cliff edge. The distance measured from the centre of the footpath to the edge of the cliff was 73 feet 6 inches.

It remains to comment further on the amount of annual erosion after the Long Groyne was built. So far we have my own recent measurements (which need taking for a longer period for proper validity) at nine inches, and the Halcrow figures (1978 to 2001) of one inch to seven inches, giving an average of say, six inches in vulnerable sections. I calculate 12 inches by scaling the Middlesex University 50-year projection from 1986, at a badly affected point west of the Dykes.

At the end of 2004, I became involved with another retired chartered surveyor, who was very concerned about erosion. After renewed research into maps and aerial photographs, we took fairly full measurements of the cliff position, using chain lines where required, from Point House Café to the base of Warren Hill. These lines can be replicated in the future to demonstrate erosion. Although the method of tape measurement is a little old-fashioned, at least it is accurate and not subject to the errors associated with computerised geo-rectification of aerial photographs. Apart from the new drawings, which will stand as a publicly available point of reference, a detailed report was produced dated March 2005 from Hengistbury Residents' Association (HENRA). It made a good case for further coast protection and was submitted to the key players. The essence of the report is that cliff armouring should now be installed from the café to the Long Groyne and new rock groynes from the Dykes to the Long Groyne. Two further erosion estimates have resulted from the exercise. Firstly, the scaled distance, on the 1962 OS map at 1/2500 scale from the kerb of Broadway at the car park entrance to the cliff edge, was 990 feet compared to the 2005 measurement on the ground of 930 feet 6 inches. Secondly, with somewhat less accuracy, the 1978 and 2001 photographs, in the Halcrow were report, were compared at two identifiable locations on either side of the Dykes. Another summary follows. Although there is some variation in figures, there is no doubt about the great reduction in erosion achieved by the Long Groyne.

Café - Dykes	2002 – 2004	Approx. 9" p.a.	My measurements
Café - Long Groyne	1978 – 2001	Approx. 6" p.a.	Halcrow report
Point west of Dykes	1986 – 2036	Approx. 12" p.a.	Middlesex University plan
Broadway - cliff	1962 – 2005	Approx. 17" p.a.	HENRA report
Point west of Dykes	1978 – 2001	Approx. 22" p.a.	Aerial photographs
Point east of Dykes	1978 – 2001	Approx. 22" p.a.	Aerial photographs

My final conclusion here is that average erosion, since the latest groynes, may now be put at 12 to 18 inches per year, near the Dykes.

Value of vegetation

For sheer low cost and high effectiveness as part of a wider policy of coast protection, it is hard to beat vegetation. Whilst it will not work on its own, it greatly enhances the other engineering. Provided it reflects local conditions, and is carried out and monitored with skill on a long-term basis, there are great amenity advantages as well. My comments here are probably more historically appropriate to cliffs in Christchurch than at Hengistbury.

The Barton Clay cliffs, dating back over 50 million years, do suffer instability and erosion, mainly through water action. Research has shown that a certain grass mixture, known as the Engineering Sward, is effective to protect clay, restrict mudflows and resist frost. To allow grass to survive the hostile sterility of the cliffs, when the slope allows, topsoil can be added to score lines in the clay before seeding. At Highcliffe, it has been found best to use this salt-resistant mixture on lower slopes, shrubs part way up and trees at the top of the 100-foot cliffs. Intelligent monitoring is essential to success, because to leave matters for only two seasons would cause a loss of benefit. Ongoing husbandry includes: checking wet spots, which can be precursors of cliff slips, by noting the appearance of water tolerant species; monitoring trees for dieback at tips, as this can indicate ground movement; deadwooding before wildlife breeding; ditching, reseeding and strimming; feeding and repairing the sward; keeping the correct balance of tree species; introducing improved salt-tolerant grasses and shrubs.

Importance of the Long Groyne

The Long Groyne deserves special mention, as it is the most significant, effective and economical sea defence of all those yet attempted. Its function is to replace the natural defence of ironstones.

Built at a cost of about £20,000 in 1938, its need had been foreseen in the Vetch report of 1854 and the Druitt one of 1869. Agreement had been reached about the need for such a barrier groyne, in discussions between Bournemouth and Christchurch in 1936. It is a substantial 17-foot wide concrete construction including tram rail reinforcement running out 700 feet from the southeast corner of the Head. Materials were taken in side tipper wagons around this corner on a temporary railway "causeway" supported by concrete and piles. In 1937, forty delegates, from the Institution of Municipal and County Engineers, were taken on this railway to inspect the works by Mr. Clowes, the Borough Engineer. The locomotive, which hauled the party around the east side of the Head, was jovially christened the Bournemouth Belle! In fact, there were two engines, and two engine sheds were built for them near the Nursery. The causeway was damaged by post-war storms (acting on the newly vulnerable coast east of Long Groyne) and not repaired quickly enough to prevent a big cliff erosion and embayment.

Within a year, its worth was proved with a large western extension of the beach below the Head. Even the 1987-1989 storms (which showed that the original construction was too light) were just a temporary setback to the increasing build-up of dunes and vegetation, which are providing improved stability. The direct effect extends west about one third of the distance from the Long Groyne to the Dykes. This cliff section, of about 550 yards, held its alignment due to an absence of wave attack. In a way, it has been too successful, because there are times when the sand drift is so great that the groyne is almost covered over and not working properly, as it can no longer retain sand within the bay in such circumstances. However, this returns to the point that groynes do not prevent, but only restrict, sand drift. Divers know that visibility at Beer Pan Rocks is low in all but still conditions, due to the suspension of sediment, as it drifts. The extremely strong currents also create a need for great caution if snorkelling. It seems that the main risk is the fast west-flowing ebb tide.

Unfortunately, due to the restrictions on building materials arising from the approaching war, the council did not take the groyne about 300 feet further out to Beer Pan Rocks, which was the old line of the Head in the eighteenth century. Whilst therefore a big help to the scouring problem of Poole Bay, the Long Groyne would have been even more effective had it been longer. A fast, deep channel (locally known as the "gutway") formed between it and Beer Pan Rocks. The sandspit beaches immediately in the lee of the groyne were soon badly eroded. The extra scouring of Christchurch Bay was also evident in the early disappearance of the large extension to the Sandbank, which it will be remembered stretched to Highcliffe Castle and protected the coast. In effect, the Long Groyne restricted sand drifting round to the benefit of Christchurch.

One man's gain was therefore another man's loss. The problem exported by Bournemouth had to be addressed by Christchurch. This has been successfully accomplished with stone groynes all along the Sandbank from the Long Groyne to the Run, together with sea walls and groynes along Avon Beach, Friars Cliff and Highcliffe. As may be imagined, Christchurch was not entirely happy with its new problem and associated costs, and therefore objected strongly and successfully to a Bournemouth plan to extend the Long Groyne in 1956.

The mere existence of the artificial headland we call the Long Groyne prevents a lengthy shoreline seeking to move landwards. The result is a long-term reduction in erosion around both Poole Bay and Christchurch Bay to the benefit of Poole, Bournemouth and Christchurch. It is important to maintain it and by so doing, limit sediment loss both at the Head and in the two bays. The council in 2005 was making a recommendation for its reconstruction in the draft Coastal Protection Strategy.

Weather conditions in the harbour

Although normally a reasonably sheltered haven, the harbour can be very inhospitable, particularly in extreme conditions of wind, tide and river flows. If there is a storm combined with floodwater trying to get out, low barometric pressure, and an unusually high incoming tide, levels can rise very seriously.

In 1916, there were such extreme conditions that the local paper published a Flood Report Supplement, from which extensive quotation has already been made in the Introduction. Figs. 45 and 49 are early photographs giving some idea of the undeveloped and unprotected nature of the quay in those days. It is because of this ongoing risk that since 1996, the terraced cottages at Mudeford Quay now have a gated concrete floodwall all around them. I am told that a combination of spring tide, south-easterly gale, and high flood levels in the rivers caused a four-foot depth of water in these cottages in 1952. I hope that this sort of thing is just isolated bad weather rather than a pointer to the future total loss of protection of the harbour. In recent years, I have witnessed water breaking over the Quay on to the tarmac car spaces and the damage the dinghies have suffered in their parks. Indeed, the flood defence works of 1995/1996 were designed to allow overtopping about twice a year. But 1916 must have been much more serious, as the waves overtopped Mudeford Sandbank and smashed up a tea room boat on the harbour side.

Christchurch Council, as the main responsible body for the Sandbank, has taken much trouble over recent years to ensure its survival. The problem is well known. For example, according to one 1936 report, there were 400 huts at Mudeford among the dunes and 20 were actually washed away, whilst 50 were moved to safety by their owners. The Engineering Services Team is acutely aware of the vulnerability. One of its publications

(*Mudeford Sandbank Coastal Defence Strategy,* 1999) comments on the eight reported cases of overtopping and breaching during the last 120 years.

In October 1976, for example, the sea swept right through near the café and destroyed 40 huts. The beach superintendent was shaken in one incident, when the hut he was in was lifted up by the waves. In the same month, only half of a sea wall remained standing at the bottom of the garden of one resident (of, I believe, Mudeford village). The council acted within 24 hours, by installing 15 cwt. granite blocks. As for the quay, a car parking charges notice was photographed under water by the local paper.

The long-term solution for the Sandbank, and very effective it has been, was to make 200 foot wide, storm-resisting beaches. This was achieved with new and strengthened rock groynes combined with putting enormous amounts of gravel below the sand on the sea side.

Although it is hard to imagine these days, the Stour has been known to freeze over. In January 1881, people walked across from Wick to Christchurch Quay. During that month, temperatures were below freezing for 21 days, and for nine days, below 20°F. In 1855, it was even possible to skate from the barracks to Mudeford, except for Wick, where the ferryman broke the ice.

History of coastal defence

Just after 1900, Bournemouth Council appointed a deputation known as a "Flying Squadron" to visit other resorts and indeed the continent to report on sea defences and cliff protection as may be applied to the town. In essence, they recommended an Undercliff Drive scheme as both a visitor attraction and a method to protect the cliffs. The first part, a drive and promenade from the Pier to the end of Meyrick Road, was opened in 1907. About four miles of promenades were built between 1907 and 1936 from Alum Chine to Southbourne at a cost of £348,700. With ongoing serious erosion, the 1950-1953 storms, and the loss of residential property near the cliff edge, the council carried out emergency protection works and continued to extend the sea wall and promenade eastwards. This has now come to an end, not least because of sheer cost, currently about £2,100 per foot run. For instance, it would cost over £7 million to extend the promenade about 3,400 feet from Solent Road to the Dykes. It is unlikely ever to be considered. Draglines and subsequent vegetation have generally been used to try and stabilise the cliffs at an angle of 36 degrees. This does not apply of course at Warren Hill, which is at least 70 degrees, nor to other parts such as the East Cliff.

Virtually no coastal defence work was done from 1939 to 1945. By the time of the Coast Protection Act of 1949, which followed a government-sponsored study by Professor Steers of Cambridge, there had been ten years of neglect. In 1951, there were fears about losing Avon Beach through storm-based erosion. The sea had reached the foundations of the café. Without delay, the council bought the freehold interest in the beach and instructed Blackford & Son (Calne) Ltd. to do the work. Steel piling, 15,000 tons of hardcore and up to 1,500 tons of concrete were placed in a difficult but successful 24-hour winter operation, resulting in a new promenade and three-foot high sea wall.

Rectangular stone filled wire cages (gabions) have been built at the slope to the sea from the Solent Meads car park, in a section on the south side of the harbour and at Double Dykes. Both wooden and Portland Stone groynes have been placed all round Poole Bay to the Dykes (current cost for both types about £200,000 each). The rock groynes are more effective as they are better at dissipating wave power but are considered to be less safe for bathers.

Sand was pumped by a dredger from the sea to replace beach losses along the bay up to Solent Road in 1974/75. The project required 654,000 cubic metres from the Dolphin Sands and was the first such scheme in the UK. There were very heavy storms in September 1974, causing the sand pipe to break up and, according to the local press, take on the appearance of the Loch Ness Monster! In the same storms, about 2,000 deckchairs were lost or damaged beyond repair. In the mid-1970s, the sea did break through due to a storm surge, to the west as well as to the east of the Dykes. This event goes against the general belief that the only real risk is to the east of them. Clearly, work was needed to prevent another flooding of the car park and risk of a tidal stream becoming established. If you look from the beach to the left of two groynes west of the Dykes, you can see it took the form of old road debris, including tarmac and kerb-stones, for about 130 feet at the top of the cliff-face (Fig.54). Beach levels were swiftly reinstated by both sea and wind driven material from the fortuitously replenished beaches to the west.

Apart from this emergency treatment of White Pits, a group of the unemployed was put to work at the sea end of the Dykes in 1976 installing and filling gabions at the back of the beach, just above the High Water line. It was a temporary solution in order to secure the Dykes for the time being. Despite this evidence, the

Fig.54 ***White Pits cliff face bolstered with hardcore after sea breakthrough, 1970s***
(Author 2002)

Whilst it is expected that one day the sea will break through east of the Dykes, it is less well known that it has already done so west of them. A quantity of road material was immediately made available for this emergency repair and remains visible near the top. In view of subsequent erosion and increased storminess in the future, the repair may not be effective to prevent flooding of the car park again.

Environment Department rejected an application for a scheme costed at £500,000 for five groynes up to the Dykes. The reason given referred to the value of the land to be protected not being enough. In 1977, the council carried out a second gabion scheme, with rubble back fill, to deal with a 33-foot cliff breach just to the east of the Dykes. The same year, two timber permeable groynes and a ramp were built near to Solent Road. This sort of groyne was useful to anchor the eastern end of replenishment, whilst allowing some drifting through them in the inter-tidal zone.

In 1980, land was reclaimed on the east side of the sandspit and three years later three reinforced groynes built at its southern end.

However much it may seem obvious that public money would be well spent on protecting Hengistbury Head, it generally seems to require a battle. There was an approach from David Atkinson, MP, to the Mayor of Bournemouth in September 1984. He was concerned at the severe erosion problem, and pointed out that the Head was just as important to the town as Bournemouth International Centre. The previous July, advice had been given to a committee about the undermining and outflanking of the 1976 gabions at the Dykes, together with a comment about erosion of three to four metres a year. A group was duly formed with the acronym DASH (Determined Action to Save Hengistbury Head). Following a public meeting on 15 December 1984, the following proposition was put forward to the Government: "We request that the minister instruct Bournemouth Council to provide the necessary details and plans for his approval by 1 May 1985."

Whilst the council was trying to consult some 30 organisations and overcome various objections to its defence proposals, which had been adopted by committee in July 1984, it was referred to the Ombudsman in 1985 for mal-administration, for not undertaking protection works. The first scheme included submerged breakwaters, which were opposed by Christchurch, due to the risk of erosion of their beaches. Hydraulics Research Ltd., Wallingford reported that expenditure of £3,900,000 was needed. There was a freeze on capital spending at the time. The revised plan, implemented from December 1985, incorporated a limited scheme of groynes up to the Dykes and new gabions to protect them. Furthermore, Wallingford was commissioned to create, in their large wave tank, a physical model of the coast from Solent Beach around to the foot of Mudeford Sandbank. In the climate of the day, this was quite a success. It is also noteworthy that Mrs. Margaret Thatcher, then Prime Minister, visited the Head when staying in Bournemouth in the 1980s. I understand that the visit assisted the council's application, at a time of financial stringency, for grant to build new groynes under the 1949 Act.

After extensive negotiations, resulting in partial government approval of the council's plans, certain works were completed in 1987: three rock groynes at the Dykes and five rock groynes, revetment and causeway north east of Long Groyne. However, English Nature persuaded the Ministry of Agriculture, Fisheries and Food that no groynes were needed from the Dykes up to Long Groyne.

To the east of Warren Hill, a Purbeck stone cascade, following the line of a large gully, can be seen from the beach. The cliff face was graded on either side, but never vegetated owing to objections from English Nature. The land drains laid behind the stone steps may now be partly blocked. Hopefully, those laid within the cliff are still clear and helping stability. If you walk along the wide gravel track from the eastern end of the top of the Head, you can see some concrete manhole covers, which are above this land drain.

In 1989/90, 998,000 cubic metres were pumped at very low cost, because the material was taken easily from the entrance to Poole Harbour, which had silted up. The beach east of Solent Road has been stabilised by shingle replacement once only, in 1989/90, when 148,000 cubic metres were used. Due to the lack of groynes east of the Dykes, it took just three years for this to be removed by the sea.

Beach monitoring is essential for the survival of the promenades. Fig.55, the latest graph available, shows net volume against time from 1974 to 2003. We do not want to go below a "critical beach volume" of about 2,000,000 cubic metres, since the promenades would begin to fail. As at 2004, we were again approaching that volume, so requiring replenishment in order to save them. Moreover, it would be more a case of replacing them than repairing them should erosion cause collapse from beneath. There really is no alternative to keeping the volume above the critical level.

The two large schemes referred to above in 1974/75 and 1989/90 are reflected in the two graph peaks. Latest thinking is that this "boom and bust approach" needs to be refined into a "robust approach", under which beaches are replenished fully and then maintained at high levels by minor schemes about every two years. This is now being planned. The least satisfactory method would be two-yearly schemes based on a low critical volume.

Mudeford Sandbank has been retained with new limestone groynes all along it. Every year sand is collected from Christchurch harbour and placed on the sandspit. In 1996, a Class A tide gauge was fitted to Bournemouth Pier to monitor sea levels. In 2003, Bournemouth could spend about £1,640 per day over the year on capital projects of which about half was government grant. Engineering repairs from the revenue budget averaged around £820 per day. Much is therefore required in the way of budgets, planning, monitoring, liaison of various parties (Bournemouth Council, Poole Council, Christchurch Council, English Nature, English Heritage, DEFRA as coast protection authority) and specialist advice (e.g. Hydraulics Research Ltd., Wallingford, Halcrow, Swindon, Bournemouth University, Proudman Oceanographic Laboratories, etc.).

The council monitors sand movement (littoral drift) along the whole of Poole Bay eight times a month. In addition, there are annual aerial photographs and a set of 50 large-scale 1/500 plans of Hengistbury Head itself. These are used whenever engineering drawings are required for a new scheme, providing better accuracy than using the Ordnance Survey. Defence plans need to reflect that whilst erosion is very slight to the cliffs above the promenades, it does continue out to sea within the bay. A continuing problem is the sheer loss from the land of eroded material. Although the coarser sand and gravel drifts along the coast, the majority of around 90% is much finer and goes out to sea.

There is a sediment sink known as Hook Sands lying off Sandbanks. Monitoring has shown that it affects wave action. But current thinking is that there is no source of sediment supply from offshore despite some westward drift, mainly because it is unable to return uphill to shore. A long tail of sediment stretches to the west of the Shingles, a bank of shingle just off the Isle of Wight amounting to more than 50 million cubic yards, but the tides do not return it to shore. Generally, it is true to say that beaches do not result from offshore supply; they are fed instead from coastal debris due to erosion. Locally, we are fortunate that such debris is golden sand and not black mud.

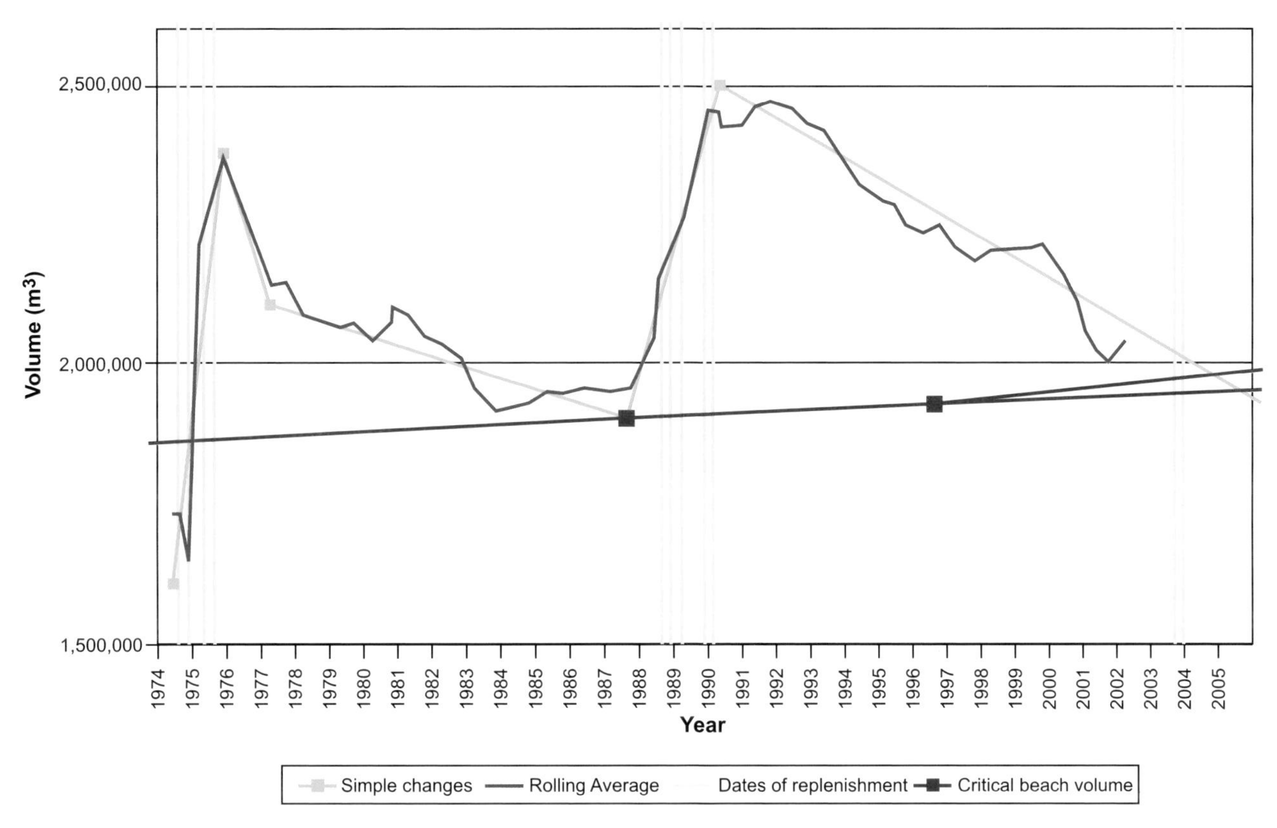

Fig.55 ***Crucial beach volume in Poole Bay, 1974 to 2005***

(Reproduced by consent of Bournemouth Borough Council)

Coastal monitoring is essential to decide how to keep the sea at bay. The graph shows that the critical volume of around 2 million cubic metres, of sand and gravel in the bay, must be maintained at least every 13 years or so (by replenishment) to prevent damage to the promenades and to restrict erosion to the east at Hengistbury. It is hoped that after a big scheme in the winter of 2005/2006, levels can be maintained by smaller schemes every two years.

Failed proposals for sea defences

A measure of the seriousness of coast protection is the fact that beach monitoring is now considered essential all round the United Kingdom, including all 88 district councils with a coastal boundary.

A number of public bodies, together known as the Poole and Christchurch Bays Coastal Group, commissioned the 1999 Poole Bay and Christchurch Bay Shoreline Management Plan (SMP). They form the Standing Conference on Problems Associated with the Coastline (SCOPAC) and comprise New Forest, Christchurch, Bournemouth, Poole, Purbeck, Dorset, and Hampshire Councils, Environment Agency South West, Environment Agency Southern, Poole Harbour Commissioners and English Nature (EN). Under the 1949 Coast Protection Act, DEFRA (formerly MAFF) consider such plans from authorities all round the coast. It is interesting that the Act does not give maritime coastal authorities any duty to protect their coast, merely a power. A decision has to be submitted for approval by DEFRA on whether to advance the coast, hold the line or operate a managed retreat. The SMP, as approved, intends to "hold the line."

After the 1989/90 shingle renourishment of the beach east of Point House Café, monitoring revealed that (as expected), within just three years, the material placed east of the Dykes was lost, due to the lack of groynes. The council produced a fresh scheme for the six suggested groynes, which had been previously rejected. After lengthy negotiations with EN and the exchange of seven draft agreements, one was finally signed for five groynes. Unfortunately, after the grant application was duly made in 1999, EN withdrew their support the following year due to science-based objections. Without their support, the plans were dropped.

What were these "science-based objections"? It seems that certain geologists do not want to lose the "geological window" as would tend to happen with coastal defence works. The Hengistbury Head Local Nature Reserve, declared in May 1991, referred to its importance as a stratigraphic bridging exposure, linking outcropping tertiary formations. Amongst all its other designations, this is a Geological Conservation Review site. Whilst the council felt protection was needed, some geomorphologists at EN believed, on a 20-year view, that the bay would stabilise after limited and acceptable erosion. The latter opinion assumed that only one or two extra groynes were needed just beyond those at the Dykes. In the end, a compromise was made into a legal agreement: the council could install short groynes, with EN managing them, adjusting length and height as required in order to allow controlled erosion. By 2003, there was no finance available and nothing could be done.

There was a lobby of EN by a joint committee of Christchurch residents' associations in 1995 to try to get sanction for these groynes, as first wanted by Bournemouth Council ten years previously. That year there had been a 1,000-ton fall below the coastguard station, shown in Fig.37. Whilst coast protection engineers pointed out that everyone else accepted the need for groynes, except English Nature, the latter said they wanted to "help establish how sea levels had changed and so increase understanding of global warming" and not "to overprotect the Head." This followed an earlier report referring to fears of the sea finally breaking through at Double Dykes. According to the Shoreline Management Plan (Section 3.C.18), both EN and Bournemouth Council spend money removing cliff falls, so increasing erosion as a matter of policy.

One policy, which does not help funding, is that such money can only be used to protect the coast if residential property is directly affected. The irony here is that property certainly is affected, albeit in a differing local authority, on the other side of Christchurch Harbour. Having had the application rejected, there was a further change to the situation justifying resubmission, without objections this time. One response to the grant application had been: "If the projected breakthrough is in 50 years time, why not apply to install the protection in 45 years time?"

A fresh technical opinion, about the speed of erosion east of the Dykes, and the need for protection measures, then arrived from Halcrow, as part of the 2003 Strategy Study following the Shoreline Management Plan (SMP). Broadly, they felt that average erosion, of only six inches p.a., did not justify new groynes, and replenishment was inappropriate on a beach without groynes. In any case, they said, the beach towards the headland received the benefit of sand drifting from the west, and was replenished naturally. If such a scheme would not attract funding, due to other coastal locations being at higher risk, there was little point in making an application. It followed that, in stark contrast to all previous policy, the plan in 2004 was to provide neither groynes nor replenishment east of the Dykes. With a low national budget for protection, no buildings behind the cliffs, and other locations deemed to be in greater need, perhaps this conclusion is not surprising.

The Shoreline Management Plan is regularly reviewed, so this latest decision might not be the last word. I am sure that the council will be closely monitoring the problem and will expect reconsideration if necessary. However cogent the reasoning for the no-action plan, I think that the low cliffs will stay vulnerable to an extreme event, and it would be better to guard against letting the sea into the harbour. If the worst does happen, an emergency repair of any cliff breach is likely to be approved at the time.

Once cliffs have fallen, they can never be replaced. If we let them go now, the choice is no longer available to our descendants. In short, "true sustainability" means that we should save cliffs unless there are compelling reasons against such a policy. The merit of spending now, to secure coastal defences, is not however as simple as indicated above. The reason is that reducing the current rate of erosion may prove to be less significant than the impact of global warming over the next 50 to 100 years.

In summary, plans for extra groynes east of the Dykes failed to attract finance, and now the scheme has been dropped. Beach recharge is also now officially considered unsuitable for this location.

Reef plan and coast protection

Since various organisations have different agendas and traditional coastal protection methods are expensive, it is possible that when protection does become essential, approval will not be forthcoming. The unfortunate result would be the Head becoming an island before necessary, with all the risks that implies for the north side of the harbour.

There is however a reef plan put forward to improve the waves for surfing, whilst at the same time (it is claimed) protecting the coast. A reef in Bournemouth would comprise bags of sand in 20 feet of water some 800 feet from the coast, with the waves diverting either side of the triangular shape. It can be designed to provide different waves types, from small, Malibu style ones to steep grinding barrels. The council's coast protection view is understandably conservative: not at this stage to remove the groynes, which are proven, even if it is decided to install a reef. This sounds right if the case for reefs is still to be made. Another restrictive factor is the sheer lack of research and experience of submerged breakwaters in this country. After all, why should an engineer, who has been consulted by a council, back an unknown quantity, when there is always advice to be given and a good flow of work concerning groynes?

At the time of writing a reef at Boscombe is approved as part of the Honeycombe Chine scheme, subject to certain conditions before the consent becomes final. The reef is seen as an integral part of the seafront regeneration proposals, with the cost met from selling the car park for residential development. The sudden listing of pier front buildings caused one delay as it implied a need to replan the leisure scheme. The next stage is a site investigation, which if successful, would allow the final design to be done. Only if all this happens would it be built, perhaps by 2006, and only if it proved satisfactory would Southbourne be reconsidered. Ongoing concerns include the risks of dangerous rip currents being created. The response from the surfing lobby is that, although such concerns are legitimate, an open mind should be kept, because they can be overcome by careful design.

So what is the case for a surf reef? Erosion followed the loss of the ironstones, which acted as a natural protecting offshore bar. A reef would in effect replace this, so restoring stability. Other advantages include no visual impact, fishery enhancement, improved bio-diversity and easy adjustment of height and extent. It is also claimed to be safer, should rubble groynes be replaced by a reef, because life guards cannot see over such eight-foot high structures. To test the concept in local conditions, it is possible to keep the groynes whilst measuring the reef's impact. It could provide coast protection as an economic benefit and enhance marine life as an environmental benefit, as well as improve surfing. However, the Boscombe upgrade scheme means that visitors would have to exchange the benefit of a car park a few yards from the promenade for a land train to the one in Hawkwood Road.

Professor Black from New Zealand has described to Wessex Surf Club the recently completed Narrowneck reef, on the Australian Gold Coast. Some 350 sandbags were placed 500 feet offshore, filling an area 1,150 feet by 2,000 feet and ranging in depth from three to 33 feet. It is claimed that the beach has widened, so creating more public open space. Marine life was also soon established. Beach replenishment was however needed.

His calculations show that the average swell is amplified 250% by the reef. This would mean that a knee-high wave would essentially become overhead. The British Surfing Association has commented that the real choice for Hengistbury beach is between a sandy shore with a reef and a shingle shore with groynes. The Bournemouth Surfing Centre commented in February 2005 about the lack of adequate surfing due to delayed beach replenishment. There is some disagreement about the short-term impact of such replenishment on the offshore sand bar (which constantly moves backwards and forwards towards the beach) and surf quality. In the end, this must be decided as a technical matter of engineering opinion, one aspect of which should be impact on the Hengistbury shoreline, which is already vulnerable to extreme events.

Current rate of erosion and plans for coast protection

As indicated earlier, I would now estimate that average historic erosion near the Dykes since the latest groynes is about 12 to 18 inches per year. The future rate will depend on protection measures and the amount of increase in sea attack. Normal waves, washing up through shingle to a low cliff (Fig.51), are not an immediate concern. Even a tremendous "one-off" storm, which causes a dramatic recession in the coastline, need be no disaster in the medium term, because any gaps could be filled. The real issue is the possibility of a basic climate change within the next century, meaning that it might become too expensive to protect the existing coastline.

Land loss by the Dykes is a special case because the part up to the edge of the gabions is reclaimed land anyway. There seem to be two options. Firstly, if the council decides only to apply for grant justified by DEFRA's criteria, then the gabions will be allowed to wear away and the unprotected and exposed reclaimed land lost to the sea within a few years. Thereafter, the cliff line at the Dykes would line up roughly with that on either side and proceed to erode at the same speed. Presumably, the existing footpath on the cliff top would be lost. Secondly, the council may install a rock revetment to protect the Dykes at its own expense. Certainly, this method ought to restrict erosion there (at the cost of less than two groynes) whilst it continued on each side.

Renourishment for Bournemouth was again delayed to 2005/06 at an expected cost of £10 million to £15 million. It would provide sand only up to the end of the promenade, because there was no perceived need by the consultants for anything further east. Although expensive, such costs are much less than the costs of repair or replacement to promenades, which have subsided after being undercut by the sea. It is thereafter hoped to keep the volume at around 75% of the initial fill, subject to DEFRA finance and the rate of loss. This means that there would be fresh, minor schemes every one, two or three years. Poole Borough and the Poole Harbour Commissioners have a report about deepening the harbour approach channel and beneficial use of the dredged material. Although the material is now to be used for Poole Bay replenishment, this will not extend to the headland. The report authors consider that the only impact on Hengistbury will be a reduction in erosion of areas which may contain archaeological remains.

The approved strategy should also see the replacement of four timber groynes at Solent Beach with three rock ones, the reconstruction of Long Groyne, and a rock replacement of the existing revetment at the Dykes. As outlined in the HENRA report of March 2005, it would now be a good idea to evaluate certain options in terms of their costs and benefits:

1. Do nothing and suffer the maximum consequences.
2. Provide rock groynes and cliff armouring now.
3. Do nothing for now, repair the breach in due course and then protect as in 2.
4. Allow the breach and then provide a suitable sea wall to protect Christchurch and Southbourne, extending as far as necessary up the two rivers.

My view is that the second option would prove to be the best.

In support of this, some more work done after the report argues the complete loss of the cliff face at particular locations in less than 50 years, i.e. a shallow mound would then provide no defence against a breakthrough.

The recommendation from the Strategy Study is known as Limited Intervention. In summary, there is to be no beach recharge, no new groynes and no protection for the low cliffs by the Dykes or the north side of the harbour. No grant would be available to protect the Dykes, which have also not attracted protection through the remits of either English Nature or English Heritage. But the Long Groyne would be maintained and the cliff erosion monitored. If there were to be a breakthrough by the sea near the Dykes, any remedial action would have to be decided at the time. My opinion is that the council would not allow a tidal stream to become established. All the above is subject to the political process and regular advice from future SMPs. Finally, it does seem strange that expensive protection for the harbour from the east side has been officially sanctioned, but not from the south.

Will the Head become an island?

Sadly, the response to this question is "yes."

In the end, the efforts of man are as nothing compared to natural forces. We will get more storms, more erosion and higher sea level, which will combine to defeat even improved defences. (The only reservation to this is the possibility that if the Gulf Stream is "turned off", storminess might or might not increase in a new icy climate.) Unless there is a total rethink on how to defend a coast and how much extra money can be spent, my own guess is we have another 50 to 150 years before the Head is cut off. The idea of providing rock armour along the unprotected cliffs might be cost-effective, but it is unlikely to attract the blessing of English Nature, and there are no plans for it. Current thinking is that a 100-year event would reduce beach width at the Dykes by about 36 feet, but the chance of a breach in any one year is below 1%.

There have been concerns about this risk since the nineteenth century. Fortunately, the more dire predictions have so far proved false. In 1977, the local press reported that there was a risk to the west of the Dykes, of a sea invasion up to Broadway. It pointed out that the sea, on the Mudeford Sandbank side, had lapped across into Christchurch Harbour in exceptional conditions. This comment seems to have come at a time of increasing pressure from the council for the necessary government support. Within the previous year, the Environment Department had rejected a proposal for five groynes up to the Dykes on the ground that the value of land to be protected was not sufficient, regardless of property on the Christchurch side.

It has been reported that erosion "continues to accelerate" at Hengistbury. Also, since its topography falls sharply inland, the headland is a finite resource threatened with destruction. (*Coastal Defence and Earth Science Conservation*. The Geological Society. 1998.) Before dismissing this as just another outdated comment in view of the Strategy Study's figure of six inches p.a. erosion, perhaps we should review the Halcrow caveats. They

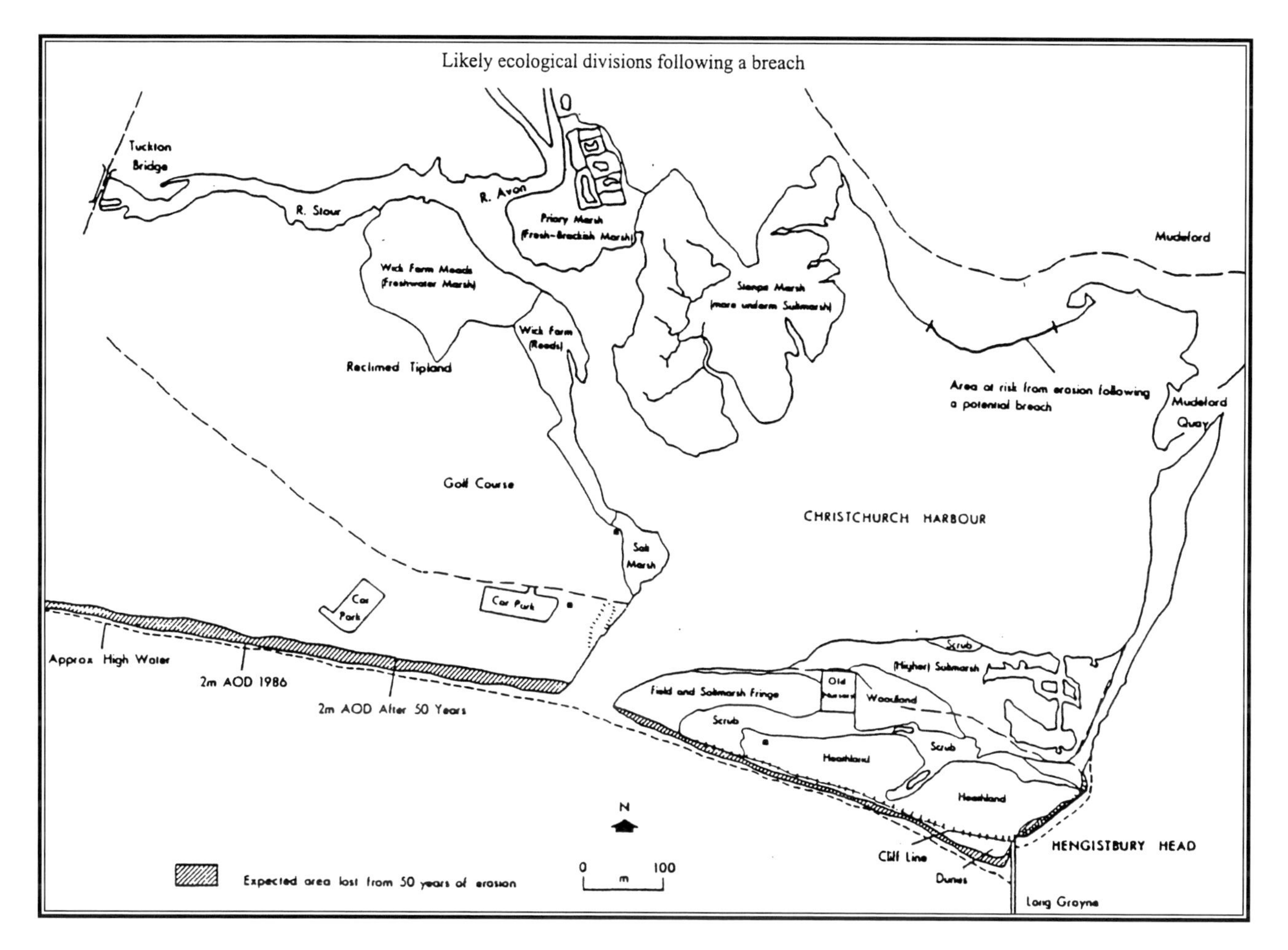

Fig.56 ***Potential Island of Hengistbury, as forecast in 1986***

(Reproduced by consent of E. Penning-Rowsell, Middlesex University)

Research concluded that in the absence of protection, Hengistbury could become an island in around 50 years from 1986. This initial phase, of an established tidal stream, assumes that the Dykes would be sliced through and the harbour frontage to the west of Mudeford Quay would be at risk. Clearly, the Centre and the ranger's cottage would become unviable without expensive safeguards. It is important to be aware that eventually it will become Hengistbury Island: the exact timing is just not yet known.

say that the estimate has had to be adjusted for error, that future rates could be different, and that monitoring is essential. Their Local Scale Shoreline Response (2002) indicated that a breach was possible within 100 years. In short, the consulting engineers are not claiming that the estimated low annual erosion rate of six inches disproves the Island of Hengistbury concept. Nonetheless, the question remains: "Is it any use spending millions to combat erosion if sea level rises and greater storms in the next 50 years are going to be lethal anyway?"

The consequence of major global warming, should it occur, is that the existing aggressive wave attacks, and storm surges operating from a higher level, are definitely expected to create the island of Hengistbury. And is there anything, which can be done about it? Is there any merit in placing new groynes from Double Dykes to the Long Groyne if they will not work? I give these questions a resounding "Yes." My belief is that a long-term plan should be financed for the benefit of the Head and Christchurch. It could include raising groyne heights, placing further ones from the Dykes to the Long Groyne and inserting a sea defence wall of Portland stone from Point House Café to Long Groyne. It would be good value compared to the consequences of letting the sea into the harbour. Indeed, the cost should not be prohibitive, being something like a quarter of the cost to the town of beach replenshment.

During a time span of 100 years, there could be a downward or upward revision of warming predictions or the invention of an effective and economical way to protect for the following century. Even if nothing beneficial happens, it is surely better to plan proper protection for a long period, such as 100 years from now, rather than recklessly leave Christchurch to be "rinsed out one morning." This turn of phrase comes from 1855, during the ironstone mining, when Christchurch inhabitants were said to "think more of the profit from the spending of the wages of a few labourers, than the danger of them being rinsed out one morning." At least such a method would permit people to make reasonable plans for the use of property.

The Flood Hazard Research Centre of Middlesex University has done work on the risk of a sea breach. Fig.56 shows the Island of Hengistbury created around 2036 following 50 years of coastal erosion at current rates. My belief is that this report was based on the defences in place at this time, including the groynes up to the Dykes. Consistent with this, the SMP is concerned about the impact on the Christchurch coast if a permanent tidal channel became established following a breach. However, such concern seems inconsistent with the advice in 2004 that no defence work is now needed east of the Dykes.

Although I have not come across any official record, the gamekeeper's son was apparently caught up in a sea breach by the Dykes, in the late 1940s. The water was pouring alongside the eastern side of the Dykes knee-deep. It reached as far as the burial mound by the cottage. Another instance is a storm in the 1970s, which caused a breach on both sides of the Dykes, including the flooding of the main car park. These examples provide simple and direct evidence of the high risk.

So, yes, the Head is going to become an island, but I do not know when this will happen. My more detailed guesses are:

With a good sea defence programme and no abnormal storms, 150 years.

With a good sea defence programme but abnormal storms, 100 years.

With no such programme but no abnormal storms, 70 years.

With no such programme and abnormal storms, 50 years.

These time limits would be greater if the authorities decided to rectify the tidal breach and improve sea defences at that time, but the level of uncertainty about that precludes me from any further appraisal.

Summary and general outlook

We are reaching the end of this tale of long and aggressive erosion by sea, weather and tourists. Current policy is in effect a "managed retreat" of the coastline, whereby the cliffs erode every year and eventually Hengistbury will become an island. Although normal erosion may not prove serious for many years, the low cliffs will certainly be very vulnerable to any 100-year storm.

Increased storminess, more extreme events and global warming may become a bigger factor than ongoing erosion in eventually causing Hengistbury Head to be cut off. The most likely breach position is just to the east of the Dykes. Should this occur, the sea could swamp Stanpit Marsh and some low-lying parts of Christchurch. However, if a sensible long-term plan is put in place to protect Hengistbury – and therefore Christchurch – for as long as practical, then future generations may just about be able to live with it. There remains an important qualification to the last sentence: by the time it is cut off, society may be facing much more serious problems anyway.

FOURTEEN

MAIN EVENTS, OWNERSHIP HISTORY AND LEGAL STATUS

What we know of the past is mostly not worth knowing. What is worth knowing is mostly uncertain. Events in the past may be roughly divided into those, which probably never happened and those, which do not matter.

W. R. Inge

THIS chapter provides a brief summary of what has happened at Hengistbury from the Stone Age onwards, who owned it from the Norman Conquest, and how it can now be used as a matter of law. The first table includes some key milestones affecting Hengistbury, but excluding archaeological investigations, covered elsewhere. The second table tells the story of the owners, and the final section includes the many legal restrictions to bring us up to date.

Main events

DATE	MAIN EVENT
18,000 BC	Height of the Devensian Glaciation. From this time, glaciers began to melt, sea level rose and the Flandrian Transgression started.
13,000 BC	Upper Palaeolithic (recent part of Old Stone Age) began.
10,600 BC	Sustained human activity began in Britain
10,000 BC	Reindeer camp established on Warren Hill above where Long Groyne is now, but then was dry land up to France.
7,700 BC	Mesolithic (Middle Stone Age) began.
7,750 BC	Flints from the Mesolithic site, the Archers' Camp, are dated at this time, plus or minus 950 years.
6,600 BC	Separation of Britain from mainland Europe, by formation from west to east of the English Channel.
5,500-4,000 BC	Isle of Wight separated from mainland Britain.
4,000 BC	Neolithic (New Stone Age) began and early farming became established at Hengistbury. Sea level reached approx. current level.
1,700 BC	Bronze Age began, together with the use of the headland primarily as a cemetery.
700 BC	Iron Age began.
700-600 BC	Settlement in lee of Head began.
700 BC	Probable start of building Double Dykes to defend Iron Age settlement.
100 BC	Hengistbury Head became major trading port and Iron Age town.
AD 43	Roman invasion and conquest by Vespasian.
AD 406	Romans withdrew and around this time Hengistbury Head was probably abandoned or at least used very sparsely.
AD 1066	Norman Conquest.

AD 1113	Legend of the Dragon of Christchurch.
AD 1457	This is one of many dates when the south coast was at risk from across the Channel. In this case, the French threatened Southampton.
AD 1664	River Avon Navigation Act passed to make it usable from Christchurch Harbour to Salisbury.
AD 1676	Yarranton Report suggesting naval base etc. Although this did not happen, his idea of a cut through the Sandbank did, i.e. Clarendon's Rocks. A warning marker pole still exists, showing the sea end of the rocks.
AD 1762	Smeaton Report on Christchurch Harbour.
AD 1777	Grose descriptive report including measurements of the Dykes.
AD 1784	Battle of Mudeford.
AD 1836	Armstrong Report on Christchurch Harbour.
AD 1836	Sylvester Report on Christchurch Harbour.
AD 1848-1856	Ironstone removal from the beach by Holloway's Mining Company.
AD 1854	Vetch Report urging the end of the "evil" of mining.
AD 1856-1870	Mining of north and west face of Warren Hill for ironstone.
AD 1857	Two fatal accidents reported at open cast mining operation.
AD 1861	Fatal firearm accident at Double Dykes, resulting in erection of fenced monument.
AD 1888	An important date in the development of Bournemouth and the inevitable increase in pressure on Hengistbury. Both Boscombe and Southbourne piers opened, as did the fast rail connection to Waterloo via Brockenhurst.
AD 1898	Marie Theresa ran aground at Beer Pan Rocks.
AD 1908	Emma Sherriff found strangled west of the Dykes.
AD 1910	Death of C.S. Rolls at Bournemouth Centenary Airshow.
AD 1913	Golf course proposed.
AD 1919	Purchase by Gordon Selfridge from Meyrick family and plans started for building two castles on the Head.
AD 1930	Purchase by Bournemouth Corporation.
AD 1935	Construction of Broadway to the Dykes, so opening up the Head.
AD 1938	Long Groyne built, so greatly reducing sea erosion.
AD 1939-1945	Full occupation of the Head, including a number of military uses, in particular as a Chain Home Radar Station.
AD 1952-1957	Waste tipping, followed by reinstatement at Wick Fields.
AD 1956	Start of systematic bird recording by CHOG.
AD 1964	Marine Training Centre opened.
AD 1968	Land train started despite strong local opposition to the plan.
AD 1969	Agricultural lease terminated on land west of Dykes.
AD 1974	Local government reorganisation transferred Bournemouth area including the Head from Hampshire to Dorset.
AD 1975	Coastguard Hut built.
AD 1976	Quarry dammed to form lake and gabions installed at the Dykes.
AD 1979	Dykes given Ancient Monument status by Archaeological Areas Act.
AD 1981	Site of Special Scientific Interest allocated.
AD 1990	Local Nature Reserve status established, including Wick Fields, which had been used for private grazing.
AD 1992	Dykes closed to public access to prevent further tourist damage.
AD 1997	Most comprehensive five year Management Plan yet produced.
AD 2003	Planning consent for the large new Hengistbury Head Centre, west of the Dykes.
AD 2004	Third big beach replenishment planned to combat coastal erosion, after 1974 and 1989 schemes.

A number of the dates above are necessarily approximate.

Ownership history and outlook

Hengistbury Head certainly seems to have a blood-curdling history following the Norman Conquest! But we must remember that the monarchs and the aristocracy had divided up the country into very large ownerships. For example, the de Redvers family owned many estates in different parts of the country apart from Christchurch and Hengistbury was just a part of Christchurch. It follows that for many of them, the Head would be an insignificant outlying part of a feudal system and the various beheadings and so forth were not connected with it.

Since Hengistbury Head was within the overriding Honour or Manor of Christchurch, its early history follows that of the Manor and its subsidiary Manors. Before the conquest in 1066, the Honour or Manor of Christchurch belonged to the Saxon kings. The main Manor included two subsidiary Manors, of the Borough (or burgh) and of Christchurch, Twynham. The former was broadly the old town and the latter included the scattered properties of the church. The events below (unless otherwise stated) broadly cover the main Manor. As for Hengistbury, it might appear to fall directly within that part of the main Manor including Holdenhurst or the Liberty of Westover, i.e. the tithings west of the Stour. However, there is evidence that it was only "indirectly" so located, because it actually formed part of the subsidiary Manor of Christchurch, Twynham. In particular, the 1791 Milne map shows the name Brander at Warren Hill and Gustavus Brander is known to have bought this Manor in 1782. Furthermore, the Christchurch Miscellany indicates that old deeds show that Hednes-Burie was part of the possessions of the Christchurch Priory.

DATE	OWNERS AND EVENTS
SAXONS	Alfred through to Edward the Confessor and King Harold.
1066	The Crown, as held by King William by right of conquest.
1086	The Crown, as stated in the Domesday Book. The king died in 1087.
1092	His son, William Rufus granted the burgh only to Flambard (only for it later to revert to the Crown, which then granted it to de Redvers around 1100). The subsidiary Manor of the Borough thereafter stayed in the same ownership as the main Manor until 1791.
c.1095	Christchurch Priory building started by Flambard and became so important that it eventually gave its name to the town.
c.1100	Richard de Redvers (granted by Henry I, youngest son of the Conqueror, to him as one of his senior advisors, as a reward for loyalty in the previous feud with Henry's brother, Robert). About this time, de Redvers transferred part of the main Manor, as "perpetual alms" to the canons of the partly built Priory. This area became the subsidiary Manor of Christchurch Twynham, i.e. church lands, which the canons added to their existing estate. It was held by the Priory until the 1539 dissolution. Succeeded by son Baldwin.
1136	The Crown, since Baldwin had fled the country having unsuccessfully sided with Empress Maud against Stephen and was an outlaw whose property automatically reverted. The king generously restored Baldwin's property to him, later.
1155	Baldwin's son Richard de Redvers succeeded him.
1162	Richard died and was succeeded by his son, another Baldwin.
1180	Baldwin died without issue, and was succeeded by his brother, Richard.
1184	Richard also had no issue, and so the estate passed to his uncle William de Redvers (who happened to be a son of the first Baldwin given above).
1200	Granted as dower to daughter Joan.
	Reverted to William.
1216	Succeeded by grandson Baldwin.
1244	Succeeded by son Baldwin.
1262	Succeeded by daughter Isabel (or Isabella de Fortibus).
1293	Conveyed to Edward I by Isabel a few hours before her death, in what is almost certainly a fraudulent transaction, arranged by the King's Chamberlain of the Exchequer. (The true heir petitioned parliament in 1315 for restitution of the estates but without success. His son renewed the petition twice in 1347 and 1364 but the result was the same).
1299	Edward I granted as dower to Margaret, his wife, who lived until 1317.
1317	Edward II granted as dower to Queen Isabel, his wife, who surrendered the Manor in 1330.
1330	Edward III granted to William de Montagu (or de Montacute) and Katherine his wife. The Manor was to stay in this family until 1541.

1337	William was made 1st Earl of Salisbury and the estate of Christchurch followed the Earls' fortunes until 1471. Succeeded by son Sir John de Montagu, 2nd Earl of Salisbury.
1389	Succeeded by Margaret, his widow.
1394	Succeeded by John, 3rd Earl of Salisbury, on her death.
1400	John de Montagu, 3rd Earl of Salisbury, beheaded at Cirencester 5 Jan.1400. Succeeded by son Thomas. (John had gone to Windsor, through loyalty to Richard II, planning to murder Henry IV and his sons. When discovered, the conspirators fled to Cirencester and secured sanctuary in the abbey. One of them, a priest, set fire to some houses in order to secure an escape route, enraging the local people, who dragged them all outside the abbey and beheaded them. It was generous of Henry to allow the succession to continue to Thomas).
1400	Thomas, 4th Earl, a great soldier, who fought at Agincourt and died at the Siege of Orleans.
1428	Alice de Montagu, his daughter.
1442	Alice's husband, Richard Newell, made Earl of Salisbury by letters patent.
1460	Richard Newell beheaded after Battle of Wakefield and his head fixed to a pole above the gates of York. Succeeded by son, Richard, Earl of Warwick.
1461	Passed to Richard, Earl of Warwick, known as "Warwick the Kingmaker." This was because he helped to depose Henry VI and put Edward IV on the throne.
1471	Warwick was killed at the Battle of Barnet, and estates passed to Isabel (daughter of the "Kingmaker" and wife of George Plantagenet) by Act of Parliament.
1476	Isabel died, leaving manor to her husband, George Plantagenet, the Duke of Clarence.
1478	George was beheaded and attainted, i.e. outlawed, so that the manor reverted to the Crown.
1478	The Crown.
1485	Henry VII came to the throne and granted manor to his mother Margaret, Countess of Richmond, who owned it probably until her death in 1509.
1509	The Crown.
1513	Henry VIII granted estate to Isabel's daughter, Lady Margaret Pole, the last of the Plantagenets and governess and godmother to the king's daughter, Princess Mary. The Catholicism of Margaret's family led to her imprisonment in 1539 at the age of 67 in the Tower, where, on the king's orders, she was executed in 1541. Since she refused to put her head on the block, saying that was for traitors, the beheading was done in a slovenly way. The scene must have been horrifying, but at least Henry knew that the Crown was secure for the Tudors.
1539 et seq.	One of the two subsidiary Manors within the main one was the Manor of Christchurch, Twynham, i.e. of the church property in Christchurch. The De Redvers family had granted it around 1100. In 1539, as part of the Dissolution, Prior Draper surrendered the Priory Church, tithes and properties to Henry VIII. Due it appears to the Prior's powers of persuasion, Henry returned the church itself to the town in 1540, but granted the rest to Wriothesley. There were a number of changes of ownership, including the Prince of Wales in 1617, the City of London by way of mortgage and Richard Fenn, who bought it in 1630. More detail from then until 1782 is given in the Summit of Warren Hill section of Chapter Six. In that year, John Compton sold the Manor to Gustavus Brander, who will be recalled as the recipient of the Grose report dated 1777 about Hengistbury. His family eventually sold to the Meyrick family in 1830. In short, for about half of the time since 1066, the headland has been part of the subsidiary Manor held by the church from the main Manor of the town.
1541	The Crown by forfeiture, i.e. the Manor reverted to Henry VIII, after the execution of Margaret, mentioned above. Christchurch Court Rolls exist from 1542 to 1546, for this period when the Crown held the manor.
1547	On Henry's death, Edward VI inherited the Manor and granted it to Edward Seymour, Duke of Somerset, who died in 1552.
1552	The Crown by escheat.
1553	Sir John Gate, Kt., who was attainted shortly after taking possession, causing reversion to the Crown.
1554	Francis Hastings, Earl of Huntingdon, and his wife Catherine, who succeeded on his death.
1576	Henry, Earl of Huntingdon, son of Francis.
1595	Succeeded by brother George.

1597	George conveyed to son Henry Hastings.
1601	Hastings sold to Thomas Arundell, later called Lord Arundell of Wardour.
1639	Inherited by Arundell's six daughters (although there followed years of legal actions, since he had purported to convey the settled estate a month before he died to one daughter's husband).
1665	The co-heirs managed to sell the Manor to Edward Hyde, Earl of Clarendon (who was responsible for Clarendon's Rocks).
1674	Succeeded by son Henry.
1708	Sold to Peter Mews, M.P. for Christchurch, who was knighted by Queen Anne.
1719	Peter Mews settled estate on his wife Lydia Gervis or Jarvis.
1751	Benjamin Clerke inherited by will. His son Joseph Jarvis Clerke inherited on Benjamin's death.
1778	Joseph died and his cousin, George Ivison Tapps inherited.
1791 et seq.	From c.1100 to this date, the Manor of Christchurch had been in the same ownership as the subsidiary Manor of the Borough of Christchurch. But in 1791, the latter was sold by Sir George Ivison Tapps to George Rose, who thereby became a Christchurch MP. Eventually, after the death of his son in 1863, it was sold to the Earl of Malmesbury, whose family still has the Manor. On the death of George Ivison Tapps, his son inherited, Sir George William Tapps Gervis.
1802	An Inclosure Act removed land (which is approximately now Bournemouth) from Christchurch Parish, although it stayed within the Manor.
1842	Again succeeded by son, Sir George Elliott Tapps-Gervis-Meyrick.
1896	Again succeeded by son, Sir George Augustus Elliott Tapps-Gervis-Meyrick.
1919	Sold to Gordon Selfridge, except for the far end of Mudeford Sandbank.
1930	Selfridge sold 430 acres to Bournemouth Borough Council, again with the far end of Mudeford retained by the Meyrick Estate.

For completeness, I should mention that other minor purchases took place by the council at the site fringes, i.e. 41 acres from Selfridge at Solent Meads in 1930, 4.5 acres at Wick from Eaton in 1944, 10 acres at Solent Meads in 1966 from Whiting and 4 acres at Solent Meads from Meyrick in 1970. It was even necessary to buy 17.5 cow runs from Whiting in 1957!

There is clearly much more history lying behind the summary above, but to tackle it would be well beyond the scope of this book. As for whether there will be any future change of ownership, nobody seems to be expecting it at present. The council already has in place its ideas about management and exploitation. But nothing stays the same forever. It is possible that the National Trust could take an interest at a time when the council needed the money, or there could be an attractive private sector bid with conservation strings attached. If and when the Head becomes an island, it may need an owner with very deep pockets. I have no inkling about any possible sale in the future: I am merely questioning the easy assumption that the status quo will continue for all time.

Legal status of Hengistbury Head

It is not possible in law for people to own land as such, merely an interest in land. Land, itself, was declared to belong to the king in 1066 by right of conquest. Having secured "absolute ownership," William proceeded to make large grants of estates, almost all to Frenchmen. The country's ruling class became French-speaking within only a few years. As in other parts of Europe, the feudal system of lords and serfs became established, with all its obligations of military service and provision of knights to the king. Frequently, an estate without inheritance would revert to the Crown on death, as happened to Hengistbury during the ownership history mentioned above. As assets other than land became important, and government became more sophisticated, the feudal system fell into decay. That said, the sheer power of landed inheritance must be recognised as part of the current fabric of society. For example, in 1719, Hengistbury fell to Lydia Gervis, along with much else, and the family still has enormous holdings in the town, including the far end of the Mudeford Sandbank.

The old concept, "an Englishman's home is his castle," harks back to simpler times, when a freeholder was almost unrestricted in his use and enjoyment of property. He could build what he liked and exclude anyone he disliked. The many reasons which now exist at the headland, to stop the owner's freedom of action, are dealt with in the next section.

Ownership restrictions and their significance

This section covers my understanding of the main restrictions now applicable to the exercise by the council of its full rights of ownership.

The first group are the restrictive covenants, etc., so far as still applicable and enforceable, imposed on the freehold sale in 1930: protection of rights for the Royalty Fishery, protection of the Double Dykes, no extraction of ironstone or other minerals, allowing access to the retained Meyrick land near to the Run, giving rights for the provision of services to premises on the spit, keeping the Lot 1 land (231.239 acres east of and including the Dykes) as public open space and ancillary buildings for that purpose, limiting Lot 2 land (190.113 acres west of the Dykes to Harbour Road) to dwellings, hotels, guest houses, doctors' and dentists' premises, recreation ground buildings, etc. This item is based on a report of a search, which it has not been possible to verify.

Next, we have the planning system, under which the council has to get consent on its own land just like any other owner, except that the procedure is somewhat different. The Public Open Space and Green Belt designations of Hengistbury are very important here, although it is generally felt that the council has more success than the average applicant when seeking consent on its own land.

Beyond this there is a variety of restrictions: the Building Regulations, which only exist to ensure good building practice; the rights for access and maintenance of the bodies responsible for electricity, water supplies, etc.; the right of access by Christchurch Council to the part of the Sandbank which they lease. In addition, others hold various rights, which the council must respect whilst still extant, such as to lay a telegraph cable and marker beacon, to build the coastguard station, to run the land train, café and golf facilities, to manage the Nursery Garden as a bird sanctuary and to provide a passenger boat service.

Public use rights are very extensive and important, including the right to walk over the whole area. Once these have become legally established due to the passage of time, affected land becomes "public open space." There is a disclaimer, under the Rights of Way Act 1932, which can be displayed on the land so that such rights do not become enforceable against the owner, but this has not been done to my knowledge at Hengistbury. In practice, the council does restrict public access for management reasons in certain fenced off sections, such as the reed beds, the Dykes, the old Nursery Garden and fields with cattle.

Public access rights are also enshrined in the "right to roam" legislation of the Countryside and Rights of Way Act 2000, now being implemented by the Countryside Agency. In the case of Hengistbury, the 2002 Draft Map showed only the area east of the Dykes and south of the tarmac road to Mudeford Sandbank as "open country." Following representations, an area to the west up to Southbourne Coast Road, including White Pits, was also so designated and appeared on the Provisional Map of May 2003 and the conclusive map of September 2004. There is thus some extra protection against the risk of development.

Since the council looks after the headland as owner and local authority, it has the duty to manage it for the public benefit, as demonstrated by the rangers following the current management plan. The council is therefore restricted to the very detailed policy laid down and approved in these documents.

Other restrictions comprise statutory designations, which apply to the Head:

- Site of Special Scientific Interest by English Nature 1986 (White Pits and the Dykes eastwards, but excluding the Sandbank).
- Dorset Heathlands Special Area of Conservation status applies to the heathlands of the Head.
- Avon Valley Environmentally Sensitive Area status applies to Wick Fields and its meadows.
- Site of Nature Conservation Interest (Mudeford Sandbank and an area between White Pits and Southbourne Coast Road).
- Scheduled Ancient Monument by English Heritage (Two round barrows north-west of the Dykes [No.820] and from the Dykes eastwards including a small part of the Sandbank [No.824]).
- Local Nature Reserve by the council 1990 (The whole area from Wick Farm Meadows to Holloway's Cut, but excluding golf facilities and car parks). The LNR is protected by Byelaws, which were confirmed in 1994.

English Nature and English Heritage, as a result of these designations, spend considerable money on site. They also have a lot of control over what the council is able to do. Although the nature reserve is a voluntary or self-imposed designation, it still makes Bournemouth Council duty-bound to manage for the benefit of both the public and wildlife.

Thus, there are many legal restrictions on the use and development of Hengistbury Head. Apart from the two councils, Meyrick Estates and the tenants and licensees, others are interested in and exercise their legal rights and powers. They include government departments and other officially funded bodies as well as the general public. For example, English Nature dictate to some extent how the Head is managed and English Heritage decide what archaeological excavations may be carried out.

When you combine the legal background with the sheer number of interested parties and the inherently controversial nature of Hengistbury, its practical significance becomes quite encouraging or depressing, depending on your point of view. My preference is to be optimistic and say things will come out for the best through co-operation. After all, the history of Hengistbury over the last 200 years is that (apart from the mining) a great number of disastrous ideas have come to nought, whilst conservation has been much strengthened. Much credit for this must go to the legal background. For completeness, however, I must mention a negative outlook shared by many local people. They feel that public consultations are lip service only and democracy simply does not work. The council proceeds to do what it likes, and protective legal restrictions are no use, because no one can afford to mount a proper legal challenge against such a large and well resourced body. I hope the reader will agree with me that, whilst some frustrations are understandable, this is not fair comment.

FIFTEEN

GEOLOGICAL SUMMARY

The great tragedy of Science - the slaying of a beautiful hypothesis by an ugly fact.

Thomas H. Huxley
(1825 - 1895)

Where does the headland fit into the world of geology? Why indeed is there a headland? How was the ironstone formed and why is it protective?

At present, Hengistbury faces a certain sea level and climate in terms of storminess. Sea level is now relatively high and slowly increasing, whilst storminess will also increase with global warming. Tidal range is modest. Beyond this, one has to look at the type and height of rocks and their resistance to such an environment. Geology provides some clues about landscape formation, current vulnerability and what the future holds. As for the sedimentary rocks, many of which are low-lying, they are mainly crumbly sand, gravel and clay. The exception is the ironstones, which have so far prevented the loss of the headland altogether. Hence, we can use science to understand something of both the formation of Hengistbury over many millions of years and indeed its future.

The planet was formed in great heat an unimaginable time ago and even now has only cooled on the surface. Tectonic plates moved various land masses across the globe, something which still continues to this day. What is now Britain has been relocated from the Tropics. Nearly all of the Earth's rocks are igneous and made from cooled molten material. There are however mainly sedimentary deposits at the surface, which are either bits worn from igneous ones or compressed life relics such as chalk. At Hengistbury, the sedimentary rocks laid down were firstly, chalk (which is now at a considerable depth) and secondly, with successive sea invasions and retreats, various sands and clays. Plate movements also created mountain ranges and folded the land, including the Hampshire Basin. Ridges have since formed from such folds as erosion features.

At different times, this area has both been near the Equator with a tropical climate, and close to the ice sheet, which came down as far as London, with an arctic climate. In relatively recent times, Ice Ages, or glacial phases, have alternated with milder weather, resulting in great changes in sea level and huge two-way movements of water. For example, there were fast outflows from melted ice. Such movements lift up in suspension, and then deposit, sand and gravel when the speed of flow drops.

"Hengistbury Hill" was eventually left as an "erosion remnant" after enormous water flows took away the land on both sides. Another landscape-forming consequence of Ice Ages is "river downcutting" leading to new floodplains and river terraces. It was due to falling sea levels, as more of the planet's water was frozen. Since the end of the latest Ice Age, the Devensian, a rising sea level created the English Channel and separated the Isle of Wight from the mainland. Aggressive erosion, of the mainly very soft sedimentary deposits, has removed most of the Head in the time since the sea broke through the chalk ridge running from Purbeck to the Isle of Wight. If it were not for the existence of the resilient ironstone within the deposits, the Head would probably not now be there: instead of Poole Bay and Christchurch Bay, we would have a single bay from Poole to Hurst Castle.

I would here mention the difference between theory and established fact in this subject. For example, identifications of river terraces at Hengistbury have changed over the years and one wonders if the latest conclusions will be reviewed in the future. An earlier theory, that originally the Stour flowed out west of the Head, has been overtaken, because most now believe that it flowed to the north instead. It is best therefore to bear in mind that parts of this subject are not an exact science and are subject to future review.

Rocks and tectonic plates

The Earth's crust is 95% igneous rock, i.e. formed from molten material. That said, about 70% at the continental surface is sedimentary, as are all the deposits found at Hengistbury. Sedimentary rocks are laid down in a horizontal fashion with younger rocks are on top of older ones, i.e. the "geological column." Fossils are found in rocks in a very definite order. The dating and composition of such material helps the tracing of geological history. It is clear that the sedimentary rocks, which form Hengistbury Head, were laid down under water. At that time, the Head did not exist in its present form of erosion remnant, i.e. after the sedimentary rocks became land rather than seabed, the land areas east and west of Warren Hill were eroded away.

When the Earth had reached about 95% of its current age, about 225 million years ago, all land was bunched together as one super-continent, Pangaea. Since then, Pangaea (a word derived from the Greek for "all lands") has gradually broken up into the five present-day continents. Land masses, or tectonic plates, have been shifting because of Mantle Convection. When plates collide on land, rocks get thrust on top of one another causing immense "folds" in the surface such as the Appalachian Mountains. On a much smaller scale, there has also been folding in the south of England, caused by plate movement, e.g. the Weymouth and Purbeck Anticlines.

Movement of the Earth's crust was therefore one factor, which alternately raised and lowered the land level in what is now the south of England. Furthermore, Eocene Britain (34 to 55 million years ago) had a very different shape from today: so different as to be unrecognisable. For example, it included what is now the sea north west of Scotland as a volcanic area of land. It was only in the Miocene Epoch that plate movement caused Britain to begin to look as it does now.

Immense geological timescale

It is hard indeed to grasp the time periods involved. To make it easier, we might take the analogy of a man aged 100 today so that each year of his life could count for a million real years. He would have been born in the Cretaceous Epoch, when the chalk was being formed. Should he look back, the English Channel was formed around three to five days ago, and Christ was teaching only yesterday!

Geological tables tend to change every few years in the light of new research. The following one extracts some information derived from a university web site.

Eras	Periods and Epochs	Million years ago (mya)
Cenozoic	**Quaternary Period**	1.8 to today
[65 mya to today]	Holocene	0.1 to today
	Pleistocene	1.8 to 0.1
	Tertiary Period	65 to 1.8
	Pliocene	5.3 to 1.8
	Miocene	23.8 to 5.3
	Oligocene	33.7 to 23.8
	Eocene	54.8 to 33.7
	Paleocene	65 to 54.8
Mesozoic	Cretaceous	144 to 65
[248 mya to 65 mya]	Jurassic	206 to 144
	Triassic	248 to 206
Paleozoic	Permian	290 to 248
[543 mya to 248 mya]	Carboniferous	354 to 290
	Devonian	417 to 354
	Silurian	443 to 417
	Ordovician	490 to 443
	Cambrian	543 to 490

Ice ages

One cause, of geological change in very recent times, is believed to relate to changes to the Earth's orbit. This has meant that there may have been Ice Ages every 100,000 years on average for the last 2,000,000 years. The Devensian (72,000 to 10,000 years Before Present [BP]) is the most recent and with most impact on Hengistbury. The current interglacial (warm period) is the Flandrian. Research on the Greenland ice cores has shown dramatic drops in temperatures on occasion, which would imply the climate of Alaska here in Britain.

During a warm period, land is flooded throughout the world due to raised sea levels. Since we are now in a warm period, such levels are relatively high, so separating us from both mainland Europe and the Isle of Wight. It is easy to see that this country was part of the European land-mass, with the sea so much lower, i.e. *a distance downwards from current sea level* of about three times the height of Warren Hill. Indeed, it is necessary to imagine a shoreline running from Cornwall to Brittany, with the English Channel abandoned by the sea during this latest Ice Age.

Being very approximate, the current interglacial seems to have started with the gradual melting of the glaciers about 20,000 years BP, causing rises in sea level to roughly current levels by about 6,000 years BP. Not only the land now under the English Channel, but that under the North Sea, was flooded. It is thought that the marine transgression was much more rapid in its middle stage, i.e. in the 6,000 years up to 8,000 BP, the sea rose from 330 feet below present level to 65 feet below present level. Separation from the continent, at Dover, is timed at about 8,600 BP, part way through the Middle Stone Age.

South of England

This country used to be in the tropics, in the Carboniferous Epoch, as evidenced by our coal, formed from tropical rain forests. Even if tectonic plates moved us north at only one inch a year, this means that a movement of 5,000 miles was possible since then!

In the Cretaceous Epoch, countless pellets digested through living organisms created chalk. At around 900 feet, it is by far the thickest deposit underlying the Hampshire Basin. It appears to have been a long and stable period, allowing the chalk to build up at a rate of about one inch every 2,500 years. It is striking to consider from this how long the chalk remnant at the Needles (Fig.57) was in the making. What is now Bournemouth was in the approximate latitude of Gibraltar at the end of the Eocene Epoch, when the Barton Clays were deposited.

An example of the surprising nature of geological history might be the deposit of the yellow sands, Warren Hill Member (Fig.58) when the sea retreated. It is easy to say: "I really cannot see the waters flowing out to sea and depositing the yellow sands at the top of Hengistbury! Can this be right?" But Eocene instability meant the uplift and subsidence of large areas of land and the invasion and retreat of the waters over a changing landscape. In short, the answer is that the yellow sands were deposited on the seabed, which greatly pre-dated the land uplift and subsequent erosion.

In the Miocene Epoch, the thick chalk stratum (together with its thinner overlying sedimentary deposits) was lifted up through plate movement and warped into the shape of the Hampshire Basin. Once the chalk and other rocks had been uplifted, the chalk ridge itself (from Purbeck to the Isle of Wight) was formed by erosion. This basin came to be drained by the River Solent. Hence it is realistic to say that perhaps about 15 million years ago the chalk was folded and much later eroded into the ridge, a remnant of which is shown in the aerial photograph of the Needles at Fig.57.

Folds occur over faults, e.g. the Purbeck Monocline runs along east to west faults. Of course, the effects in the South of England were much less dramatic than elsewhere during the same period, e.g. the formation of the Himalayas. Whilst the folding was going on, it seems that the whole area was also being uplifted, but most of the uplift was cancelled out by erosion.

Geology of Hengistbury Head: introduction

Starting with the Cretaceous Epoch some 100 million years ago, the biggest deposit of the Hampshire Basin is chalk, which begins at a depth of about 1,000 feet below the Head and then goes down 900 feet or so [after R. Agar]. The land then rose into shallow water, as evidenced by shallow water fossils. This was well before sediments such as Barton Clay were laid down. Being very approximate, we can say that such sediments were deposited from Bournemouth to Highcliffe about 50 million years ago, but that erosion on both sides of the Head swept much of these strata out to sea much more recently.

Fig.57 ***The Needles, Isle of Wight, a remnant of the chalk ridge***
(Picture by www.patrickeden.co.uk)

This spectacular sight is all that remains of the eastern end of the chalk ridge running across the bay to Old Harry. Originally part of a land fold due to tectonic plate movement some 15 million years ago, the chalk became a ridge through erosion. Following the last Ice Age and the rise in sea levels, nearly all the ridge was demolished. The process was part of the colossal sea invasion, which created Poole and Christchurch Bays in place of the Solent River valley. If the ridge had held, Hengistbury would now be a rather uninteresting inland hill.

Hengistbury Head does not therefore result from landscape-folding plate movement. Instead, it has been left whilst immense quantities of water eroded wide and shallow valleys on either side of it. Broadly, the land is "high" at Southbourne, Warren Hill and Highcliffe. The two large valleys in between show the sheer power of this erosion.

This is why the river valley gravel by the Dykes is not only a lot *lower*, but also a lot *younger* than the Warren Hill Member, i.e. the sand at the top. Hence, although we still have the usual "geological column" at Warren Hill with the most recent deposits at the highest level, this does not apply at the Dykes, where the old sediments have been partially washed away and replaced by much younger valley gravel.

When looking at the cliff from the beach, there are other misleading indications. Ironstones can *appear* to be within gravel at the base of the cliff, but they have actually fallen from the Barton Clay above. Also, the lowest part of windblown sands form a grey line close to the top of the cliff, but strangely dip some six feet below the top at one section west of the highest point. The explanation is that this southern edge of the Batters was mined for ironstones and the top six feet are quarry spoil from the nineteenth century.

Geology of Hengistbury Head: strata identification

Before dealing with the nature of the sedimentary rocks at the Head, I feel that it is best to mention an identification issue, connected with the Christchurch Fault, which has only fairly recently [after Curry 1976] been addressed. The significance is that it has now been possible to establish the geological succession of deposits consistently at both Highcliffe and Hengistbury.

The Christchurch Fault (also known as the Stour Valley Fault), as indicatively shown in Fig.58, runs along the Stour Valley. The British Geological Survey refers to it as a fault, although Curry says it could be a fault, a downfold or even a combination of both. It dates back to an uncertain time, except to say that it must be younger than the sedimentary rocks of the Eocene Epoch, mentioned below. At the Head end, it may run out to the east or the west of the Long Groyne: this is not yet established definitely. (It may be relevant that although most of the outer third of Christchurch Ledge is as shallow as about 25 feet, divers have found a number of holes, going to a depth of 75 feet.) Either way, it seems that it originally caused what is now Hengistbury Head to be much lower than it would otherwise have been. Due however to the enormous amounts of erosion since the fault caused the land subsidence, one cannot say whether the Head would have been much higher today without it. In other words, the extent of erosion may well have levelled the land, anyway. After all, Highcliffe, Hengistbury and West Southbourne are all about the same height now. I believe that the explanation, which follows and is illustrated in Fig.58, is the latest view.

The best way to understand the identification problem is to work through the sketch shown in Fig.58:

East of Steamer Point (and beyond the sketch) the name Highcliff Sands was given to the light yellow sands visible in the higher part of the cliff. This is fair comment. We can think of this stratum as the "true Highcliff Sands." They are actually known now as Burtons A3 and form one of the higher sections of the Barton Clay.

Issue One at Steamer Point

Below the Barton Clay are pebbles and then another different stratum of sands, which were again named the Highcliff Sands. Now that more has been established, they have been identified as the Boscombe Sands.

Issue Two at Hengistbury Head

The light yellow sands, towards the top of Warren Hill at Hengistbury Head, were associated on the previous theory with this lower stratum at Steamer Point and so named the Highcliff Sands. They have since been recognised as the same stratum as the true Highcliff Sands mentioned above. These light yellow sands are now classified as the Warren Hill Member, i.e. this higher section of the Barton Clay is at the same level as Burtons A3 in the geological column.

The irony in all this is that consistency appears to have resulted from these two aspects, i.e. the recognition of the light yellow sands of the Head as the Highcliff Sands. But the result was problematic, because it took no account of the fault or downfold and created strata anomalies.

Using the latest identifications and allowing for the fault, it all becomes clear because the succession of strata is the same in both Hengistbury and Highcliffe, as indeed it should be. Applying the geological convention of going from the bottom (oldest) to the top (youngest) we have:

Top. Barton Clay, which includes a high level section of light yellow sands, now known in Highcliffe as Burtons A3 and at Hengistbury Head as the Warren Hill Member.

Pebble Bed.

Bottom. Boscombe Sands.

This latest interpretation given here is simpler than it seems, because it can be summarised by stating: "The land, which is now eroded into the shape of Hengistbury Head, had subsided relative to Highcliffe due to a fault or downfold or combination of both. Hence, the same sequence of strata appear as at Highcliffe but the whole batch are lower down."

Geology of Hengistbury Head: sedimentary rocks

The names given here are based on the most up-to-date classifications of the British Geological Survey. They are generally sloping down to the east at a shallow angle, which is variously reported at about one degree or three degrees. This is to be expected as we are on the western side of the Hampshire Basin. A most striking indication of this slope can be seen from the position of the Point House Café at the south end of Harbour Road. When the Head is in broad sunlight, the strata beneath the top sands can be seen clearly going downwards to the east in straight lines. Indeed, they are so clearly cut off at the headland's edges on left and right, this viewpoint also demonstrates that it is an erosion remnant. Geologists consider the Head to be very important as a "bridging exposure," since it exposes sequences shown on the cliffs of Poole and Christchurch Bays. If you look at the Head from the beach (Fig.59) you can see its make-up in successive strata:

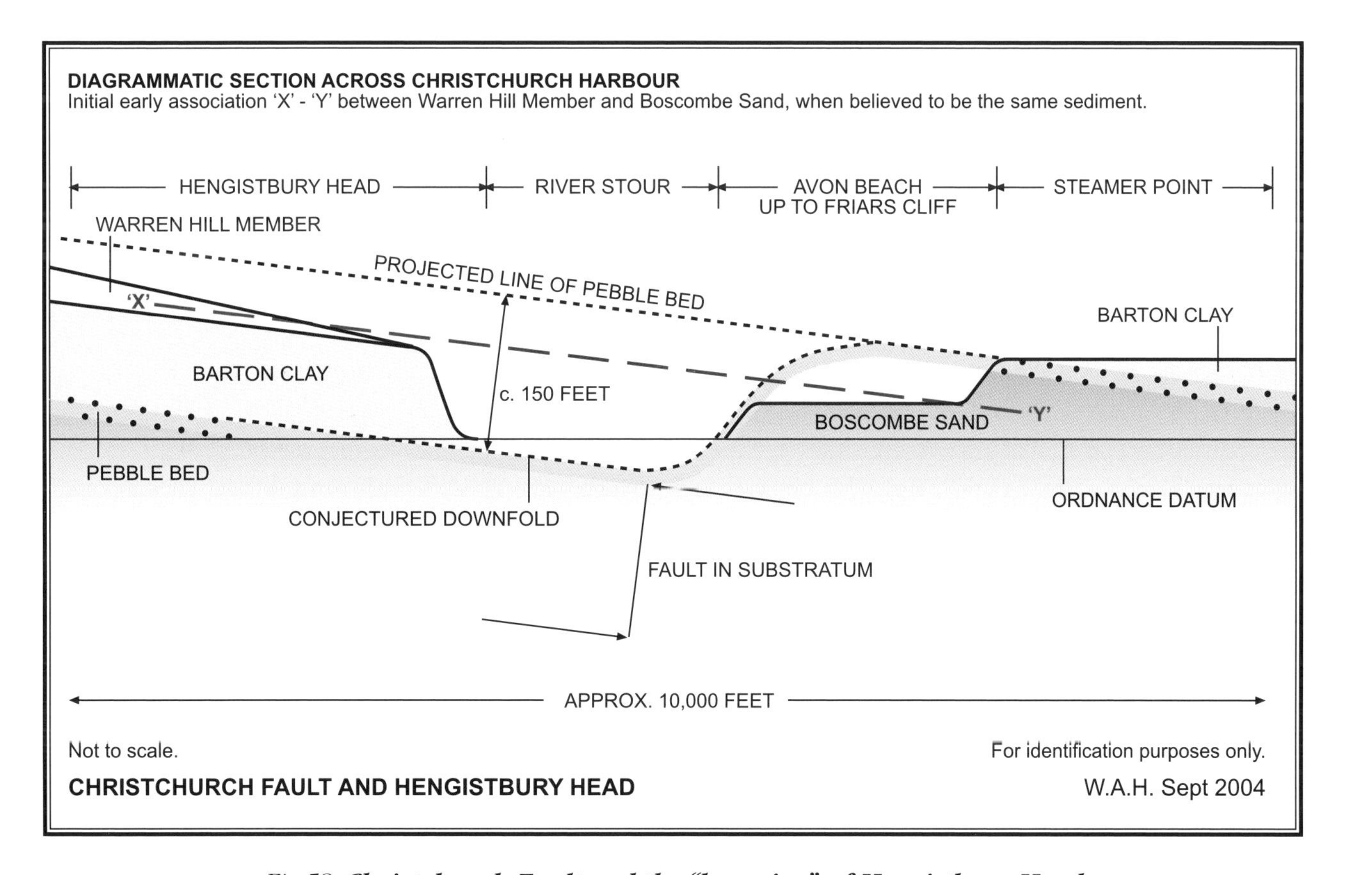

Fig.58 ***Christchurch Fault and the "lowering" of Hengistbury Head***

(Author 2002, after M. Hinton)

The result here appears to be that Warren Hill is now about 150 feet lower than would have happened without the fault. So, did the tectonic plate movement, which caused the fault, really mean that the Head is now "sitting low in the water"? No, we cannot conclude this, because it is hard to say what impact the erosion would have had without the fault or downfold. The double pebble layer shown here appears also in Figs. 50 and 59.

Fig.59 ***Strata at Warren Hill***
(Author 2002)

The cliff exposure varies as you walk east. In one photograph, the double strata of pebbles are more prominent and in the other, the ironstones and gullies. In both, the order of deposition, from the bottom, is Boscombe Sands, pebble strata, Barton Clay, Warren Hill Member. These sediments were put down some 34 million to 55 million years ago, before immense erosion took place. Warren Hill was left as an "erosion remnant" after much of the sediment was swept away on both sides. Much more recently, the cliff itself has been exposed to erosion, as the sea formed Poole Bay and the hill became a headland.

The lowest is the buff-purple **Boscombe Sands** [lowest part of the Barton Group: after Edwards and Freshney 1987], carried down a tidal river in tropical conditions. The landmass was then much closer to the Equator than it is now. Plant remains, such as conifers from the Eocene Epoch, show that the sediment was carried down from the land to the sea. Parts of these sands are very dark, almost black, smelling of bitumen. Although not remotely commercial, they are of interest to show a possible stage of arrested development in the formation of oil. If this is indeed bitumen, it is most unlikely ever to have become oil, which needs a great depth to form. Fig.31 shows the position of the Menrod 85, some five miles south of the headland, a platform-type trial oil well, which was capped in 1993. The water became shallower, eventually leaving an exposed beach, as evidenced by a stratum of bleached pebbles. There are actually two strata of pebbles (Figs.50, 58 and 59), which are the definitive boundary between Boscombe Sands and Barton Clay referred to next. Due to the occasional similarity in colour of the two deposits, the pebbles are very useful for identification purposes from the beach.

The next sediment, to be laid down, was the lowest part of the **Barton Clay**, the Barton Beds. This sediment also goes back to the Eocene Epoch. There has been some debate about classification, with the conclusion moving in favour of Barton Clay rather than the Bracklesham series (which is below), largely due to an examination of mollusc remains and dating evidence. The indications, this time, are of a sea invasion due to land subsidence caused by crustal movement and the creation of a deep estuary. The presence of glauconite is known to prove that the Barton Clay was deposited under marine conditions. It also helps dating. This lowest part of the Barton Clay has two strata:

The dark green sandy clays and purple-grey silts, which originally were named the Lower Hengistbury Beds.

The greenish sandy clays, which were known as the Upper Hengistbury Beds. This stratum has about four rows of ironstone nodules.

At that time, there was no land to be seen for many miles: the cliff face we see today was merely part of a normal seabed then. It seems that iron compounds were first set down in deep water, but they changed into iron nodules, due to the water being active when it became a shallow river delta.

On its retreat, still during the Eocene Epoch, the sea deposited further white-yellow sands known as the **Warren Hill Member,** which is now towards the top of the cliff. It is actually possible to demonstrate the Stour Valley Fault, mentioned above, by projecting the continuance of the pebble bed and Barton Clay strata from Steamer Point westwards at the same gradient (Fig.58). It can be seen that these strata are actually some 150 feet lower at Warren Hill than would be expected if there were no fault, albeit still sloping up westwards at the same gradient.

The next thing to happen was the folding of the Miocene Epoch, which created the Hampshire Basin, referred to above. Thus, after the deposits had been laid down in successive strata, plate movement shaped the Hampshire Basin. The result, at Hengistbury, was that the strata sloped down to the east.

After the Miocene folding, the Head still did not exist, being merely part of a plateau. But above the main deposits, we have the **river gravel** that lies on the top of the Head and to a greater extent on the low land by Double Dykes. During the Pleistocene Epoch, the gravel was transported with rivers, possibly created by melting ice. It is easy to imagine such enormous flows of water, with the climate changing from very cold to sub-tropical and back again. Before the last Ice Age, there was a very high sea level, but as it took hold, the level dropped, so creating the river terraces. Being more specific, it means that the top of Warren Hill was a gravel-covered flood plain. It follows that the land around it was eroded to a height close to sea level. Once more, we are back to the headland being an erosion remnant. To be clear, however, this is an older and different process from the relatively recent erosion by sea and weather of the south of the Head.

The wind-blown sand, light poor soil and vegetation are at the very top.

Throughout most of this enormous time-span, the Hengistbury area was under water, with the depth varying at different times. It only turned into land with falling sea levels due to the onset of the various Ice Ages, during the last two million years.

Geology of Hengistbury Head: the ironstones

"Gold is for the mistress – silver for the maid –
Copper for the craftsman cunning at his trade."
"Good!" said the Baron sitting in his hall,
"But Iron – Cold Iron – is master of them all."
Rudyard Kipling

These are one of the most important geological features of the headland. Ironstone nodules, or concretions, comprise mainly siderite or ferrous carbonate, which originated in warm, tropical, deltaic conditions. One must imagine the iron layer trapped in shallow seas and the ferrous carbonate forming.

It is quite different from the local copperas, which is ferrous sulphate, mined in the sixteenth century and used for tanning and dye making. Overton shows two mines on his 1600 map: Allom Chine Copperas House and Bascomb Copperas House. A certain Mr. Medley, by forecasting huge profits, persuaded some rich investors that he could convert the iron of copperas into true copper. When this never happened, it became clear that the whole thing was a swindle and they lost their money.

The ironstone nodules are brown on the exterior and include some fine sand and clay, occasionally some pebbles and only rarely, fossils or sharks' teeth. In addition, analysis has shown other content: carbonised wood, pyrite and, within the fine sand, green non-oxidised glauconite grains. It will be recalled that the presence of glauconite means a sea invasion when the middle-Eocene strata were laid down. Occasionally, a nodule can be seen on the beach tending to break up naturally with several skins appearing like onion peel. When broken artificially, the nodules are found to have a different internal appearance, rather like compact limestone. Nonetheless, the Hengistbury Mining Company found the iron content to be commercially viable at about 30%. A piece of this ironstone will produce a lump of iron, if placed in considerable heat, such as that generated by coke in a domestic boiler.

Geology of Hengistbury Head: river terraces

Any river in a valley will have a flood plain alongside. This will be a fairly shallow stretch of land that will take the water in conditions of heavy rain, before drying out during normal times. Perhaps the main local existing example is the water meadows by the River Avon at Christchurch. When rivers had to "down-cut" their valleys due to falling sea levels, a new flood plain would develop at a lower level, leaving the original one as a river terrace. The identification and significance of river terraces at Warren Hill is controversial. It now appears [after *Geology of Country Around Bournemouth*, 1991] that there are only two terraces: firstly, number ten, previously known as Boyn Hill, at the top, and secondly, number six, previously known as Berry Hill, to the east. It is believed that the Stour, Avon or Solent Rivers laid down the terraces.

In summary, from the sedimentation phase, the order of events was the laying down of the various deposits, the folding of the land and finally, the erosion and movements of sediment and gravel due to heavy water flows as part of the Ice Age/interglacial changes. We can think of the landscape as relatively fixed at this extremely recent stage of geological history. The scene is therefore set for seeing the impact on the landscape of events up to and beyond the channel breakthrough near Dover.

Creation of Poole Bay and Christchurch Bay

Before looking at how the sea accomplished this stupendous erosion task, we must look first at the background. As mentioned earlier, land in the south of England had a number of folds, which eroded to form chalk ridges. They were produced in the Miocene Epoch due to plate movement. One of these (Fig.60) originally ran between and beyond two existing chalk outposts, i.e. the Needles (Fig.57) and Old Harry, Ballard Point, south-east of Studland village on the Isle of Purbeck. The outposts are all that now remain.

A lot of research has gone into the breach of the chalk ridge, with various opinions on when, why and how it happened. Views have varied from late Miocene (say 6 million years BP) to the Flandrian Transgression (say 10,000 years BP). As this matter also concerns coastal erosion, it is mentioned in that chapter under the section, *Impact of tides*. What follows is one opinion of the most likely course of events.

Not only does there exist a submerged coastal feature nearly 20 miles south of the ridge, but also it is believed that the ridge (comprising chalk) was up to about 500 feet high. It seems that the sea was highly effective here before the last Ice Age. If there was a very large tidal range in the warm period before the last Ice Age, together with stormy weather, this could explain the sheer volume of erosion. It is quite possible that these were very violent and destructive tides, due to the effect of "resonance," i.e. the very large tidal range arising from an "enclosure" such as the Bristol Channel, or indeed the English Channel prior to the Dover breakthrough. Moreover, the modified landforms would have made the next incursion of the sea much easier, because some obstructions were already destroyed.

At the height of the last Ice Age (the Devensian), the Frome, Avon, Stour and other rivers to the east such as the Test, drained into the Solent, which flowed from the west to well past what is now the Isle of Wight. Britain was part of mainland Europe. The rivers were forced by the low sea level to "down-cut" on their way, so creating valleys. A major significance of a down-cut valley at a time of low sea level is that the riverbed is much lower than would ever occur today. However, when the next Ice Age arrives, the rivers will tend to scour out their post Devensian deposits, when repeating the down-cutting process. The English Channel was then dry land, except for a large river (known as the English Channel River) draining the south coast and France. Having first collected the waters from tributaries such as the Solent, it flowed west to the sea at a coastline running from Brittany to Cornwall.

As the ice retreated, the sea rose in the same fashion that had occurred in the later stages of previous Ice Ages. This again meant the creation of an increasingly enormous inlet from the west towards Dover, a much larger version of the Bristol Channel. At this time, the coast was still a long way south of the chalk ridge (Fig.61). The process continued with river valleys increasingly becoming sea inlets. Research from 1999 (again Fig.61) has shown that there were three substantial rivers in Poole Bay, running right through the chalk ridge before the end of the last Ice Age. Finally, the river valleys could no longer retain the ever higher waters of what had become sea inlets and the big valley of the old River Solent was flooded as part of this whole process known as the Flandrian Transgression.

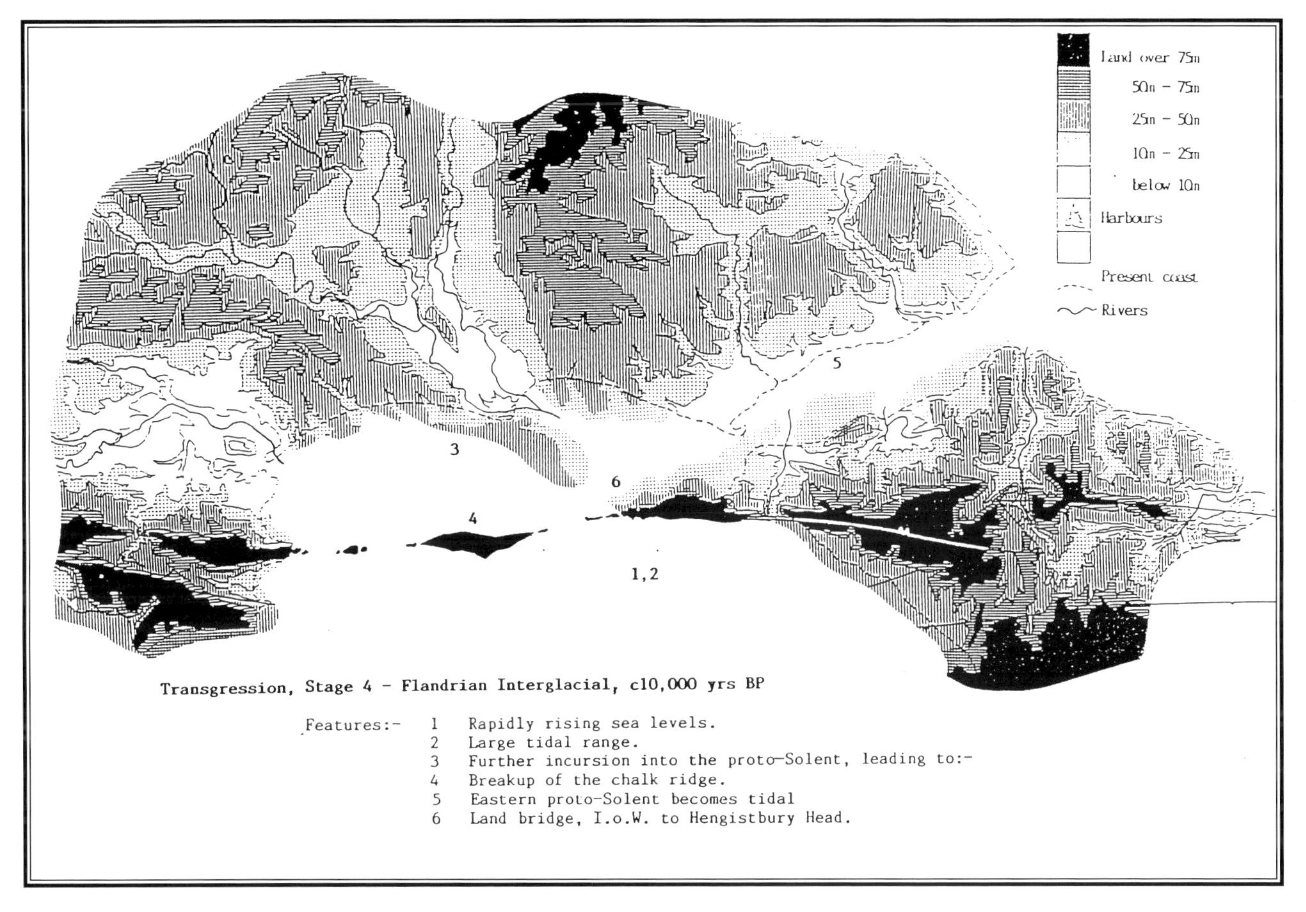

Fig.60 ***Chalk pillars remaining across Poole Bay, c. 8,000 BC***

(Reproduced by consent of F. Tyhurst & M. Hinton)

The intermediate stage, of the sea incursion known as the Flandrian Transgression following the last Ice Age, shows enormous chalk pillars, over 250 feet high, still then existing. Although Poole Bay had roughly formed, Christchurch Bay was perhaps 7,000 years in the future, whilst Hengistbury may still have been joined by land to the Isle of Wight. On this theory, violent tides had still to erode tremendous areas of land, up to the broken line of the present coast.

Fig.60 shows the middle phase about 10,000 years ago, when sea channels had been made through the ridge, but intermediate chalk pillars had not yet been demolished. The erosion would have been spectacular, including dramatic cliff collapses and the creation and destruction of chalk stacks. One reason for the severity of erosion was the enormous tidal range, running at perhaps ten times the present one. Before that time, Hengistbury Head was merely a hill surrounded by miles of countryside in all directions, like its twin St. Catherine's Hill, Christchurch, today. Indeed, it may still have been connected to what is now the Isle of Wight by a land bridge.

Hence, the retreat of the ice caused a big rise in sea level, turning river valleys into sea inlets. The biggest example was the English Channel River, which became an inlet suffering from resonance. Working from a much higher sea level, the destructive action of the violent tides must have been awesome, as the waters rose a typical amount of perhaps 65 feet, twice a day.

Following the creation from west to east of the English Channel, around 8,600 years ago, the Purbeck Ridge remnants slowly disappeared. A fresh coastline had developed. Of course, the new coastline and hills were subject to erosion, albeit relatively slowly now that the tidal range had reduced to the current figure of about six feet only. When the sea came to attack the soft sediments of the coast, the ironstones of Hengistbury defended the headland, slowing down erosion at that point. The ironstones only became effective when they had fallen from the cliff and formed a protective skirt. Consequently, two bays were formed from the Purbecks to Hurst Castle instead of just one. The ironstones are still there in great number, stretching out from the Head

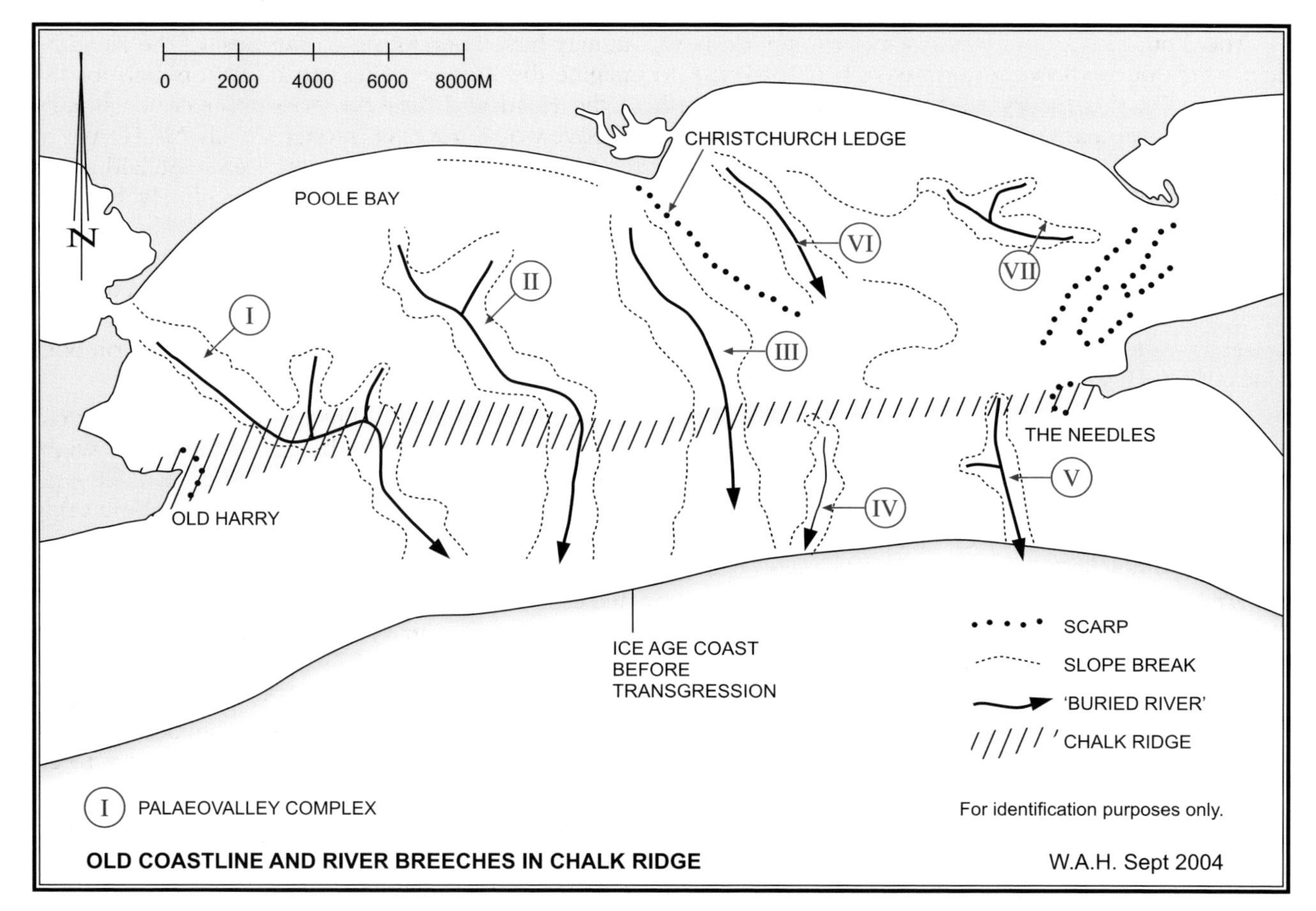

Fig.61 ***Ice Age coast, chalk ridge and river breaches***

(after Velegrakis, Dix and Collins 1999. Reproduced by consent of the Geological Society)

This diagrammatic sketch shows the coast around the end of the Ice Age and before completion of the sea incursion through the old Purbeck Ridge. Major findings, in 1999, were three buried river valleys in Poole Bay, which carried south flowing rivers through the high ridge. The complexes, marked I to III, mean that the upper reaches of the Solent River were captured before the end of the last Ice Age. The rising sea must have first flowed up these old rivers to inundate the land of what is now Poole Bay. Before such capture, the old Solent River had flowed during the Late Quaternary, simply from west to east and on the north side of the ridge. Having passed to the north of what is now the Isle of Wight, it had joined the west flowing English Channel River as a tributary.

beyond the Long Groyne in the form of Christchurch Ledge (Figs. 11, 31 and 61).

If the previous paragraphs covered what appears to have happened, the next ones are intended to make clearer the processes and reasons for them. The 1999 research shown in Fig.61 suggests that a large upstream section of the Solent was already flowing directly south to the English Channel River before the Flandrian Transgression. At three points, between Old Harry and the eastern end of Christchurch Ledge, rivers breached the chalk ridge. The process took place, probably in the late Devensian, but possibly earlier and effectively disrupted the River Solent. The three fluvial palaeovalleys of Poole Bay were drowned and their estuaries filled during the Transgression. This is known because there were river deposits found beneath estuarine ones. The river breaches might only have happened with a very high water level north of the ridge, implying that much of existing coastal land was previously under water.

It follows that the ridge was not a strong bastion at all, being flawed and vulnerable to the process of sea incursion. For example, the waters of the Frome originally joined the Solent and travelled east around what is now the Isle of Wight, before turning southwards to find the west flowing main river in what is now the English Channel. Later, they went directly south, straight through the ridge to this west flowing river. The ever-rising sea would have flooded through the valleys to the main Solent valley beyond, so enabling an attack on the ridge from both sides at once.

The Stour and Avon originally met as they do now, but may have been joined to the west of the Head by the River Bourne flowing north-east. It is hard now to imagine the Bourne being substantial enough for the purpose. On this theory, all three rivers joined north of the Head and then flowed south-east, eventually becoming a tributary of the Solent. The disruption outlined above would not have interfered with this. However, according to Pepin (1967) there was a previous stage when the Stour ran out west of the Head and laid down the river valley gravel, which we can still see in the low cliff west of the Dykes. This may be less likely, because the land rises from the Stour towards the sea. Others (such as King 1974) prefer the view, as I do, that the valley between Southbourne and Warren Hill was cut by a river draining north to the Stour from higher land, which has since been eroded. The landscape section, in the chapter about the Iron Age, refers to this. For good measure, there is another possibility about the valley of the River Solent being shallow enough to permit its water to wander substantially, laying down the valley gravel at the Dykes as it did so. In short, erosion on both sides of the Head clearly happened, but its exact process is not proven.

We can now consider the bay formation. Poole Bay was the first to form as a direct result of the valleys cut through the chalk before the rise in sea level. There is likely to have been a land bridge to the Isle of Wight from Hengistbury Head (Fig.60). Although the first incursion of the sea was before or during the last Ice Age, most of the development of Poole Bay would have happened since. At a much later stage, Christchurch Bay was submerged, but in a more abrupt way and in association with the separation of the Isle of Wight from the mainland, 7,000 to 7,500 years BP (Velegrakis). It could have followed the establishment of a very strong tidal stream from the encroaching sea in Poole Bay to the drowned estuary to the east. The formation of Christchurch Bay was altogether less drastic, progressing much later from a drowned estuary to a bay that even now is on average only about half of the depth of Poole Bay. Recent research has suggested that the bay formation itself may have started only some 3,000 years ago and it will one day be twice its existing depth.

One local resident recalls a time from the 1930s when large ocean liners could be seen from Southbourne on their way to Southampton. They ran fairly close to the headland in the days before it was necessary to go south round the Island, due to a shingle bank having built up at the Needles. People could easily be made out on deck, with the aid of a telescope. It appears therefore that even recently, strong currents have greatly changed the seabed where the old River Solent once flowed.

Another factor is the final breakthrough from the North Sea to form the English Channel. It may have been catastrophic due to a great amount of glacial floodwater suddenly rushing west down the Channel. The degree of violence involved has raised the thought that this was enough to cause the two bays to join. The Head had to change from being a local hill (a lot longer than existing since it went over what is now Christchurch Ledge) at least four miles from the sea, to being a headland under aggressive wave attack. One further piece of the jigsaw, concerning the separation from the Isle of Wight, is some pollen evidence from beneath the sea (Devoy 1987). It suggests that the separation took place more recently, only about 6,000 years ago.

It is quite a thought that the reindeer hunters of 12,000 years ago looked out in all directions from the top of Warren Hill on to land and rivers only. But although they were miles from the sea, they would have been aware of great tidal flows, flooding in and out of the gaps between the gigantic pillars of the chalk ridge to the south. They would probably have found conditions too dangerous to venture out on to the water very often, particularly if tidal flows caused sea level to rise and fall at the rate of 10 feet an hour. After all, at that time, the land bridges remained both to the continent and the Island.

APPENDIX

Summary of excavations and collections

DATE	DESCRIPTION	LOCATION OF FINDS
1909-43	Herbert Druitt was well known locally and collected many items brought to him over the years. A tremendous quantity was thrown up by the ploughing in 1913.	Entire collection and notebooks at Red House Museum.
1911-12	J.P.Bushe-Fox published in 1915. This was the biggest dig, which had been done by then and was instigated by Druitt as a rescue due to the impending sale of the Head. It was mainly in Barn Field and Long Field.	Mainly Meyrick Estate at Hinton Admiral. Some on loan to British Museum from Society of Antiquaries. Some at Red House, Poole and regional Museums. Surviving excavation records at Society of Antiquaries.
1918-24	H. St. George Gray, in and near the Nursery Garden at the request of Gordon Selfridge. Results never published.	Red House Museum and Taunton Museum including both finds and records. Only some of the limited records have survived.
1950's	J. B. Calkin dug trial pits, finding Upper Palaeolithic flints near cliff edge above the Long Groyne.	
1957	Angela Mace confirmed this as an Upper Palaeolithic Site by a full excavation, published in 1959.	British Museum.
1968-69	Dr. John Campbell further dug the site, as a rescue because of its cliff edge location.	University of Oxford, to be sent to Bournemouth Museum Service (Russell-Cotes).
1970-71	Dr. David Peacock dug the south shore of the harbour, again to rescue the remains before they were lost to erosion.	University of Southampton, to be sent to Bournemouth Museum Service.
1977	Ronald Powell made many finds on the Early Mesolithic campsite.	
1979-84	Prof. Barry Cunliffe & Dr. Nick Barton excavated the Long Field vicinity and the two Stone Age sites respectively.	Finds to be sent to Russell-Cotes Museum when provision has been made. Dataset held at Institute of Archaeology, Oxford.
Various	Mr. A. Nobili-Vitelleschi held a large private collection.	Dorset County Archaeologist and Red House Museum.
1985	Prof. Cunliffe investigated marsh to east of previous dig.	
1982-85	Prof. Cunliffe and Mr. Tooley arranged dig at Rushy Piece.	
1986	Prof. Cunliffe and Mr. Tooley looked into changes to geomorphology of headland.	
2001	Wessex Archaeology dug pitch and putt site west of the Dykes	Bournemouth Museum Service
Various	Thousands of coins have been collected and dispersed widely, with many lost and others held at locations not mentioned here. For example, Mrs. C. Draper holds a private collection. A definitive, complete list of coins and locations is unlikely to be possible.	Ashmolean, Bristol City, British, Red House, Russell-Cotes and Winchester Museums. Also the Meyrick Estate.

Bibliography

Birds of Hengistbury Head. Peter Hawes and Mark Holloway, 1998.

Bournemouth 1810 – 1910. C.H.Mate and C.Riddle, 1910

Bournemouth and the Second World War 1939 -1945. M. A. Edgington, 1994.

Bournemouth Railway History. L. Popplewell,1973

Christchurch: A Millenium Trail around a Saxon Town. Christchurch Borough Council, 2000

Christchurch Miscellany. June 1922.

Discover Dorset. Shipwrecks. Maureen Attwooll,1998.

Dive Dorset: A Diver Guide. John and Vicki Hinchcliffe, 1999.

*Domesday: A Search for the Roots of Engl*and. Michael Wood, 1999.

Dorset Shipwrecks. David Burnett, 1982.

Dorset Shipwrecks. A Comprehensive Guide. Steve Shovlar, 1996.

Excavations at Hengistbury Head, Hampshire in 1911-12. J.P. Bushe-Fox, 1915.

Fire Over Dorset. Frank Kitchen, 1988.

Hampshire & Dorset Shipwrecks. Graham Smith, 1995.

Hengistbury Head. Barry Cunliffe, 1978.

Hengistbury Head, Dorset, Volume 1. The Prehistoric and Roman Settlement 3,500 BC – AD 500. Barry W. Cunliffe, 1987. Monograph No.13.

Hengistbury Head, Dorset. Volume 2. The Late Upper Palaeolithic and Early Mesolithic Sites. R.N.E.Barton, 1992. Monograph No.34

Hengistbury Head Management Plan. Bournemouth Borough Council, 1997 (and draft new plan, 2004).

Hengistbury Head, The Coast. Peter Hawes, 1998.

Hengistbury Head Archaeology Trail. Peter Hawes and Mark Holloway, 1994.

Hengistbury Head Nature Trail. Peter Hawes and Mark Holloway, 1990

Hengistbury Head. Cecil Pepin, 1985.

Ironstone Canyon. Lawrence Popplewell, 1986.

International Aviation Meeting Southbourne Aerodrome,11th – 16th July 1910. Ian Andrew, 1999.

Poole Bay and Purbeck 300BC – AD 1660. C. Cochrane, 1970.

Poole and World War II. Derek Beamish, Harold Bennett and John Hillier, 2004

RAF Fighter Command Losses of the Second World War. Volume 1-3

Operational Losses. Franks N.L.R., 1997-2000.

Reminiscences of Christchurch and Neighbourhood. W. Tucker, 1921.

Saving Mudeford Quay from the Sea. Frank Tyhurst, 2004

Shipwreck Index of the British Isles. Richard & Bridget Larn, 1995.

Smuggling Days. K. Merle Chacksfield, 1984.

Smuggling in Hampshire and Dorset 1700-1850. Geoffrey Morley, 1983.

Tales of Old Mudeford, Some Fishy Stories. Olive J. Samuel.

The Battle of Mudeford 1784. Mike Powell, 1993.

The Christchurch Coastal Path. Frank Tyhurst, 2004

The Manors of Christchurch. Mrs. G. Dear, 1972.

The Ringwood Christchurch and Bournemouth Railway. J.A.Young, 1992.

The Smugglers of Christchurch, Bourne Heath and the New Forest. E. Russell Oakley, 1944.

The Smuggler: No Gentleman. Smuggling with Violence around Christchurch and Poole Bays. M. A. Hodges, 1999.

True Remembrances: the memoirs of an architect. Philip Tilden, 1954

Victoria County History, Hampshire, 1912.

Warren Head and Christchurch Haven. Lawrence Popplewell, 1992.

Wrecks and Rescues around Solent-Wight to Christchurch Bay. Olive J. Samuel, 1998.

Wick, Last Village on the Dorset Stour. Lawrence Popplewell, 1995.

Useful web sites

- **Black House, Mudeford**
  www.theblackhouse.co.uk
  Site giving background & holiday letting information.
- **Bournemouth Council**
  www.bournemouth.gov.uk
  Constantly updated local authority site.
- **Bournemouth Echo**
  www.thisisbournemouth.co.uk
  Local newspaper site, including archives.
- **Bournemouth Natural Science Societty**
  www.bnss.org.uk
  Large local society to promote science and natural history. Includes museum, library, lecture hall, etc.
- **Bournemouth Surfing**
  www.bournemouth-surfing.co.uk
  Enthusiasts' site with webcam, news on reefs etc.
- **Bovington Tank Museum**
  www.tankmuseum.co.uk
  Has had restored Valentine Duplex Drive tank on display from 1944.
- **Christchurch Harbour Ornithological Group**
  www.chog.org.uk
  Extremely comprehensive wildlife site, including much more than birds.
- **Christchurch Council**
  www.christchurch.gov.uk
  Constantly updated local authority site.
- **Christchurch Local History Society**
  www.communigate.co.uk
  A major site for local history, found by "list all sites" on the umbrella communigate site.
- **Dorset County Council**
  www.dorset-cc.gov.uk
  Main county site, including archaeological research section.
- **Dorset Coast Forum**
  www.dorsetcoast.com
  Detailed environmental and coastal history site, with many links.
- **English Heritage**
  www.english-heritage.org.uk
  Official site including function to protect Double Dykes as an Ancient Monument.
- **English Nature**
  www.english-nature.org.uk
  Government agency promoting conservation of geology and wildlife.
- **Environment Agency Flood Advice**
  www.environment-agency.gov.uk.floodline
  Slightly scary web site showing government concern about public awareness of risks.
- **Google**
  http://google/
  Perhaps the best search engine on the net. Over 5,000 results from inputting Hengistbury.
- **Greenlink**
  www.greenlink.co.uk
  Conservation site including events for the Christchurch Volunteers Group.
- **Hampshire Record Office**
  www.hants.gov.uk/record-office
  Considerable archives.
- **Hengist Kites**
  www.hengistkites.com
  Local supplier of many types of kite.
- **Hengistbury Head Geology and History**
  www.hengistbury.head.btinternet.co.uk
  The web site of the book of the same title by Bill Rees. 2001. Chalk Ridge Publications.
- **Historical Association**
  www.history.org.uk
  Major local history site with 60 branches.
- **International Panel on Climate Change**
  www.grida.no/climate/ipcc_tar/index.htm
  Very technical site to advise governments about global warming, sea level rise etc.
- **Joint Nature Conservation Committee**
  www.jncc.gov.uk
  UK government wildlife advisory body.
- **Marine Conservation Society**
  www.mcsuk.org
  Body concerned with all aspects of conserving marine life.
- **Maritime and Coastguard Agency**
  www.mcga.gov.uk
  Comprehensive government site covering safety at sea, Coastguard function, etc.
- **Mudeford Beach Huts**
  www.mudeford-beach-huts.co.uk
  Community site for hut owners, huts for sale, AGM etc.
- **Mudeford and Sandbank News**
  www.msbnews.co,uk
  Detailed newspaper and information site covering Mudeford, harbour and the Head. Editor Tim Baber.
- **National Coastwatch Institution**
  www.nci.org.uk
  Charity, which maintains partial coastal watch and hopes to reopen all closed stations.
- **Ordnance Survey**
  www.ordsvy.gov.uk
  Full details of maps available.
- **Personal Watercraft Club**
  www.mudeford.org.uk
  Site for active jet-ski club, based at Mudeford.
- **Planning Portal**
  www.planningportal.gov.uk
  Planning guide, which includes approved local development plans and policies in detail.
- **Proudman Oceanic Laboratory**
  www.pol.ac.uk
  Research facility including tide predictions, sea levels etc.
- **Public Records Office**
  www.pro.gov.uk
  National archives HQ.
- **Red House Museum, Christchurch**
  www.hants.gov.uk/museum/redhouse
  Full information on displays and events. This excellent museum is now open free to the public.
- **RAF Museum, Hendon**
  www.rafmuseum.com
  Research resource and display areas.
- **Royal National Lifeboat Institution**
  www.rnli.org.uk
  A clear site giving full particulars of the work of this charity.
- **Stanpit and Mudeford Residents' Association**
  www.bluetrain.co.uk/samra
  Local association promoting local causes.
- **Southampton University**
  www.soton.ac.uk
  The geology section (Ian West) gives considerable research information.
- **UK Hydrographic Office**
  www.ukho.gov.uk
  National naval records, including original historic

Aspects of property development and market

Before the days of detailed town planning, estate companies laid out residential areas to a certain standard. In this way, a pleasing consistency and density was achieved. Unfortunately, now that the estates have been built and the companies wound up, all that remains are some limited residual restrictive covenants. This is nothing like as effective as the previous need to gain the company's approval of submitted plans. Despite the enormous technical structure of the town planning system we now have, it is poor at maintaining existing densities on redevelopments. This is why it is inevitable that the character of the Hengistbury part of Southbourne must change. For example, in recent years it has become common for old houses and hotels to be used as sites for flats with a much greater building mass. I am sure readers can think of examples. It is a moot point whether an estate company, today, would go along with such schemes to gain the benefit of a high land value, or would prefer to keep the character of the area intact.

In the early part of the century, there was very little residential property to the east of Belle Vue Road. It seems that there was a farm gate from this road leading to a track, as far as Sunnylands Avenue, beyond which, the track petered out into a footpath up to the Dykes. This track, which the 1924 OS map shows as serving allotment gardens, has become the start of Broadway. Moreover, we must visualise Carter's chicken farm behind a high wire fence on the eastern side of the footpath up to where the Saxon King was later built! There were two large houses. Broom Close dates from about 1908 and was occupied by Lt. Col. W.T. Digby. It was later taken over during the war for bombed out families and is now the popular Tuckton Library. The other is Col. Brander's old house to the east known as West Close and now converted into flats in Branders Lane. Otherwise, the area was mainly farmland giving a clear view of the harbour, the headland and the sea. Even by 1953, a walk from Broom Close to the isolated Saxon King was across fields, fringed by the rear gardens of Broadway houses. The cinder car park at the end of Broadway was free and, on the Head itself, one was lucky to be able to find Lily Pond, as it was so overgrown!

A resident remembers buying a plot in Sunnylands Avenue for £175 in 1931 from the Brightlands Estate and building a bungalow for £575. Since all the plots were the same price, he and his wife chose one at the south-west end. The mortgage was fixed at 4% for 23 years, amounting to 16s. 6d. per week, which was well covered by an income of £3 10s! Even the subsequent road charges were a mere £15 for the 40-foot frontage. During the 1930s, houses were put up on the south side of this road and sold for between £850 and £950. Whilst it may be amazing to imagine now, the emptiness of the area then allowed our resident to have an unrestricted outlook. The south-east aspect of the bungalow's bedroom covered the harbour, Sandbank, headland, Hurst Castle, the Needles and St. Catherine's Point. Hence, although there was some pre-war housing, this was very limited and most was built from the 1950s onwards.

Interestingly, although what is now Harbour Road and Wildown Road were clearly built on the line of old tracks, Nugent Road was new and apparently followed a line of sunken blackberry bushes. Indeed, the gardens of those dwellings on the western side of this road closest to Broadway are much shorter than those further south owing to a "dogleg" in the field boundary of the 1924 OS map. Presumably, it is this field boundary, which provided the blackberries of local recollection and now provides the rear garden boundaries for the houses! No doubt it was also an ownership boundary at the time.

The section of the market covered below is the historic level of residential values in a few local roads, where I have come across and analysed a number of actual sale prices. It does indicate a large percentage uplift occurred from the 1930s, discussed above, to the 1950s.

This table can only be read together with some comment. It includes only a few roads in Southbourne, mainly towards Hengistbury, where there was a reasonable amount of evidence and properties in the road are similar. The analysis is not statistically valid, but an approximate guide only. State of repair and features (such as property size, garden, garage and central heating) are not known. Nor is the state of modernisation for any particular sale. Average prices must also be treated with caution because they derive from differing ranges of years with differing emphasis towards certain years within the range. Hence, it would not be correct to make straight comparisons between these average prices for different roads. Even if a lot more information had been available to allow adjustment of the sale prices and thereby give some validity to relative values, it would not apply to the present day. This is because supply and demand factors are no longer the same.

It is also worth stressing that the table is only intended to be a general look at what was happening in a fairly stable market from 1945 to 1960, with fairly minor increases in value. The data is not sufficient to draw detailed conclusions about particular roads. It is however undeniable that prices have increased enormously since those early post-war years. People would not then have believed the high values current in 2003, e.g. £290,000 for a 2-bedroom bungalow or £330,000 for a 3-bedroom house!

Otherwise, I would restrict myself to a few general comments concerning the local property market. The Hengistbury part of Southbourne is sure to stay popular with the public; the bungalows in particular will always sell to the retired whilst the 1930s and 1950s detached houses having large gardens will always sell to families. The easy, level access to the relatively quiet beaches near the Point House Café is unique within Bournemouth and reflected in values. Southbourne is becoming more residential now with the increased closure of hotels for redevelopment as flats, which at least doubled in value in the six years to 2003. The Bournemouth market generally has been more volatile than the Home Counties, i.e. it can fall further in bad times.

Hengistbury sale price evidence for the 1950s

Road (No. of Sales)	Typical Type of Property	First sale	Last Sale	Middle Year	Average Price
Baring Road Odd (10)	2 bed. Mainly early post-war detached bungalows	1946	1963	1954	£3,700
Baring Road Even (8)	Mainly 1930's but some 1950's detached 3 Bed and 4 Bed. houses	1954	1964	1959	£3,800
Carbery Avenue (34)	Large good quality mainly 4 bed. 1930's detached houses	1945	1964	1954	£4,550
Harland Road (17)	Mainly 1930's but some 1950's detached 3 Bed and some 4 Bed. houses	1945	1961	1953	£3,450
Hengistbury Road (32)	Mainly 1930's detached 3 Bed and 4 Bed. houses	1945	1964	1954	£3,750
Solent Road (17)	Mainly 1930's detached 3 Bed and 4 Bed. houses	1946	1962	1954	£3,600
Southlea Avenue (12)	Mainly 1930's detached 3 Bed houses	1946	1965	1955	£3,200
Watcombe Road (23)	Mainly 1930's detached 4 Bed and some 3 Bed. houses	1945	1961	1953	£3,450

Birds at Hengistbury

Alpine Swift
American Golden Plover
American Wigeon
Aquatic Warbler
Arctic Skua
Arctic Tern
Atlantic Puffin
Baird's Sandpiper
Balearic Shearwater
Barn Owl
Barn Swallow
Barnacle Goose
Barred Warbler
Bar-tailed Godwit
Bearded Tit
Black Guillemot
Black Kite
Black Redstart
Black Scoter
Black Tern
Black-billed Magpie
Blackcap
Black-crowned Night Heron
Black-headed Gull
Black-legged Kittiwake
Black-necked Grebe
Black-tailed Godwit
Black-throated Diver
Black-winged Stilt
Blue Tit
Bluethroat
Blue-winged Teal
Bohemian Waxwing
Bonaparte's Gull
Brambling
Brent Goose
Broad-billed Sandpiper
Buff-breasted Sandpiper
Canada Goose
Carrion Crow
Caspian Tern
Cattle Egret
Cetti's Warbler
Chaffinch
Chiffchaff
Cirl Bunting
Citrine Wagtail
Coal Tit
Collared Pratincole
Common Blackbird
Common Bullfinch
Common Buzzard
Common Crane
Common Crossbill
Common Cuckoo
Common Eider
Common Goldeneye
Common Grasshopper Warbler
Common Greenshank
Common Guillemot
Common Gull
Common Kestrel
Common Kingfisher
Common Linnet
Common Moorhen
Common Pheasant
Common Pochard
Common Quail
Common Raven
Common Redshank
Common Redstart
Common Rosefinch
Common Sandpiper
Common Shelduck
Common Snipe
Common Starling
Common Swift
Common Tern
Common Whitethroat
Common Wood Pigeon
Coot
Corn Bunting
Corn Crake
Cory's Shearwater
Curlew Sandpiper
Dartford Warbler
Dotterel
Dunlin
Dusky Warbler
Egyptian Goose
Eurasian Collared Dove
Eurasian Curlew
Eurasian Golden Oriole
Eurasian Hobby
Eurasian Jackdaw
Eurasian Jay
Eurasian Marsh Harrier
Eurasian Oystercatcher
Eurasian Penduline Tit
Eurasian Reed Warbler
Eurasian Siskin
Eurasian Sparrowhawk
Eurasian Spoonbill
Eurasian Teal
Eurasian Tree Sparrow
Eurasian Treecreeper
Eurasian Wigeon
Eurasian Woodcock
Eurasian Wryneck
European Golden Plover
European Goldfinch
European Greenfinch
European Honey Buzzard
European Nightjar
European Robin
European Serin
European Shag
European Storm-petrel
European Turtle Dove
Ferruginous Duck
Fieldfare
Firecrest
Gadwall
Garden Warbler
Garganey
Glaucous Gull
Glossy Ibis
Goldcrest
Goosander
Great Bittern
Great Black-backed Gull
Great Cormorant
Great Crested Grebe
Great Egret
Great Grey Shrike
Great Northern Diver
Great Reed Warbler
Great Skua
Great Spotted Cuckoo
Great Spotted Woodpecker
Great Tit
Greater Scaup
Greater Short-toed Lark
Greater White-fronted Goose
Green Sandpiper
Green Woodpecker
Greenish Warbler
Green-winged Teal
Grey Heron
Grey Partridge
Grey Phalarope
Grey Plover
Grey Wagtail
Greylag Goose
Gull-billed Tern
Hawfinch
Hedge Accentor
Hen Harrier
Herring Gull
Hoopoe
Horned Lark
House Martin
House Sparrow
Iceland Gull
Icterine Warbler
Jack Snipe
Kentish Plover
Lapland Bunting
Leach's Storm-petrel
Lesser Black-backed Gull
Lesser Crested Tern
Lesser Redpoll
Lesser Spotted Woodpecker
Lesser Whitethroat
Lesser Yellowlegs
Little Auk
Little Bunting
Little Crake
Little Egret
Little Grebe
Little Gull
Little Owl
Little Ringed Plover
Little Shearwater
Little Stint
Little Swift
Little Tern
Long-billed Dowitcher
Long-eared Owl
Long-tailed Duck
Long-tailed Skua
Long-tailed Tit
Mallard
Mandarin Duck
Manx Shearwater
Marsh Sandpiper
Marsh Tit
Marsh Warbler
Meadow Pipit
Mediterranean Gull
Melodious Warbler
Merlin
Mistle Thrush
Montagu's Harrier
Mute Swan
Northern Fulmar
Northern Gannet
Northern Goshawk
Northern Lapwing
Northern Parula
Northern Pintail
Northern Shoveler
Northern Wheatear
Nuthatch
Ortolan Bunting
Osprey
Pacific Golden Plover
Pallas's Leaf Warbler
Pectoral Sandpiper
Peregrine
Pied Avocet
Pied Flycatcher
Pink-footed Goose
Pomarine Skua
Purple Heron
Purple Sandpiper
Razorbill
Red Kite
Red Knot
Red-backed Shrike
Red-breasted Flycatcher
Red-breasted Merganser
Red-crested Pochard
Red-eyed Vireo
Red-footed Falcon
Red-legged Partridge
Red-necked Grebe
Red-necked Phalarope
Red-rumped Swallow
Red-throated Diver
Red-throated Pipit
Redwing
Reed Bunting
Richard's Pipit
Ring Ousel
Ring-billed Gull
Ringed Plover
Rock Pipit
Rook
Roseate Tern
Rose-ringed Parakeet
Ross's Gull
Ruddy Duck
Ruddy Shelduck
Ruddy Turnstone
Ruff
Rufous Nightingale
Rustic Bunting
Sabine's Gull
Sand Martin
Sanderling
Sandwich Tern
Savi's Warbler
Sedge Warbler
Short-eared Owl
Skylark
Slavonian Grebe
Smew
Snow Bunting
Song Thrush
Sooty Shearwater
Spotted Crake
Spotted Flycatcher
Spotted Redshank
Spotted Sandpiper
Squacco Heron
Stock Dove
Stonechat
Stone-curlew
Subalpine Warbler
Surf Scoter
Tawny Owl
Tawny Pipit
Temminck's Stint
Terek Sandpiper
Tree Pipit
Tufted Duck
Tundra Swan
Twite
Velvet Scoter
Water Pipit
Water Rail
Western Bonelli's Warbler
Whimbrel
Whinchat
Whiskered Tern
White/Pied Wagtail
White-winged Black Tern
Whooper Swan
Willow Tit
Willow Warbler
Winter Wren
Wood Sandpiper
Wood Warbler
Woodchat Shrike
Woodlark
Yellow Wagtail
Yellow-browed Warbler
Yellowhammer
Yellow-legged Gull
Zitting Cisticola

INDEX